The Lake District

RED GUIDE

THE LAKE DISTRICT

ORIGINALLY COMPILED BY
M. J. B. BADDELEY, B.A.

Twenty-sixth edition

Ward Lock Limited · London

PLANS

© Ward Lock Ltd 1978
ISBN 0 7063 5072 3

This edition published in Great Britain in 1978 by
Ward Lock Ltd, 116 Baker Street,
London W1M 2BB, a member of the
Pentos Group.

Printed and bound in Great Britain by Butler & Tanner Ltd.,
Frome and London.

CONTENTS

Page

INTRODUCTION

The Lake District of England is generally understood to be that portion of the country which has for its boundaries, on the west and south, the Irish Sea and Morecambe Bay, on the east the main line railway from Carnforth to Penrith and Carlisle, and on the north a line drawn—say—from Penrith to Cockermouth, and thence to St. Bees. In reality, its area is much smaller than that. The traveller from Carnforth to St. Bees has certainly fine distant views as he crosses the various estuaries opening on to Morecambe Bay, and skirts the Irish Sea, as well as a dash of real lake scenery in the foreground from the mouths of the Kent, the Leven, the Duddon and the Esk; but between Carnforth and Penrith, and from Penrith to St. Bees, except for a few miles on either side of Keswick, he will see little but mountain-tops to suggest the proximity of such a district. The actual boundary is the range of fells south-east of Windermere, and thence a line drawn round the ends of Coniston, Wastwater, Ennerdale, Crummock, Loweswater and Bassenthwaite Lakes; over the tops of Skiddaw and Saddleback, then southward, over the Dodds of Helvellyn, turning again so as to include the whole of Ullswater and Haweswater, and back to Windermere, the only outlying parts being the Lower Duddon valley on the south-western border, and the vales of Kentmere, Long Sleddale, and Swindale on the east. Within these limits *all* is typical Lake scenery; without, none. The newcomer should remember this, or he may be disappointed on arriving at such towns as Kendal, Penrith, or Ulverston to find that he has barely touched the hem of the magic garment of Lakeland proper, interesting as the surroundings of those towns are in their own way.

In the effect which it produces on the eye and mind of the spectator, mountain scenery is much more dependent on the proportion of its component parts than on the foot-and-line measurement of any of them, and in this attribute of proportion there is probably no beauty-spot in the world which can equal English Lakeland. Such epithets as " stupendous," " sublime," we may at once dismiss as unsuitable in a description of our Lake scenery, though it is wonderful, considering the small dimensions of the district, how near it comes, under certain atmospheric conditions, to meriting them. The head-to-foot steepness of the mountains, often bringing their full stature before the spectator's eye at a glance, and the absence of any disproportionate width in the valleys from which they rise, give them, when subject to the magnifying effect of intervening mist, a grandeur which those who, perhaps, only see them basking beneath a summer sun, or rising peak after peak from a far distance, cannot realise.

To the walker the small scale of the English Lake scenery is an invaluable boon. It gives him that infinite variety which is, as it were, the salt of his exertions. In a six-days' tour he can wander from lake to lake and from valley to valley, and see so many utterly different views that he may think he has exhausted the district. The leisurely tourist, however, may roam for six weeks or even months, and still find fresh scenes of beauty to delight his eyes. Only those who have spent whole days in ascending one long *Thal* or crossing a snow-field in a party, can thoroughly appreciate the charm of their native land in this respect.

This smallness also has the effect of bringing into close proximity features of widely differing kinds, with the result that each is, as it were, keyed up by the other. The ferns and birches of Borrowdale are beautiful in themselves; but how much more lovely are they when seen against a rugged background of fells. Those fells, rugged as they are, feel even wilder as one looks down from them into the vivid green strath of Rosthwaite, dotted with white farmsteads and cut into innumerable meadows by strong stone walls.

Another characteristic of the English Lake mountains, investing them with a beauty far in excess of that which a mere consideration of their height would indicate, is the rich and glossy appearance of their slopes. This is far more noticeable in the southern part of the district, where the geological formation is due to a combination of igneous and aqueous influences, than in the northern, where the rocks are more entirely of aqueous origin: there are not, perhaps, in Britain two mountains more thoroughly pleasing to the eye than the fells of Coniston Old Man and Wetherlam.

The Weather and the Seasons.—That part of the year in which the Lake District is most frequented by tourists is certainly not the best from a scenic point of view. There is more than one reason for this. The months of July and August are not freer from rain than other months, and much of the fine weather is accompanied by atmospheric conditions which place the scenery at the greatest disadvantage. We have known many successive days of fine weather pass without affording a single glimpse of mountains merely half a dozen miles distant, so thick has been the haze. Another reason is that during the period of the year which may be described as the " bracken season," lasting from the end of June till the middle of September, the district only possesses in a modified degree that charm of colour variety which at all other times is one of its most striking characteristics.

In this matter of colour there is a tradition, as delusive as it is popular, that the heather districts are superior to the fern districts. While admitting that the heather, during the month or two of its efflorescence, is the most beautiful livery which a mountain-side can assume, we cannot shut our eyes to the fact that for the greater part of the year it is the dullest and heaviest of vestures. The fern tribe, on the contrary—such portion of it, at least, as finds its home on the fell-side—is more beautiful, when taken *en masse*, in death than in life; and ferns are the almost universal clothing of the English Lake District. Under an October sun many of the fell-sides, notably those in the neighbourhood of Crummock and Buttermere, are all aglow with the bright sienna tints of the dying bracken, and the same effect, gradually diminishing, is continued all through the winter and spring till the light and warmth of returning summer uncurl the fresh fronds. Add to this the bright brown tints of the oak leaves, still clinging to their twigs, and the purple hues of the hazel and birch, and we obtain a richness and variety of colour far surpassing the pervading green of the summer months, which differs in shade only. It is only glen scenery, such as that of Killiecrankie and Glen Affric, which really loses its attractiveness during the leafless period of the year, and of glen scenery, strictly speaking, English Lakeland has but little. In the early spring the vivid green of the larch is a welcome harbinger of that general return to life and vigour during the progress of which the district wears, perhaps, its most beautiful aspect. The chances of good weather are greater in May and June than at any other time of year, and in no other months except, perhaps, October, does the scenery appear to such advantage. June is, on an average, the finest month of all, and during the first half of it nothing can surpass the freshness and variety of the immediate environs of the Lakes. Windermere, especially, owing to the sylvan character of its shores, is seen at its very best. Nor is the depth of winter without its charm. Never, perhaps, does the Windermere scenery appear to such advantage as when the lake is covered with transparent ice from end to end, and the glint of sunshine, investing its surface with bright and changeful colours, makes it appear like an opal set in a wreath of virgin white. Towards sunset the snow-clad fells assume every tint the sun can create, from deepest crimson to palest gold. Several of the " Days on the Fells " described at the end of the book were originally the results of walks undertaken during the depth of winter. Taking an average of years the Lake Country boasts a great deal of beautiful and thoroughly enjoyable weather in the winter season.

As a Winter Resort, there is a general impression that the Lake District is not to be thought of. Quite a number of the hotels remain open, and, except at the rock-climbing centres during

the Christmas and Easter holidays, one is sure of a bed. There
is, as above stated, a more than average share of bright weather
(the views are splendid : " how different are the firm outlines
of those distant peaks from the hazy indistinctness which usually
falls to the lot of the summer tourist ! "), very little fog, and
a fair quantity of entertainment—dances, lectures, and hunting
being the most popular amusements. Most of the hunting is
of necessity done on foot, and the mountain-tops afford to the
active follower a view-point from which he can often follow
a run almost from end to end. Participants who are less energetic
may see a great deal from the valleys. When the weather hardens
skating and other ice sports are indulged in, and during most
winters ski-ing is possible on some slopes.

The Rainfall of the district is of course considerable, the
annual downpour varying from about 50 inches in the outlying
to nearly 150 in the central parts, the wettest inhabited spot
being Seathwaite in Borrowdale (average 125 inches), and the
wettest spot in Britain where a rain-gauge is kept being " The
Sty " (1,077 ft. ; record 247·3 inches in 1923), on the Pass of that
name. In February 1920 6·81 inches fell during 24 hours at
Dungeon Ghyll, but in 1936 at the same place there was no rain
from April 29 to May 14. Compared with other parts of the
country floods are infrequent and of short duration. The number
of wet days is much less than may be supposed from the volume
of rain, and " absolute droughts " (periods of 15 or more rainless
days) occur from time to time. On the other hand, the downpour
on wet days is often torrential. It is comforting also to reflect
that to this excessive rainfall the district owes no small share of
its beauty in production of cascading waterfalls.

Preservation of the Scenery.—Considering its popularity, the
Lake District is, perhaps, not more troubled than other resorts
with the untidy habits of a certain class of visitor ; but there is
still plenty of work, for those who appreciate the beauty of this
wonderful playground, in checking the popular custom of casting
bottles and tins and other picnic débris into the nearest stream,
or leaving it lying about the fells, and even more important,
in curbing the practice of wrecking bridges and signposts.
Travellers who deplore the lack of finger-posts on the fells may
care to reflect that such posts are, apparently, considered fair game
by certain hooligans, who unhesitatingly take huge delight in
destroying them ; with the result that the labours of the County
Council are restricted by the need for *replacing* such posts, and
the erection of further new ones has to be postponed.

There is, however, real cause for thankfulness in the Lake
District's freedom from modern " development." For many
years Canon Rawnsley championed the natural beauty of the
district with fierce courage, although at times the difficulties were

such that even Ruskin wrote to him : " It's all of no use. You will soon have a tourist railway up Scafell, and another up Helvellyn, and another up Skiddaw, and then a connecting line all round."

But Canon Rawnsley persisted, and to him, with Miss Octavia Hill and Sir Robert Hunter, is due the inception of the National Trust, 1895, in which so much Lakeland property is now vested on behalf of the public. From time to time the Trust is able either to acquire land by gift or purchase or to prevent its spoliation. In 1923 it was the recipient of a magnificent gift from the Fell and Rock Climbing Club, to wit, the summits of Kirkfell, Great Gable, Green Gable, Brandreth, Grey Knotts, Base Brown, Seathwaite Fell, Glaramara, Allen Crags, Great End, Broad Crag, Lingmell, above the height of 1,500 feet, except at the Sty Head, where the contour is slightly raised. This land was first purchased as a memorial to members of the Club who fell in the 1914–18 War, and any word of commendation of the taste and dignity of this gift would be impertinence. Somewhat similarly the summit of Scafell Pike was presented by Lord Leconfield to the nation as a memorial of the men in the Lake District who gave their lives in the 1914–18 War. The Lake District Safeguarding Society used to do excellent work in dealing with encroachments on the amenities of the District, *e.g.* unsightly advertisements, unnecessary roads and railways, misplaced individual efforts, etc. etc. The County Councils are responsible for the provision of direction posts, bridges, etc., whilst the Friends of the Lake District participated with other amenity bodies in the successful legislation which resulted in the Lake District becoming the first of Britain's great National Park areas. This area is now under the administration of an established National Parks Board. The Nature Conservancy also proposes the establishment of Nature Reserves in the Lancashire part of the Lake District National Park, also certain sylvan-shored lakes, to preserve the distinct deciduous character as compared with " State " afforestation.

Geology.—Writing, as we do, entirely for the benefit of those who visit the Lakes for purposes of recreation, we have thought it best to discard altogether scientific geology.[1] " What sort of chisels," to quote the language of John Ruskin, " and in what workman's hands, were used to produce this large piece of precious chasing, or embossed work, which we call Cumberland and Westmorland," it is not our province to inquire. Students of geology will provide themselves with one or more of the excellent books which have been written on the subject. Our duty as guides to the picturesque is simply to point out those differences of formation which have a visible effect upon the scenery.

[1] Those interested should see J. E. Marr's *Geology of the Lake District* (Cambridge University Press), also L. Dudley Stamp's *Britain's Structure and Scenery* (Collins New Naturalist Series No. 4).

A remarkable peculiarity of the district is the absence of limestone from the central part, and consequently of that class of scenery which is characteristic of a limestone formation. Rough and rugged as the ground is from end to end, there is not, we think, a single instance of an inaccessible height in it. The wonderful isolated rocks of Dovedale, almost untrodden by man, and the needle-pointed rocks of Cheddar, have no counterpart in the Lake Country. The limestone district may be said to enclose the Lakes, as it were, in a ring-fence ; but in no case does it encroach on them. Travelling from the south, we leave it behind at Cartmel and Whitbarrow, and from the north soon after quitting Penrith. There is, to be sure, a narrow belt of what is called Coniston limestone extending from Broughton-in-Furness, past the heads of Coniston and Windermere, to Long Sleddale, but the effect upon the scenery is only visible in isolated escarpments on the fringe of Kendal, and just outside Ambleside at Pull Scar.

Granite is also somewhat scarce, only appearing round the foot of Wastwater, whose strand in that part is entirely paved with it, whence it extends eastward to Burnmoor Tarn and Hardknott ; southward along the western slopes of the line of fells to near Bootle ; northward to Ennerdale and the N.W. corner of Buttermere. It also occupies a strip near the summit of Scafell and a patch or two of Skiddaw Forest behind Saddleback, and at Threlkeld, where there are quarries, near Keswick. Where it does occur, the felspar part of it has a red tinge and is seen to best advantage in Eskdale which has the largest exposure of granite in the Lake District. The red tinge is due to haematite. The Shap granite quarries are, however, famous.

Another variety of igneous rock, syenite, has forced its way through the stratified formation between Buttermere and Ennerdale, and forms a portion of the range of which High Stile is the highest summit. The same rock extends some way south of Ennerdale Lake.

Broadly speaking, the Lake District, as defined in the introductory paragraph, is divided into three bands. The Skiddaw Slates on the north of a line from the foot of Ullswater on the east-north-east to Egremont, west-south-west ; the Bannisdale Slates south of a parallel line between Shap Wells and Millom ; and between these are the rocks of the volcanic series. Roughly, this central band just clears the southern end of Derwentwater and the northern extremity of Windermere. The northern section is characterised by bold clear-cut contours and comparatively smooth slopes. In ruggedness and variety of aspect these are far inferior to the central band of mountains. These features are specially marked in the western group around Sty Head and Wasdale and become less pronounced on the eastern fells.

History and Antiquities.—From the point of view of the archæologist the chief interest of Cumbria (Cumberland, Westmorland and N. West Lancs), is in the traces of the early people who lived hereabouts before the Norman conquest. Of the Stone Age, the earliest period of all, there are no visible remains within the Lake District proper, but there were settlements on the perimeter, notably near Beckermet on the Cumberland coast. The inhabitants of these settlements are believed to have penetrated into the fells for the peculiarly hard stone of which their axes were made : roughed-out axes have been found below the Langdale Pikes, but polished axes only at lower levels, and even these cannot be dated with certainty. In the Early Bronze Age the large stone circles were set up, and the finest example is the Castlerigg Stone Circle outside Keswick. Another one, less well known, is the Swinside Stone Circle on the lower slopes of Black Combe. The Bronze Age is also represented by small stone circles and cairns, evidently burial-places, the best examples being on Burnmoor (between Eskdale and Wasdale) and Moor Divock (above Ullswater). At Banniside near Coniston excavation revealed urns, a food vessel, and bits of woollen stuff. In the 18th century bronze implements presumably of this period were found at Ambleside and Troutbeck.

In the Early Iron Age there were "British Settlements," villages of a primitive type, at Kentmere, Heathwaite near Coniston, and Lanthwaite Green near Crummock Water. Hillforts at Peel Wyke on Bassenthwaite, Castle Crag overlooking Haweswater and others in the Derwentwater district are believed to have been places where the Britons took refuge from invaders during the Roman period or perhaps a little later.

The Roman remains in the Lake District are chiefly on the line of a road which Agricola drove northwards from Lancaster and Kendal to Ambleside, continued later over the Wrynose and Hardknott passes to the Cumbrian coast, and this was the connecting link with a port at Ravenglass. The Ambleside fort has been excavated and the more interesting parts of it are left exposed for visitors to see ; Hardknott too has been excavated, its foundations are clearly seen, but at Ravenglass the bath house is practically all that survives. There was a secondary Roman road from Ambleside to Brougham near Penrith, which is still traceable on the mountain called (for this reason) High Street, much of which is over 2,000 feet above sea-level.

The Dark Ages after the Romans left were remarkable for little except the raiders who came to this part of the country from the still wilder regions farther north. In the middle of the 7th century Anglian settlers colonised the outskirts of the District, for we know that St. Cuthbert found Angles at Carlisle in 685, and there are stones with Anglian carving at Dacre and Irton. In the 10th century an even more eventful settlement was made by the Vikings who, having already established colonies in the Hebrides, Ireland and the Isle of Man, came to Cumbria about 925 and came to stay. A cross of the 10th century is

standing in the churchyard at Gosforth and many other fragments of crosses are in various local churches, but the most
interesting memorial of the Norsemen is in the place-names and
dialect. The *thwaites* and *becks* and *ghylls* are all Norse in origin,
and so are many of the words still used by the farmers in the
fells.

There is a tradition that St. Kentigern preached at Crosthwaite,
Keswick, in 553 and if this be so his converts may have been the
first Christians in the district. The church now standing where
he set up his cross was not founded till 1175, but it is one of the
finest parish churches in the Lake District. The majority of the
ancient churches are on the circumference of the Lake District,
as at Barton, Kendal, Cartmel, St. Bees and Brigham, and these
gradually established "chapels" in the inner valleys. The
mother church at Kendal, for instance, started daughter chapels
at Windermere and Grasmere which in their turn founded other
chapels at Troutbeck and Langdale. The existing churches at
Wasdale Head and Newlands illustrate the smallness and simplicity of the places of worship in the dales down to about a
hundred years ago. The only abbeys that can be claimed for
the Lake District are Furness, (1127) to the south; Calder,
(1134) to the west ; and Shap, (1199) to the east (the remains of
which are described in the main part of the guide). These three
abbeys, together with Fountains Abbey in Yorkshire, were
considerable landowners and great sheep farmers.

Castles, like the parish churches, are only on the fringe of the
fells, for instance Penrith, Kendal, Dalton, Egremont, all of
which are now preserved by their respective towns. Only
Muncaster and Cockermouth Castles are still occupied as such,
and Millom and Dacre Castles are now farm-houses. Owing to the
many Scottish raids throughout the Middle Ages the larger houses
were fortified as a matter of course, and there are a number of
pele-towers—peculiar to the Border Counties—round Penrith
and elsewhere. Kentmere Hall is an example of a pele in the
midst of the fells.

Good domestic architecture of the later periods is almost
non-existent. The old halls at Coniston and Rydal were both
built by the le Flemings, Hawkshead Hall apparently dates back
in part to the days of Furness Abbey, there is a fine old hall
at Dalegarth in Eskdale and another at Calgarth on Windermere, but these have all become farm-houses—with the exception
of Rydal which is now a retreat for the clergy. The typical
white farm-house of the Lake District, built of stone and roofed
with slate, usually dates from about 1600 to 1700, a period
when there was much building activity after the Restoration.
Before that time probably everyone except the gentry lived in
wattle-and-daub cottages thatched with turf or bracken.

Sheep farming has been the traditional local industry from the
Viking Age to the present day. Some claim that the Herdwick

sheep were brought here by the Norse settlers, others that they are descended from a flock that escaped from a ship in the Spanish Armada, said to have been wrecked on the Cumbrian coast. But there have always been other industries too. In Norman times some of the valleys were royal forests and this meant employment for hunters and fishermen; in Elizabeth's reign there was much mining for copper and other metals, especially in the Keswick and Coniston fells, and German miners were imported and settled here. There are lead mines still working at Greenside above Ullswater and a barytes mine in Coledale, near Braithwaite. Stone and slate quarrying is a more recent industry and a very considerable one, as may be seen at Honister Crag and on Coniston Old Man, where some of the quarries have been worked for at least two hundred years. But the principal industry to-day, second only to sheep farming, is the business of catering for the visitors who for more than a century and a half have been coming to the Lake District in increasing numbers every year.

Fauna.—Visitors to the Lakeland mountains may count on seeing the raven, the peregrine falcon, the buzzard and the kestrel, all of which nest in the crags. Meadow pipits are everywhere abundant and the commonest bird of the fells. The skylark nests on the hill-tops, often at high elevations, and wheatears are to be seen from the edge of cultivation well up the hills.

On the lower moors the merlin, red grouse, blackcock and snipe nest. The ring ouzel is found locally only. Curlews and lapwings come to the fells to nest in considerable numbers and leave for the coast in August. The golden plover is not a bird of the Lakeland mountains though it is common in eastern Cumbria.

The wild geese of the Solway Estuary and Morecambe Bay have regular flight lines over the fells during the winter, and snow buntings are winter visitors to the tops. Large flocks of rooks and jackdaws fly daily from certain roosts along regular lines, in some cases for many miles, to disperse over the fells and dales, returning in the evening.

On every beck the dipper may be seen all the year round, and in summer the grey wagtail. Herons are common. The common sandpiper frequents the shores of the lakes and tarns and wild swans and various kinds of diving ducks visit the lakes in winter. On some lakes cormorants have become a menace to trout and char. Mallard, teal, shovellers, a few tufted duck, grebes, moorhens and coots all breed.

The characteristic summer visitor to the Ambleside district is the pied flycatcher, whose numbers have been greatly increased by the placing of nesting-boxes in gardens. Two birds which have become moderately common throughout the district in suitable surroundings in recent years are the hawfinch and the great spotted woodpecker. Corncrakes have almost vanished. Redstarts may be seen in most of the dales.

Of the owls the tawny is common, the longeared is decreasing, and the barn owl often nests in crags. The woodcock has become a very common nesting species.

Several species of warblers are found, but the commonest everywhere is the willow warbler and in lesser numbers the garden warbler. Some warblers are found in gills and hillside woods at considerable elevations.

There are large colonies of blackheaded gulls at Ravenglass and Walney Island, and lesser blackbacked and herring gulls at Walney and Foulshaw Moss, where also some pairs of the greater blackbacked gulls breed. The blackheaded and lesser blackbacked gulls are common visitors to the hills in most months of the year. The former are trying to establish themselves in smaller colonies inland. Common gulls are seen in the fields of the lowlands from late summer to early spring.

The list of mammals comprises some twenty-five species, to which may be added the mountain hare, which has been introduced. The pine marten still exists in some of the wilder parts of the mountains and is occasionally found in the lowlands. The polecat or foumart, formerly common, now seems to be extinct. The badger, being a creature of nocturnal habits, is seldom seen and is more common in the areas immediately surrounding the Lake District proper. The red deer of Martindale are the survivors of the original wild stock of the country. The fox and the otter are fairly numerous.

Fish of various kinds are found in the lakes and becks. The gwyniad of Ullswater and Haweswater is known locally as the " skelly," and perch—which abound in most of the lakes—are known as " bass." Windermere char were formerly considered a great delicacy and char pies and potted char were even sent to London.

Books to refer to are : Macpherson's *Vertebrate Fauna of Lakeland* (now out of print) ; Collingwood's *The Lake Counties* ; and Astley's *From a Bird Lover's Diary.* Fish are dealt with in Watson's *Lake District Fisheries*, and *Life in Lakes and Streams* by T. T. Macan and E. B. Worthington.

Flora.—Lakeland possesses probably the largest variety of flowers, ferns and mosses of any area in Britain ; it would therefore be impossible to give in limited space a complete list of Lakeland plants. Many famous botanists have published their notes on the Westmorland Flora : one of the earliest local lists is by Thomas Lawson, who in 1661 was schoolmaster at Great Strickland, near Shap. It is remarkable that many of the plants he recorded are still growing in the same locality.

The Lake Poets have made famous the Lakeland Flora. Wordsworth immortalised the daffodil, primrose, daisy and celandine.

What can surpass the golden daffodils, the woods of wild hyacinths, or the brilliant array of foxgloves in their summer glory ? Lily of the valley still grows wild in secluded woods in Lakeland.

May is the month of spring flowers, and woods are gay with anemone, primrose and violet. In June old pack-horse lanes are radiant with wild roses, honeysuckle, blue borage, and comfrey ; ragged robin, red and white campion ; blue speedwell and forget-me-not ; wild geranium, herb robert, stitchwort, globe flower and the dainty yellow poppy.

On marshy ground at the heads of the dales you find the lovely grass of parnassus, and where the limestone merges towards the slate grows that charming pink flower *Primula farinosa* or mealy primrose, also the field gentian. Butterwort raises its purple head by mountain streams along with several alpine plants, the lovely white mountain saxifrage, tormentilla, bird's-foot trefoil, purple ling and bell heather. About the higher rocks grows the giant bearberry with its cluster of white and pink wax-like flowers and dark evergreen leaves. On the lower slopes are three colours of milkwort—pink, blue and white—and bog bean and lousewort.

The fields are gay with eyebright and mayflower, the hedges full of blossom such as mountain ash, bird cherry, crab apple and wild plum.

The characteristic fern of the district is the parsley fern (which grows here more abundantly than in any other part of Britain). Bracken is increasing everywhere and often covers whole mountain-sides. Lakeland however has long been famous as the haunt of both ferns and mosses, a subject on which many useful handbooks may be obtained to assist the student.

Hotel Accommodation and Charges.—Throughout the main centres of the district, there is an abundance of good class hotels. The smaller inns are invariably clean and ready to provide simple fare and accommodation as desired. Almost everywhere are farm-houses and cottages which pride themselves on their hospitality—some of these are, in their way, almost as famous as the hotels. A prevailing feature is little limitation of good quality fare. On later pages of this book we mention the principal hotels, etc.

The Country-wide Holidays Association, the **Holiday Fellowship,** the **Youth Hostels Association,** and other similar bodies have hostels of various types and sizes for their members throughout the district. Campers will find that permission to camp is not difficult to obtain : indeed many farmers provide sites and give special facilities. In addition, many clubs have climbing- and rambling-centre huts at accessible points to the mountains. Of particular note is the spacious caravan site on the shores of Windermere at White Cross Bay.

GLOSSARY

Band, an elevated tract of land forming a division between two areas of less elevation, the fundamental idea being *bourn* or boundary; often a high, rocky flat.

Barrow, a hill. The elongated ridge of a fell; sometimes a tumulus.

Beck, a stream.

Bield, a shelter for men or animals. In fox-hunting it signifies a fastness in the rocks inaccessible for hounds.

Bink, a grassy ledge on a precipitous face.

Blea, cold blue.

Borran, a heap of stones.

Brant, steep.

Burn, probably the same word as *borran*. It does not appear to mean brook.

Cairn, a pile of stones, generally erected to mark the way, or to denote the summit of a fell.

Cam, the crest (cock's *comb*) of a hill.

Combe, a hollow enclosed on three sides by a hill or hills.

Den, a valley.

Dodd, a high, bare rounded summit—*e.g.* Stybarrow Dodd, Watson's Dodd, and Great Dodd on the Helvellyn range. Often a dependency of the main fell.

Dore or *Door*, an opening in a ridge between walls of rock. The Great Dore, Mickledore, is between Scafell Pike and Scafell, two mountains.

Dub, a river pool.

Dun, a dune or down.

Edge, a narrow ridge.

Fell, a high open pasture giving name to the hill above it.

Force, a waterfall.

Garth, an enclosure. It seems to be in some way connected with garden. In Norway " gaard " is the regular word for a farm-house.

Gate, a way. These two words possibly occur in conjunction at Gatesgarth, near Buttermere; "the enclosure by the way."

Gill or *Ghyll*, a mountain stream; a narrow ravine or gully.

Grain (a prong), the fork of a stream.

Grise (a common prefix), wild boar, *viz.* Grisedale.

Hag, a wood; enclosed ground.

Hause, a pass or defile.

Heaf, a sheep pasture on a mountain.

Holme, an island.

How, a low hill.

Intack, an enclosure on a fell-side surrounded by stone walls; a piece of waste land "taken in."

Keld, a spring.

Knock, a hill.

Knott, a rocky excrescence on a hill; a "knotted" hill.

Lath, a barn.

Man, a cairn on a summit; a summit. Not necessarily the highest point of the mass. The terms High Man and Low Man are not uncommon.

Mere, a lake.

Nab, a projection, a promontory, an extremity.

Ness (a nose), a projection, not necessarily into a lake.

Pitch, an abrupt ascent ; a sudden drop.
Raise, a heap of stones, or a hill marked by one.
Rake, a straight passage through rocks or rough ground (just as the straight portions of a winding river are " reaches," the fundamental idea being " reach ").
Rigg, a ridge.
Scale, a rough hut on a hill (Scotch, " shieling ").
Scarth, a notch in a ridge.
Scree, the débris of cliffs, a talus of loose stones fallen from the cliffs above.
Sike, a rivulet in marshy ground.
Slack, a slight depression between two elevations.
Slape, smooth, slippery.
Stickle, a sharp peak.
Tarn, a small mountain ake.
Thwaite, a clearing.
Walla, sad-coloured, grey.
Wath, a ford.
With, a wood.
Wray, a landmark ; generally a prominence.
Wyke, a bay.

HEIGHTS OF MOUNTAINS

	ft.		ft.
Scafell Pike	3,210	Harter Fell (Mardale)	2,539
Scafell	3,162	Wandhope	2,533
Helvellyn	3,118	Caudale Moor	2,502
Skiddaw	3,053	Wetherlam	2,502
Great End	2,984	High Raise	2,500
Bowfell	2,960	Red Pike (Buttermere)	2,479
Great Gable	2,949	Ill Bell	2,476
Pillar	2,927	Dale Head	2,473
Esk Pike	2,903	High Crag (Buttermere)	2,443
Fairfield	2,863	Robinson	2,417
Saddleback	2,847	Seat Sandal	2,415
Crinkle Crags	2,816	Harrison Stickle	2,403
Dollywaggon Pike	2,810	Hindscarth	2,385
Grasmoor	2,791	Ullscarf	2,370
St. Sunday Crag	2,756	Froswick	2,359
Eel Crag (Grasmoor)	2,749	Pike o' Stickle	2,323
Little Scoat Fell	2,746	Pike o' Blisco	2,304
High Street	2,718	Seatallan	2,266
Red Pike (Wastwater)	2,707	Place Fell	2,154
Lingmell Crag	2,649	Harter Fell (Eskdale)	2,140
High Stile	2,643	Fleetwith Pike	2,126
Old Man	2,635	Honister Crag	2,070
Kirkfell	2,631	Yewbarrow	2,058
Swirl How (Coniston)	2,630	Causey Pike	2,000
Haycock	2,619	Black Combe	1,969
Grisedale Pike	2,593	Haystacks	1,750
Carrs	2,575	Wansfell	1,581
Glaramara	2,560	Catbells	1,481
Kidsty Pike	2,560	Latrigg	1,203
Red Screes	2,541	Loughrigg	1,101

HEIGHTS OF PASSES

(APPROXIMATE.)

	ft.		ft.
Esk Hause [1]	2,490	The Stake	1,576
Sticks	2,420	Kirkstone	1,476
Nan Bield	2,100	Garburn	1,450
Greenup Edge	1,995	Scarth Gap	1,400
Walna Scar	1,990	Floutern Tarn	1,300
Gatescarth	1,950	Hardknott	1,290
Grisedale	1,929	Wrynose	1,270
Black Sail	1,800	Honister	1,190
Coledale	1,800	Buttermere Hause	1,096
Scandale Head	1,700	Whinlatter	1,043
Sty Head	1,600	Dunmail Raise	782

[1] 2,490 feet is the height of the actual hause, the summit of the pass between Borrowdale and Eskdale. The height of the cairn on the Esk Hause route is 2,386 feet.

MEASUREMENTS OF LAKES

	Volume in millions of cubic ft.	Greatest Length and Breadth.	Height above sea-level ft.	Depth. Max. ft.	Depth. Aver. ft.
[1]Windermere	12,250	10½ by 1¼	130	219	78
[1]Ullswater	7,870	7½ „ ¾	476	205	83
[1]Coniston	4,000	5¼ „ ½	143	184	79
[1]Bassenthwaite Water	1,023	4 „ ¾	223	70	18
[2]Thirlmere	—	3⅝ „ ½	583	158	—
[3]Haweswater	3,630	4 „ ½	790	198	135
[1]Derwentwater	1,010	3 „ 1⅛	244	72	18
[1]Wastwater	4,128	3 „ ½	200	258	135
[1]Crummock Water	2,343	2½ „ ⅝	321	144	88
[1]Ennerdale Water	1,978	2½ „ ¾	368	148	62
Esthwaite Water	—	1½ „ ⅜	217	80	—
[1]Buttermere	537	1¼ „ ⅜	329	94	55
Loweswater	—	1¼ „ ⅜	429	60	—
Grasmere	—	1 „ ½	208	75	—
Rydal Water	—	¾ „ ¼	181	55	—
Brothers' Water	—	⅜ „ ¼	520	70	—

[1] The depths of these lakes are taken from Dr. H. R. Mill's " Bathymetrical Survey " of the Lakes, the first complete and regular survey of the kind. The "earliest record of regular soundings " appears to have been made in 1787.

[2] Original Area, 330 acres. When raised 20 feet, 565 acres; 35 feet, 679 acres; now raised 50 feet, 793 acres, with a length of 3 miles 5 furlongs.

[3] The old lake had a length of 2½ miles and a breadth of ⅜ miles.

HEIGHTS OF WATERFALLS

(APPROXIMATE.)

	ft.		ft.
Scale Force	125	Dalegarth Force	60
Barrow Cascade	108	Dungeon Ghyll Force	60
Lodore	90	Rydal Upper Fall	60
Aira Force	70	Colwith Force	45
Stock Gill Force	60	Skelwith Force	15

SPORT IN LAKELAND

CLIMBING

BRITISH rock-climbing has long been recognised as an important branch of mountaineering, and on many of the Lakeland
fells splendid climbs are possible. It must be remembered, however, that here " the art has been highly elaborated, and the
standard of difficulty and dexterity is even dangerously high. If
men would be content to serve an apprenticeship and to feel their
way gradually from the easier climbs onward, they would excite
less apprehension in the minds of those who know what these
climbs are. If, on the other hand, they rush—as too many do
—straight from the desk in a crowded city, with unseasoned
lungs and muscles, in the cold and the wet, to attack alone or with
chance companions whatever climb enjoys for the moment the
greatest notoriety, frightful accidents are certain to occur."

Graduated lists of routes from " easy " to " very severe " have
been published in standard volumes comprising a series of
climbing guides by the Fell and Rock Climbing Club. Such
lists, if intelligently followed, are valuable. On the other
hand, it is objected that they encourage " cramming," that " they
tend to concentrate upon a few climbs, placed towards the end
of the list, the attention which ought to be spread over the whole."
We have here adopted a middle course, and contented ourselves
with indicating such of the climbs as may, in our opinion, be
safely attacked by novices of average strength, average nerve,
and average *sense*. In climbing, as in everything else worth the
doing, one has to go to school, and ignorance or neglect of the
rules—*e.g.* carelessness about belaying—may make even a simple
climb risky, and bad weather conditions may make any climb
excessively dangerous.

First-class climbing on first-class rock is to be found on Pillar,
Scafell Crags, Great Gable, Gimmer and Dow Crags. Good
climbs may be had also on Bowfell and Pavey Ark, around
Buttermere and in the Borrowdale valley. Before, however, attempting any form of rock climbing we would advise
the complete novice to secure the services of one of the professional
guides whose names and addresses are advertised in the hotels
and boarding-houses ; and with him to attempt some climb under
instruction. He will then be able to judge his ability to under-
take any of the climbs mentioned in the following list (which is
far from complete, and is intended to indicate some of the better

23

known climbs, whilst omitting any reference to crags which are for various reasons unsafe for climbers).

Pillar.—Slab and Notch ; Old West ; Climbs out of Jordan Gap ; North and New West (more difficult) ; the outlying climbs on Pillar Fell, Steeple and Scoat Fell.

Great Gable.—Needle Ridge, Arrowhead Ridge ; Kern Knotts Chimney ; Napes Needle (more difficult).

Gimmer.—Yields good climbing, but the majority of the routes are for experienced climbers only. Excellent climbing may, however, be obtained on Pavey Ark, Middle Fell Buttress, Scout and Tarn Craggs.

Dow Crag.—C. and E. Buttresses ; The Chimneys in Easter Gulley (Blizzard, South and Black).

Scafell.—(*a*) *Scafell Crags* ; Broad Stand ; North : Deep Gill and Professor's Chimney ; Pinnacle from Steep Gill by Slingsby's.

(*b*) *Pikes Crag.*—A. C. and D. Gullies.

(*c*) *Great End.*—Custs ; South-East, and Central Gullies (care should be taken on account of loose rock).

Outlying Climbs.—Burtness Comb ; Climbs in Borrowdale valley ; Castle Rock, Thirlmere : on Bowfell.

BOOKS ON CLIMBING.—*Rock Climbing in the English Lake District*, O. G. Jones (Abraham, Keswick) ; *Climbing : Part I, England*, W. P. Haskett-Smith (Longmans) ; *The Complete Mountaineer* and *British Mountain Climbs*, George D. Abraham (Mills & Boon) ; J. E. Q. Barford, *Climbing in Britain* (Pelican books) ; and the *Journals* of the Yorkshire Ramblers', Climbers', Fell and Rock-Climbing, Rucksack, and other mountaineering clubs, and paramount, the series of guides issued by the Fell and Rock Climbing Club of the English Lake District.

FELL-WALKING

As long ago as 1864 the Rev. J. M. Elliot gave a definite start to the gentle art of peak-bagging. Since that time strong walkers have delighted in bagging, or attempting to bag, all the three-thousand-footers within twenty-four hours. (It may be noticed that Scafell was for many years, by a pleasing convention, included under the head of Scafell Pikes.) Record was piled on record, till in 1904 and again in 1905, Dr. A. W. Wakefield beat all previous performances, only to end by coaching Mr. E. Thomas to beat him in 1920. Subjoined is a list of some of the most notable fell walks. It will be understood that the distances given are only approximate.

1895.—Dawson, Poole, and Palmer : Elterwater, Bowfell, Scafell Pikes, Skiddaw, Helvellyn, Grasmere, Elterwater (*via* Rydal and Ambleside). Time, 19 hours 18 minutes.

1898.—Broadrick : Windermere, Bowfell, Great End, Scafell Pikes, Scafell, Great Gable, Skiddaw, Helvellyn, Windermere. Time, 20¼ hours. (12 miles were done on a cycle.)

1899.—Westmorland, Johnson, Strong, Beaty : Seathwaite, Great Gable, Great End, Scafell Pikes, Scafell, Bowfell, Wythburn (*via* Langdale Combe

Head and High Raise), Helvellyn, Saddleback, Skiddaw, Keswick. Time, 19 hours 25 minutes.

1899.—Westmorland and Beaty: Threlkeld to Threlkeld over the same fells. Time 23¾ hours

1902.—Johnson: Threlkeld, Helvellyn, Fairfield, Bowfell, Great End, Scafell Pikes, Scafell, Pillar Fell, Great Gable, Skiddaw, Saddleback, Threlkeld. Time, 22 hours 7 minutes.

1904.—Wakefield: Keswick, Great Gable, Kirkfell, Pillar Fell, Scafell, Scafell Pikes, Great End, Bowfell, Fairfield, Helvellyn, Saddleback, Skiddaw, Keswick. Time, 19 hours 53 minutes.

1905.—Wakefield: Keswick, Robinson, Hindscarth, Dalehead, Brandreth, Green Gable, Great Gable, Kirkfell, Pillar Fell, Steeple, Red Pike, Yewbarrow, Scafell, Scafell Pikes, Great End, Bowfell, Fairfield, Helvellyn, Saddleback, Skiddaw, Keswick. Time, 22 hours 7 minutes. Ascents, 23,500 feet. Distance, 90 miles; equivalent to nearly 120.

1920, May 29.—Eustace Thomas, 21 hours 25 minutes, over practically the same course as Dr. Wakefield's 1905 walk.

1922, June.—E. Thomas ascended 30,000 feet in 28 hours 5 minutes, completing Wakefield's round, with the addition of the tops on the ridge running N. from Helvellyn to Clough Head and of Gt. Calva, continuing over Grisedale Pike, Grasmoor, Wandhope, Eel Crag, Sail, and Causey Pike.

1932, June 13.—Robert Graham created what was then probably a world's walking record. The route was: Keswick, Skiddaw, Great Calva, Saddleback, Wanthwaite Pike, Helvellyn, Dollywaggon Pike, Fairfield, Seat Sandal, Steel Fell, Calf Crag, High White Stones, High Raise, Sergeant Man, Harrison Stickle, Pike o' Stickle, Rossett Pike, Hanging Knotts, Bowfell, Esk Pike, Great End, Scafell Pike, Scafell, Wasdale, Yewbarrow, Red Pike, Steeple, Pillar, Kirk Fell, Great and Green Gable, Brandreth, Honister Hause, Dalehead, Hindscarth, Robinson, High Snab, Keswick. Time, 23 hours 39 minutes.

1965, July 24.—Alan Heaton of Accrington beat Bob Graham's record by walking 90 miles, and climbing approx. 34,000 feet of fell in 24 hours. His route was from the Old Dungeon Ghyll Hotel in Langdon up Pike O'Blisco, Cold Pike, Crinkle Crags, Bowfell, Great End, Scafell Pike, Scafell, Lingmell, Wasdale Head, Yewbarrow, Red Pike, Pillar, Kirk Fell, Great Gable, Green Gable, Honiston Hause, Dale Head, Robinson, Newland Hause, Aitken Knott, Saal, Grasmoor, Hobcarton, Grisedale, Lairthwaite Road, Little Man, Skiddaw, Saddleback, Threlkeld, Great Dodd, Raise, Helvellyn, Dollywaggon Pike, Seat Sandal, Dunmail Raise, Steel Fell, High Raise, Sergeant Man, Harrison Stickle, Pike O'Stickle, Old Dungeon Ghyll Hotel.

1975, June 22–23.—Jos Naylor, a farmer of Wasdale, set up a new record of 72 peaks in 23 hours 11 minutes, walking 105 miles and a total ascent/descent of 40,000 feet.

HUNTING

There are eight packs of Fell Fox-hounds, one pack of Harriers and three packs of Beagles, which all hunt within the district. The meets of the fox-hounds are generally held early in the morning and are advertised in the local papers. It may be mentioned that the Blencathra Fox-hounds (Threlkeld) are descendants of John Peel's pack and cover some of the Skiddaw Country, etc., which he hunted.

The **Blencathra** (Kennels: Gategill, Threlkeld). District: Saddleback, Skiddaw, and the fells about Derwentwater, Thirlmere, and Bassenthwaite, etc.

The **Coniston** (Kennels: Greenbank, Ambleside). District: the fells round Coniston and the head of Windermere.

The **Eskdale and Ennerdale** (Kennels: Brantrake, Eskdale). District: Broughton-in-Furness to Ennerdale, including Langdale (by invitation) and Wasdale Head.

The **Melbreak** (Kennels: Lorton). The fells about Buttermere, Loweswater, Lorton, and to the east of Cockermouth.

The **Ullswater** (Kennels: Grassthwaite How, Patterdale). District: Helvellyn and High Street Ranges, and over towards Long Sleddale, Shap, and Swindale. Also Pennines and Appleby district.

North Lonsdale (Kennels: Penny Bridge near Greenodd).

Lunesdale; a little riding is done with this pack, but it is mainly a fell pack.

The **Windermere Harriers** (Kennels: Burneside). District: Windermere and Kendal.

These hounds must obviously be followed on foot, and provide grand sport and abundance of exercise to hard workers. Much of the hunting, however, may be enjoyed, under favourable conditions, by climbing some suitable elevation, or following (at a distance) on the main road by cycle or car.

To those who wish to ride to hounds, the *Cumberland and Cumberland Farmers'* and *West Cumberland Fox-hounds* are reasonably accessible.

The fox-hunting season lasts from about the end of September to Easter.

There are also the **West Cumberland Beagles** with kennels at Seascale and covering a very large area, the **Furness Beagles,** with kennels near Cartmel, the **Bleasdale Beagles** and the **Caldbeck Fell Beagles.** The **Kendal and District Otter Hounds** (Kennels at Milnthorpe) cover the district, while occasionally the **Dumfriesshire Otter Hounds** pay visits to the River Eden, etc.

ANGLING

Though the angling in the Lake District cannot be described as first-class, there is plenty of tolerable sport to be had. The fish most commonly caught in the district are as follows :—

Salmon.—All rivers connected with the sea, and sometimes in the lakes and in the Eamont.

Trout.—Sea trout in the salmon streams. Brown trout everywhere—in lakes, rivers, becks, and tarns—running from five to the pound to five-pounders.

Char.—Buttermere, Coniston, Crummock, Ennerdale, Haweswater, Ullswater, Wastwater, Windermere.

Pike and Perch (Bass) in all the lakes. Esthwaite has a reputation for pike, Bassenthwaite for perch.

Licences and Permits

All waters within the Lake District area come, for licence purposes, under the jurisdiction of the North West Water Authority, and before commencing to fish anglers must have the necessary licence from the Authority. These licences can be obtained from distributors throughout the area or from the office of the clerk to the Authority.

The address is:—

North West Water Authority, Rivers Division, P.O. Box 12, Newtown House, Buttermarket Street, Warrington, WA1 2QG

Schedules of licence duties, particulars of close seasons, etc., are also available from this office.

In addition to the holding of a Water Authority licence it is necessary for anglers to obtain permission from riparian owners or fishing associations to fish in these waters. Though considerable parts of waters are, apart from the Water Authority licence, still free to anglers, for the most part rights are held by local corporations, the National Trust, fishing clubs and associations and hotel proprietors. Addresses of secretaries of associations and owners are obtainable by local enquiry or from the fishing offices of the Water Authority. In any case it is advisable to make careful enquiry.

ICE AND SNOW SPORTS

The winters in the Lake District are often extremely severe, and splendid skating is to be had on many of the lakes, except Wastwater, the deepest of the lakes, which is reputed never to be frozen over. Curling also is very popular at Keswick and there are instances of competitions having been decided on the higher tarns when the ice on the lakes was melting. There are several fair toboggan courses, but the sudden alternations of temperature and frequent storms tend to make this sport an uncertain quantity. Ski-ing is possible in most winters and the long slopes about Helvellyn are worth attention. The High Street range is also possible, but as yet has not been used to any extent. Practically every peak has been ascended on ski. The difficulty is that the slopes are very steep and rough, and the snow rarely lies long enough to mature for real sport. There is in existence a flourishing Lakeland Ski-Club, which holds regular meets when snow conditions permit.

GOLF

Golf is to be had rather more on the outskirts than actually within the district. The best courses are at Seascale and Windermere. There are 18-hole courses at Appleby, Grange-over-Sands. Kendal, Penrith, Seascale, Ulverston, Walney Island, Barrow, and Windermere. Play on 9-hole courses at moderate charges may be had at Cockermouth, St. Bees, Sedbergh, Silecroft and Silverdale. Full particulars may be obtained on application to the secretaries of the various clubs, of which there are now 21.

YACHTING AND BOATING

Boating of various kinds is to be had on almost every lake, and yachting is a favourite pastime, especially on Windermere, where also motor boating has become very popular. It is well to remember that mountains make their own weather, and that the lakes are liable to squalls of extreme suddenness and violence. The Royal Windermere Yacht Club hold races every Saturday in summer. The headquarters of the club are at Bowness. Bowness-on-Windermere and Waterhead at Ambleside are the chief pleasure craft hiring places. There is a popular yacht club at Bassenthwaite Lake.

TENNIS, BOWLS, AND PUTTING

There are public tennis courts at Windermere, Ambleside, Keswick, Kendal, Grange-over-Sands, and elsewhere, and at most of the principal centres are bowling and putting greens. Visitors are made welcome by the local clubs.

SPORTS MEETINGS

Summer visitors will be interested in the sports meetings and other gatherings which are held at Whitsuntide and during August and September. The most famous of these is the Grasmere Sports, usually on the third Thursday in August, which is notable for a very stiff Fell Race to the top of Butter Crags and back : it is also the *locus classicus* for the Cumberland and Westmorland style of wrestling. Sheep Dog Trials take place at Applethwaite Common near Windermere, Rydal, Patterdale and elsewhere. At all of these meetings the day is incomplete without one or more *Hound Trails*, which are spectacular events peculiar to this part of England.

WALKING TOURS

Routes.—Newcomers to the district should not assume that in all cases where a route is referred to in the Guide, or even where a path is marked on the map, there is a definite and identifiable track for the whole distance. On some much-frequented routes (*e.g.* the path over Scarth Gap) there is a well-marked track for the whole way, and a further safeguard is provided by means of cairns placed at short intervals. On other routes a definite track may exist for only a part of the way, and cairns, if they exist at all, are a long way apart. In many places it is necessary to plan a route convenient to oneself, having regard to gradients, swamps, streams, etc., and if one plans a good route one will frequently find evidence that it has been trodden by previous users.

The following week-end walking tours are designed to allow the tourist to see as much of Lakeland as is possible in three full days. For these short runs there are only two reasonable approaches—from Windermere and Keswick. The approach from Windermere is the best and a most panoramic introduction to the Lakes ; but from Keswick, in the limited time at his disposal, the walker can cover more country. It is worth while to consult current time-tables of transport services.

Times.—The journey times quoted throughout the Guide are those given by the late Mr. Baddeley with a few revisions. Some walkers will find them comfortable estimates ; others—especially during the first few days—may consider them rather fast. It is obviously impossible to give a " standard " time for even the simplest walk ; but we would suggest that if readers compare their own times with Mr. Baddeley's when making their first few expeditions they will have no difficulty in making the necessary adjustments to the printed estimates on subsequent occasions.

Telephones.—For list of public telephones, see p. 42.

A WEEK-END FROM KESWICK

Note.—It is suggested that those for whom the following tour is a trifle strenuous should conclude the Saturday tramp at Wasdale Head : on Sunday cross Scafell Pike to Langdale and Grasmere, and on Monday tramp by Fairfield to Patterdale and Penrith.

Saturday.—Transport to Seatoller (*Derwentwater* and *Borrowdale*) ; walk up to Honister Hause ; thence over Brandreth, Green Gable, and Great Gable (*Buttermere, Crummock Water, Ennerdale Lake, Wastwater*), descending to Sty Head. Thence to Esk Hause (viewing *Upper Eskdale*), Rossett Gill, Great Langdale (visiting Dungeon Ghyll if time permits), Hunting Stile

(*Elterwater*), Grasmere. (Buses run between the Dungeon Ghyll *Old Hotel* and Ambleside, etc.)

Sunday.—Grasmere to Ambleside (*Grasmere* and *Rydal Water*), and to Coniston by Barn Gates Inn (*Coniston Lake*), returning by Hawkshead and Far Sawrey (*Esthwaite Water*) to the Ferry (*Windermere*) for Bowness and Windermere.

Monday.—By bus (summer service only) to the inn on the Kirkstone Pass. Thence over Red Screes and Fairfield, descending to Patterdale, preferably by Cofa Pike and St. Sunday Crag. An alternative descent for people who are not blessed with steady heads is from Fairfield to Grisedale Tarn, and so by the Pass to Patterdale ; thence to Penrith by bus or by boat and bus.

Alternative in case of mist on the high fells: *Saturday*—By mini-bus over Newlands Pass to Buttermere ; thence walk to Gatesgarth, at the foot of the Honister Pass, and on by Scarth Gap and Black Sail to Wasdale Head. *Sunday*—Walk over Esk Hause to Grasmere. *Monday*—Bus and boat to Bowness, walk to Patterdale and to Penrith as above.

If an extra day is available, it may be occupied by making the Furness round from Grasmere (*Coniston* and the whole length of *Windermere*) or Ambleside. Or the Red Screes and Fairfield round may be made on Monday, and the boat taken to Howtown ; and Tuesday may be occupied by crossing High Street to *Haweswater*, and thence to Penrith or Shap. It will also be found possible to arrange a visit to *Thirlmere*. Those who wish to see Thirlmere, and are restricted to three days, may drive to Wythburn and cross Helvellyn to Patterdale ; but the expedition is not as extensive as that by Red Screes and Fairfield.

A WEEK-END FROM WINDERMERE

Saturday.—Bus by Troutbeck and the Kirkstone Pass to Patterdale (*Brothers' Water* and *Ullswater*), and thence by either Striding or Swirrell Edge over Helvellyn to Wythburn (*Thirlmere*) and so (either afoot or by bus) to Grasmere, from which Rydal Water may be visited if time permit.

Sunday.—Grasmere to Wastwater. If fine, by Easedale, Sergeant Man, round Langdale Combe by the Stake and Esk Hause, with fine views of Windermere, Coniston, etc. ; or in mist, by Hunting Stile, Langdale, Rossett Gill, and Esk Hause, thence by the Sty to Wasdale Head. Strong walkers, on a fine day, may reach Wasdale Head from Esk Hause, over England's summit, Scafell Pike (*Wastwater*).

Monday.—From Wasdale Head (*Wastwater*), by Black Sail and Scarth Gap to Honister Pass (*Buttermere* and *Crummock Water*), through Borrowdale to Keswick (*Derwentwater*).

In case of an extra day being available : *Alternative first day*—Furness round (*Coniston* and the whole length of *Windermere*), or Ambleside, Barn Gates, Coniston, Esthwaite Water, and the Ferry to Windermere.

Alternative Monday—From Wasdale by Black Sail and Scarth Gap, and thence over High Crag, High Stile, and Red Pike, descending by Scale Force to Buttermere. *Tuesday*—Buttermere to Keswick by Honister Pass and Borrowdale.

TEN DAYS IN THE LAKES

The following notes are intended for those who are not primarily concerned with arranging a holiday afoot, but would wish to make full use of public transport services or have their own means of transport.

Newcomers to the District are recommended to approach the Lakes from the Windermere end, and spend the first half of their holiday there, moving on to Keswick for the latter half. The sail up Ullswater also offers a fine approach. The Keswick approach by Derwentwater and Borrowdale affords also an ideal entrance to Lakeland.

Expeditions from Bowness, Ambleside, or Grasmere.—1. The first clear day, the drive to Patterdale and back, *viâ* Troutbeck, including a sail up and down Ullswater. It is better to take this expedition from Bowness, travelling *viâ* Troutbeck both ways. 2. Coniston by Barn Gates, returning by Hawkshead and the Ferry, or *vice versa*. 3. The round of the Langdales. 4. The Furness round. 5. Circular trip by Newby Bridge, Lake Side, and the Ferry House, returning by the Ferry or right round the lake, the route being continued through Hawkshead and Ambleside. The expedition may, of course, be taken in the reverse direction.

Expeditions from Keswick.—1. The Honister round. 2. Round Bassenthwaite. 3. Round Thirlmere. 4. Round Derwentwater. It is also possible to visit Patterdale from Keswick by bus to Penrith hence to Patterdale, time being available for a sail up and down Ullswater.

These expeditions occupy nine out of the ten days available, and, unless the weather is exceptional, the tourist will be lucky to get them all in. If any extra days are available, the following mountain ascents are recommended :—From Windermere or Bowness, *Ill Bell* ; from Ambleside, *Red Screes* or *Caudale Moor* ; from Grasmere, *High Raise* and the *Langdales*, *Fairfield* or *Helvellyn*, etc. ; from Keswick, *Grasmoor*. Less ambitious ascents are : From Windermere or Ambleside, etc., *Wansfell Pike* ; from Grasmere, *Loughrigg* or *Silver How* ; from Keswick, *Latrigg*.

A FORTNIGHT'S WALKING TOURS

We give these route suggestions, not with any idea of their being strictly followed, but as an indication of convenient tracks for those who wish to see as much as possible in a given time.

Making allowance for wet weather and other occasions of delay, we have only reckoned ten walking or bus expedition days. It is assumed that for some of these routes, transport will be taken part of the way.

Starting from Windermere or Bowness

1.—Windermere, Garburn Pass, Kentmere, Nan Bield, Mardale ; 4½–5½ hrs.
2.—Kidsty Pike (or High Street), Patterdale ; 3½–4 hrs. Patterdale to Aira Force, or to Howtown, and back by the Lake.
3.—Helvellyn, Thirlspot, Keswick ; 6–7 hrs.
4.—Watendlath, Rosthwaite, west side of Derwentwater, Portinscale, Keswick ; 5–6 hrs.
5.—Buttermere Round by conveyance or on foot, 23 m.
6.—Whinlatter Pass, Scale Hill, Floutern Tarn, Ennerdale Lake Car Park ; 5–6 hrs.
7.—Black Sail Pass (or the Pillar), Wasdale Head ; 4–5 hrs.
8.—Scafell Pike, Dungeon Ghyll, Grasmere ; 7–8 hrs.
9.—Red Bank, Elterwater, Colwith Force, Tilberthwaite, Coniston, Tarn Hows, Skelwith Bridge ; 6–7 hrs.
10.—Ambleside, Stock Gill, Wansfell Pike, Troutbeck, Windermere Village ; 4–5 hours.

Starting from Lake Side

1.—Graythwaite, Hawkshead, Tarn Hows, Coniston (Waterhead), 12 m. Ascend the Old Man ; 5–6 hrs.
2.—Walna Scar, Seathwaite, Woolpack, Strands ; 7–8 hrs.
3.—Wasdale Head, 6 m. Ascend Scafell Pike ; 4–6 hrs.
4.—Black Sail, Scarf Gap, High Crag, High Stile, Red Pike, Scale Force, Scale Hill (Crummock) ; 6–8 hrs.
5.—Buttermere, Honister, Borrowdale, Keswick ; 18 m.
6.—Watendlath, Rosthwaite, W. side of Derwentwater, Keswick ; 5–6 hrs.
7.—Thirlspot, Helvellyn, Patterdale ; 6–7 hrs.
8.—Grisedale Pass, Grasmere, Red Bank, Elterwater, Little Langdale, Blea Tarn, Dungeon Ghyll ; 7–8 hrs.
9.—Great Langdale, Skelwith Bridge, Ambleside, Kirkstone Pass, High Street, Mardale (Haweswater) ; 9–10 hrs.
10.—Nan Bield, Kentmere, Garburn, Windermere ; 4½–5½ hrs.

Starting from Coniston

1.—The Old Man, Walna Scar, Seathwaite, Woolpack or Boot (Eskdale) ; 6–7 hrs.
2.—Stanley Ghyll and back, 3 m. Santon Bridge, Strands, Wasdale Head, 14 m. ; or to Wasdale Head over Scafell Pike ; 5–6 hrs.
3.—Black Sail, Scarf Gap, High Crag, High Stile, Red Pike, Scale Force, Scale Hill (Crummock) ; 6–7 hrs.

4.—Whinlatter Pass, Keswick, 10 m. Row or motor boat on Derwentwater.

5.—Buttermere Round (conveyance or on foot); 23 m. Full day.

6.—Watendlath, Armboth Fell, Thirlmere, Thirlspot, Helvellyn, Patterdale; 8–9 hrs.

7.—Aira Force and back (boat), 6 m. Howtown (steamer), 6 m. Fusedale, Measand, Haweswater, Mardale; 3–4 hrs.

8.—Nan Bield, High Street, Kirkstone Pass, Ambleside; 4½–5½ hrs.

9.—Rydal, Red Bank, Grasmere, Easedale Tarn, Dungeon Ghyll; 4–5 hrs.

10.—Langdale (Great or Little), Skelwith Bridge, Ambleside, Wansfell, Troutbeck, Windermere; 6–7 hrs.

Starting from Boot (or Wasdale Head)

1.—Stanley Ghyll and back, 3 m.; Wasdale Head over Scafell Pike, 5–6 hrs.; or by Santon Bridge and Strands, 14 m. If starting from Wasdale Head the tourist may devote the first day to the ascent of Scafell Pike, descending into Eskdale, 6–7 hrs.; visiting Stanley Ghyll, 3 m.; and returning from Boot to Wasdale Head by Burnmoor Tarn.

2.—How Hall Farm (Ennerdale), over the Pillar, 4½–5½ hrs.; or by Black Sail Pass and Ennerdale Valley, 4 hrs.; How Hall Farm to Scale Hill Hotel, by Floutern Tarn, 6 m.

3.—Buttermere, Honister, Borrowdale, Keswick; 18 m.

4.—Ascend Saddleback by Threlkeld, returning under Latrigg, 5–6 hrs. (bus to Threlkeld).

5.—High Lodore, Watendlath, Armboth Fell, west side of Thirlmere, Thirlspot, Helvellyn, Patterdale; 8–9 hrs.

6.—Aira Force and back, 6 m. Boardale Hause, Howtown, Measand, Mardale Green; 5–6 hrs.

7.—Kidsty Pike, High Street, Kirkstone, Ambleside, Grasmere (by Loughrigg Terrace and Red Bank); 8–9 hrs.

8.—Easedale Tarn, Codale Tarn, Stickle Tarn, Dungeon Ghyll, 2½–3½ hrs. Blea Tarn, Tilberthwaite, Coniston; 9 m.

9.—Ascend the Old Man; 3–4 hrs. Tarn Hows, Oxenfell, Colwith Force, Elterwater, Ambleside; 12 m.

10.—Wansfell Pike, Troutbeck, Windermere Village; 3–3½ m.

Starting from Ennerdale or Crummock

1.—Scale Force, Red Pike, High Stile, High Crag, Scarf Gap, Black Sail, Wasdale Head; 6–7 hrs.

2.—Scafell Pike, descending to the Woolpack Inn at Eskdale; 6–7 hrs. Stanley Ghyll and back, 3 m. Burnmoor Tarn, Wasdale Head; 6 m.

3.—Sty Head Pass, Seatoller, Honister Hause, Buttermere, Newlands, Keswick; 21 m. (or Styhead Pass, Great Gable, Green Gable, Brandreth, Grey Knotts, Honister Hause, etc.).

4.—Ashness Bridge, High Lodore, Watendlath, Rosthwaite, the Bowder Stone, Lodore, Keswick; 15 m.

5.—West side of Thirlmere, Wythburn, 8 m. Helvellyn, descending to Patterdale; $3\frac{1}{2}$–$4\frac{1}{2}$ hrs.

6.—Aira Force and back (boat if available), 6 m. Boardale Hause, Howtown, Measand, Mardale Green (Haweswater); 5–6 hrs.

7.—Kidsty Pike, Hayeswater, Patterdale, Grisedale Pass, Grasmere; 8–9 hrs.

8.—Round Grasmere by Loughrigg Terrace, 5 m. Easedale Tarn, Codale Tarn, Stickle Tarn, Dungeon Ghyll; 3 hrs.

9.—Blea Tarn, Little Langdale, Fell Foot, Wetherlam, Coniston, Old Man; 5–6 hrs.

10.—Tarn Hows, Ambleside, 9 m. Wansfell Pike, Troutbeck, Windermere Village; 3–$3\frac{1}{2}$ hrs.

Starting from Keswick

1.—Castlerigg Stone Circle, Vale of St. John (detour to Thirlmere Dam), Thirlspot; 8 m. Over Helvellyn to Patterdale; $3\frac{1}{2}$–$4\frac{1}{2}$ hrs.

2.—Howtown (steamer), 6 m. Fusedale, Measand, Mardale Green (Haweswater); 3–4 hrs. Kidsty Pike, Hayeswater, Patterdale; 3–4 hrs.

3.—Grisedale Pass, Grasmere, 3–4 hrs. Ascend Helm Crag, or walk round Grasmere Lake by Red Bank; $1\frac{1}{2}$–2 hrs.

4.—Easedale Tarn, Codale Tarn, Stickle Tarn, Dungeon Ghyll; 3–4 hrs. The Stake Pass, Rosthwaite; $2\frac{1}{2}$–$3\frac{1}{2}$ hrs. Keswick, $6\frac{1}{4}$ m.

5.—Scale Hill by Whinlatter Pass, 10 m.; or by Coledale Pass, 3–4 hrs.; or over Grisedale Pike, 4–5 hrs. Scale Force, Buttermere, 2–$2\frac{1}{4}$ hrs.

6.—Honister Pass, 4 m. Grey Knotts, Brandreth, Green Gable, Great Gable, Sty Head Pass, Wasdale Head; $4\frac{1}{2}$–$5\frac{1}{2}$ hrs.

7.—Burnmoor Tarn, Boot, Stanley Ghyll, Birker Moor, Ulpha, Seathwaite, Walna Scar, Coniston; full day.

8.—Tarn Hows and back, 5 m. Furness Abbey, 21 m. Lake Side (Windermere), 15 m. Ambleside (steamer), 11 m.

9.—Skelwith Bridge, Colwith Force, Blea Tarn, Dungeon Ghyll, Chapel Stile, Red Bank, Rydal, Ambleside; 20 m.

10.—Wansfell Pike, Troutbeck, Windermere Village, 3–$3\frac{1}{2}$ hrs.; or back from Troutbeck to Ambleside by Low Wood, same time; and drive to Keswick, 16 m.

Starting from Patterdale

1.—Aira Force and back, 6 m. Boardale Hause, Howtown, 6 m. Fusedale, Measand, Mardale (Haweswater); 3–4 hrs.

2.—Nan Bield Pass, Kentmere, Garburn Pass, or over High

Street to Queen's Head, Troutbeck; 3½–4½ hrs. Low
Wood, Ambleside, 3 m.

3.—Barn Gates, Tarn Hows, Coniston, 9 m. Furness Abbey
(rail), 21 m. Lake Side (Windermere), 15 m. Ambleside
(steamer), 11 m.

4.—Red Bank, Grasmere, Easedale Tarn and back, Skelwith
Bridge, Colwith Force, Blea Tarn, Dungeon Ghyll; 20 m.

5.—Rossett Gill, Esk Hause, Scafell Pike, the "Woolpack"
(Eskdale), 7–8 hrs.

6.—Stanley Ghyll, Santon Bridge, Strands, Wasdale Head;
16 m.

7.—Ennerdale Lake (car park), over the Pillar, 4½–6½ hrs.; or
by Black Sail Pass and Ennerdale Valley, 4½–6½ hrs.
Ennerdale Lake to Scale Hill (Crummock) by Floutern
Tarn, 6 m.

8.—Buttermere, Honister, Borrowdale, Keswick; 18 m.

9.—Ascend Saddleback or Skiddaw, 5–6 hrs.; or visit High
Lodore and Watendlath, returning by Rosthwaite and
west side of Derwentwater; 15 m.

10.—Ride or walk to Windermere Village, 21 m.; Bowness, 22 m.

Starting from Shap

1.—Rosgill, Haweswater, Mardale (Haweswater); 9½ m.
Kidsty Pike, Angle Tarn on the fringe of Martindale
Common, Boardale Hause, Patterdale; 4½–5½ hrs.

2.—Aira Force and back (boat if available), 6 m. Kirkstone
Pass, Troutbeck, Low Wood, Ambleside; 14 m.

3.—Grasmere (by Loughrigg Terrace), 5 m. Dunmail Raise,
Harrop Tarn, Watendlath, High Lodore, Ashness Bridge,
Keswick; 5–6 hrs.

4.—Buttermere Round by coach or on foot, 23 m.

5.—Whinlatter Pass, Scale Hill, Anglers' Hotel (Ennerdale);
16 m.

6.—Over the Pillar, 4½–6½ hrs.; or by Cold Fell, Calder Bridge,
Gosforth, and Strands to Wasdale Head; 16 m.

7.—Scafell Pike by Esk Hause, descending direct to Wasdale
Head; 5–6 hrs.

8.—Burnmoor Tarn, Boot, 6 m. Stanley Ghyll, Birker Moor,
Ulpha, Seathwaite, Walna Scar, Coniston; 5–6 hrs.

9.—Furness Abbey and back (rail), 40 m.; or ascend Coniston
Old Man, 3–4 hrs. Tarn Hows, Tilberthwaite, Fell Foot,
Blea Tarn, Dungeon Ghyll; 11 m.

10.—Great Langdale, Waterhead (Ambleside), 8 m. Low Wood,
Windermere Village by Troutbeck, 5–6 m.; or Bowness (by
boat), 4½ m. Orrest Head and Windermere Village, 4 m.

MOTORING AND CYCLING

WHILE the main roads through the Lake District are, on the whole, excellent, motorists should bear in mind that by-roads are often surprisingly steep, giving very little or no hold even for cars with efficient brakes. Roads like the "Struggle" from Ambleside to Kirkstone are a severe test, whilst the route over Hardknott and Wrynose, though having an excellent surface, consists of hair-pin bends and steep gradients. Inquiries should be made before setting out on any but the recognised motor roads, and almost everywhere constant care is called for by winding roads and steep hills. For all that, motoring in the Lake District is well worth while—there is hardly a mile of road that is not worth following either for itself or for the views it commands. There are well-equipped garages at all the principal centres—Windermere, Ambleside, Grasmere, Keswick, Coniston, etc. Among smaller resorts, accommodation is generally provided by the hotels, but spares and petrol are not always supplied.

Cycling in the Lake District is noteworthy in two ways—its keen interest and its limited area. There is no finer run anywhere than the twenty-one miles of high road between Windermere and Keswick, which may be commenced anywhere you like south of Windermere and continued to Cockermouth, etc. The routes within the district often incorporate steep "pass" roads, but on the whole are varied and interesting, some ending at the foot of the mountains, others completing inter-valley circuits. Pleasant circuits may be taken round Windermere, Coniston, Esthwaite, Thirlmere, Derwentwater, and Bassenthwaite, the easiest being those of Thirlmere and Bassenthwaite.

On the chief frequented routes through the District, the most dangerous places for cyclists are Kirkstone Top down to Ambleside (known as "The Struggle" and in parts prohibitive) or Ullswater or Windermere; the hills between Skelwith and Colwith Bridges, the Graythwaite hill between Lakeside Station and the Ferry on the west side of Windermere, and also the direct descent to Keswick on the road from Windermere. The danger of riding down the "break-neck" Red Bank to Grasmere must be obvious to anyone from the top of it, as also at Honister Hause, Hardknott Pass, and Wrynose Pass. We conclude with the remark that perhaps the most fascinating little run in Britain is the first half of the road from Windermere to Keswick, by Grasmere, to the foot of Dunmail Raise.

Some notes on the routes *through* the district will be found on *pp.* 38–42, but we first enumerate a few from the North of England and the South of Scotland *to* the district.

ROAD ROUTES TO THE DISTRICT

In the following summary of main roads of approach to the Lake Country, Keswick is the centre chosen, because from all sides it is easily reached over easy passes and by good roads.

The roads from Liverpool (*viâ* Ormskirk, 31 *m.*), Manchester (*viâ* Bolton and Horwich, 31 *m.*), and Warrington (*viâ* Ashton-in-Makerfield and Wigan, 29½ *m.*), converge on **Preston.** The scenery in South Lancashire is tame, and the roads are marred by industrial traffic. The M6 Motorway has done much to alleviate congestion, and provides welcome stretches of unhindered driving to beyond Penrith and Carlisle with views of the distant fells across Morecambe Bay. From Carnforth (27¾ *m.*), through Milnthorpe (35 *m.*), the A6 passes Levens Hall, and at Kendal (42¾ *m.*) reaches the edge of the real Lake Country. The route (A591) to Keswick (72 *m.*) is through Windermere (51 *m.*) and Ambleside (55½ *m.*).

From London and Southern England the fastest route is via Point 36 on the M6 motorway through to Kendal and Windermere, with a new road link completed two years ago. Another route for those who avoid motorways is via the A5 or A6 (which runs from London to Kendal, a distance of 269 *m.*).

From the south-east, the best road may be taken as starting from Leeds, and passing through Otley and Ilkley to Skipton (25 *m.*). Beyond Settle (42½ *m.*) a long and steep hill is tackled. Thence through to Kirkby Lonsdale (60 *m.*) the road (A65) is hilly. At Kendal (72¾ *m.*) the road for Windermere (81 *m.*) and Keswick (102 *m.*) is joined.

Another and longer route from Leeds to Keswick passes east on the hill country through Harrogate (15 *m.*), Ripon (26½ *m.*), Middleham (44¾ *m.*), to Leyburn (47 *m.*), where the beautiful Wensleydale is entered and traversed to Hawes (63½ *m.*). From this village to the Moorcock Inn (69 *m.*) is mostly rise, and at the inn the road forks, a direct route west falling down Garsdale to Sedbergh and Kendal (89½ *m.*), whence the Windermere (98 *m.*) road is followed to Keswick (119 *m.*). The north fork at the *Moorcock* (69 *m.*) leads to Kirkby Stephen (80½ *m.*), Brough (84½ *m.*) and traverses the lovely Eden Valley to Penrith (105 *m.*), thence west by Troutbeck and Threlkeld to Keswick (123 *m.*).

From Newcastle and the North-east the most direct route is by Alston (45 *m.*) to Penrith (64¾ *m.*) and Keswick (82¾ *m.*), but the road is very hilly, and between Alston and Penrith passes over Hartside at a height of 1,889 feet. There is an alternative route (A69) *viâ* Hexham (21½ *m.*), Haltwhistle (37 *m.*), Brampton (50 *m.*), Carlisle (59 *m.*) and Keswick *viâ* Bothel (91½ *m.*). The alternative route *viâ* Penrith (95¼ *m.*) is a slightly better road but affords no saving of time.

From Scotland Carlisle is the converging point. From Glasgow there is a pleasant "Burns Country" run *viâ* Kilmarnock

(22 *m.*), Mauchline (31 *m.*), Cumnock (38 *m.*), Sanquhar (45 *m.*), Dumfries (81 *m.*), Gretna (104½ *m.*), to Carlisle, (115 *m.*) and Keswick (147½ *m.*).

There is a shorter Clyde route over Beattock : Hamilton (12½ *m.*), Abington (37½ *m.*), Beattock (57½ *m.*), Lockerbie (70½ *m.*), Carlisle (95 *m.*), Penrith (113¼ *m.*), Keswick (131¼ *m.*). From Edinburgh there are also alternative routes south, *via* Liberton (3¼ *m.*), Leadburn (13 *m.*), Romanno Bridge (19¾ *m.*), Crook Inn (35½ *m.*), Moffatt (52 *m.*), Carlisle (91½ *m.*), Keswick (124 *m.*).

Another route traverses the Scott Country, through Dalkeith (6 *m.*), Galashiels (32 *m.*), Melrose (36 *m.*), Abbotsford (40 *m.*), Selkirk (44 *m.*), Hawick (56 *m.*), Langholm (79 *m.*), to Carlisle (100 *m.*), and Keswick (132½ *m.*). On these routes the best scenery from Glasgow lies between Sanquhar and Thornhill.

There are innumerable variations and side-routes quite recommendable, but the roads named have been chosen from personal acquaintance.

ROUTES WITHIN THE DISTRICT

(For descriptions of the roads enumerated on following pages, see Index.)

From Windermere the finest road is that **to Keswick (21 miles)** It is, indeed, the finest in the district, leading as it does by the shores of Windermere to Ambleside, with noble mountain views ahead, thence by lovely Rydal Water to Grasmere, with its beautiful lake. Thence northward the road takes on a sterner aspect, climbing by the long Dunmail Raise between Steel Fell on the left and, on the right, Seat Sandal. Beyond Dunmail Raise is Thirlmere, with good roads on either shore (the western road—bad corners—gives the best views of Helvellyn). The two roads unite beyond the farther end of the Lake and in about five miles come to Keswick, which is entered by a steep 1-9 descent requiring care. (The road is described on *pp.* 80–87.)

It may be added that this road is busy during the height of the season with all kinds of traffic, and the wise motorist will endeavour to choose a time when he can raise his eyes to the scenery without unduly imperilling his car and its occupants.

Round Windermere (about 35 miles). An enjoyable tour may be had by rounding Windermere Lake by Waterhead and Clappersgate, thence by High Cross and along the east shore of Coniston to Greenodd ; thence to Newby Bridge, at the southern end of the Lake. The road northward thence to Bowness lies along the eastern shore of Lake Windermere. Another but shorter round is by Waterhead, Clappersgate, Hawkshead, down west shore of Esthwaite Water, by Graythwaite Hall, Lakeside, Newby Bridge, up east shore to Windermere town, thence to Ambleside by the low lake road from Bowness.

To Patterdale and Penrith.—From Windermere there is a long and often very steep climb over Kirkstone (the average gradient is 1–8, rising to 1–5½ in places—the worst part is the descent north from the *Kirkstone Inn*), but this road is well worth following for the magnificent scenery unfolded. From Windermere to Glenridding is 13 miles; to Penrith, 26½. (*See pp.* 88–90.)

Caution.—The road *from Ambleside to Kirkstone is dangerous for cars*, having among other features a 1–4 gradient and an uneven surface.

Langdale.—For the greater part of the way the road through *Great Langdale* is good, though none too wide for the traffic (including buses and coaches) it is called upon to bear. The road through *Little Langdale* is not nearly so good; it is very steep in places and there are a number of points where two vehicles would find it difficult to pass. The road between Great and Little Langdale rounding Side Pike and on by Blea Tarn is narrow and well-surfaced but deteriorates to track near Little Langdale.

Ambleside to Coniston (7½ miles) and Broughton (16½) is a route with fine retrospective views, but few bad hills, though there are one or two 1–7 and 1–8 gradients.

Ambleside to Wasdale and Ennerdale.—Ambleside is but 12 miles from Wasdale Head—as the crow flies. For motorists the intervening fells make it necessary to take a roundabout route *viâ* Broughton-in-Furness and Bootle to Holmrook, just short of which turn off to Santon Bridge and Wasdale. For Ennerdale pass through Gosforth to Calder Bridge where the Ennerdale road branches off over Cold Fell.

Having circumnavigated the south-western portion of the Lake District in reaching Ennerdale from Ambleside, many motorists return *viâ* Keswick and Thirlmer

Keswick is the best centre for motorists bent on exploring Lakeland, and the first run from Keswick is certain to be—

Round Derwentwater, extending southward through **Borrowdale** to Seatoller. The roads bordering Derwentwater call for no remark, except that the western road is best taken from south to north. On the return to Keswick the choice of roads alongside Derwentwater is made at Grange, the western road crossing the bridge.

The Honister Pass and Buttermere.—The direct Borrowdale–Buttermere route presents no great terrors, and the " Buttermere Round " has become very popular.

Alternative routes between Keswick and **Buttermere** are by way of Newlands and Keskadale (but the road is steep and winding) or *viâ* the Whinlatter Pass, leaving Keswick by Braithwaite, or *viâ* Bassenthwaite and Embleton (where turn southward) and across to the Vale of Lorton. The road is the usual Lakeland highway, on which it is constantly necessary to be on guard against steep gradients and sharp turns.

Round Bassenthwaite is almost a tame ride after the thrills of Honister, but the round opens up some fine views. The outward journey should be made by the western road. The return might be made to include Caldbeck.

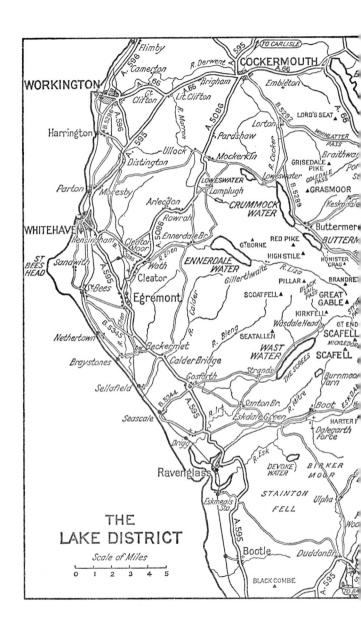

THE LAKE DISTRICT

Scale of Miles

0 1 2 3 4 5

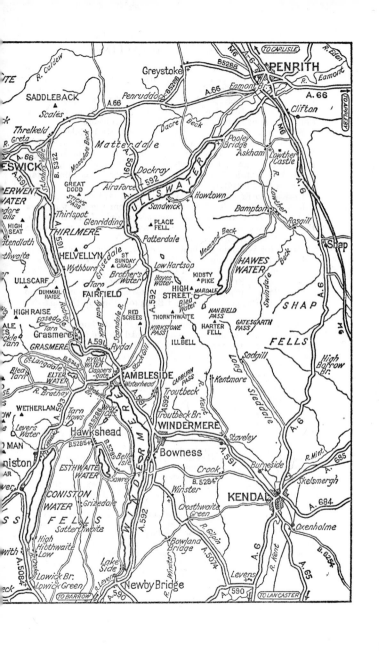

Keswick to Windermere (21 miles). The usual route out of Keswick is by the Penrith road, turning up to the right about a mile from the Town Hall. The ensuing climb is steep (fine views), but thenceforward the road gives little trouble, though due to the fact that it winds round rocks, etc., the narrow west-side Thirlmere road must be driven with caution.

Keswick to Penrith (18 miles). A pleasantly undulating road with no bad hills, but it cannot be said to run through typical Lakeland scenery. But affords fine distant views of Helvellyn Mountain Range and the Fells round Vale of Keswick. From Troutbeck Station (9 miles out) a road runs across Matterdale Common to Ullswater.

Keswick to Ennerdale and Wasdale Head (41½ miles). Ennerdale and Wasdale Head are *culs-de-sac* from the point of view of the motorist and can be approached only from the west. From Keswick the road is *viâ* Cockermouth, where turn south for Ennerdale Bridge, at the entrance to Ennerdale.

Hence for Wasdale the best road (and, in fact, the only available one) is *viâ* Egremont and Gosforth, where we turn eastward.

Eskdale, a few miles south of Wasdale, may be reached from Wasdale *viâ* Santon Bridge, where join the main road from Gosforth.

Mardale is reached from Penrith (14½ miles) by a pretty road *viâ* Eamont Bridge, Askham and Bampton, then up the east side of Haweswater past the Haweswater Hotel.

Mardale is a *cul-de-sac* for motorists, but at Bampton a road turns eastward to the main Carlisle road at Shap [whence one may run north to Penrith or south to Kendal, and re-enter the Lake District from either of those places].

PUBLIC TELEPHONES

The following is a short list of some public telephone kiosks in the central parts of the Lake District.

Ambleside (Market Square)	Grange-in-Borrow-dale	Portinscale
Bampton	Grasmere (Red Lion Square)	Rosthwaite
Bassenthwaite Village	Hartsop	Seathwaite (outside Newfield Inn)
Boot (outside Post Office)	Hawkshead (Market Square)	Skelwith Bridge
Braithwaite	Hawkshead Hill	Thornthwaite
Buttermere (near Post Office)	Kentmere (near Church)	Threlkeld
Coniston	Loweswater (near Kirkstyle Inn)	Torver
Eskdale	Martindale	Troutbeck (Village Institute)
Eskdale Green (outside Post Office)	Nether Wasdale	Ulpha
Glenridding	Patterdale	Wasdale Head (outside Wastwater Hotel)

At Elterwater and at Little Langdale there are Call Offices at the Post Offices. There is neither Kiosk nor Call Office in Great Langdale but the telephone at *Dungeon Ghyll Hotel* may be used by courtesy of the proprietor.

LOCAL BUS SERVICES

Ribble Motor Services Ltd. cover most of southern Lakeland and also run an Eight Lakes Tour from Ambleside and Windermere and a Ten Lakes Tour from Penrith in the season. Enquiry offices at Ambleside, Kendal, Keswick, Penrith and Ulverston. See current announcements and timetables. Principal services run by this company include those—

From Ambleside to Windermere and Kendal; to Barrow-in-Furness by Newby Bridge and Ulverston; to Dungeon Ghyll; to Coniston by Skelwith or Hawkshead; to Grasmere and Keswick.

From Ambleside to Hawkshead, Sawrey and the Ferry.

From Coniston to Ambleside by Skelwith or Hawkshead; to Torver and Ulverston.

From Grasmere to Keswick; to Ambleside and Windermere.

From Kendal to Windermere, Ambleside and Keswick; to Shap and Penrith; to Kentmere; to Crook, Bowness, Bowland Bridge.

From Keswick to Grasmere, Ambleside, Windermere and Kendal; to Troutbeck and Penrith.

From Penrith to Keswick; to Patterdale and Brotherswater, continuing (summer only) over Kirkstone Pass to Windermere.

From Ulverston to Newby Bridge, Windermere and Ambleside; to Torver and Coniston.

From Windermere to Ambleside, Grasmere and Keswick; to Kendal; to Newby Bridge, Ulverston and Barrow; to Troutbeck continuing (summer only) over Kirkstone Pass to Brotherswater, Patterdale and Penrith.

Cumberland Motor Services Ltd. service much of the northern and western parts of the district. Services include those—

From Penrith to Troutbeck, Threlkeld and Keswick.

From Keswick to Threlkeld, Troutbeck and Penrith; to Threlkeld, Troutbeck, Aira Force and Patterdale (summer only); to Lodore, Grange Bridge, Bowder Stone, Rosthwaite and Seatoller (in conjunction with local operators); to Braithwaite, Lorton and Buttermere (summer only); to Braithwaite and Cockermouth, and to Bassenthwaite and Cockermouth. *Note :* these last two services from Keswick to Cockermouth run alternately on the west and east sides of Bassenthwaite Lake respectively.

From Cockermouth to Lorton and Loweswater; to Lorton and Buttermere; and to Whitehaven.

From Whitehaven to Cockermouth and Keswick (*see above*); to Ennerdale Bridge (Thursdays only), and Cockermouth; to Egremont and Ravenglass; to Nether Wasdale (Thursdays only).

There are other local bus services including those—

From Penrith to Bampton and Haweswater; and to Dockray and Matterdale (Tuesday).

APPROACHES TO THE DISTRICT

Road Routes to the Lake District are indicated on *pp.* 37-8

CONSIDERING the great advantages in point of accessibility and accommodation which Windermere and Keswick, and, in a minor degree, Coniston and Patterdale, possess, it is small wonder that the tourists who enter the Lake District at other points are not numerous. At the same time it is a fact that, by sticking so pertinaciously to this " sheep-through-a-gap " custom, thousands visit the district over and over again without seeing some of its most striking features. Two lakes, in particular, suffer greatly from this habit—Wastwater and Haweswater. Travellers who descend Sty Head or Black Sail to Wasdale Head, and set off up the fells again next morning, under the impression that they have seen Wastwater, labour under a grievous delusion. Wastwater, to be judged of at all, must be approached from Strands, at its lower end ,and to get to Strands a train may be taken to Seascale, and from there the journey made by car, or. the road taken from Santon Bridge or Gosforth. Haweswater, again, is, even though the Corporation of Manchester have converted it into a reservoir, a veritable gem ; and a walk of five or a drive of eight miles from Shap station on the main railway line brings us to the foot of the lake, and to a scene which, for picturesque and bold simplicity, is hardly surpassed in Britain. Stanley Ghyll, too, in Eskdale, the finest scene of its kind in the district, is usually missed through this lack of originality in planning approaches. It is within a mile of Beckfoot.

We might multiply instances, but enough has been said to warrant our devoting a chapter of this book to a brief description of the various routes by which English Lakeland can be reached. For the order in which these are taken, readers should see the list of Contents, *p.* 5.

Current railway arrangements must be ascertained ; but here it may be pointed out that British Railways (London Midland Region) run through trains or through carriages from many large centres to Windermere and Penrith.

APPROACHES FROM THE SOUTH

The three principal approaches from the South are:

1. *viâ* Kendal to Windermere village.

2. To Lake Side by road and thence by boat up Lake Windermere to Bowness (for Windermere) or to Waterhead (for Ambleside).

3. By the road either right through to Coniston, or the road (bus route) from Greenodd to Coniston.

The route *viâ* **Kendal** (*see p.* 95) is that most familiar to motorists coming from the Midlands and the South by way of Skipton and Settle and to the majority of railway travellers bound for Windermere, since so many prefer to go right through to their destination without a change of conveyance. The approach *viâ* Lake Side, however, offers one of the strongest arguments in Britain for taking a longer and slower journey, for the boat trip (described on *pp.* 71–3) up Lake Windermere to Bowness or to Ambleside (Waterhead) affords a very lovely introduction to the beauties of Lakeland.

APPROACHES FROM THE WEST COAST

The west coast of Cumbria is cut off from the rest of the country by the long range of fells which extends from Black Combe, at the south-western extremity of the county, to Lord's Seat, 5 miles north-west of Keswick, a distance of nearly 30 miles as the crow flies. The highest and roughest ground in England lies in this range. The coast itself, except in the immediate vicinity of St. Bees, is flat and uninteresting ; but it is from this side that some of the finest of the Lakeland valleys are most suitably approached. Wastwater, Ennerdale, and Crummock can only be properly appreciated by being *first* seen from their lower ends. Wildness of scenery, to be thoroughly effective, must burst suddenly upon the eye. Disappointment is always the lot of those who walk from the grand to the tame end of a wild lake, and expect, by the simple process of turning round, to feel all its force.

Seascale (*Scawfell Hotel*) is a small resort with extensive sands but its character is changing, owing to industrial development in the neighbourhood. From here the heart of Eskdale (Boot, 1 *m.* from Stanley Ghyll) may easily be reached by road. Calder Abbey is only 5 miles away (see *p.* 47).

St. Bees (*Abbots Court*) is the nicest starting-place for Ennerdale. At St. Bees is the fine old church of St. Bega, who founded the monastery in 650 and the old-established *St. Bees School*. It is an interesting walk from St. Bees to Whitehaven (3 hours) by cliff and shore, crossing St. Bees Head and visiting the little smugglers' bay at Fleswick.

1. Ravenglass to Boot (6½ *m.*). By adopting this approach, walkers may first explore Stanley Ghyll and the beauties of Eskdale, and then, crossing to Strands, see Wastwater to full advantage. *For paths, see p.* 126.

The 7-mile miniature Ravenglass and Eskdale Railway conveys passengers up the beautiful Mite and Esk Valleys between Ravenglass (*Pennington Arms Hotel*), Eskdale Green (*King George Hotel*), Beckfoot and Dalegarth (Woolpack Inn). Its Preservation Society, founded 1960, runs a summer service. The road leads past Muncaster Fell to *Eskdale Green* (inn), where it is joined by the Gosforth road, and so by *Beckfoot* to *Boot*.

2. Drigg to Strands and Wasdale Head.—Drigg is the best station on the main line from which to start for Wasdale Head. The road is a mile shorter, and more attractive than that from Seascale, the next station, and easier.

From Drigg the road goes eastward for a mile to the hamlet of **Holmrook**, where it descends to the river Irt, the stream by which Wastwater has its outlet. The wooded park of now demolished Holmrook Hall, is passed on the right, and just beyond it, about 1½ miles from Drigg, the Wasdale road goes off square to the right. The mountain basin in which Wastwater lies is conspicuous wherever the view is not intercepted by higher ground or trees, the first good view of it being obtained from Holmrook hamlet. Great Gable, one of the most beautifully shaped of the Lake mountains, forms the centrepiece, lying back at the head of the lake. To the right are the Screes, and to its left Kirkfell, Yewbarrow, and Seatallan. The lake itself is not visible until its shore is reached. Another wood-embowered hall is passed on the right, and then at **Santon Bridge,** where there is a small inn, capable of affording a night's accommodation, the river is crossed. Beyond it, take the narrow road to the left. At this point the Wrynose route from Ambleside *viâ* Eskdale converges (*see p.* 128).

3. Seascale to Wasdale Head (*by road,* 13 *m.* ; *inns at Gosforth,* 3 *m., and Strands,* 7 *m.*). The road is a fair one for cars throughout.

From Seascale to **Gosforth** (*Globe,* and other *inns*) the road is unmistakable. At the east end of the village, where the road forks, diverge to the left, and pass by the church. In the church-yard is the famous cross of the Viking age, 14 feet high, showing in its carvings a remarkable confusion of the Christian and pagan religions. On the one side, for example, is Loki and the serpent, on the other the Holy Rood. It is assigned to about A.D. 1000.

In another half-mile the river Bleng is crossed at a house called *Wellington,* and thence the road, after a long and steep hill, proceeds with little variation in the direction of the basin of Wast-water. The mountains surrounding the lake become more and more conspicuous—the Screes and the Scafell range on the right,

Seatallan, Buckbarrow, and Yewbarrow on the left. Great Gable is hidden by the latter. The lake itself is not visible until its actual shore is reached, being hidden by intervening knolls and copses. About 3 miles from Gosforth the road through *Strands* diverges on the right. The direct route misses Strands, and rejoins the road through that village 1¼ miles up the lake. The route by **Strands** (or Nether Wasdale) is the more effective one. In the village, which is picturesquely placed at the foot of a slope, are *Strands Hotel*, a temperance *Inn*, and a tiny church. Hence to Wasdale Head, *see p.* 128.

4. Sellafield to Wasdale Head by Calder Bridge. Tourists who wish to pass Calder Abbey on their way to Wastwater should take this route. The road is a cross-country one by Calder Bridge (on the main road from Egremont to Gosforth) and is plainly shown on the map.

Calder Abbey (ruins : Saturdays and Sundays, 2–6) is nearly a mile from the main road. It is reached by a turning, signposted to Ennerdale, at Calderbridge Church. Admission (*charge*) is by the Lodge gate, one mile from the village. The ruins are attractive from their position in the well-wooded valley rather than extensive or remarkable in themselves. The Abbey dates from the 12th century, and was affiliated to Furness Abbey. The remains include the central tower with fine pointed arches, the south transept, and the arches forming the north side of the nave. The Abbey is in the grounds of a large private house.

The road from Gosforth to Wasdale is the same as that described in the preceding route.

5. To Ennerdale Lake from Egremont (8 m.), or from Seascale by Calder Bridge (15 m.). From St. Bees by Cleator and Wath (10 m.) ; from Whitehaven, 10 m.
The distance to be walked from Whitehaven may be reduced by using the Lamplugh bus for part of the way. It should be noted that the rail services are now confined to one route.

This approach is to be recommended only to those who, being already on the western side of the district, wish to see Ennerdale Lake properly ; and it is well worth seeing. **Egremont** is a dull, commonplace town except for the Castle ruins in a public park, and during the first half of the eight miles between it and Ennerdale there is little to indicate the proximity of beautiful scenery. A more interesting but longer approach is from the hotel at Calder Bridge, whence a road, skirting the fells and affording occasional glimpses of the Wastwater Mountains, leads over Cold Fell to Ennerdale Bridge. It is described the reverse way on *p.* 199. To avoid disappointment, however, the stranger should recollect that he is not in the Lake District till he has reached the lake of Ennerdale itself.

From Egremont take the road passing under the old railway south of the station. The Ehen is soon crossed.

A round-shaped mountain to the far right, which appears soon after the town is left, is Dent Fell. *Cleator Moor* is on the other side of the stream, which is crossed in about three miles by the road from Whitehaven and St. Bees at *Wath Bridge*. Nearing **Ennerdale Bridge** (6 m.; *inn*) the pyramidal peaks of Red Pike and High Stile, the Buttermere Fells, appear; and after crossing it, and turning to the right, the depression of the Ennerdale valley, nobly flanked by the Pillar on the right, is revealed. Bearing slightly to the left at the next junction of roads, about half a mile farther on, and turning to the right in another three-quarters of a mile, you come to a farm-house, facing you, called " How Hall." A cross over the gable of a barn, and a pointed window or two on the far side, indicate its antiquity. Formerly it was a mansion of some note. Keeping the farm-house on the left, you soon descend to the lake, a good view of which is obtained during the descent.

6. Cockermouth to Scale Hill (Crummock Water), 8 *m*. Crummock Water, like all other outlying lakes, except Loweswater, must be approached from the direction of its lower end to be appreciated. This is usually done by adopting the Whinlatter route from Keswick (*p.* 184). The view from Lanthwaite Hill, just above *Scale Hill Hotel*, is most charming.

To some, however, Cockermouth may be a more convenient starting-place. By this approach the scenery increases in interest with every mile till, before Crummock is reached, it attains a very high degree of excellence. The pike which is seen right ahead on leaving Cockermouth is Lady's Seat, on the Grasmoor group just below Hope Gill Head.

Cockermouth (*Globe*; *Trout*; pop. 6,480) is a small town situated 29 miles from Penrith, 12 from Keswick, and 13 from Whitehaven. Cockermouth is the native place of Wordsworth, who was born at " Wordsworth House," (*National Trust*) in the main street, in 1770, and here spent his early boyhood. The house is rented to a tenant but is open to visitors on certain days in the summer. *Cockermouth Castle* is a most interesting building with a very long history. It has not been used as a fortification since 1648 when it was dismantled. A modernised wing is still occasionally used as a residence by Lord Leconfield. The gardens and ruins are open daily to the public.

For the first 3 miles the road is identical with the Whinlatter route to Keswick, and then a divergence to the right is made, soon followed by another in the same direction, to **Lorton** village (Inn: *Horse-shoe*). What remains of " The yew-tree, pride of Lorton Vale," occupies the corner of a field near the village. Under it George Fox, founder of the " Society of Friends," preached to a vast crowd of the dalesmen in 1653. Its girth is 13 ft. 2 in.

From Lorton the road proceeds due south, and there is no fear of mistaking it all the way to **Scale Hill** (*hotel*), about a mile short of which the direct route to Buttermere branches off on the left. On the way Red Pike and High Stile becomes more and more conspicuous in front, Whiteside and Grasmoor on the left, and Melbreak on the right.

APPROACHES FROM THE NORTH AND EAST

Visitors entering the Lake District from the north almost invariably select either Keswick or Patterdale (Ullswater, *via* Pooley Bridge) as their starting-point, and indeed motorists would find it difficult to discover a third course. Pedestrians, however, who wish for a little originality, may try Shap.

The balance of convenience, as far as travelling facilities go, is in favour of Keswick, though Penrith and Patterdale are connected by regular bus services. In other respects the Ullswater route has a decided advantage, inasmuch as it lands the tourist on one side of the district and not half-way between the eastern and western sections. At Keswick the visitor who wishes to see all the panoramic prizes is in the awkward position of having them on both sides of him, and he must exercise good strategy to avoid travelling over the same ground twice.

Derwentwater, again, is almost too good to begin upon. Its beauty, unlike that of Windermere, which works gradually to a climax during the voyage up the lake, bursts suddenly on the eye in its entirety, and should consequently rather be worked up to than made the first object of interest encountered in the tour. The case is different with those who wish to make one particular spot their headquarters, and to take daily excursions from it. Keswick is quite an interesting town, with well-laid-out parks and a museum; and is very close to the loveliest of English lakes and the most strikingly chiselled of English mountains. The numerous excursions from it, its hotels, and abundant transport services render it a deservedly favourite centre for those who wish to see the best of scenery without the trouble of finding out for themselves where it is or how it is to be reached.

(*a*) **Oxenholme** to **Penrith** by rail. Beyond Oxenholme the line rises and affords on the left a good view of the grey town of Kendal, lying beneath its limestone scar, with the Lake District fells, from the Old Man to Langdale Pikes, in the background. Beyond *Tebay* comes the sharp ascent to **Shap Summit** (1,000 *ft.*), about a mile short of which the *Shap Wells Hotel* is passed on the left. On the same side, at the summit, are the well-known Shap Granite Works, and then we look up Sleddale to the north-east barriers of the Lake District, the monotonous outline of which is only broken by the peak of Kidsty Pike. (For *Shap see p. 53.*) Hence the line descends all the way to Penrith. On the right the flat top of Crossfell may be seen; on the left farther on, Helvellyn and Saddleback.

(*b*) Many now approach **Penrith** *via* the M6 motorway. The interchange (No. 40) is about a mile west of the town. This is also the junction with the A66 from Teesside and Scotch Corner to the east, and Keswick and Workington to the west.

Penrith can be reached from **Appleby** by bus and from **Carlisle** by bus or train.

Newcastle to **Penrith** and **Keswick** by road. The Stainmore (A66) can be used, but the more interesting route is by the Hartside Pass (A686), one of the highest carriage roads in England. From it are impressive views of the Lakeland Hills, the Vale of Eden, and the Solway from the summit. Cross Fell can be climbed from various points along this road.

Penrith [Hotels : *George, Hussar* in main street, *Glen Cottage,* also (smaller) *Gloucester Arms*[1] ; Banks : *Barclays, Lloyds, Savings Bank, Midland, National Westminster* ; pop. 11,400 ; buses to Patterdale and Keswick] is a pleasantly-placed red-sandstone town with a busy market on Tuesdays. The Castle, acquired by the town, stands in a public park near the station. Those who spend a night at Penrith on the way to the Lake District should by all means ascend the **Beacon** (1½ *m.* from the station) for the sake of the view.

The top, on which stands a square tower, is 937 feet above the sea (the town is about 450 *ft.*). The way to the Beacon is quite easy to find, about ¾ mile to the east of the Town Hall. The feature of the view is the lowest reach of Ullswater, with St. Sunday Crag directly behind it, and the long billowy Helvellyn range stretching away to the right. Westward is the ridge of Saddleback and, farther away to the left, the peak of Grisedale Pike. In olden times this was one of the beacons in the fiery line of communication between the Cheviots and Lancashire, though Macaulay, with a poet's licence, has substituted Skiddaw for its less pretentious but more accessible little neighbour.

" Till Skiddaw saw the fire that burnt on Gaunt's embattled pile. And the red glare on Skiddaw roused the burghers of Carlisle."

Penrith is a good centre for exploring eastern Lakeland : Saddleback is very near, and with the help of motor transport, the Helvellyn and Fairfield group of mountains, the High Street range and also the little known Swindale area, are all easily accessible. To the east, the lovely Eden Valley, and the long wall of the Pennines are well worth exploring.

Among objects of interest in the neighbourhood of Penrith are *Long Meg and her daughters,* a prehistoric circle, between 6 and 7 miles to the north-east, composed of 65 stones, exclusive of Long Meg (height 12 feet), and nearly 400 yards in circumference ; *Brougham Castle,* a ruin, (Department of Environment), 1¾ miles from Penrith on the Appleby road ; and at Eamont Bridge two mysterious ancient remains, *Mayburgh* and *King Arthur's Round Table,* respectively on the right- and left-hand side of the Pooley

---

[1] The *Gloucester Arms* was once the residence of Richard III, as is testified by the arms of that much abused monarch—a couple of boar pigs, *very* "rampant," hung over the entrance. The oak wainscoting in some of the rooms further attests the antiquity of the building.

Bridge road, close to the point at which it diverges from the main road to Kendal and the south, about 1½ miles from the town. They are a couple of mound-encircled areas, about 20 and 100 yards in diameter respectively, and both of them capable of taxing the brains of the archæologist to the utmost.

Penrith to Lowther Castle, 5¼ m.   and Pooley Bridge, 10.   *See below.*

1. Penrith to Keswick by road.

The approach to this famous little Cumbrian town needs very few words of description. After leaving Penrith, a good view of the fells surrounding the head of Ullswater, including St. Sunday Crag and Helvellyn, is obtained on the left. The red sandstone of the Eden valley has been quickly left, and the limestone—an index to so much beautiful scenery in other parts of England, but up here a sign that we have either just left or not yet entered the limits of Lakeland proper—takes its place. At Troutbeck we then rise to the top of a desolate moor, relieved only by the round-topped height of Mell Fell, and the Dodds of Helvellyn more to the west ; and it is only when we near **Threlkeld**, and the many-ridged Saddleback to the right competes for our attention with the opening of the narrow Vale of St. John on the left, that we realise our proximity to the beautiful land we have come to see. The moorland is quickly left, and the Greta is crossed and then comes Keswick and the mountain cordon of Derwentwater. For **Keswick**, *see p. 162.*

2. Penrith to Pooley Bridge (Ullswater), 6 *m.* (road), and to Patterdale (boat), 13½ *m.*

There is a public footpath from the west side at Penrith Station through the fields to Stainton and Dalemain and also a path from Skirsgill near the M6 interchange to the River Eamont at Ironbridge and out to the Eamont Bridge–Pooley Bridge road at Tirril. At Eamont Bridge a wide footpath strikes off to the right on the south bank of the river which cuts off an angle and rejoins the same road at Yanwath.

From Penrith take the road to the Motorway interchange and from there the Keswick road (A66) as far as a roundabout at Stainton where the Ullswater road runs off to the left. In about 2 miles is the manor house of Dalemain, in whose park pedestrians will find a foot bridge (permissive) across the river, and from it a footpath to Pooley Bridge. The road continues to reach the shore of Ullswater at Waterfoot.

An alternative route is to go south on the A6 over the Eamont to Eamont Bridge, where the Pooley Bridge road turns right at the *Crown Hotel*, and near to the " Round Table " and " Mayburgh " (*see above*). In about 5 miles the road reaches **Pooley Bridge** (*Sun, Crown* and *Waterfoot Hotels*). Here the lowest reach of Ullswater comes into view, and the fells crowd round the other two reaches, the lateral ridges of Helvellyn, St. Sunday Crag and Place Fell being conspicuous.

From Pooley Bridge an enjoyable walk of about 4 miles may be taken along the eastern shores of the lake to **Howtown**. Pass through a gate a little short of the bridge, and follow a footpath by the water's edge for nearly a mile, till you reach a farm-house. Here join the road, which continues along the lakeside to Howtown (*Howtown Hotel*). From Howtown the walk may be continued to Patterdale either by Boardale (*see p.* 215) or along the lake-side.

It is also a fine walk from Pooley Bridge over **Moor Divock** (1,050 *ft.*) (*see p.* 222) to **Bampton** (6 *m.*; *Crown and Mitre*) and **Haweswater**. Fine views of Ullswater. In the reverse direction, there is an excellent approach to Ullswater from Penrith, by way of Lowther Park, the pretty village of Askham, and the green track past the prehistoric monuments of Moor Divock.

From Pooley Bridge to Patterdale by road is 9 miles (8 to *Ullswater Hotel*). Bus service.

Whether it is made by road or by boat the journey from **Pooley Bridge to Patterdale** is one of increasing interest throughout. The lowest reach of **Ullswater** is part of the transition region from ordinary to " Lake " scenery, not—like that of Windermere —thoroughly identified with the peculiar charm of the district (*see also p.* 212).

The wooded hill which rises to the west at the outlet of the lake is *Dunmallet*,[1] commanding a fine prospect. Later, as the view of the middle reach opens up, the overlapping ranges of fells assume a more imposing appearance ; a kind of mystery enshrouds the scene, caused by the sharp angles of the lake ; nor is the feeling dispelled when, instead of keeping up the reach which has just disclosed itself, the boat plunges boldly into a watery *cul-de-sac* (Howtown).

The middle and longest reach of the lake extends from Howtown and Skelly Nab to Glencoyne Park. It is commanded at the upper end by Helvellyn and its north-eastern spur, Catchedicam. Hallin Fell stands boldly out on the left as we leave Howtown, and beyond it the waters of Boardale and Rampsgill find an outlet in the lake near the hamlet of Sandwick. Farther on the same side comes Birkfell, and on the other side the sylvan glades of Gowbarrow Park, Lyulph's Tower, and the stream of which Aira Force forms part. Then, turning sharply to the left, the boat enters the shortest and grandest reach of the lake, a scene which, in its own style, rich and at the same time severe, is perhaps the finest in the district. The semicircular depression of Glencoyne and the nobly wooded Stybarrow Crag are the most striking features on the right. Opposite them Place Fell descends steeply from head to foot to the water's edge, while Patterdale

---

[1] Here is the site of a British hill-fort. *Caerthanock*, near at hand, may be also a British fort, but not of the hill type.

and St. Sunday Crag, the presiding fell of Ullswater, supply a beautiful background. Beyond Patterdale the ascent of the Kirkstone Pass to Ambleside and Windermere commences. Red Screes is conspicuous at the head of it.

After passing three islands, of which one is apparently divided into two, the landing-stage is reached just beyond the *Ullswater Hotel* and close to Glenridding.

For the route *via* Lowther Castle, *see p.* 56: for Patterdale, *see p.* 212.

3. Shap to Haweswater.

Walking : *Shap Station to Rosgill Bridge*, 3 m. ; *foot of Haweswater*, 5½ ; *Haweswater Hotel*, 7½ m. ; *Mardale (Gatescarth Foot)*, 9¼. Driving : *Shap Station to Bampton Grange* (" *Crown and Mitre* "), 4½ m. ; *Mardale*, 10¼ m. Conveyances can be had by previous arrangement from Shap to Haweswater.

Haweswater, in spite of its completed conversion in 1940 into a reservoir for Manchester, is, in its own style, quiet but decisive, ranking high among the sisterhood of lakes for beauty, and, like most of the other outlying ones, can only be seen to advantage from the lower end. **Shap**, too, is an excellent starting-point for a walking tour, being well on one side of the district, and not introducing the walker too suddenly to the *crème de la crème* of the scenery. It is on the main " A6 " road, 16 miles from Kendal and 10 miles from Penrith.

Shap Wells (*hotel*) is situated in a hollow of Shap Fells, between 3 and 4 miles south of the village. The surrounding scenery is bleak, but the air is salubrious.

At the north end of Shap's long street a signpost indicates the divergence of the Bampton road to the left. In 300 yards along this road a barn is passed on the right. Thirty yards beyond it is a wicket. Pass through this, and take the right-hand one of the two paths—that to the left leads to Shap Abbey, ¾ mile distant, whence the main route may be regained in about 25 minutes at Rosgill, by recrossing the stream and keeping along its east bank.

Shap Abbey, situated at the bottom of the valley on the far side of the river Lowther, consists of a square tower and the scattered masonry and foundations of the church and convent built here for Premonstratensian (White) canons. It was founded in 1150 under the name of Heppe, derived from the Old English " *heap* " and not now thought to have any connection with " hip," alluding to the thorn-bushes which, planted at regular intervals, and guarded by stone walls, still remain to show the means adopted by our forefathers to guide their steps across the desolate tracks of Shap Fells. The earliest part is the eastern end of the church (about 1200) ; the *West Tower*, which is contemporary with that at Fountains, " was built quite at the end of the 15th or early in the 16th century." It had long had alarming cracks in the fabric, but has now been well restored. The great slab on the floor of the church " doubtless covered the high altar." The kitchen " probably stood on the site of the present farm-house."

After the Dissolution the Abbey appears to have been regarded, like many other structures in similar circumstances, as a public stone-quarry to be drawn from by all comers at the simple cost of carting away the material.

Shap Abbey to Haweswater.—The head of the lake may be reached by average walkers direct from Shap Abbey in from 2 to 2½ hours, passing through Swindale, and over the heights (1,600 ft. above sea-level) between it and Mardale. The route is interesting, but misses the view of Haweswater from its lower end, which is generally the chief object of those who make Shap their starting-point.

The route from the Abbey leaves the stream and, passing through a gate two hundred yards from the ruin, crosses a common, over which there is no regular track. Take a south-westerly direction, keeping a clump of trees, at first prominent but shortly disappearing, considerably to the right. In about 10 minutes the new concrete road to Haweswater is crossed, and in another 10 minutes the cart-track from Keld to Swindale is entered a little to the left of a farm-house called *Tailbert*. Do not pass by the farm-house, but, where the track forks, keep to the greener left-hand branch, which gradually ascends the fell-side, and then, bending slightly to the left, descends obliquely into Swindale, crossing the main beck of the valley by a bridge near another farm called *Truss Gap*. The church, which used to stand close by, has been demolished.

Swindale is a wild, secluded, and thoroughly characteristic valley, with a head dominated by Selside Pike, and suggestive of Great Langdale on a small scale. It contains only three farmsteads. A portion of the Mardale water scheme decrees that Swindale must be flooded some day for compensation and reserve water.

There are some waterfalls at the head of Swindale which, but for their remoteness from beaten tracks, would be more appreciated than they are at present.

On the other side of the bridge the regular road through the valley is joined. Follow this for about ¾ mile, and then turn up a horse-track, to the right, close to a half-ruinous farm-house. This track climbs the steep part of the fell, bending first to the right and then to the left, to ease the gradient, and when it has reached the comparatively level ground at the top, becomes difficult to trace for a time. The best direction is to keep straight on in a line with the track by which you descended into Swindale, distinctly visible on the other side of the valley, at the same time making for the most depressed part of the range which you are crossing. Selside Pike rises on the left, and beyond it the mountains surrounding the head of **Mardale** soon come into view. Named in order, from left to right, they are Branstree, Harter Fell, High Street (long and almost flat-topped), and Kidsty Pike, with its sharply peaked summit. Mardale itself soon follows far below, and the extended head of Haweswater contrasts finely with the splendid array of encircling fells, but the green pastures of Mardale are no more. This is one of the most striking of the near mountain-views in the

district, and all the more so from the suddenness with which it
bursts upon the eye.

In descending there is a steep but good and easily found peat-
road, which should not be neglected. Its course is to the right of
and considerably above the beck, which is seen running into the
valley a mile north of the end of the new road (Gatescarth Foot).

The direct path, after crossing three fields, re-enters the
Bampton road, which it leaves again in less than 100 yards, proceeding in the same direction as before, and passing between
a quarry and a limekiln, with a gate on the left, which must be
avoided. As it leaves the first field at its far corner, two valleys
appear on the left; the nearer is Swindale, the farther Mardale, in
which lies Haweswater. Beyond the latter rise High Street and,
to the right of it, the sharp peak of Kidsty Pike. In front is spread
the wide and pleasant vale of Bampton, with the limestone Knipe
Scar overlooking it on the right. On reaching Rosgill, descend to
and cross the bridge over the Lowther. Thence make straight
across the moor by a faint track for the farm-house (Rawhead) on
its brow. Pass through the yard and out of it through a farm-
gate. Keep a fence on the left for a few yards, and then bear
down in the same direction towards the Haweswater depression,
which has reappeared. The path, a faint one, leaves a block of
farm-sheds on the left and joins a cart-track at the bottom of the
valley. Follow the cart-track as far as the first bridge, crossing
which you will pass by *Thornthwaite Hall* into the new road from
Bampton to Haweswater, at a point 2 miles from the *Haweswater Hotel* and 5 miles from the head of the valley.

Thus far the scenery has been merely rather wild in a commonplace way, though indeed suggestive of good things ahead; but
by continuing and by passing through Burn Banks Village and
taking the " Ramblers' Path," you come, most suddenly, into
full view of one of the most striking pictures in Lakeland.

Haweswater, stern and solemn, and almost immured in lofty
mountains, lies before you. On both sides the fells rise steeply
out of it. Those on the right are bare of everything but grass
and bracken and heath and parsley fern; the lower ones, on the
left, craggy, precipitous, and richly draped with forest-foliage—
oak, larch, ash, and sycamore all lending their varied hues to
enhance the scene. This is Naddle Forest, and the rock is
Wallow Crag. The features are few, simple, and unpretentious,
but all good of their kind, and well knit together. There is no
aping of the grandeur of Windermere, the loveliness of Derwentwater, or the wildness of Wastwater, but—although it is a reservoir and somewhat artificial—not to have seen Haweswater
would have been to fall short of a just appreciation of the beauties
of English Lakeland. A little way up the lake the waters of
the upland valley of Measand come tumbling down the fell-side
in a series of Lodore-like cascades. In front, Harter Fell lords

it over Mardale. At the head of the lake Whelter Crags are an imposing feature on the right. High Street and Kidsty Pike appear when Riggindale opens in the same direction ; about a quarter of a mile beyond the head of the lake the site of a British hill-fort on Castle Crag is passed above on the right; the path then crosses from Riggindale into the head of Mardale and joins the new road 2 miles south of the *Haweswater Hotel*. Beyond the end of the road there are only two tracks : to the left for Gatescarth and Long Sleddale, to the right for Nan Bield and Kentmere.

As already stated, Haweswater has been converted into a reservoir for Manchester. The Dam, which is 1,550 feet long and has a maximum height of 120 feet, was completed in 1940 and cost about £500,000. The lake has been raised 96 feet above its natural level. Through the mountains on the south there has been bored the longest tunnel of its kind in Britain, and by this tunnel the waters are led to the aqueduct buried on the eastern side of Long Sleddale. Along the eastern side of Mardale a new road has been built, at a considerable height above the original lake-level. The old road on the western shore and the sites of Mardale Church, the hamlet of Mardale Green, and the *Dun Bull* have been covered by the extended area of the lake following the construction of the dam. The later hotel, opened in 1937, is half-way along the eastern side of the lake.

Penrith, 10 *m.*, or Shap, 12, to Pooley Bridge by Lowther Castle (5½ from Penrith—an interesting drive). The point of departure from the main (Penrith and Shap) road is ¾ mile on the Penrith side of Hackthorpe (*inn*). There a road strikes off square, and, passing through a gate into the *Park*, leads close past the front of the Castle. Much of the Park is now a Wild Life and Nature Park (*daily in summer, charge*).

From the Park, the road, crossing the *Lowther*, enters the picturesque village of Askham (*Punch Bowl, Queen*), whence it is 3½ miles round the N. end of the High Street range to Pooley Bridge (*p.* 52).

WINDERMERE AND BOWNESS

Banks : *Barclays, Midland, District.*
Bathing Centre, near Millerground Landing.
Boats at Bowness, or Millerground Landing.
Bowls : Queen's Park and Longlands.
Buses connect Bowness and Windermere with Ambleside, Grasmere, Keswick, Kendal, Newby Bridge, Grange-over-Sands, Ulverston.
Car Parking-Places.—*Bowness :* Rectory Road, adjoining the Promenade ; Church Street. *Windermere :* Broad Street.
Coaches run to Grasmere, Keswick, Patterdale, Furness Abbey, and many other places. For particulars of fares, etc., *see* current announcements.
Churches.—WINDERMERE: *St. Mary's.* BOWNESS: *Windermere Parish Ch. ; St. John's,* half-way between the two; also *Congregational* and *Roman Catholic* half-way from Windermere to Bowness; *Methodist* at Windermere and Bowness ; etc.
Distances.—From WINDERMERE STATION *by road,* Bowness, 1½ m. ; Low Wood, 3 ; Ambleside, 4¾ ; Rydal, 6 ; Grasmere, 8¼ to 9 ; Wythburn, 12¾ ; Thirlspot, 15½ ; Keswick Station, 21. Troutbeck Village, 3 to 4 m. ; Kirkstone Pass, 7 ; Patterdale, 13 ; Ullswater steamer pier, 14.
From BOWNESS PIER : Windermere Station, 1¾ m. ; Ambleside, 5¾ ; (by the Ferry) *Ferry House,* 1¼ ; Hawkshead, 5¼ ; Coniston, 9¼ ; *Storrs Hall Hotel,* 2 ; Newby Bridge, 7. By the Lake : Lake Side Station and Hotel, 6; Waterhead (¾ m. from Ambleside), 5 m.
Early Closing.—Thursday.
Ferry.—Between Ferry Nab, about a mile below Bowness, and the Ferry House on the western shore, a ferry plies regularly. First ferry 7 a.m. ; last ferry 8.40 p.m. and 9.40 p.m. in summer. Cars and caravans carried.
Fishing.—Pike, perch, char, and trout are the chief fish caught. (*See p.* 26.)
Golf.—(*See* p. 27.) Putting and Miniature Golf Course at the Glebe, close to Promenade. Windermere Golf Club at Cleabarrow.
Height above Sea.—Bowness from 140–350 feet ; Windermere, 350–500.
Hotels.—WINDERMERE : *Windermere, Applegarth, Elleray, Greywalls,* etc.
BOWNESS.—*Old England ; Belsfield,* overlooking lake ; *Crown ; Royal,* in village ; *Windermere Hydro.* All within 300 yards of pier. *Beech Hill,* on road to Newby Bridge.
Low Wood and *Langdale Chase,* on margin of lake, 3 miles on Ambleside road ; *Storrs Hall,* 2 miles S. of Bowness.
The whole neighbourhood abounds in **private hotels and apartment-houses** and there are several good **boarding-houses.**
Lake District National Park Centre—at Brookhole between Windermere and Ambleside.
Population.—Windermere and Bowness, 7,900.
Postal Address.—As there is more than one Bowness in the district, letters for *this* Bowness should be addressed " Bowness-on-Windermere." Similarly, Post Office Orders intended for Bowness should be made payable at Bowness-on-Windermere.
Post Offices.—WINDERMERE, head office Crescent Road.
BOWNESS : Ash Street.
Railway Station at Windermere town ; **Boat Pier** at Bowness ; 1¾ m. apart. Buses between the places to meet all trains, and nearly all ferries.

Regattas.—The Royal Windermere Yacht Club holds races from Whitsuntide till September. The usual starting- and finishing-places are the *Ferry House*, and Hen Holme, a little above Bowness. The headquarters of the Club are at Bowness. The Windermere Motor Boat Club also holds Regattas.

Passenger Boats ply up and down the lake about six times either way daily.

Tennis.—Public Courts beside Bowness Promenade ; Windermere Queen's Park ; and at Ellerthwaite.

To all intents and purposes, Bowness and Windermere form parts of the same town. From Windermere Station to the centre of Bowness is a mile and a half, but the two places are practically united and have a joint Urban Council. Nor is there any material difference in the travelling facilities afforded by them, a short ride representing the balance of advantage possessed by either as a starting-point. Most of the bus services call at both places. Bowness is better placed for the lake itself ; Windermere will appeal to those desiring a high situation and distant as well as near views.

Both Bowness and Windermere provide easy access to the lake itself. Windermere is also somewhat more convenient for the High Street range of fells and for Haweswater. Either may be taken as the starting- or finishing-point in the Ullswater excursion. For the central, northern, and western part of the district, however, comprising the Cumberland lakes, Grasmere, Helvellyn, and the Langdales, Ambleside is the nearer by 5 miles.

The village of **Windermere** is little more than a century old, having sprung into existence since the opening of the railway from Kendal in 1847, prior to which date it was known as Birthwaite. Though situated on the very skirts of the district, the entire prospect commanded by it—and a very extensive prospect it is—is within the limits of Lakeland proper. Its position on the western slope of Orrest Head shuts out all view of the less interesting country to the south-east. It is between 400 and 500 ft. above sea-level, and about 300 higher than the lake, the nearest point of which by road is at Bowness, a mile and a half away, though it may be reached by footpath, described on *p.* 65, in less than half that distance.

Bowness—rightly pronounced Bówness by the inhabitants, and wrongly Bo-ness by nearly everybody else (*see p.* 173)—consists of one curving main thoroughfare with a labyrinth of small streets branching out of it—a confused mass of building in which every contributor has done that which seemed best in his own eyes, without regard to his neighbour. Busy as this main thoroughfare generally is, there are times when things are even more lively on the **Promenade,** which is probably the most characteristic corner of Bowness. Here one gains a fair impression of the importance of Lakeland boating and motoring—on the one hand are coaches, cars, buses, and bicycles ; on the other are rowing boats, sailing boats, motor-launches, and other craft, all in great number. For cars there are several large parking places, and overlooking the Pier are tennis courts and putting greens, while in the Glebe, a few yards southward, is an excellent miniature golf course.

Only 100 yards from the pier is *St. Martin's Church*, a large, long-roofed, gable-towered structure, of the true Westmorland type. It is the Parish Church of Windermere.

The church was built in 1483, to replace a considerably older building destroyed by fire. The upper tower, the vestry, and the end of the chancel were added in 1869–73, when the building was thoroughly repaired and redecorated as also in 1960. The War Memorial Chapel and a new clergy vestry were consecrated in 1922.

Entering by the **south porch**, which is later than the nave, note the rough stone seats and the older arch above the inner door.

The special feature of the **nave** is the simplicity of the plastered arches and their pillars : over these are some curious texts (note the spelling). These quaint extracts, which were discovered under the plaster and carefully preserved in 1870, are probably from a book by R. Openshawe of Weymouth (1548). At the west end is a modern mural representation of Christ in " Majesty." Near the entrance door is the *font*, with a very ancient top decorated with four rudely carved faces.

Close to the lectern is a case containing three " Breeches " Bibles, two books of Homilies (one by Latimer, Ridley, and Cranmer, the other by Bishop Jewel), and two chained books : *Paraphrase of the Gospel*, by Erasmus, 1516 ; and Bishop Jewel's *Apology for the Church of England*, 1562.

Notice the modern windows of the **south aisle**. At the east end of this aisle are Flaxman's slab to Bishop Richard Watson of Llandaff (1816), who lived at Calgarth ; and right of the small door, a wall-tablet to Robert Philipson (1631) with the following remarkable inscription :—

" THE AVTHORS EPITAPH VPON
HIM-SELFE, MADE IN THE
TYME OF HIS SICKNESS.

A Man I was, wormes meate I am,
To Earth retvrn'd from whence I came
Many removes of Earth I had,
In Earth at length my Bed is made
a Bed which Christ did not disdaine
Altho' it covld not him retaine,
His deadlie Foes might plainlie see,
Over Sinn, and Death his Victorie.
Here mvst I rest, till Christ shall let mee see
His promised Iervsalem and her Fœlicitie.
Veni Domine Iesv, veni cito.
Robert' Philipson gent ; xiiito Octo-
bris Ano Salvtis 1631 : Anno
Ætatis Svæ 63tio."

On the under-side of the arch opposite this same door is the most interesting inscription in the church, a jubilation in Latin upon the failure of the Gunpowder Plot, dated 1629, twenty-four years after that event. It was put up by Christopher Philipson, kinsman of " Robin the Devil." [1]

The following is a literal translation :—

This is the day [the anniversary of the Gunpowder Plot], more famed as each year brings it round, which God himself appoints and marks with his peculiar favour.

Rejoice, ye who are good ! The mischief conspired in (or *by*) Stygian darkness has been now made an empty tale by the hand of Providence. England, which was shortly to be conspicuous for the greatness of its ruin, may now sing hymns since she has remained free by the aid of Heaven.

England expresses her great joy.

I am delivered from the jaws of Faux as from the prison of death. Glory to God in the highest. Hence is my secret safety.

Christopher Philipson, junior, Gentleman, 1629.

(From the History of Windermere Parish Church, by Rev. E. J. Nurse, M.A.)

In the *north aisle* is a well-cut bust of Fletcher Raincock, Q.C. (1844) ; and in a window, west of this, is a bit of glass on which is painted, tradition says, the trade-mark of the pack-carrier who brought the old roof-lead from Whitehaven over Wrynose Pass.

The eastern end of the chancel was added in 1870, and decorated with mural pictures—the Adoration of the Magi (north), and the Entombment (south). Two handsome carved oak prayer desks were presented in 1908 by Mrs. Baddeley in memory of her husband, Mr. Mountford Baddeley (" Thorough Guides "), and of her brother, Captain Michaelson Yeates. The best thing here, however, and in the building, is the deeply interesting **East Window**. The details are best seen with the aid of field-glasses. The window was carefully restored in 1872 by Henry Hughes, who wrote :

" Having visited and studied all the principal works in glass both in England and on the Continent, I am able to say that this, both in effect and interest, stands quite unique." By its " remarkable symbolistic character " the faith of saints and martyrs is represented by individual figures instead of groups. It is a combination of several old windows, and it may be accepted as established that the major proportion of the stained glass came from Cartmel Priory. From Cartmel probably came some Cartmel Fell glass also (*p.* 104).

Below the main transom there are six large figures in the central lights. These, and the seven lowest panels, with the exception of small bits added by Hughes, date from A.D. 1480 ; the canopies above them are rather later. The figures, taken from left to right are : St. Barbara (probably), St. George, St. Mary, The Christ (face restored ; note the angel on the left hand), St. John (much restored), St. Catherine (with torture-wheel) ; the next four heads are earlier. The first (l.) of the lower panels is inscribed " Jno. Plo. P'or of Kyrkmell " ; the second " Willm Thornboro " (of Cartmel) ; the third represents a Prior with monks, all named ; then follow knights and their ladies.

Above the bar is a heraldic hotch-potch in which are found the arms of Cartmel Harringtons, of the Middletons, and of William Marshal, the protector, who founded Cartmel. In the central upper light is the circular blue garter with the combined arms of

[1] *See* White's " Lays and Legends of the Lake Country," and *p.* 73.

France and England. These are either the arms of Edward V when Prince of Wales, or of Prince Arthur, the elder brother of Henry VIII.

To the left of this latter light is a bit of darker glass representing the Virgin and Child. This is the most treasured bit of the whole, and priceless. It is Early English in character, originally shaped for a lancet window, and, according to Mr. Hughes, of date A.D. 1260, *temp.* Henry III. It is therefore only 24 years later than the oldest glass at Canterbury. In the entire window are 21 coats of arms, nearly all of Cartmel families.

In the right-hand top corner of the 3rd light, from the right, is the coat of arms of John Washington. From the arms of this family originated through George Washington the " Stars and Stripes " emblazoned on the flag of the United States of America.

To sum up : although it may be called in general terms a " Late Perpendicular " window (1430–1480), the glass above the transom is much earlier. The panel containing the Virgin and Child is of about the year 1260. The four trefoils of the upper lights are Decorated. The right-hand group of four heads is 1430 work, and the six large figures and lowest panels are of 1480 date.

Outside the porch, notice a curious inscription on a dark grave-slab ; and, outside the east end the lines to Rasselas Belfield the slave (1822).

> A Slave by birth : I left my native Land,
> And found my freedom on Britania's Strand.
> Blest Isle ! Thou Glory of the Wise and Free
> Thy Touch alone unbinds the Chains of Slavery."

WALKS FROM WINDERMERE VILLAGE

(*For walks starting from Bowness, see pp. 67–71.*)

1. Orrest Head, 1 *hr. up and down* ; 400 *ft. above station* ; **650** *above lake* ; 784 *above sea.* The finest extensive view-point in the Lake District, and, perhaps, the finest in Great Britain. On the top is a diagram indicating the mountain-tops.

Take the broad gravel path (sign) which turns out of the Ambleside road, to the left of the *Windermere Hotel*, and 80 yards from the station gates. Immediately after entering, follow the broad right-hand path, which winds up and up for nearly half a mile to the *Woodman's Cottage*, 100 yards beyond which a narrower path on the right leads to the boundary wall of Elleray Woods. Here the path doubles back behind and above the Woodman's Cottage, and lands you on open ground a few feet below the top.

The View. (*See Panorama on pages 314–15.*) The gem of the view is Windermere itself, visible from end to end. Around and beyond it spreads a landscape containing every characteristic feature of English scenery, and all in perfect harmony, none unduly over-powering another. Trite and worn though they be, we cannot forbear quoting Scott's famous lines (*Lady of the Lake*, Canto I, xiv) on Loch Katrine, where that fairy-like lake—

> " In all her length far winding lay
>   With promontory, creek, and bay,
>   And islands that, empurpled bright,
>   Floated amid the livelier light,
>   And mountains that like giants stand
>   To sentinel enchanted land."

Which answers better to the description—the Scottish loch or the English mere ?

But to the details. Beginning at the south end of the lake we have the Finsthwaite Tower rising just above Lake Side (p. 76). To the right of it the Furness Fells, with wood and knoll, extend to the first prominent height which rises behind them, almost over a white cottage on the far side of the lake. This is Coniston Old Man.

Behind the Old Man, to the left, are Dow Crags and Walna Scar, and still farther in the same direction a strip of Black Combe appears over the Claife Heights, whose wooded slopes sink steeply down to the margin of the lake. The massive rounded fell to the right of the Old Man, and rather more prominent, is Wetherlam, behind whose southern ridge is a sharp angular peak called Carrs, forming the northern spur of the former mountain. All these are in Lancashire, but to the north of Wetherlam, where a slight depression marks the position of the Wrynose Pass into the Upper Duddon valley, Westmorland and Cumberland begin, the boundary of the counties being pretty nearly the skyline of the fells. The first summit north of Wrynose Gap is Cold Pike, and to the right of it, a little in advance of the direct chain, Pike o' Blisco is prominent. Both these fells are characterised by short flat tops and sloping shoulders. Then come the correctly, if not euphoniously, named Crinkle Crags, three or four distinct humps, diminishing in size from left to right.

Northwards of Crinkle Crags is a depression, the right slope of which rises steeply to the peak of Bowfell, one of the finest mountains in the district, and a landmark from the whole north-eastern shore of Windermere. The mountain rising to the left of it, behind the depression, is Scafell Pike, the comparative remoteness of which prevents its asserting its pre-eminence among the neighbouring fells. Then, what appears to be the northern buttress of Bowfell, is in reality Great End, a mountain forming the northern shoulder of the Scafell group. Close underneath Great End, in a dip of a few hundred feet, are Esk Hause and Allen Crags, the former the great watershed of the district, whence flow the Esk and the Derwent, and within a short distance of which the waters of Wasdale have their source. The mountain rising behind Allen Crags, and just to the left of Langdale Pikes, is Great Gable, which overlooks the wild Cumbrian lake of Wastwater.

The line of fells now draws nearer, and the eye rests upon two peaks which together, probably, constitute the finest mountain of its size, not only in Lakeland, but in the whole kingdom. These are the Langdale Pikes. They have been likened to a lion *couchant*. They are both under 2,500 feet high, and when looked at from the neighbouring fells dwindle into two inferior humps ; but they are decidedly the lions of the famous mountain-screen of Windermere, from whatever point on that lake they are seen.

The valley leading up to the Pikes is Great Langdale. To the right is a precipitous rock-face called Pavey Ark, and then a long almost level ridge, broken only by one little excrescence in front of High White Stones, strangely named Sergeant Man, extends as far as Dunmail Raise, the dip over which the Windermere and Keswick road passes, almost north of our present point of observation. This long ridge is the one fault of the view, but it is amply atoned for by the beautiful little Loughrigg Fell, which rises in front of it at the head of the lake, and separates the Brathay valley leading up to Great Langdale from that of the Rothay, whose course may be traced in the direction of Dunmail Raise, though its strath is invisible. In the midst of it, below the farthest ridge, rises Helm Crag, overlooking Grasmere ; and eastwards the fells again rise steeply to Nab Scar and the Fairfield group, behind which, and unseen, is Helvellyn. The lower and nearer ridge of Wansfell Pike all but hides Fairfield itself, only a strip of its highest part being visible. The fell sinking boldly to the east, to the right of Fairfield, is Red Screes, between which and the next high part of the range is the Kirkstone Pass, on the way to Ullswater. The green valley and long straggling village of Troutbeck lie between us and Wansfell ; and then come the steep smooth slopes of High Street, at the head of the valley, Froswick, and Ill Bell, the two last-named recognisable by the pyramidal form of their summits. Behind them lie Kentmere and the track to Haweswater, with Harter Fell still more to the right. Then comes a wide stretch of Shap Fells, the Howgills and the Pennines, retiring farther and farther, till the flat square summit of Ingleborough is seen far away in the south-east. Southward, seen over the depression of the Winster valley, is a part of Morecambe Bay, and more to the right, Gummer's How, a little to the left of Finsthwaite Tower, with which we began our description, and whence the Furness Fells extend to Coniston Old Man.

Descent.—A descent to the west can be made by entering a broad path at the entrance to the wood (4 min. from top). This path descends by a boundary wall and joins the public path to the Common at the gate by which the latter passes out on to the open fell. Turn down to the left, and, passing a gate, you will descend steeply by a circuitous but unmistakable gravel path into the wide track that starts from near the station. Go to the left for the station. In the other direction the track passes Christopher North's cottage at Elleray and leads into the Patterdale road.

2. **Miller Brow,** 120 *ft. above lake.* Follow the Ambleside road for ⅔ mile to cross-roads, and there turn left along the Bowness road. The Miller Brow view is 300 yards from the turn. The main features of this view are the same as those which we have just described in connection with Orrest Head, but being obtained from lower ground, the panorama is less extensive, and the lake itself, from its closer proximity, forms a much larger proportion of it. A richer foreground than that furnished by the *Calgarth Woods,* immediately below the eye, cannot well be imagined, and the islands, with their luxuriant drapery of foliage, save the wide expanse of still water from all suspicion of sameness. The modern turrets of Wray Castle are very effective on the far side of the lake.

From Miller Brow the road at once drops, and, passing the *Cemetery*, is crossed by a footpath (*see below*, route 4) 300 yards above the *Millerground Landing-stage*. A little farther, a bare green hill to the right is known (in commemoration of a visit by the Queen Dowager) as Adelaide Hill. It is now vested in the National Trust. Beyond this we pass by the rich woods of *Rayrigg* and enter Bowness.

3. Through Rayrigg Wood to the Lake. From the junction of the roads to Bowness, about a third of a mile below the station, turn to the right down Birthwaite Road. After crossing the Bowness and Ambleside road a footpath leads across a field just south of Adelaide Hill to the lake shore. From this point the margin of the lake may be followed northward.

4. To the Millerground Landing, ¾ *m.* (*boats and bathing*). Turn down out of the Ambleside road by the third opening, just beyond the church (¼ *m.*). The first opening leads to the College Grounds, and the second is a private drive with a gate. The third opening descends through wooded grounds, with the Cemetery to the right, crosses the Bowness and Ambleside road, and drops thence by a beck-side to the Landing. The *Miller Brow* view (*see above*) is about 300 yards to the right from the crossing of the Bowness road.

5. Views from the Troutbeck Road (1¼ to 1½ *m.*). These are obtained without climbing by following the route next described as far as two depressions in the wall, 200 yards or so beyond the point at which the Elleray path enters the road. The views are deservedly famous. By returning along the road, without turning into the Elleray path, and crossing the main Windermere and Ambleside road, you may include the Hammar Bank view.

6. By the Troutbeck Road to Low Wood (4½ *m.*), or **Ambleside by Skelgill** (6 *m.*). One of the finest walks in Britain ; road or path all the way.

Enter the **Elleray grounds** to the right of the Ambleside road, close to the station gates and the *Windermere Hotel*, and keep along the main path till you come out on the upper Troutbeck road by an iron gate (¾ *m.*), avoiding on the way a turn up to the right, which leads to Orrest Head, just short of Christopher North's Cottage. A little way along the road there are two openings in the wall made for the sake of the view, which, perhaps, reaches its climax at Borrans (1¾ *m.* ; *p.* 88). Nearly ¾ *m.* farther are some stepping stones below on the left, to which a path strikes off through a gate 80 yards beyond the junction of a road on the right. Descend to and cross the footbridge and climb the steep pitch beyond, entering the other Troutbeck road through a farmyard. Crossing this road at once we climb by a rough lane into the main Troutbeck and Low Wood road, which, as we proceed, bending to the right where a narrow road goes on direct, discloses an exquisite full-length view of the lake. From this point to **Low Wood** the distance is 1¾ *m.* (A footpath, *see map at end of the book* ; *and p.* 88, cuts off the last corner.)

For **Ambleside** by Skelgill, however, we turn up a lane on the right 250 yards after joining the Troutbeck and Low Wood road, and proceed along it for about half a mile, avoiding a tempting blind alley on the left, and leaving the lane at a direction-post, whence a track (scarcely marked in places) descends to the Holbeck stream, which it crosses at another direction-post, where it enters a cart-track that winds down from High Skelgill Farm towards Low Wood. The view westward is of surpassing loveliness. In the distance are the Coniston and Bowfell ranges, the Langdale Pikes, shading off gracefully into the lesser heights which slope to the glittering foreground of Windermere. Passing through High Skelgill farmyard we enter bosky ground on the slope of Wansfell. On the left, led up to by stiles, is Jenkin Crag (*see p.* 111). Then comes a rough descent to a beck. Keep the upper track just before crossing it, and in 10 minutes more you are in the main road half-way between Waterhead and Ambleside, or you may drop almost direct to Waterhead.

7. Footpaths to Bowness.

(*a*) **To Bowness by Heathwaite.** *2 miles ; a delightful and dry walk.* From the station turn down the Bowness road, and 200 yards beyond the *Queen's Hotel* (3 min.) take the straight street (*Broad Street*) on the left.

At the end of this turn right, and a few yards farther left again along the road that skirts the Park and continues through **Heathwaite** (1 *m.* from station). At the top the road ends at a stone wall with a turn-stile into a lane, after ascending which for 50 yards turn right. Proceeding through a gate, we bend down by *footpath* below *Lickbarrow Farm*. Pass through a stile beneath a tree, and enter a field from which there is a splendid view over the finest part of the lake. From the near side of the next stile a gravel path drops to **Bowness** direct through two more fields, connected by wicket-gates, and a wood, entering the upper part of the village close to Biskey How and the Hydro.

A very pleasant but somewhat longer route to Bowness or the Ferry is that by the track which those following route (*a*) leave between Heathwaite and Lickbarrow. The lane continues upward then goes past Matson Ground, a private residence (¾ *m. from Windermere Station*), into the Kendal and Bowness road, by which either the Ferry or Bowness may be reached (*total distance about 4 miles*). It makes a nice walk, and affords a charming view in descending towards the lake. The map will be sufficient guidance. Three-quarters of a mile beyond Matson Ground is the **Windermere Golf Course** ; from the road past the Club House there are excellent views of the fells. (The general public are not allowed on the Course.)

(*b*) **To Bowness by Mill Beck** (" Sheriff's Walk ") (2 *miles*). A pleasant variation to the high road. Follow the main road as far as (¾ *m.*) St. John's Church, on the right, and, a few yards farther, take the path that goes square across a field into Rayrigg

Wood, and then turn down to the left alongside the beck. 300 yards down, the stream divides and forms an islet. Here diverge on to the narrow path that hugs the stream, and where the streamlets meet again you will come to a couple of pretty miniature falls. Returning to the main track, you drop into the lower (Rayrigg) road, ⅛ mile north of Bowness.

8. Windermere Station to Bowness Pier (1¾ *miles*; bus service). The road from Windermere to Bowness affords charming views across the lake to the Fell country behind, the chief heights visible being Coniston Old Man, Wetherlam, Crinkle Crags, Scafell Pike, Great Gable, and the Langdale Pikes. From the station gates the road turns downhill to the left through the village. All the divergences meet again. At the road junction about half-way to Bowness is a memorial clock tower to the late M. J. B. Baddeley, the author and editor of earlier editions of this and other Guide Books bearing his name. *St. John's* is a modern church, with some good windows. A little farther down, on the left, is the War Memorial. Then the road descends through Bowness to the boat-landings and steamer-pier, passing the parish church on the right hand.

9. Kendal to Bowness over Scout Scar. ("Underbarrow Scar" on maps.)

A thoroughly clear day should be selected for this 10–12 mile walk, which passes through simple yet beautiful scenery, and affords, from Scout Scar, one of the finest views of the Lake mountains.

Take train or bus to Kendal (*see p. 95*), and turn up the street opposite the Town Hall—All Hallows Lane. At the fork just above take the steep left branch to the top of the rise, where an open space will be found with three roads. The central (Brigsteer) is that to be followed, and in ⅔ mile cross the by-pass bridge and go through the farm gate on the right, past the farm to the top of the **Scar**. The view bursts on the eye with fine effect. On the top of the Scar is a small "mushroom" shelter. As a fore ground we have the alluvial flats, green valleys—Underbarrow, Lyth, etc.—and limestone ridges—Whitbarrow in particular—which lie between the Lake District proper and Morecambe Bay ; behind these, the whole range of fells, from Black Combe to the Old Man group, Scafell, Bowfell, Langdale Pikes, Helvellyn, High Street, Harter Fell, the Shap and Sedbergh fells, and, in the S.E., Ingleborough.

Following the ridge northward the Kendal–Newby Bridge road is entered, 2 miles from Kendal, and after descending nearly a mile we pass a public-house, the *Punch Bowl*, and 2 miles farther reach the village of **Crosthwaite**, with another *Punch Bowl*, and an interesting modern church, built by the Argles family of **Heversham**. Notice the tower, reredos, and windows.

Hence the nearest walking way is to turn right in half a mile; then left over a curious stone bridge and a steep brae, dropping to **Winster** (*Brown Horse*), 2½ miles from Crosthwaite ; 3 from Bowness (*p.* 69).

In descending the hill to Winster by the main road, Bowfell stands boldly out in front without a trace of any of the neighbouring mountains.

Another route over Scout Scar. Instead of going through the gate mentioned above, continue along the Brigsteer road, which after an almost continuous rise of 1¾ miles makes two wide curves across limestone country, and then, bending sharp to the right, makes a very steep winding descent to the picturesque village of **Brigsteer** (*Wheatsheaf Inn*), 3½ miles from Kendal—" Brigsteer Pee-at," as it is called, from the quantity of that fuel which is cut just below the village. During the *ascent* there is a wide view over the Kent valley to the Yorkshire fells, including the flat-topped Ingleborough, nearly 20 miles away; in the valley the square tower of Natland Church, and, higher up, the long flat roof of Oxenholme Station, are conspicuous. In the *descent* the wide flat alluvial strath of **Lyth**, with the limestone Whitbarrow Scar backed by the Lake mountains (*see view from Scout Scar*), is spread like a map, with Morecambe Bay and Arnside at its southern end. The valley is noted for its damsons, and the blossoming week, early in May, is the annual feature.

From Brigsteer it is 2 miles north into the main (Kendal and Newby Bridge) road, which is entered about 4 miles from Kendal. In another 1½ miles we come to the *Punch Bowl* at Crosthwaite, whence to Bowness (5½ *m.*), *see* preceding route; or we may proceed from Brigsteer to Bowness by **Crook** and the Kendal and Bowness road as shown on map.

From Crosthwaite to **Newby Bridge**—by Bowland Bridge (2½ *m.*) and Strawberry Bank (3) is 7 miles. Newby Bridge on to **Ulverston, 9**; Newby Bridge to Bowness, 8; *see p. 69*—east side of lake.

To return to Kendal. On reaching the escarpment return along the edge of the Scar to the left through a gate. About ¼ mile farther is a path turning sharply to the left which leads back to the Brigsteer road.

Cunswick Scar commands equally fine views. Start as for Scout Scar, but before reaching the top of the hill turn to the right at a triangular piece of grass—the old cattle-market was held here. Then turn left, cross another stretch of grass, and ascend by a twisting lane to the Golf Course. Cross this, keeping on the upper side. In about a mile the edge of the Scar is reached with its tarn nestling below. The traverse of the two Scars occupies a full afternoon.

WALKS FROM BOWNESS

1. **Biskey How,** 170 *ft. above the lake*; 300 *above the sea.* Turn to the right out of the Windermere road at the Chestnut Tree on Crag Brow, 100 yards above the *Royal Hotel.* Passing the Hydro on the left you come to **Biskey How,** behind and above it, laid out as a park. From the big boss of rock that forms its top there is a fine, almost full-length, view of the lake

and of the mountain semicircle from Crinkle Crags to the Trout-beck and Kentmere ranges, the heights, taken in order, being Crinkle Crags, Scafell Pike (in the dip to the right), Bowfell, etc.

A similar view is to be had from **Post Knott**, a craggy hill-top south-east of the village. To reach it take the Kendal road for ¼ mile and climb up left-handed at a direction sign. The view-point was given to the National Trust in 1929.

2. The Ferry, 1 m. A pleasant stroll, which may be continued by road along the east side of the lake without crossing the water, or from the *Ferry House* either up or down the lake, or by the Hawkshead road to Sawrey (1 m. from ferry. p. 78), etc.

Pass the boat-pier at Bowness, walk southward, avoiding the road to the right (leading to the car park) and the main Newby Bridge road which goes off to the left. At the far end of the Glebe, with its miniature golf course, is the cemetery, where is the grave of the late M. J. B. Baddeley : the tombstones were conveyed with great labour from the summit of Scafell Pike. Beyond this take the footpath which rejoins the road after crossing a field and passing the ancient *Windermere Rectory*. The ferry is 250 yards to the right.

An alternative way is to pass the car park and walk along the shore of the lake at **Cockshott Point** (National Trust), emerging in the field mentioned above. Cockshott Point is a pleasant spot at which to linger, and there are views both down the lake and up to the Troutbeck Fells. (The ferry boat crosses at regular 15 to 20 minute intervals.

From the Ferry House to Lake Side, at the foot of Windermere Lake, the distance by road is 6 miles, by a very pleasant route mostly through wood. [The distant views are not so good as those along the east side (*see below*), where the road is carried at a higher average level and looks across the water to some of the finest mountain-outlines in the district.] The way is quite easy to find. Pedestrians cut off a corner and avoid a hill by going through a gate at the point where the main road leaves the lake-side, a good ¼ mile from the *Ferry House*.

From near *Graythwaite Hall* (3½ m.) a road crosses the hill to Thwaite Head in the Rusland valley, whence it is 7 to 8 miles by **Oxen Park** (*inn*) to the foot of Coniston Lake. The route is a quiet and picturesque one across hill and dale.

Beyond Graythwaite the road passes (5 m.) *Stott Park* and *Fins-thwaite Corner*, where it branches to the left and, ¾ m. farther reaches **Lake Side** Station and Hotel (*p.* 71).

3. Bowness to Newby Bridge, (8 m.) and Lake Side, (9 m.) *by road along east side of Lake.*

Recent widenings and other improvements to this road tempt the motorists to neglect the views which the road commands, but those who walk along it, or take the car along for an after-dinner "jaunt," will find leisurely going well repaid. By reason of the elevation of the road above the water, the mountain-background is much better seen than from the steamer-track, while the lake itself is a lovely foreground. Pedestrians should go by boat to Lake Side, cross the river at Newby Bridge, and walk back. (Infrequent bus service between Windermere and Newby Bridge.)

A good **Circular Drive** is to cross by the Ferry, thence skirt the west shore to Newby Bridge and return by the east side ; *total distance* 17 *m.*

The road goes south out of Bowness above the *Belsfield Hotel* and the one direction needed is to keep as straight as you can the whole way.

Continuing along the main road, we reach (3½ *m.* from Bowness) the charmingly placed *Beech Hill Hotel,* from the neighbourhood of which are obtained the clearest and best views.   Beyond the hotel the route is hilly, till at 6 miles we are directly under **Gummer's How** (1,054 *ft.*), the slopes of which are delightfully sprinkled with rock, bracken, whins, and other wilding growth. The ascent (*p.* 77) is easy and remunerative.   Then on the right comes *Town Head* and on the left our road is joined by the old road from Kendal to Ulverston.

At Fell Foot is the National Trusts' Country Park with information centre, café and other facilities.

Newby Bridge (*Swan* ; *Newby Bridge* ; *Landing* ; *Lakeside*) is a mile farther, and **Lake Side** (*hotel*) a mile back beyond the bridge. *For details of this neighbourhood, see pp. 76–7.*

4. To Winster, 3 *m.* ; Strawberry Bank, 6 *m.* ; Newby Bridge 8½ *m.* ; *and* Lake Side, 9½ *m.*   A very enjoyable walk ; a splendid view may be had by diverging to the top of Gummer's How.

Leave Bowness by the Kendal road, which passes below the *Crown Hotel* ; avoid the turn to the right just beyond the hotel, and in 10 minutes, when the Kendal road ascends to the left, keep straight on, crossing, ¼ mile farther, the road from Kendal to the Ferry.   Two-thirds of a mile farther the Winster (" Milnthorpe ") road strikes uphill to the left, and in a short 1½ miles we come to **Winster**.   At the *Brown Horse* we diverge to the right out of the main road, and passing Winster Church, keep on as straight as we can till we enter another road (1¾ *m.* from the inn) at right angles. Turning down to the right we cross the stream, and, after ascending for 350 yards beyond it, pass through a gate on the left on to a footpath that takes us by the left side of a wall and across some fields to *Hollins Farm,* whence an occupation road ascends into the public road to the prettily placed inn at **Strawberry Bank** (3 *m. from Winster*).

It is worth going a mile farther south to **Cartmel Fell Church** which is always open, on the eastern slope of Cartmel Fell, a quaint little building of much interest, which figures in the pages of Mrs. Humphry Ward's *Helbeck of Bannisdale.*   Of the ancient chapels in England north of the Thames, this is the only one dedicated to St. Anthony, who was the patron of basket-makers, charcoal-burners, hermits, and swineherds.   Doubtless the church was one of " the chapels " erected by monks from the Priory of Cartmel. Its most interesting feature is the remarkable glass of the east window, which, like that of Bowness, has been probably transferred from Cartmel Priory.   It is thought that the pictures of the Five Sacraments were copied from R. Van der Weyden's triptych at

Antwerp; that the figure of St. Anthony (*first left*) is probably English, of date between 1300–1400; and the figure of Christ appearing in the Garden may be even Early English (say, 1260 ?) Notice also the Jacobean woodwork.

(For route from Newby Bridge to the church *see p. 78.*) About a mile to the north-east of the Church is *Cowmire Hall,* a pele tower with a Caroline House built on.

From Strawberry Bank the road to Newby Bridge, beginning with a sharp zigzag, reaches in 1½ miles a height of 700 ft., and then sinks to a shallow depression, beyond which on the right is **Gummer's How,** from which there is a splendid view across and up Windermere. To reach it leave the road as soon as the lake comes in sight.

A little farther our road again attains 700 feet, and then begins a long descent to the foot of the lake, entering the Bowness and Newby Bridge road a mile short of the bridge.

5. Over Claife Heights (*west side of the lake*). There is a network of rather confusing tracks over this beautifully wooded little range, which lends so much grace to the west side of Windermere. To enjoy a good walk over the top, follow the Hawkshead road as far as Far Sawrey, 1½ miles from the Ferry, and there turn up a lane to the right. This will take you over the ridge, and, in about 2½ miles, into the wood-track between Belle Grange and Colthouse (*see below*), crossing which you soon reach High Wray. Several routes have now been waymarked.

By *Colthouse and Belle Grange,* longer but very interesting (8 *or* 9 *m.,* 3 *to* 4 *hrs.*), starting and ending at the *Ferry House.* Follow the Hawkshead road past Far and Near Sawrey and along the east side of Esthwaite till, beyond the second turning for Hawkshead (visible ½ *m.* to the left), a sharp bend to the right takes you to the hamlet of *Colthouse* (4 *m.*), and, a furlong farther, a house called *Crag.* Here turn up to the right by a rough track. This track crosses the heights to Belle Grange. At a fork about ½ mile up, after entering open ground covered with gorse, heath, juniper, etc., keep the left branch, which soon crosses the beck, and, passing a small tarn on the right, ascends through some larch trees. Where they end bear left at another fork over open ground to a gate at the highest point of the walk (700 *ft.*). Both in front of us and behind the mountain-view is very fine ; on the left front is the valley leading up to Kirkstone.

From the top, Low Wood is seen across Windermere, but growing trees will gradually obscure the distant views ; in 12 or 15 minutes you will drop into a plain cart-track, that has been visible some way off in front, and which takes you down to *Belle Grange,* a long 2 miles (by road) north of the Ferry. The track which is crossed at right angles is a bridle path from Sawrey to High Wray.

6. Bowness to Coniston by Grizedale, 11 *m.* ; 3¼–4 *hrs.* As a variation of the walk or ride through Hawkshead, this affords the best view of Esthwaite and a splendid prospect of Coniston in descending from the moor between Grizedale and the shores of Coniston Lake. There is no inn between Sawrey and Coniston and Forestry Commission Woods have obliterated many tracks.

Proceed as directed on *p. 77,* until you have skirted the south

shore of Esthwaite and left the lake-side in approaching Esthwaite
Hall. Here cut off a corner by crossing a stile and climbing to
the left of a house, beyond which you at once cross the road from
Hawkshead to Rusland. Then, entering a moorland cart-track,
cross the ridge between Esthwaite and Grizedale—the latter a
green, narrow valley, at the bottom of which is the hamlet of
Grizedale (*inn* at Satterthwaite, 1¼ *m.* down the valley by high-
road). Turning left down the road for a few paces, resume your
previous direction by a road that starts almost opposite Grizedale
Hall, and, after crossing the stream, rises up a rough hillside. In
half a mile turn right and ascend obliquely. After a long ascent
(1¼ *m.*) the track leaves the Grizedale Valley at a height of about
900 feet, and crossing open ground you see soon after the whole of
Coniston Lake spread below, with the Old Man and other of the
chief Lancashire and Westmorland fells forming a grand background. Brantwood is below on the left, and after a charming
descent, the main east-side road of Coniston is entered at *Bank
Ground*, ¼ mile short of *Tent Lodge* (*p.* 135). Thence the road goes
round the north end of the lake to the Waterhead Hotel.

WINDERMERE

(*Map at end of the book.*)

Windermere is 10½ miles long. Its width varies from ¼ to
1¼ miles, and its greatest depth is 219 feet. Its volume is equal
to that of Ullswater and Wastwater together and twelve times
that of Derwentwater.

Lake Side to Bowness (6¼). *Time 35 min. Several boats a day.*
The pier is alongside the station, and from the former there is a
charming view across and up the lake. The grounds on the
other side of the water, and close to the outlet of the lake, are
those of *Fell Foot* (the house was demolished many years ago),
and the next residence north, *Town Head*. This end of the
lake is remarkable for its luxuriant timber. On the eastern side
the holly in particular grows to a great height. The prominent
height beyond Town Head is *Gummer's How*, the loftiest summit
south of Bowness. Then, looking northward up the lake, we
see several of the chief mountains of the district. Fairfield is
on the left ; next to it Red Screes ; then Caudale Moor ; and
lastly the High Street range, of which the most conspicuous
height is the pyramidal Ill Bell. High Street derives its name
from a Roman road, which ascends by the left of Ill Bell, and
then continues along the ridge in the direction of Penrith. It
is still to be traced in places.

Soon after we leave the pier, Helvellyn appears to the left of
Fairfield. It drops gently to the west, but two or three little
notches, which break the regularity of its slope, indicate the
precipitous character of its descent in the opposite direction.

Close at hand on the west shore of the lake, soon after starting,
we have *Stott Park*, a modern house on a greensward dotted with

numerous wooded knolls, and the village of *Finsthwaite*, beyond
which the Finsthwaite Heights present a picturesque outline.
Behind us rises the Finsthwaite Tower, described on *p.* 76,
while on the east Gummer's How sinks abruptly to the water's
edge. There is nothing grand or wonderful about this part of the
lake, but look which way you will you cannot detect a dull
outline or a bare acre of ground to mar the general effect of
rich and tranquil beauty. Bobbin manufacture and charcoal
burning were formerly carried on in these woods.

The next object of interest is the little islet of *Blake Holme*,
clothed with oak-scrub and firs. It lies to the right of our course.
Then on the left side we pass near *Graythwaite Hall*, below which
is a picturesque little group of cottages on the edge of the lake,
and embowered in trees. A slight projection, a little farther on,
is *The Grubbin's Point*, beyond which, on the opposite side of the
water, is the charmingly placed *Beech Hill Hotel*, on the road
from Bowness to Newby Bridge. In front *Storrs Hall Hotel* is
conspicuous.

As we proceed, Helvellyn gradually disappears behind the
Claife Heights, which rise from the west shore of the lake. Almost
simultaneously a glance over the hollow on the left front will
detect in rapid succession the two peaks of the famous Langdale
Pikes, the most striking features in the view of the head of the
lake between Bowness and Ambleside. From this part they come
and go in a moment, but their place is supplanted by the fine
bluff of Wetherlam and the companion height—more pointed—
of Carrs. Both these are in Lancashire. Then, to the right of
them, apparently lower but in reality 400 feet higher, the
eminently graceful peak of Bowfell comes into view, with Scafell
Pike in the gap between it and Wetherlam. South of Wetherlam
the Old Man reappears. The islet on the left is *Grass Holme*.

Our course now continues past *Rawlinson Nab*, a low fairly
wooded promontory on the left. As we pass it, the central portion
of the lake quickens in interest. Beyond Rawlinson Nab we
gain a still better view of the Lancashire fells—the Old Man,
Carrs, and Wetherlam. The Old Man, by the way, has no human
association to account for the name. It is perhaps a corruption
of " Alt Maen," which is Celtic for High Crag (*see footnote, p.* 135)·

A little beyond Rawlinson Nab the *Cunsey Beck*, by which the pleasant
Esthwaite Water has its outlet, falls into the lake.

The boat next passes **Storrs** (*hotel*). In front of it a causeway projects to a little observatory called the **Temple** and interesting as the place where, in 1825, Wordsworth, Southey, Scott,
Canning, and Professor Wilson (Christopher North) gathered to
witness a regatta held in honour of the 54th birthday of the great
Scottish novelist and poet.

The wooded island passed on the right, ¼ mile short of
the Ferry, is *Ramp Holme,* in the neighbourhood of which are

several reefs visible when the water is low, and marked by red buoys.

We are now at the **Ferry**, one of the loveliest spots on Windermere, the Ferry House (Headquarters of the Freshwater Biological Association) being on the left.

At the Ferry two narrow promontories reduce the width of the lake to a little more than a quarter of a mile. This is part of the highway between Kendal and Hawkshead. There is a ferry-service, carrying cars, across the water at regular 15 to 20 minute intervals. (For details *see* p. 57.)

From the Ferry to a little north of Bowness the lake is at its shallowest, and here are nearly all the islands, the chief of which is *Belle Isle*. From the western shore of the lake rise the Claife Heights, wooded from head to foot with native trees and conifers. The islands are also richly clothed and the whole scene is one of great sylvan beauty and variety.

" **Belle Island** was formerly the property and residence of the Philipsons, an ancient Westmorland family. During the Parliamentary War two members of this family, brothers, had espoused the royal cause. The elder, to whom the island belonged, was a colonel, and the younger a major in the royal army. The latter, from some of his desperate exploits, had acquired among the Parliamentarians the appellation of ' Robin the Devil.' A certain Colonel Briggs, an officer in Oliver's army, and also a magistrate resident at Kendal, having heard that Major Philipson was secreted in his brother's house on Belle Isle, went thither to apprehend him. The major, however, was on the alert, and gallantly withstood a siege of eight months, until his brother came to his relief. Thereupon the major raised a small band of horse, and set forth one Sunday morning in search of Briggs. Upon arriving at Kendal, he was informed that the colonel was at prayers. He at once posted his men at the church door, and himself rushed down the main aisle into the midst of the congregation. The colonel was not present after all, upon discovering which fact the intruder made a dash for another door, which happened to be lower than the one by which he had entered, and in attempting to force his exit came into violent contact with the arch and lost his helmet. The congregation tried to seize him, but with the aid of his followers the indomitable major made good his escape, leaving the helmet as a perpetual voucher for the truth of the story."

More anciently the island was called Longholme, and from about 1250 onwards it was the seat of the lord of the manor of Windermere. The present circular house was built in 1777, and a few years later it passed into the ownership of the Curwen family.

We are now in sight of **Bowness** (*p.* 59). On approaching the pier, the upper part of the lake reveals itself as it were in the twinkling of an eye—a surprise view unsurpassed in Britain. Above and a little to the left the village of Windermere is conspicuous.

1. Bowness to Lake Side (6¼) by boat.

This part of the lake is more particularly described in the reverse route, *from* Lake Side (*pp.* 71–3), but for the benefit of those making the journey in the reverse direction we add a few notes on the principal features.

In passing through the strait between Belle Isle and Cockshott Point, the southern horn of Bowness Bay, a fine glimpse is obtained of the northern reach of the lake. Immediately behind it rises Loughrigg Fell, east of which is the Rothay valley, backed by the Fairfield group of mountains. The richly wooded park-like *Belle Isle* forms a delightful foreground, notwithstanding the " tea-caddy " mansion erected upon it in 1777 by Thomas English. The small island, close at hand, is *Crow Holme*. Passing the Ferry, the steamer crosses to the **Storrs** side (*Storrs Hall Hotel*), passing the beautifully wooded *Ramp Holme* and the *Storrs Estate* on the way. Beyond the pier is the " Temple " (*p.* 72). Then, on the right, the stream flowing from Esthwaite joins the lake, and beyond it is a promontory called *Rawlinson Nab*, and another island, *Grass Holme*. From hence the familiar outlines of the Old Man, Wetherlam, Bowfell, Scafell Pike, and the Langdale Pikes are recognisable for a few moments. Hence to the foot of the lake the scenery is unique but unpretentious. The shores on both sides are clothed with an almost unbroken fringe of wood, and the hills slope to them in a succession of outlines graceful and varying, but shrinking from any approach to the sensational. The highest and steepest of them is *Gummer's How*, on the left (1,054 *ft.*) a mile or so before the end of the lake is reached.

The lake maintains its character to the very end. There is, in fact, if possible, less marsh and uninteresting ground at its foot than at its head. The retrospect from **Lake Side** is very beautiful (*see p.* 71). The hotel lies close to the pier. For excursions in the neighbourhood of Lake Side see *pp.* 76–7.

It is a delightful *river-row* from Lake Side to Newby Bridge.

2. **Bowness to Ambleside (Waterhead)**, 4½ *m.*   *Time,* 30 *min.*
This, the upper reach of Windermere, is without doubt the most striking example of diversified beauty in the British Isles. Winding shores wooded to the water's edge ; a trio of valleys, vying in beauty, but distinct in style ; lower hills covered to their summits with copse-wood, crag, or bracken, and the whole girdled round by as shapely an array of mountains as the eye can wish to rest upon—these are the features which, taken separately, are surpassed elsewhere, but in combination are matchless.

Putting out from the pier at Bowness we have on the left *Belle Isle* (*p.* 73) ; in front Fairfield, at the end of a deep valley flanked by Nab Scar and Scandale Fell ; and on the right, close at hand, the grounds of *Fallbarrow*. The first islets passed close at hand are **Hen Holme**, with a vesture of oak and laurel, and **Lady Holme**, on which a " hospital " was founded by one of the Lindesay family in 1256. Later there was a chantry or chapel, dedicated to the Virgin Mary. It was standing up to the reign of Henry VIII, but there are now no traces of it. Then on the same side come the grounds of *Rayrigg*, Adelaide Hill (*p.* 64), and the *Millerground Landing* for Windermere village, the towers and villas of which peer above the trees at the foot of the green crest of Orrest Head. Beyond this the view up Troutbeck opens. Below Caudale Moor, at its upper end, this valley is broken by a beautiful rounded hill called Troutbeck Tongue. Troutbeck is famed for the sturdy independence of its (e)statesmen, as the hereditary farmers of the district are called ; amongst them was the uncle of Hogarth, the painter. To the left of the dale Wansfell rises in front of Red Screes, while away across the lake the Langdale Pikes begin to assume that pre-eminence which they jealously maintain over the head of Windermere, though they are as much as 500 feet lower than some of the neighbouring heights. Usually, and especially after heavy rain, a white streak may be seen descending from the cliffs to the right of the chief Pike. This is Mill Gill. Under the cliffs above it is Stickle Tarn, and in the next hollow on the left, between the two peaks, lies Dungeon Ghyll.

On the far side of the Trout Beck is *Calgarth Park*, built by Bishop Watson of Llandaff, now the " Ethel Hedley Orthopædic Hospital."

Wray Castle is now prominent on the west side of the lake. It is a modern building with tower and battlements, and is more impressive from a distance than near at hand. It was given to the National Trust in 1929, but in 1958 was opened as " *R.M.S. Wray Castle* ". It is now however little more than a shell. Beyond it the mountain-outline stretching southwards from the Langdale Pikes has become particularly fine. Next to the Pikes themselves Bowfell is the most prominent height. It rises from the right to a slight but graceful peak and sinks abruptly to a hollow on the left, over which the summit of Scafell Pike, the monarch of English mountains, may be seen. The left side of the dip between Bowfell and the Langdale Pikes is Esk Hause, over which passes the wild fell-route to Wastwater. The square fell beyond the dip is Great Gable. Then the nearer range of Bowfell is continued by Crinkle Crags, a cluster of humps close together. Pike o' Blisco, with a short square top and sloping shoulders, is a little in front of these, and farther south is the depression of Wrynose, over which the old pack-road from Kendal to Ravenglass passes.

South of the Wrynose Pass the Lancashire fells of Wetherlam, marked by a bold round bluff, and the Old Man—its cairn visible even at this distance—come into view. The High Street range now disappears behind the lower height of woody Wansfell, and in another minute or two we are opposite the *Low Wood Hotel*. The view across the lake from the pier is very fine, but those who stay here—and it is only 1¾ miles by high road from Ambleside—will find it still finer if they climb the hill behind the hotel by road or path for half a mile or so (see p. 81).

The lower skirts of Wansfell are beautifully fringed with wood and broken with bosses of rock. So, too, are those of that most delightful rambling fell, Loughrigg, which rises immediately from the head of the lake, in colour and clothing a gem of beauty. Quite bold enough for its situation, it is not of sufficient height to break the fine outline of distant mountains which is one of the strong characteristics of Windermere scenery. Every English lake has its individuality, and a rugged mountain sinking abruptly to the water's edge like those around Wastwater would be aggressive in Windermere, whose paramount charm lies in the easy and graceful transition from the softest to the sternest features of nature.

Hereabout, if we measure across the lake into the recesses of **Pull Wyke Bay,** conspicuous on which is the villa of *Pull Woods,* we have its widest part, 1¼ miles. Beyond this little bay, the water is bordered by the park-like grounds of *Brathay Hall,* and the opposite shore-line is broken by several tiny inlets, and by the channel through which the combined waters of the Brathay and the Rothay slide noiselessly into the lake. Up the former valley the bell-tower of *Brathay Church* rises very prettily above the trees, marking the route to Great and Little Langdale. The line of houses sheltering under Loughrigg is Clappersgate. To the right of Loughrigg is the Rothay valley, in which the spire of Ambleside church is a prominent object. As our boat goes round the buoy we shall see, high up, a barer valley on the right, and at the head of a road which is appropriately called the *Struggle,* a little white house. This is the *Kirkstone Inn* on the top of the Kirkstone Pass, one of the highest of its kind in the country (see p. 89).

And now we draw up at the pier of **Waterhead,** from which buses run to Ambleside (¾ mile), Grasmere, etc.

Excursions from Lake Side

The best view-points are Gummer's How and Finsthwaite Tower, though foliage may limit the prospect in certain directions. There is also the drive or walk up either side of the lake. Bus services run between Newby Bridge and Bowness.

(a) **Finsthwaite Tower** (1½ m., 605 ft.). On the north side of the railway bridge at Newby Bridge pass through a wicket gate, and in fifty paces turn up to the right and again steeply in the same direction twenty paces farther. Then, after a climb for about 100 yards, turn sharp to the left along a wider track, which winds up to the top. The tower (reduced in height some years ago) was originally built in honour of the naval campaigns of 1799. The view through the foliage is good—Windermere as far as Belle Isle and Bowness, with Storrs Hall and Temple conspicuous on its eastern side, and not a bare strip along its entire shore. The line of the lake is continued by the green valley of Troutbeck, with the conical Ill Bell and High

Street flanking it on the right, and Wansfell with Red Screes over it on the left. Then come the Fairfield group and Helvellyn—a slight notch marking its summit—the head of the dip of Dunmail Raise, the Langdale Pikes, Wetherlam, Grey Friar, the Old Man, and Dow Crag. To the right of the High Street range is Harter Fell.

The view of the foot of the lake is obscured by trees, but the Leven estuary, the Hoad monument over Ulverston, Morecambe Bay, and the Lancashire fells complete the panorama.

(b) **Gummer's How** (1,054 ft., 2 hrs. there and back). Go round the foot of the lake by Newby Bridge, then follow the steep Kendal road as shown on map. The view of the lake and mountains is splendid. Just across the water on the Finsthwaite Heights, are the seldom seen High Dam and Bortree Tarn. These heights are a designated reserve area by the Nature Conservancy Board. Esthwaite Lake and the Leven valley look their best. For the way down to Strawberry Bank or back to Lake Side by Newby Bridge, etc., see p. 70.

(c) **To Cartmel Fell Church.** (See p. 70.) Go over the bridge, and follow the Kendal road to just beyond the brow of the hill, where is a guide-post directing down Sow How Lane (fine eastern view), past Sow How Farm, and Foxfield Farm. Continue along the lane for about half a mile, avoiding a rough track to the right a short distance beyond Foxfield, until a beck is crossed. Just beyond this turn to the right till a second post is reached. Here turn left to a third white post on a road. Here again turn left to a fourth post by a stile near the old Vicarage. The church itself is a little farther on, beyond the school-house. The hill, with a cairn on it, is called " Raven Barrow Old Man." Within a short distance of the church is " Hodge Hill," an ancient residence containing some fine old oak.

The Lakeside and Haverthwaite Railway runs a steam-hauled service in the summer season.

ROAD EXCURSIONS FROM BOWNESS AND WINDERMERE

1. Bowness to Coniston by the Ferry and Hawkshead ; returning by Waterhead.

Bowness to Ferry Nab, 1¼ m. ; Ferry House, 1½ ; Hawkshead, 5½ ; Coniston (Waterhead), 9 ; Return route by Oxenfell, Skelwith Bridge, and Waterhead (Windermere), 13 m.

This is, perhaps, the best route for those who wish to visit Coniston for a few hours only. The return route (pp. 139–40) by Oxenfell and Skelwith Bridge affords very fine views for a great part of the way. Those who contemplate paying a visit to Coniston from other parts are recommended to make a special journey along this route as far as Near Sawrey, and thence to drive round Esthwaite Water by Hawkshead, and back to the Ferry. The tour abounds in soft, sylvan beauty of a pleasing type. The distance, out and in, from Bowness is about 12 miles.

The views in crossing from **Ferry Nab** are very fine both ways. The long southern reach of the lake, with lessening hills and shores, draped to the water's edge with a flowing robe of wood, displays no startling features of beauty, but it never degenerates, as so many lakes do at their lower end, into commonplace. Northwards, over the beautifully timbered Belle Isle, appear Fairfield, Hart Crag, Red Screes, and the High Street range, the green valley to the left of the latter being Troutbeck.

From the Ferry the road ascends sharply round the south end of Claife Heights, and, passing **Far Sawrey** [1] (*hotel*) and *Near Sawrey* (*inn*)—Beatrix Potter's house, Hill Top Farm (*National Trust*), open in summer, 11–5.30, Sundays from 2 p.m., fee— drops down again to the shore of *Esthwaite Water*. From between the two Sawreys Bowfell in front presents a very striking outline.

For the road along the western side of Esthwaite Water, take the left-hand road at Near Sawrey, and, avoiding a second turn on the same side about a quarter of a mile farther on, skirt as nearly as possible the shores of the lake. The road is for some distance fringed with wood, on emerging from which it leaves the water's edge and passes a farm-house called Esthwaite Hall. Beautiful views—including the Langdale Pikes and Bowfell range, with a peep of Scafell Pike—across the lake are obtained. The mountain due north is Fairfield. Half-way up the lake, where the road again approaches it, a peninsula, looking from many points like an island, agreeably diversifies its surface and in another mile, three miles after quitting the high road at Near Sawrey, Hawkshead is reached.

From half a mile south of Hawkshead a road commanding fine views strikes over the fell (*800 ft.*) to *Grizedale* (3 m.), *Satterthwaite* (4½, *inn*); *Oxen Park* (8½, *inn*); **Newby Bridge** (10), etc. In its last part it passes through a fine beech avenue.

The "east coast" route of Esthwaite, after passing *Lake Fields*, draws near the shore at *Lake Bank*, a villa just opposite the promontory described in the above detour, and thence skirts the lake almost to its head.

Esthwaite Water is rather more than 1½ miles long and less than half a mile wide. Its attractions are the soft sylvan character of the scenery immediately surrounding it, and the fine view it commands of the fells to the west and north, from Coniston Old Man to Red Screes.

A short distance beyond the head of the lake is a small tarn, rather mysteriously called *Priest Pot*. The name is probably a reminder that the pool was a fish-preserve for the monks of Hawkshead Hall, but the popular idea is that it held just the *quantum* of good liquor which a priest could comfortably consume at a sitting. Close by is a small *Quakers' Burial Ground* and meeting-house at Colthouse.

Our road diverges to the left just after passing the Pot and in less than half a mile we are in **Hawkshead** (*Red Lion*, *Queen's Head*), passing on the left, as we enter the town, the *Grammar School* (small fee for admission) in which Wordsworth was educated from 1778 to 1783. The building (date 1675) has been restored. In front are a coat of arms, a sundial, and an inscription recording the foundation of the school by Edwin

[1] Far and Near Sawrey take us back to the time when Hawkshead, and *not* Windermere, was the centre of this district.

Sandys, Abp. of York, 1585. On a desk Wordsworth's name is cut, reputedly by the poet.

Hawkshead is one of the quaintest of English "towns," though modern improvements have somewhat spoilt it. Such an extraordinary arrangement, or rather disarrangement, of houses was probably never seen elsewhere. The whole effect is far more reminiscent of Robin Hood's Bay or Polperro than of any other Lakeland feature.

The following stanza, from the pen of A. C. Gibson, in his amusing "Rambles round Coniston," is no exaggeration :—

"A quaint old town is Hawkshead, and an ancient look it wears;
Its church, its school, its dwellings, its streets, its lanes, its squares
Are all irregularities—all angles, twists, and crooks,
With penthouses and gables over archways, lanes, and nooks."

The *Church* occupies an eminence behind the School.

It is certain that a Norman Church once stood at Hawkshead for as early as 1200 the foundation is referred to as an *old* one In that year, at the time when Carlisle was still bishopless, and hordes of Scots were constantly swooping down upon the farmers in these "daals," the priest here was placed under the control of the Cistercian monks of Furness. At different times the chapel of "Hawksett," or "Hoxet," was connected with Dalton-in-Furness, and later with Ulverston. In spite of the statement in Baines's "History of Lancashire," that the present walls are Norman, it is contended that this structure only goes back to the time of Elizabeth. And notwithstanding the older appearance of the rough pillars of the nave, without bases and capitals, and the undressed arches, it is insisted that lack of funds, and not antiquity, has given its shape to the masonry. Probably the moulding of the north door of the nave is the only part of the earlier church now remaining, unless it be the lower part of the tower, upon which a new top was built in 1873. In this year great changes were made, the east wall and window and part of the south aisle being built afresh, and the interior recoloured.

The most interesting feature to the antiquary is the altar-tomb, in the north-east angle, with effigies of Wm. and Margaret Sandys— 1578. A legend in questionable elegiacs runs round it, and it has been enclosed by a light screen. Note also a curious dugout chest (1603) near the organ, placed in the church some years ago.

The Methodist Chapel has been in continuous use since 1862.

The house in which Wordsworth lodged stands back on the right, 20 yards beyond the arch in the following walking route.

Walking Route.—Between Hawkshead and High Cross the walker may save a quarter of a mile, and greatly enhance the pleasure of his walk, by turning to the left up the lane opposite the *Red Lion*, passing under an arch, and, after proceeding ¼ mile, taking an unmistakable footpath on the right, which climbs the hill and rejoins the high road 250 yards short of the Baptist Chapel at **Hawkshead Hill,** as the hamlet is called. During the walk there is a beautiful mountain-view, from Helvellyn to Ill Bell and Harter

Fell on the right, with part of the Coniston Range on the left, which is not visible from the road.

On reaching the chapel, those who wish to include the exquisite scenery of **Tarn Hows** in their day's programme should diverge to the right from the main road, and, crossing the Ambleside and Coniston road almost immediately, proceed according to the instructions given on *pp.* 135–6.

From Hawkshead the main road continues northwards over a bridge to *Hawkshead Old Hall* (*see below*), just short of which the turn to the left must be taken. The road straight on leads to Ambleside, 5 m. from Hawkshead; *inn* at Outgate, 1½ m. Climbing the hill we reach Hawkshead Hill and, ¼ mile farther on, *High Cross*, where the route from Ambleside to Coniston (*p.* 122) is joined. For **Coniston** *see p.* 134.

Hawkshead Hall stands near the first bridge on the Ambleside road. It has long been a farmhouse but the thick walls, the round chimneys and a Jacobean staircase are proof of its former importance.

The Hall was originally probably quadrangular, erected about Henry III's reign. Little is recorded of the place, but it seems that this, with the whole manor of " Hawkr's-Seat," [1] was under the direct control of the monks at Furness ; and a document of Henry VIII's reign, called " The Custom of High Furness," was actually drawn up in this place. This house was no doubt occupied generally by a few monks up to the year 1537, and there is every reason to think that in its rooms the abbot lodged, when on circuit.

The large building near the road—the **Gate** or **Court House**— is thought to have been added in the 15th century to the older buildings near. The building is now in the care of the National Trust, and the interior may be inspected for a small fee.

It has at the village end (south) a pretty little window of Early Perpendicular tracery, and above its rude and ancient gateway-arch are some curious bits of carving. Perhaps the sprigs carved on the keystone may represent deadly nightshade in allusion to the connection with Furness Abbey. The upper storey within is a long room containing an unusually interesting fireplace decorated with dog-tooth moulding. The latter might have been cut as early as 1250, but for the shape of the arch, which cannot be put earlier than 1400.

2. Windermere or Bowness to Keswick.

(*Map at end of the book.*)

Windermere to Ambleside, 4¾ *m. ; Grasmere,* 9 *; Wythburn,* 12¾ *; Thirlspot,* 15½ *; Keswick,* 21¼.

Good service of buses and private coaches. Approximate journey times: Bowness to Keswick in 2¼–2½ hrs. ; from Windermere, 1¾–2 hrs.

The above mileage is reckoned through Grasmere village. If the direct route to the right of the village be taken, ¼ mile is saved.

This is the only really first-class road through the Lake District, and provides, without doubt, one of the most beautiful and varied

---

[1] " Hawk " is almost certainly a corruption of " Hakon."

drives in Britain. In its length of twenty-one miles five lakes are seen, and, from one point or other, the summits of nearly all the principal fells. At the same time, no delusion can be greater than the idea that by taking this one journey through it the tourist has exhausted all that is most beautiful in the district. Let the northward-bound traveller break his journey, by all means, for this excursion, as he speeds on his way to the land of wild sea-lochs and incomparable glens, but let him not come home and make comparisons. The characteristic beauty of Scotland is of that broad, dashing type which challenges admiration at first sight, and sometimes has a tendency to pall with familiarity. That of English Lakeland is of a finer tissue. The very diversity of the threads which compose it is apt to disappoint the rushing tourist, but there is probably no scenery in Europe which so grows upon the thoroughgoing lover of nature as that of Westmorland and Cumberland. One hurried journey, though it be through the midst of it, is apt to establish a very false impression. The true one is only gained by lingering, and leaving the beaten tracks.

Even the habitual pedestrian will do well to drive the first part of the route we are describing, especially Windermere to Ambleside which is a wide motoring road, often busy with traffic.

The Route.—The mountain straight ahead, as we follow the main road from Windermere station, is Wetherlam, in Lancashire. On the right are the grounds of Elleray ; on the left the church, and then (⅔ *m.*) we come to cross-roads ; that on the left comes up from Bowness ; the right branch goes to Ullswater. Leisured pedestrians should diverge for 300 yards along the Bowness road for the splendid view from Miller Brow (*see p.* 64). From the cross-roads the highway descends, with a large housing estate between it and the lake, and then in full view of the mountain range from the Old Man to the Langdale Pikes (Great Gable fills the gap to the left of the latter), to **Troutbeck Bridge** (*Sun*). On the left is Calgarth, now the Ethel Hedley Hospital. Thence there is nothing particularly noteworthy, except, from the more open ground, a good view of Bowfell, the Langdale Pikes, etc., until just beyond one or two fine houses and the convergence of the Troutbeck road, the lake-side is reached at the beautifully situated *Low Wood Hotel* (3 *m.*). The lake is here at its widest, and the mountain-view extends from the Old Man to the Langdale range. It is, with a few variations, the same as the one from Orrest Head (*p.* 61). Carrs has vanished behind Wetherlam, to reappear shortly on the right of it. Wray Castle, Brathay Hall, and the campanile of Brathay Church are conspicuous objects on the other side of the lake, between the two former the deep recess of Pull Wyke retires. The lesser heights of Brow Fell, Lingmoor, and Loughrigg prevent all abruptness in the transition from the rich foreground to the wild fells behind.

Footpath into Troutbeck Road, $\frac{1}{4}$ *m.* The view from this is still finer than from the main road. Go through the arch in the centre of the hotel, cross the car park to a gate into the field. Turn right to a kissing gate leading into a lovely dingle threaded by a streamlet which forms a number of pretty little cascades. This is *Holbeck*. Crossing by stepping stones you ascend steeply to the Troutbeck road.

Low Wood to **Troutbeck Village, or Windermere,** by Troutbeck. The road between Low Wood and Troutbeck village ascends about 400 feet, and is justly celebrated for the exquisitely beautiful and almost full-length view of Windermere which it commands, best seen about $1\frac{1}{2}$ miles on the way. The *road* quits the highway 300 yards south of the hotel : pedestrians should cut off the corner by the above footpath. The drive can be extended beyond Troutbeck to the Kirkstone Pass, and return made through Ambleside.

The walk from Troutbeck to Windermere is described the reverse way on *pp.* 64–5.

Low Wood to Wansfell Pike (1,587 *ft.*, 2 *m.*). A very pleasant climb. Go through the arch in the centre of the hotel, cross the car park to the gate into the field. Bear left to the ladder stile, above which the course of the Thirlmere aqueduct is crossed. Then, passing through *High Skelgill* farm, take the right-hand track and ascend over the open ground. There is a wall or two to be dodged.

On the main road is **Brockhole,** the National Parks Information Centre with café and picnic area.

From Low Wood to Waterhead the main road skirts the lake along the base of Wansfell Pike and passes below *Dove Nest* (hidden amid trees), which years ago had some celebrity as a residence of Mrs. Hemans, the poetess.

Waterhead (Hotel : *Waterhead*) is the pier for Ambleside. The road branching off to the left joins the Ambleside and Langdale road at Rothay Bridge, half a mile away. The cluster of white cottages just over the head of the lake is Clappersgate, and beneath it the streams of the Brathay and Rothay meet, and, in $\frac{1}{4}$ mile, pour their combined waters into the calm depths of Windermere. Waterhead is the point where the road and lake routes from Windermere and Lake Side converge. On a fine summer day the scene is a lively one from morning till night, with its constant flow of passengers and officials to and fro, and *mêlée* of steamers, row-boats, cars and conveyances of every sort gathered round the landing-stage. Immediately after passing Waterhead, the road enters the Rothay valley, and the higher western fells retire one by one behind the rugged and picturesque slopes of Loughrigg.

Ambleside (*p.* 106) is reached in less than a mile. The mountain with the deep hollow in front, and extending two parallel arms towards us, as we approach it, is Fairfield, and the valley thus enclosed Rydal.

Quitting Ambleside we cross the Stock Gill stream, spanning which is the quaint little *Old Bridge House.* On the left, the *Knoll* once of some local importance as the residence of the writer Harriet Martineau. On the right is *Scale How* (Charlotte Meson College), a teacher training college. The road proceeds up the richly-timbered Rothay valley, crossing the Scandale stream, and affording in half a mile glimpses of *Fox How* and *Fox Gill*, lying under Loughrigg on the left.

Then, on the right, after crossing Rydal Beck, we have before us *Rydal Hall*, the ancient seat of the le Flemings, now leased by the Diocese of Carlisle and, passing Pelter Bridge on the left, we enter the pretty little village of **Rydal** (*Glen Rothay Hotel*).

Rydal Mount, the home of Wordsworth from 1817 to 1850, is a house which retires from the road about 200 yards above the church, and is almost hidden by a mass of foliage. It is open in summer. The *Rashfield* (*National Trust*) once belonged to the poet's daughter Dora and is well worth seeing at daffodil time.

By crossing Pelter Bridge and turning to the right, one reaches a charming path which skirts the west side of Rydal Water, and goes on to Grasmere by **Loughrigg Terrace** (*see p.* 148).

Pedestrian Route from Rydal to Grasmere. This, a more enjoyable one than the main road, ascends the hill past Rydal Church for 300 yards, as far as a turn just behind Rydal Mount. Here take the narrow lane to the left. After getting clear of the Mount, lovely peeps of Windermere and Rydal Water are visible through the trees. In 4 minutes from the turn follow the upper track to the right of a wall and keep on as straight as possible, avoiding a divergence to the left, until you enter a by-road at White Moss and descend into the main road again 150 yards beyond the *Prince of Wales Hotel*, Grasmere. The main road will be seen making a wide divergence to the left round the head of Rydal Water. The only thing lost by adopting this route is the first view of Grasmere from the main road.

Rydal Water now appears through a thick foreground of trees and over the hills in front appears Harrison Stickle, with Crinkle Crags and Pike o' Blisco to the left. From a rock on the left of the road (*Wordsworth's Seat*), climbed by some natural steps, there is a lovely view over the lake, behind which rise Silver How and Sergeant Man.

Some distance along the lake-side we reach **Nab Farm**, once the abode of Hartley Coleridge and de Quincey. Thence the road winds round the west end of the lake and through a wood to Grasmere Lake.

The low-lying land at the head of Rydal is very ragged in appearance. As it is one of the few places open to the road between Windermere and Keswick, this is a popular picnicking spot. There is no access for cars, but a car park is situated opposite.

Across the lake **Loughrigg Terrace** is seen skirting the northern slope of Loughrigg some way up, and is easily reached from the end of Rydal Water by an obvious footpath and footbridge (*see p.* 148).

There are two other routes from the end of **Rydal Water** to

Grasmere : (*a*) the most direct by *White Moss Tarn*—very steep for a bit ; (*b*) ascending out of the main road a few yards farther and passing, at a bend, the *Wishing Gate* (*p.* 149), whence there is a charming view over the lake. This route, ¼ mile shorter than the main road, is the best for pedestrians, the only thing missed being the fine burst of the lake-view mentioned below. Both routes descend to the main road again a furlong beyond the *Prince of Wales Hotel*. In the cottage on the right just before entering the main road Wordsworth lived from 1799 to 1808 (*p.* 145).

A sharp turn to the right brings the whole of **Grasmere** and the rich valleys beyond suddenly before the eye. The valley over the island is Easedale. Silver How rises to the left of it, Helm Crag to the right. The rocky hump seen from this side on the top of the latter represents the " Lion and the Lamb." The line of a track along the slope of Loughrigg, some few hundred feet above the lake, is visible. This is Loughrigg Terrace (*see p.* 83). Soon after leaving the shores of Grasmere the main road goes straight ahead ; for Grasmere turn to the left (the road rejoins the main route about ¾ mile on) ; for Wordsworth Cottage turn up the lane which strikes back on the right. The lake and village of **Grasmere** are described on *pp.* 145-7.

Two-thirds of a mile beyond the *Swan Hotel,* where the roads rejoin, and just beyond the little inn called the *Traveller's Rest,* the Grasmere ascents of Helvellyn and of the Grisedale Pass to Ullswater begin through a gateway on the right.

Then the long ascent of **Dunmail Raise** (780 feet) begins. As we climb, the peculiar rock-outlines on the summit of **Helm Crag** assume a greater reality than from any other point of observation. The most striking similitudes are of lion and lamb, and of an old woman playing the organ. Towards the summit the rock changes to another and a better lion, which, however, seems to have eaten the lamb.[1] The course of an old road (mistermed " Roman ") may be traced along the slope of Helm Crag and farther, almost as far as Dunmail Raise, approaching which the moraine heaps are numerous and clearly defined.

The summit, which the division line between Westmorland and Cumberland crosses about 3 miles beyond Grasmere, is marked by a pile of stones between the dual carriage way, said to cover the remains of Dunmail, " last king of rocky Cumberland." The battle was fought in 945 against King Edmund. " Cumbria thus became a fief of the crown of England."—*Ferguson.* The views from the summit-level are good, though not extensive. At no one point are both Grasmere and Thirlmere visible. The fell on the right is Seat Sandal, on the left Steel Fell. **Thirlmere** comes into view in front almost immediately after Grasmere has disappeared in the rear, and very attractive it looks, embosomed between the stalwart shoulder of the huge Helvellyn and the lesser but more

[1] This rock is not the same as the one we noticed when approaching Grasmere.

rocky heights of the crags on the western side—chief amongst them Fisher Crag and Raven Crag.

Thirlmere is the property of the Corporation of Manchester, of which city it is now the chief reservoir. The level of the lake has been raised fifty feet, and it is really a noble sheet of water, though the thick fringe of trees by which it is surrounded is making it less visible from the roads. Even more to be deplored is the closing of the famous old Nag's Head at Wythburn, so long a head-quarters of climbers and walkers.

The reservoir was 10 years in construction, and the whole scheme cost about 3 million pounds. The total length of the aqueduct is 95¾ miles. The *Aqua Marcia* and the *Anio Novus*, the two longest aqueducts of ancient Rome, measured 57 and 54 miles respectively; the *Aqua Claudia*, 42½; the one between Loch Katrine and Glasgow is 34½ miles long; that between Lake Vyrnwy and Liverpool, 67; and the one from Mid-Wales to Birmingham, 73¼.

The distant mountain filling up the dip beyond Thirlmere is Great Calva in Skiddaw Forest, with Littledale Pike (Lonscale Fell), on Skiddaw, to the left of it.

About a mile beyond the Raise we reach the entrance to the road skirting the—

West side of Thirlmere. This fine road, 5¼ miles in length, and all but level throughout, affords one of the most beautiful drives or walks in the District. It was made by the Manchester Corporation as an acknowledgment of the withdrawal of the local opposition to the conversion of the lake into a reservoir, and cost between £20,000 and £30,000. Cyclists making the tour of the lake should take this road northward and return along the east side.

In recent years, the Manchester Corporation have planted the embankments of the lake and portions of the lower slopes of Helvellyn with larch and spruce. These add greatly to the charm of the prospect from a distance : but, as already mentioned, they have grown so luxuriantly as in parts completely to shut off the view from the road.

Route.—Leaving the main (east side) road, ⅓ mile south of Wythburn, the road crosses the head of the lake, then turns north and crosses (1 *m.*) **Dob Gill** (a fine cataract after rain), which brings down the water from Harrop Tarn. On the way we pass beneath the farmsteads of *Steel End* and *West Head*. In front Great How, Raven Crag, and Saddleback are imposing features. At Hause Point we cut through the rock by *New Nick* (an isolated rock on the right has steps and seats and is a good view-point), beyond which, bending to the left, we pass under the precipitous **Rough Crag,** splendidly draped with trees and flowers in due season. Half a mile farther, the stream of **Launchy Gill** comes rushing down from a fine fall several hundred feet above the road. The fall may be reached by a stiff climb on the near side.

After crossing the gill, the road overlooks a charming little inlet called *Deergarth Bay*. Then, beyond *Fisher Gill*, we pass the site of Armboth House—now removed and the site submerged by the extension of Thirlmere. Hereabouts the road is joined by the mountain-track from Borrowdale, by Watendlath and Armboth Fell (*p.* 159).

Thence the road goes on to the foot of **Raven Crag,** which towers 900 feet above it. The retrospect of Thirlmere from about here is exquisitely beautiful. Over Dunmail Raise Loughrigg Fell reappears. Helvellyn Low Man is conspicuous across the lake, and the sharp-ridged Saddleback northwards. The wooded height of Great How, almost exactly opposite, is a fine feature in the view. Raven Crag is easily ascended by fetching a compass round it on the north side, or by starting up some way on the south. The road then proceeds past the great **Dam** of the lake—a fine piece of engineering work 260 yards in length, 100 feet from foundation to summit, and 50 feet wide at the bottom (20 at the top), with a good road 16 feet wide across it. The main road is entered 4¼ miles short of Keswick.

₊ The road crossing the dam joins the main road close to Smeathwaite Bridge (where turn sharp left for Keswick), continuing into St. John's Vale under the Castle Rock.

Passing the entrance to the western road, the main route reaches, 1¼ miles beyond Dunmail Raise, the hamlet of **Wythburn** (the favourite starting-place for Helvellyn). The church was once one of the many aspirants to the doubtful honour of being the smallest in England. Some years ago, however, it was enlarged by the addition of a chancel.

Some strange stories are told of the Lake clergy of a past generation, and, as they are in no way applicable to those of the present, we may be excused for relating one. By the side of the old pulpit at Wythburn was a narrow slit, locally called a " grike," into which, on one occasion, the preacher had the misfortune to drop his sermon when he was about half-way through it. Finding all efforts to recover it futile, he turned to the congregation, and, taking up his Bible, remarked, " Brethren, I've dropped t' sermon doon t' grike, but I'll read a chapter in t' Bible that's worth twal' of it."

Thirlmere is now 3⅝ miles long, and about half a mile broad. It is 583 feet above sea-level, the only one of its sister lakes exceeding it in this respect being Haweswater. The side of Helvellyn, along which the main road runs, remains unattractive, despite the Manchester plantations, and the only building is the *Straining Well,* designed to look like a castle. On the opposite side, the shores of the lake are gracefully fringed with wood diversified with rocky knolls, while the line of hills is broken by picturesque gills.

Only occasional glimpses are caught, through the trees, but towards the northern end of the lake there is a gap in the plantation and from this point there are excellent views both of the lake and of the lovely western shore. The road, after rising, now falls to reveal a splendid view of the " narrow valley of St. John," backed by the razor-like edges of Saddleback. Thirlmere is seen no more.

Half a mile beyond the top, the *King's Head* at **Thirlspot** lies to the right of the road. Here a track from Helvellyn joins the highway. In less than another mile the road down St. John's

Vale, through which flow what can be spared of the waters of Thirlmere, strikes off on the right.

Great How, 509 ft. above the lake, is well worth a climb. Leave the road by short lane ⅓ m. beyond inn, and opposite Post Office. Then bear right across a field and up through the wood. From the top you command the length of the lake and the dam.

Just short of **Smeathwaite Bridge** a road strikes off to the big dam and into the west-side road (*p.* 85), and from this point is one of the best views of the famous " Castle-rock of Triermain," so called, which rises sharply above the St. John's Vale road. For the next two or three miles, through *Naddle*, there is a marked falling-off in the landscape, its only attraction being the simultaneous view of the tops of Skiddaw, Saddleback, and Helvellyn Low Man, which is obtained after the first mile beyond the bridge. A glimpse of the Castlerigg Stone Circle (*p.* 170) may also be obtained just short of Shoulthwaite Bridge. On the left *Shoulthwaite Gill* comes down from behind Raven Crag. High up the gill and close against the Crag is the site of an interesting British hill-fort. Here for a short distance the scenery deteriorates, except for the massive shoulders of Saddleback to the north-east and Skiddaw straight ahead; Naddle Fell shuts out the valley of St. John, and neither Thirlmere nor Derwentwater gives any sign of its proximity. The road soon begins to rise for **Castlerigg,** the ridge between us and Keswick. A few more minutes and we are at the top of it, and then, at Moor Farm, just as the eye is becoming listless, there bursts upon it a vision of beauty as rich and varied as it is sudden and startling. Low down in front, the vale of Keswick, wide, flat, and fertile, fills up the space between the lakes of Derwentwater and Bassenthwaite; Skiddaw looks its loftiest, and is seen from head to foot. Over Derwentwater the Crummock and Buttermere Fells appear, the latter in the opening formed by the vale of Newlands; and farther back to the left, the fells that cluster round the head of Wasdale and Ennerdale, with Scafell Pikes and Great Gable pre-eminent. Below the latter lies the entrance to Borrowdale. The steep green slope of Catbells descends to the south-western shore of the lake, and farther back to the right rises the knob of Causey Pike.

The range of Causey Pike trends westward, culminating in the long flat top of Grasmoor, which overlooks Crummock Water, and then, working round to the right to the tapering summit of Grisedale Pike and the Whinlatter Fells, between there and Skiddaw are Bassenthwaite Lake and the vale of Keswick, completing a magnificent panorama.

From Castlerigg into Keswick there are two roads—the direct one, very steep, to the left; the other, the more usual route, dropping into the Greta valley on the right. For **Keswick,** *see p.* 162.

3. Windermere (or Bowness) to Patterdale (Ullswater).

Map at end of the book.

Windermere to Troutbeck Church, 3 m. ; Kirkstone Inn, 7 ; Brothers' Water, 9½ ; Patterdale Hotel, 12½ ; Ullswater Hotel, 13½. Bus service from Bowness and Windermere in summer.

This is undoubtedly the finest route to Ullswater. The road from Ambleside is shorter by 4 miles, but misses two of the most attractive features of the district—the valley of Troutbeck itself, and the view of Windermere from the road leading up it. The Ambleside–Kirkstone road is also extremely steep and is not recommended for cars. The route here described is steep but quite safe.

The Troutbeck road goes off to the right from the high road to Ambleside at the cross-roads, two-thirds of a mile from Windermere Station. Those starting from Bowness keep straight ahead at this cross-roads, which is about half a mile beyond the path leading down to the Millerground landing (*see p.* 64).

Walkers who have already seen the Miller Brow view should start from Windermere by the **Elleray** footpath (*see* Walk 6, *p.* 64). In two minutes, after passing a turning to Orrest Head, keep straight on by the narrow path, past " Christopher North's " old cottage of Elleray. Lovely peeps of the lake are gained from time to time. The track soon descends through a wood, and then crossing Winlass Beck enters the high road.

A short distance from the cross-roads we pass out of the woods, and beyond the convergence of the above path obtain splendid lake and mountain views. On the right, above us, are the mansions of Chapel Ridding and Brow Head. In two places the wall is lowered for the sake of the view, which, however, can be seen nearly all the way to the *Borrans* (2 *m.*), at the top of the rise and, perhaps, the most beautifully situated house in Britain. A feature of the view is the green, undulating, and richly-wooded foreground, while the gradual transition from the brimming luxuriance immediately beneath the spectator's eyes to the wild and rugged grandeur of the fell amphitheatre that forms the limit of the prospect, gives a wonderful impression of diversity without incongruity, and of majesty without overbearingness. The scene is especially beautiful in the morning hours, when it is " dappled o'er with many a passing cloud," or almost equally so in the full sunlight.

From Borrans the road goes up and down, with pretty views into the glen below, and then drops to and crosses the stream at **Troutbeck Church**, which has been sensibly restored, and boasts a large east window and a smaller window, each by Burne-Jones. Notice the three lych-gates.

At the church a road comes down from that which, starting from Troutbeck Bridge (*p.* 82), runs above the west side of the beck and goes the length of Troutbeck village. Our direct route joins this road at the far end of the village, just beyond the *Queen's Head*.

The village of **Troutbeck** [*Mortal Man, Queen's Head*, both at north end of village] is one of the most picturesque in Britain.

The main street is nearly a mile and a half long, and consists of cluster after cluster of low-roofed white and grey cottages contrasting beautifully with the emerald verdure of the valley. Sycamores, the tree *par excellence* of Westmorland, yews, and other veterans of the forest, grow in profusion around.

The population of Troutbeck is about 450. The most notable house in the village is *Townend* (*National Trust*), a 17th-century yeoman's house with much of the original oak furniture still intact. The interior may normally be seen. *Charge.*

Beyond the *Queen's Head* begins the climb for the **Kirkstone Pass**—steep pitches varied with level stretches. Lovely views into the valley, which is split into two by **Troutbeck Tongue**, and flanked on the far side by Ill Bell, Froswick, and Thornthwaite Crag.

The road next ascends over a depression in the hills till, losing sight of Troutbeck, we look down Stockdale on the left to Ambleside and the highest strip of Windermere. Beyond it are Blelham Tarn and the Old Man.

At the *Kirkstone Inn* we are 1,468–9 feet above the sea. Here the road, or " struggle," from Ambleside comes up. Beyond the inn there is a good echo from the slopes of Red Screes, which towers a thousand feet above the inn.

This inn, by the way, is not the highest inhabited house in England. Setting aside many private houses, it must yield pride of place as an inn to *Tan Hill*, in Yorkshire (1,727 *ft.*), the *Cat and Fiddle* (1,690 *ft.*), and the *Traveller's Rest* (1,535 *ft.*) at Flash Bar—both near Buxton—the *Shaw House* on the Pennines, between Alston and Penrith (1,485 *ft.*), and the *Isle of Skye* (1,480 *ft.*) in the West Riding.

The **Top of the Pass** (1,476 feet) is about 200 yards beyond the inn, and the *Kirk Stone* (*see p. 218*) about twice as far beyond, and a little to the left of the road. The pass itself is more wild than rugged. The Red Screes descend steeply to it on the left, and Caudale Moor on the right. Brothers' Water lies directly in front, and Place Fell, sinking steeply into Ullswater, with Mell Fell to the left of it, forms the background. Then, separated from Red Screes by Caiston Beck, comes High Hartsop Dodd on the left. Beyond it is Dovedale, nobly headed by Dove Crag.

The road now descends somewhat steeply for just on two miles and at the foot of the hill reaches **Brothers' Water**, the squareness of which detracts from its beauty, when seen close at hand. It is rather more than a quarter of a mile in length and breadth. A derivation of the name is the drowning of two brothers. An older form is, however, *Broad Water*. A little farther on is *Low Hartsop*, an attractive hamlet where a few houses still show their old spinning galleries. Here we cross a considerable stream which descends from High Street and the mountain tarn of Hayeswater on the right, and then the road turns sharply to the left, and crossing the Goldrill Beck, which unites Brothers' Water and Ullswater, enters the beautiful strath of Patterdale. The glen to the left, which is crossed after emerging from the wood, is *Deepdale*, a valley which cuts deep into the recesses of Fairfield and St. Sunday Crag. The precipices of the former are very fine, and give a more rugged impression of the same mountain in comparison with its smooth-backed summit seen from the Windermere side. Hence we pass along the well-cultivated valley to **Patterdale** village (*see p.* 212). The *Patterdale Hotel* is about half a mile from the lake ; the boat pier about a mile farther. A very pleasant alternative route from the top of the pass down to Patterdale is as follows. From the inn descend the road for about half a mile. Where the stone wall on the left gives way to an iron fence is an opening with sign post " To Patterdale." A pathway here passes a small ruin and descends on the left of the stream, then bearing away left to a junction (sign-post) with the Gaiston Glen path. This is a far better route than by the hard road.

Windermere or Bowness to Coniston, by Millerground, High Wray, and Tarn Hows.

To Millerground (from Windermere), ¾ m. ; Belle Grange (other side of lake), 2 ; High Wray, 3 ; Hawkshead Hall, 5 ; Tarn Hows, 7 ; Coniston (Waterhead), 9 ; Coniston Village, 9½. From Bowness hire a boat to Belle Grange.

This is a charming walk, and for those who wish to obtain the best views, or have already visited the Ferry, Esthwaite Water, and Hawkshead, a most agreeable variation of the better-known routes. The prospect both from the neighbourhood of High Wray, on the north slope of Latterbarrow, and from Tarn Hows, on the high ground to the north of Coniston, is very beautiful, especially from Tarn Hows, which commands perhaps the finest of all the near panoramic views of the fells of Lancashire and Westmorland, and a most exquisite prospect down the lake itself. The walk may also be extended to include Tilberthwaite and Blea Tarn, as far as Dungeon Ghyll, the extra distance from Tarn Hows to Dungeon Ghyll being about 7 miles.

Cross the lake from the *Millerground* landing (*see p.* 64), or from Bowness, to Belle Grange. (No boats *at* Belle Grange.) On landing take the road along the west shore of the lake, which begins to ascend in a north-west direction. Hence it gradually works round the slope of Latterbarrow—a somewhat featureless hill—passing the picturesque village of **High Wray.**

During this part of the walk a very fine view is obtained of the amphitheatre of fells which become so familiar to those making excursions round Windermere. The High Street range is particularly impressive in the rear, and just above the head of the lake, the road over the Kirkstone Pass is seen climbing the dip between Wansfell Pike and Red Screes. The level road joining it at the top from behind Wansfell is the route from Windermere to Kirkstone and Patterdale. Helvellyn is prominent to the left of Fairfield.

Beyond High Wray, Blelham Tarn appears in the hollow to the right. Avoid descending towards it. After walking southwards about half a mile, turn to the right by a narrow lane, crossing the valley and joining the Ambleside and Hawkshead road a little to the north of Hawkshead Hall (see p. 80).[1] Just beyond the Hall, turn to the right on to the Hawkshead and Coniston high road. Continue along it, ascending Hawkshead Hill for nearly a mile. Then take the lane which branches to the right beyond the Baptist chapel. In a few hundred yards you will cross the Ambleside and Coniston road.

Tarn Hows, *etc.* Climb the lane straight in front of you. It ascends rapidly between stone walls, and soon reaches an eminence whence, by diverging to the right for a few yards you will obtain a view through trees of Coniston Lake to the south, the Old Man and Wetherlam immediately before you to the west, and then, starting northwards from behind the latter, Pike o' Blisco, Glaramara (in Borrowdale), the Langdale Pikes, with their long eastern shoulder of almost level moorland, followed by the familiar shapes of Helvellyn, Fairfield, Red Screes, High Street, and Ill Bell, with a host of intervening heights which it would be tedious to mention in detail. Windermere appears to the east, and Esthwaite southeast. Saddleback may also be seen over Helm Crag between Helvellyn and Steel Fell.

Descending slightly from this view-point, the road soon discloses, on the right, the tarn popularly known as Tarn Hows (see p. 136).

Just beyond the tarn the road bends to the left, and in rather less than a mile the Ambleside and Hawkshead road to Coniston is joined nearly opposite the entrance-gate of Monk Coniston Hall, and a short mile on the Hawkshead side of the *Waterhead Hotel.* For the descent by Tom Gill see p. 136.

Windermere to Mardale (Haweswater)

Windermere to Troutbeck, 3 m. ; Kentmere, 6 ; Mardale, 12½;
Haweswater Hotel, 14½ m. ; 5 to 6 hours' walk.
 Height of Passes :—Garburn, 1,450 ft. ; Nan Bield, 2,100 ft.

This is a most interesting walk, abounding in beautiful views. The intermediate descent into Kentmere valley may be avoided by crossing High Street, near its summit, and dropping into Mardale, as described in the " High Street Ascents " (p. 244). Those for whom the whole walk is too long may walk down from

---

[1] For **Hawkshead** direct enter a cart-track ¼ m. along this road. The path hence crosses a road and enters Hawkshead through the yard of the *Red Lion.*

Kentmere to Stavely and thence return to Windermere by train
or bus.

The Patterdale route (*p.* 88) must be followed as far as about 200
yards short of Troutbeck Church (or you may turn up a mile
sooner just beyond Borrans, *see Map*). Here turn sharp up a
lane to the right, and, passing a residence called the Howe, make
an equally acute angle to the left. The road then climbs between
two walls to the top of the **Garburn Pass.** The view during the
whole ascent is very fine. Troutbeck, lying deeper and deeper
still at every step, between the steep green declivities of Ill Bell
and Wansfell, with High Street, Caudale Moor, and Red Screes
overlooking its upper reach, has a most striking appearance.
Over Wansfell, as we pursue our long ascent, appear the Langdale Pikes and Bowfell. Windermere itself, backed by the
Lancashire fells—the Old Man, etc.—charmingly diversifies the
scene. Scafell Pike, bracket-shaped, showing Mickledore (the gap
between the Pike and Scafell itself), and Great Gable, an isolated
block, soon become prominent objects in the far west.

From the top of the pass rocky knolls block the view northwards, and the distant view eastwards is tame. The descent,
however, into **Kentmere** is delightful.

Many people, on entering this valley, will ask, why Kent*mere* ?
Except for a modern reservoir at the head of the valley, there is
no mere at all. Look down the valley, however. More than a
century ago the valley possessed a lake a mile long, the delight of
the fisherman, and an adornment to a scene which, with it, was
beautiful—without it, is bare and desolate. However, "Hodge"
set to work, and at vast trouble and expense scooped out a deep
channel at the foot of the lake. The waters rushed down it, and
lo ! in place of a lake, a marsh ! Some of that damage has been
repaired since for excavations by the modern diatomite works
have extended a sizeable lake in the valley.

Down below, on the right, as we approach the bottom of the pass,
is the sycamore-girdled **Kentmere Hall,** of which the old " Pele "
tower and other parts date back to the 14th century. The Hall
was the birthplace (1517) of Bernard Gilpin, " one of the most
able and most gentle of the reformers," and called " the Apostle
of the North."

At the foot of the pass, *Kentmere Church*—a whitewashed
building with lancet windows and a 16th century roof—is passed.
Then, after crossing the bridge beyond, we climb the steep road
to the left.

Another route is by a good road up the west side of the valley to
the reservoir. For this turn to the left through a gate about ¼ mile
short of the church, just past the first farm. At the quarries a little
short of the reservoir the way crosses the valley into the Nan
Bield track.

A third of a mile above the bridge at Kentmere, the river forms
two very beautiful **falls,** for a close inspection of which it is worth
while to cross the fields, through a gate on the way up from the

bridge. The main track may be regained through a gate higher up, which cuts off a sharp corner.

On breasting the hill, Upper Kentmere comes into view. Kentmere, like the Duddon valley, is divided into two distinct portions, separated, as it were, by a cross-bar of rock. The lower part, now that the lake is gone, is featureless ; the upper, however, is more attractive. The flat extension of High Street is at the head of the valley ; Ill Bell, Froswick, and the almost sheer Rainsborrow Crag on the left, and Harter Fell on the right. Remembering how steep Ill Bell and Froswick are on the Troutbeck side, one is astonished to find them dropping still more precipitously into Kentmere. Altogether, the head of Kentmere is thoroughly characteristic.

Those who wish to cross into **Long Sleddale,** and thence proceed northward to **Mardale,** by Gatescarth, or southward to **Burneside** (3 syllables) or **Kendal,** must take the road to the right about ¾ mile beyond the Bridge, after ascending the hill. It is a pleasant breezy walk across a turfy track, and the view during the descent into the valley is charming. Long Sleddale is narrow and deep, and in parts well wooded. The view up it will be an agreeable surprise to those who fancy that they have passed the limits of the Lake District, The distance from Kentmere Bridge to *Sad Gill Farm,* on the main road up the valley, is 4 miles, and thence to Mardale, over Gatescarth, 6 miles ; to Burneside 8 miles, and to Kendal 10.

The road (or, rather, lane and track) now descends slightly and passes below several farmsteads. Keep to the lowest track as far as *Overend Farm (see Map at end of the book),* where take the right-hand fork.

A third of a mile farther, just above the junction of two tiny becks, and almost hidden from our track, are a series of charming but nameless little **falls,** worth the few yards' necessary diversion.

Beyond this we work round a sort of tongue that projects from Harter Fell, in commencing the climb of which avoid a distinct track that bears to the right to some old quarries. Our route is for some way indistinct. Then, after looking down upon the Kentmere reservoir, it climbs steeply to the lowest part of the dip between Harter Fell and High Street—**Nan Bield** (2,100 *ft.*).

On reaching the summit of Nan Bield, **Small Water** appears below—an almost perfect specimen of a tarn, deep-set in crags, and softened by the rich tufts of parsley-fern with which the surrounding ground is carpeted. Blea Water, similar in its characteristics, and worth a visit, lies over a ridge to the left.

Keeping Small Water on the right, the path rapidly descends till, at the end of the new road along Mardale, it joins the Gatescarth Pass track from Long Sleddale, which comes down from

the other side of Harter Fell. For the *Haweswater Hotel* follow
the new road for two miles.

Readers of Mrs. Humphry Ward's *Robert Elsmere* may probably recognise
that in " Long Whindale " and " Marrisdale " she described Long Sleddale
and Bannisdale.

Windermere to Mardale (Haweswater), by Long Sleddale.

Windermere to Burneside (bus), 6 m. ; *Kendal*, 8 ; *Burneside
to Mardale*, 14½ ; *Kendal to Mardale*, 16. *Height of Gatescarth
Pass*, 1,950 ft.

Long Sleddale presents a charming picture of thriving hus-
bandry in the midst of beautiful and secluded scenery. The
entrance to the valley is about four miles from Kendal on the
old north road (the Penrith bus may be used thus far), and
two miles and a half from Burneside by a cross-country one.
It is narrow, but scarcely more so than the valley itself, the
cultivated portion of which extends for half a dozen miles between graceful and luxuriant hills, and is brought to a termination by a couple of towering crags—Goat Scar, on the left,
and Buckbarrow, on the right—but little less striking than
the best in the district. Farmsteads dot the valley throughout. The church occupies a prominent position half-way up it,
and altogether, it is difficult to picture a scene in which peace,
contentment, and beauty are more happily combined.

It is to the credit of Manchester Corporation that in bringing
their Mardale water conduit (*see p.* 56) through the valley, they
have covered their tracks as far as possible, so that practically
the only alteration in the scenery of the valley is the building at
the point where the sub-mountain tunnel joins the conduit.

Those who desire to return to Windermere without crossing
Gatescarth (for Mardale) should cross the intervening ridge, which
seldom attains a greater height than 1,150 feet, to **Kentmere**, and
thence proceed over the **Garburn Pass** (1,450 *ft.*), as described in
the reverse direction on *p.* 92. The best plan is to leave Long
Sleddale at Sad Gill, the highest farm-house in the valley.

A little beyond **Sad Gill** cultivation ceases, and the cart-track
mounts steeply, with a picturesque gill and the towering *Goat
Scar* and *Raven Crag* on the left hand, and the crags of Buckbarrow on the right, to the summit of the **Gatescarth Pass**, between Harter Fell and Branstree. The track over the head of
the pass is very vague ; special care must be taken not to turn,
soon after leaving the course of Wren Gill, to the right, in which
direction there are traces of a rough track leading into the desolate Mosedale valley and thence to Shap.

Descending Gatescarth, the view over Blea Water to the High
Street range is very fine. The track from Kentmere to Mardale

by Nan Bield converges on the left just short of the end of the new road alongside Hawes Water, and the *Haweswater Hotel* about 2 miles farther on.

Kendal to Shap, 16 *m.,* **and Penrith,** 26 ; by the old North road, which attains its summit-level (the " Demmings," 1,304 *ft.*) 11 miles from Kendal.

Passing under the bridge at the station, take the left-hand fork and in a mile cross the river Mint. For some way the road scenery is dull, but between the fourth and fifth milestones, where the road has attained a height of nearly 600 feet, there is a charming view southward over Kendal, and northward up Long Sleddale, the narrow entrance to which is rendered additionally effective by *Garnett Bridge* and the mills. Then, after passing *Forest Hall,* a sharp descent is made to *High Borrow Bridge* (8¾ *m.*)—whence we rise steeply for two miles to the summit-level. Along the old road— first below on the left, then above on the right—the luckless Charles Edward made his disastrous retreat from Derby in the " '45."

Then we come to the railway just beyond Shap Summit and the granite works, and travel alongside it to (16 *m.*) Shap (*see p.* 53).

From Shap to **Penrith** (*p.* 50) the road is good but unremarkable. In 6 miles we pass Lowther Castle—a mile away on the left.

Windermere to Kendal and Levens Hall

Kendal is 9 miles south-eastward from Windermere by road (ample bus services) or rail. Levens Hall is 5 miles south of Kendal by road.

KENDAL (Hotels : *Kendal,* ⅓ *m.* from Station—*Woolpack Inn,* Stricklandgate ; pop. 22,440 ; P.O.). Kendal, which properly prides itself on being a "gateway to the Lake District," is a busy old market town, chiefly noteworthy as an agricultural centre, but with some industries—boots, woollen goods, snuff, etc. The once famous "Kendal Green" has long since ceased to be made. The chief objects of interest are the church and the castle, the former for itself and the latter for the pleasant views from it.

The **Church** (Holy Trinity) dates from the 13th century, but is mostly of Perpendicular character. Its most remarkable feature are four distinct aisles, all the same length as the nave, so that the chancel at first looks like part of the nave. The reredos arcade of stone is quite modern and very graceful work. There are traces of fresco work in the oldest (south-east) part : four chapels with carved oak screens, and the pews are all of pitch pine, and the roof of oak, which is new, except for some of the bosses.

A well-preserved brass within the altar-rails has the following autobiographical inscription :—

"Here vnder lyeth ye body of Mr. Ravlph Tirer, late vicar of Kendall, Batchler of Divinity, who dyed the 4th day of Jvne, Ano. Dni., 1627.

> " London bredd me, Westminster fedd me,
> Cambridge sped me, my sister wed me,
> Study taught me, Living sought me,
> Learning brought me, Kendall caught me,

Labour pressed me, sickness distressed me,
Death oppressed me, and grave possessed me,
God first gave me, Christ did save me,
Earth did crave me, and heaven would have me.

At the E. end of the N. aisle are the complete colours of the 55th (Westmoreland) regiment running from its raising in 1755, to 1881. The helmet and sword of Robin the Devil (*see p.* 73) also hang in the church.

For the **Castle** cross the river by the double footbridge 200 yards north of the church ; go back 50 yards, and then straight up by street and footpath. The ruins date from the 12th century onwards and consist of fragments of an old wall built up so as to form an enclosure, a round tower and scraps of two others and a dungeon or two, the whole surrounded by a wooded moat. There is a good view of the Lakeland fells, the most conspicuous being Ill Bell and Red Screes. The castle was the birthplace of Catherine Parr. The ruin, and a large portion of the surrounding land, are now public property.

On the opposite side of the main street, 5 minutes up All Hallows Lane, is a **mound** with a fosse, and a plain obelisk erected in 1788 in honour of the Revolution of 1688.

For some years Kendal was the home of George Romney and here he died in 1802. Some of his paintings and drawings hang in the Town Hall. In the Town Hall also is preserved Queen Catherine Parr's prayer-book. There is a museum near the station.

Benson Knott (1½ *m.*) commands a fine panoramic view. Take the Sedbergh Road under the railway bridge and turn up a lane to the left after about 200 yards.

Sizergh Castle, the ancient home of the Strickland family (about 4 miles S.), is one of the most interesting houses in Westmorland.

Originally built as a border castle, it has sustained many major additions and alterations since then, notably in Elizabethan times, but still retains its 14th century Pele tower. It has now been donated to the National Trust, and is open Thursdays in summer, 2–6.

Levens Hall (5 miles S.) should be visited, if possible, either from Kendal or on the way to the district by road from the south.

The *house* is open to visitors on Tuesday, Wednesday, Thursday and Sunday afternoons, 2–5. The *gardens* are open daily, May to mid-September.

The history of this interesting old house dates back to about 1170, when William de Lancaster granted land at Levens to Norman de Hieldand (or Yealand), later called Redman. The oldest remaining part of the house—the Pele tower, parts of which can still be seen at the road end of the mansion—was probably built, like Sizergh, as defence against the Scots, Mathew de Redman having been made Commissioner of Array for Lancashire and Westmorland in 1300. In 1415, Richard de Redman became Speaker of the House of Commons. Nearly 150 years later the house was sold to the Bellinghams ; but in 1689 Alan

Bellingham—the "ingenious but unhappy young man"—sold it to James Grahme, a soldier, an M.P., and Privy Purse to James II. Then came the later owners, the Howards, Earls of Suffolk and Berkshire, by marriage with the heiress, Colonel Grahme's daughter, whom Richard Bagot, brother of the 1st Lord Bagot, married in 1783; whence the succession of the Bagots, the present owner being Mr. Robin Bagot.

The **Entrance Hall**, with adjoining rooms, was decorated in oak and plaster work by Sir James Bellingham (1585). Here stood the original Great Hall : but the great transformation made by the Bellinghams has changed almost all that is seen.

Of the two **Drawing Rooms**, the larger is perhaps the most striking, with its fine overmantel (1595) and oak panelling. The smaller one, also fully panelled, has an elaborately carved overmantel of later date (about 1640). The **Dining Room** walls are covered with bright Cordova leather (1688), and the overmantel bears John Bellingham's initials, and the date, 1586. The **Library** was panelled in 1807—at the same date as some of the bedrooms, several of which are also open to the public.

Among items of interest on show are pictures by well-known artists, including a portrait by Rubens ; Colonel Grahme's Charles II and William and Mary furniture, still in the house, and the Sèvres coffee service brought to England by the Duke of Wellington for his niece, Lady Mary Bagot, having been originally intended for Napoleon's mother.

The **Gardens**, in the topiary style, and probably the best specimens of their style in the country, are almost exactly now as they were originally designed by Beaumont, who claimed to have laid out the grounds of Hampton Court for James II. The ancient Park is the only remaining one of the fifteen deer-parks which surrounded Kendal in the time of Elizabeth. It contains a breed of peculiarly dark fallow-deer, which figures among the legends of the district. The birth of a white fawn, tradition has it, forecasts great good or evil to the house of Levens. There was also specimens of the Bagot wild goats from Blithfield, Staffs.

Mrs. Humphry Ward's *Helbeck of Bannisdale* was written at Levens Hall, and the story is laid in the district. [See *History of Levens*, by J. F. Curwen, 1898 ; *Colonel Grahme of Levens*, by J. Bagot (Wilson, Kendal).]

To Furness Abbey

The beautiful ruins of Furness lie, strictly speaking, outside the Lake District, near the southern end of the tongue of land between the estuaries of the Leven (which flows out of Lake Windermere) and the Duddon, to the west. Furness may be reached by bus from Bowness. It is also visited by the coaches and included in several circular tours embracing road and steamer.

FURNESS ABBEY

Admission.—10–4.30, Nov.–Feb. ; 9.30–5.30, Mar., Apr., Oct. ; 9.30–7, May–Sept. ; Sundays, in winter, from 2 p.m. ; May–Sept., 9.30–7. Small charge.

Of all the monastic ruins in Great Britain there are few which combine extent and beauty of detail to a greater degree than Furness. To a Yorkshireman it is, of course, high treason to name any other abbey in the same breath as Fountains, which has the advantage in size ; voyagers down the lovely reaches of the Wye, between Ross and Chepstow, will probably admit that in compact and symmetrical beauty Tintern is unequalled ; Melrose has its keen supporters ; but everyone, whatever his individual choice, must admit the claim of Furness to a place in the foremost rank.

The Abbey is placed in a small cup-shaped hollow—the " Vale of Deadly Nightshade "—which is entirely occupied by the ruins, and an hotel.

The ruins were given to the nation by Lord Richard Cavendish and have been carefully treated by the Department of the Environment.

History. The Abbey was founded by Stephen, afterwards King of England. The monks were of the Order of Savigny in Normandy, and originally settled at Tulketh near Preston in 1123 but four years later they re-established themselves at Furness. Eventually they adopted Cistercian rule.

The district of Furness comprises all that part of Lancashire which lies north of Morecambe Bay except the strip between Carnforth and the Leven estuary. Over all this wide region, bounded by the Duddon, Wrynose Pass, the Brathay, Windermere, and the Leven, the Abbots of Furness held lordship. Besides which, the Abbey had several minor monastic institutions either emanating from or annexed to it, some as far distant as the Abbey of Corcomroe, near Galway. In wealth and importance Furness ranked second to Fountains, and its abbots enjoyed almost feudal power for centuries.

It is a strange sequel to such a history that, at the time of the Dissolution, Furness was the first of the larger monasteries to yield to the pressure brought upon them. Two of the monks were committed to Lancaster Castle, and the abbot, Roger Pile, signed away his place and his power to the king and accepted instead the adjacent living of Dalton—one of his own dependencies, and valued at £40 a year ! As to the Abbey itself, there is a tradition that a part of its destruction is attributable to fire, the molten lead falling from the roof and damaging the substructure.

The date of the present remains ranges over a period of four centuries, exhibiting specimens of the Transitional (1145–1190), to which the splendid round arches and a part of the nave belong ; the Early English, which is beautifully exemplified in the Chapter House ; the Decorated in the chancel sedilia ; and the Perpendicular in the Belfry Tower at the west end of the nave, and the far eastern end (the Presbytery).

Before entering the main area of the ruins, a visit should be paid to the *Gateway Chapel*, a few yards to the north and a common feature of Cistercian Monasteries but here unusually well-preserved and lacking only its roof. It is entered by a round

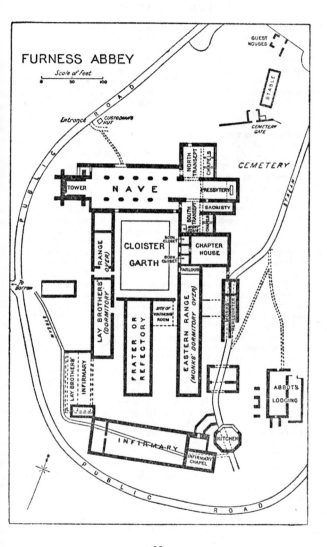

FURNESS ABBEY

Scale of Feet

0   50   100

GUEST HOUSES

STABLE

Entrance · CUSTODIANS HUT

CEMETERY GATE

CEMETERY

TOWER · NAVE · NORTH TRANSEPT · CHAPELS

PRESBYTERY

SACRISTY

SOUTH TRANSEPT

NIGHT STAIRS · CHAPEL

To Barrow

RANGE (OVER)

LAY BROTHERS' (DORMITORY OVER)

CLOISTER GARTH

BOOK CLOSET · BOOK CLOSET

PARLOUR

CHAPTER HOUSE

FRATER OR REFECTORY

SITE OF WARMING ROOM

EASTERN RANGE (MONKS' DORMITORY OVER)

MONKS' REREDORTER

ABBOTS LODGING

LAY BROTHERS' INFIRMARY

INFIRMARY

KITCHEN

INFIRMARY CHAPEL

PUBLIC ROAD

99

archway, over which is a trefoiled niche, vacant. The lower part of the east window remains, and in the south wall there are three pointed windows, with a little tracery ; also a small round-headed doorway. Inside we may notice the steps of the altar, three sedilia, and the usual niches for the sacred vessels.

Returning from the Gateway Chapel to the entrance to the ruins, the foundations of the great northern Gatehouse are passed. Farther to the left is another group of foundations where the guest-houses and stables formerly stood, and where a smaller gateway gave access to the cemetery east of the abbey. We then come into full view of the **Church,** consisting of nave, transepts, and chancel. The uniformity in height of such of the walls as remain standing, and the absence of gables, are apt to mar one's first impression of the building as a whole, there being no picturesque skyline to please the eye. The dimensions of the church are as follows : Total length, 290 ft. Width, nave with aisles, 70 ft. ; transept, 130 ft. ; chancel, 25 ft.

The chief entrance is by a round-headed doorway in the north transept, but, before entering, our attention will probably be attracted by the massive keep-like erection which forms the west end of the nave, called the **Tower.** This is evidently of a much later date than the rest of the church, and its heavy walls and buttresses, though relieved by canopied niches, harmonise but ill with the lighter and eminently graceful examples of earlier styles which prevail everywhere else. A stairway leads to the top of the south side of this tower, and, as we shall see from the interior, there has been a Perpendicular west window, the frame-work of which, showing the ends of a transom, still remains.

By a fine *Norman door,* recessed four-deep, and generally to be found in this position in Cistercian churches, we now enter the north transept. Passing through it, and standing at the inter-section of the transept with the nave and choir, we get the best idea of the church as a whole. Of the **Nave**—apart from the Tower—all that remains is the blank wall of the south aisle, separating it from the cloister court, a foot or two in height of the corresponding north wall, and the stumps of the pillars, nine on the north, five on the south side, alternately round and clustered. Marks along the walls that separate the aisles from the transept show the former pitch of the roof below the clere-story. On the floor of the north aisle at its east end are some curiously sculptured round panels, and at the choir end of the nave are floor-marks of the screens which once stood there.

Of the four pointed arches which supported the Central **Tower,** the only remaining one is that on the side of the choir, which is still perfect and rises to a height of 52 feet.

The **Transepts** are very like one another in plan, though the ill-advised attempts to convert parts of them from the Transitional to the Perpendicular style, and the connection of the two chapels with one and of the vestry with the other, prevent their matching exactly. The east sides have each three pointed arches with clustered columns—those in the north transept surmounted by two round arches, one of which retains in one of its two subdivisions a beautiful trefoil arch. The large *North Window*, 30 feet high, is perfect in its framework, but its mullions and nearly all its tracery are gone. Two chapels on the east side of the north aisle were those of the Lancasters of Kendal. Little more than the ground-plan remains.

The **Choir** or **Chancel** has some splendid details. Its *East Window*, stripped of its mullions, was nearly 50 feet in height, and still rises some feet above the spring of its arch. Outside, just at the spring, are two figures possibly meant to represent the founder, Stephen, and his wife Maud. With the exception of two pillar-niches in the south transept this is the only instance of the Furness monks breaking the Cistercian rule which forbade statues, pictures, and coloured glass. The two windows on the north side are almost as high but very much narrower. Their mullions, too, are gone, but they are otherwise complete and very beautiful. There are also two pointed windows on the south side. In the south wall are four splendid *sedilia*, with canopies in the richest style of the Perpendicular period; a piscina (for rinsing the sacred vessels), under the same row of canopies as the sedilia; and two aumbries (for stowing them away).

Next to the choir, on its south side and connected by a doorway, is the *Vestry*, which contains also a piscina. Thence, passing through the archway (reduced from its original size to a small one) that connects the transept with the south aisle of the nave, we turn at once through a round doorway into the *Cloister Court*, which has little to show except a few foundations scattered about, and come at once to the trio of **Transitional Arches**, which are perhaps the grandest features of the Abbey. They are deeply recessed, each showing the remains of five shafts with foliated capitals, the arches themselves forming complete semicircles, and being splendidly moulded in lines that run parallel with their curve. The recesses behind the left- and right-hand arches were probably used as book cupboards.

The middle arch introduces us to a *Porch*, from which we enter the **Chapter House** (1220–1240 ?), another gem of the Abbey, and one of the most exquisite examples of Early English in the kingdom. It measures 60 feet by 45, and the sides are as far as possible uniform in design. All round is an arcade containing four arches on the longer (N. and S.) sides, three on the east, and two—one each side of the doorway—on the west. The spandrels are ornamented with medallions, and the capitals generally are decorated with an uncommon and pretty crossed stem foliage, which occurs also at Cartmel Priory. Above is what remains of a series of smaller windows. The roof has fallen in, but one of the six slender clustered shafts which supported it is complete to the top of its capital; four of the others are still erect up to a height of from four to six feet, and the remaining one is a mere stump. Fragments of the old moulding lie about on the floor.

Returning to the cloister court, and noting the foundations, on the grass to the left, of the Frater we find two smaller round-headed arches adjacent to the larger trio. By the second of these we enter a room 200 feet long by 30 feet wide beneath the great *Dormitory*. In the upper part of the wall on both sides of the north half of the room are rows of narrow deep-splayed pointed windows belonging to the dormitory.

Beyond the farther (south) end of this and not square with it is the site of the *Infirmary* with entrance hall and chapel attached. Each has a groined roof, and the latter three angular-headed windows (south). In the chapel are two effigies in Caen stone of knights in armour, probably of the 12th century, the only ones of the kind in England. Note also the rings fastened in the walls, which were used by the farmers to tether their cattle after the Dissolution. At the opposite or railway end of the chapel are the foundations of the octagonal *Kitchen*, and next beyond this are the remains of the *Abbot's Lodging*. Visitors should return by the winding walk that rises above them, passing the *view-point* marked on the plan. Hence the ruin displays almost its full extent, but the loss of its gables detracts from its picturesqueness.

Furness Abbey is in the borough of **Barrow-in-Furness** which is a town of modern growth, and busy industrial centre. The principal industrial concern is Messrs. Vickers, whose shipbuilding and engineering works have a worldwide reputation. At present the Barrow Shipyards are responsible for the building of the nuclear and Polaris submarines for the Royal Navy. There are steelworks in the town as well as large paper works and industrial plants producing soft tissues and cellophane. Other concerns produce micro-electronic circuits, chemicals and clothing. A recent introduction into the town has been spinning, which now gives employment to nearly 2,000 people.

The **Docks** occupy nearly the whole of Barrow Island. The road-stead is one of the safest in Britain. The harbour is protected by **Walney Island** (included in the borough of Barrow), a flat sand-bank, about ten miles in length and one in breadth, which acts as a natural breakwater. An extensive housing estate occupies the central portion and there is an aerodrome at the northern end. At the southern end is a well-known bird sanctuary. The island is joined to Barrow by bridges with lifting spans. On another of the islands is 14th-century **Piel Castle** built by the monks of Furness. An enormous ridge of pebbles at the southern extremity of the island is believed to have given rise to the name (literally "walled island").

At **High Cocken** (1¾ miles from Barrow, 1½ from Furness Abbey) is the early home of *George Romney*. Here the famous portrait painter lived from 1742-1755.

Near the mouth of the Leven Estuary is **Ulverston** (Hotels: *Sun, King's Arms, Lonsdale House*), administrative centre of the

Furness district on the northern shore of Morecambe Bay. Its only attractions for the tourist are the fine old parish church and the view from *Hoad Hill*, on which is a monument erected in 1850 to Sir John Barrow, sometime Secretary to the Admiralty.

The **Church** has rather remarkable glass, *e.g.* at west end of north aisle, subject, the " Resurrection "—allegorical. The oldest monument is to Miles Dodding, *d.* 1606. There is also one to Wm. Sandys, Conishead Priory, 1638: also worn and tattered flags, and a copy by Ghizardi of a Vandyke picture in Rome.

From the church **Hoad Hill** is gained by a steep climb from a little beyond the churchyard by obvious paths.

The top of the hill commands splendid views across the Leven Estuary, by which the waters of Windermere find their way into the sea. In clear weather, when the tide is up—a small part of the day, we must confess—the view of this estuary is very fine indeed. The lower hills have the true Westmorland characteristics ; and round them is a noble range of fells, of which the chief summits— from west to east—are Coniston Old Man, with Dow Crag on its left, bold and graceful in shape ; Helvellyn, almost due north; Fairfield, flatter than the rest ; Red Screes, bold and bluff; and, as we proceed, the High Street range, in which the cone of Ill Bell is the most recognisable feature.

Just outside Ulverston is **Swarthmoor Hall,** where George Fox, founder of the Society of Friends, preached in 1652. One of his converts was Margaret, wife of Judge Fell. In 1669, ten years after the death of her husband, she married the great preacher, and in 1675 he returned to Swarthmoor Hall.

Two miles south of Ulverston, and close to the sea, is *Conishead Priory*, built on an ancient site as a private house, and variously used as a Hydro and convalescent home.

To Cartmel Priory Church and Grange-over-Sands

No one interested in architecture should fail to visit the grand old church of Cartmel, which lies about 5 miles south-east of Newby Bridge and between 2 and 3 miles north-west of Grange-over-Sands. From Bowness or Windermere the excursion can be made by rail or bus (Grange-over-Sands) or by coach ; or the journey may be varied by using the steamer to Lake Side and motoring thence to Cartmel.

Cartmel Priory Church

" St. Mary's, Kertmel," or Kyrkmell, is an exceptional specimen of Transition-Norman architecture. It was built, for the most part, in 1188, sixty years after Furness Abbey, when the severe Norman features were giving way to the developed forms and graceful decoration of the Early English work. Cartmel Church is also interesting as being, with the exception of Lancaster, the only priory church in Lancashire now in use as a parish church. The church and priory of the Augustinian canons who used it were founded by William Marshall, Earl of Pembroke and Baron of Cartmel, who afterwards, as Protector for the boy Henry III, rescued England from the French. Before that time, however, there had been a still earlier church, probably on the same site. Camden says that St. Cuthbert received Cartmel "with all the Britons in it" from Egfrig, son of Oswig.

Externally its characteristics are loftiness, fine proportions, and the massive construction of the remarkable **Tower**, unique in Britain. The original Norman part of this rises very little above the transept roof, and the present upper tower was placed diagonally upon it 200 years later.

The present building, if we except the nave, roof, and some additions to the choir, represents the original 12th-century church. The very handsome *south doorway* opens into the later portion of the church, the **Nave** (15th century). According to high authorities this has replaced the older nave, which was, perhaps, the earlier parish church.

In the **Transepts** notice the entrance arches of the side aisles, most graceful specimens of Transition, and the best things in the whole building.

The choir is enclosed by magnificent carved screens, some of the finest made since the Reformation, and the work, tradition says, of a Flemish carver. The older stalls below have good *miserere* seats, especially the "Elephant and Castle," the "Hedgehog," the "Mermaid," and a remarkable Trinity.

The main **Choir**, which was probably the first part built (1188–1190), contains some splendid round arches, which opened into the (then smaller) side chapels; and, above these, a very fine arcade. On the north side is the "Piper choir." Between 1300 and 1400 the short south choir-aisle was doubled in size, adorned with Decorated windows, and for a long period used as the Parish Church. To this latter fact is due the preservation of the whole church.

Note the *sedilia*, and the *Harrington Tomb*, which may be that of a 14th-century Harrington, of Gleaston, an ancestor of Lady Jane Grey. Round its base are monks chanting a requiem from books; when opened it contained bones of man, and of a bird, probably the earl's favourite falcon. Opposite is the earlier tomb of a "Prior de Kertmel," William de Walton, First Prior.

Early in the 15th century the present east window replaced the six old Norman lights. It is one of the finest in England: only three feet shorter than that at Carlisle. High authorities have found conclusive evidence that the unique glass now in the east window of St. Martin's Parish Church, Windermere, originally filled this and other windows in this church; most of it dates *c.* 1450, but an upper light is as old as 1260 (*see pp.* 59–61).

The Priory was dissolved in 1537, and this choir, stripped of its roof, left open to the weather (note the injured seats). Eighty-one years afterwards George Preston of Holker came to the rescue, and most liberally restored the building.

The *Priory Gatehouse*, over an archway in Cavendish Street, is the property of the National Trust, and is shown on weekdays.

Grange-over-Sands (Hotels : *Grange, Grand, Crown,* etc.) lies some 2½ miles south-east of Cartmel, with which it is connected by bus. Walkers will find a pleasant route over Hampsfell, on which is a square tower, commanding an extensive panorama

of the fells and intervening country as well as a pleasant seascape.
Grange is outside the Lake District proper, but those with cars
who desire to combine sea and mountains as far as possible might
find themselves well suited here. Whatever one may say or
think about the far-receding tide, Grange is definitely the prettiest
of the seaside resorts on the fringe of the Lake District. Landwards the limestone cliffs with their rich covering of foliage, and
the pleasant villas that rise everywhere, may remind the passer-
by of Torquay. There are facilities for practically all sports.
There are two excellent golf courses. Recent developments
include a bathing pool, good tennis courts and bowling and putting greens. There are riding schools in the area, and a cinema.
From the Promenade, which is over a mile long, there is a fine
panorama, especially at high tide.

AMBLESIDE

(Map—*at end of the book*)

Angling.—*See p.* 26.
Banks.—*Midland, Barclays, National Westminster.*
Boats for hire.
Buses, etc., to Windermere Station (20 min.), Bowness, Grasmere, Keswick, Hawkshead, Coniston, Langdale ; also motor-coaches to Patterdale, Coniston, the Langdales, etc.
Churches.—*St. Mary* ; *Holy Trinity* (Brathay), 1½ m. on Langdale road ; *St. Mary's* (Rydal), 1½ m.
R.C. Church on Wansfell road ; *Methodist,* Millans Park, etc., etc.
Distances.—(*By road*), Waterhead, ¾ mile ; Low Wood, 1¾ ; Windermere Station, 4¾ ; Bowness (direct), 5¾, (by Windermere), 6¼.
Kirkstone Top, 3 m. ; Patterdale Village, 9 ; Ullswater Hotel, 10.
Rydal Village, 1¼ m. ; Grasmere (Town End), 3½, (Village), 4 ; Dunmail Raise, 6½ ; Wythburn, 7¾ ; Thirlspot, 10½ ; Keswick, 16¼.
Elterwater Village, 4½ m. ; *Dungeon Ghyll New Hotel,* 7¼ ; *Old Hotel,* 8.
Skelwith Bridge, 2¾ m. ; Coniston (*viâ* Oxenfell), 8.
Hawkshead, 5 m. ; Coniston, Waterhead (direct), 7 ; Station, 8.
Fell Foot, Eskdale, etc., *see p.* 123.
By Water.—(From Waterhead), Bowness, 4½ m. ; Lake Side, 10½.
Early Closing.—Thursday (in winter months).
Hotels.—In the town : *Salutation, White Lion.* Many boarding-houses, and private hotels.
At Waterhead : *Waterhead* and several unlicensed hotels.
Population.—2,700
Post Office.—Market Place.
Boats ply up and down the lake about six times a day either way, to Bowness ½ hr. ; Lake Side, 70 min. **Boat-pier** at Waterhead, ¾ m. from the town.
Tennis.—Hard courts on Recreation Ground near St. Mary's Church, Also putting greens. Bowling green near Rothay Bridge.

Ambleside is a thriving little town beautifully situated in the park-like vale of Rothay, nearly a mile from the head of Windermere, and except southwards, in the direction of the lake, encircled by fells varying in height from 1,000 to nearly 3,000 feet, all richly garbed with wood and purple crag. As a headquarters for touring it has the advantage of a more central position than Windermere and Bowness, but this is purchased at the loss of the fine command of Windermere lake which the two last-named places possess. From Ambleside the lake is not seen, and from the drives out of it only the upper reach, with a monotonous background, is in view. Those, however, who ascend Wansfell, one hour's walk, obtain one of the finest views of the lake, while from behind Low Wood, 2 miles, and nearer still, from Jenkin Crag, on the slope of Wansfell, the views are almost equally good. Loughrigg, on the opposite side of the Rothay valley, affords beautiful views.

106

There is little calling for comment in the town itself. *St. Mary's Church* dates from 1854 and has a good peal of bells ; but to most visitors it is memorable on account of the annual *Rush-bearing Festival*, usually held on a Saturday in July. A procession of children moves to the church in the afternoon, carrying crosses and designs formed partly of rushes, but mostly of flowers. (*See also pp.* 146-7.) Inside the church is a mural illustrating the ceremony : it was executed in 1944 by Gordon Ransom. The Wordsworth Memorial Chapel was dedicated in 1952. There are stained-glass windows in memory of the poet and his family.

At the Rydal end of the town is the *Old Bridge House*, an interesting structure built on a bridge spanning the Stock Beck and now cared for by the National Trust and used as an Information Centre.

The convergence of the Windermere and Keswick high road with the Langdale road from the Brathay valley and the Patterdale road over the Kirkstone Pass renders Ambleside a most convenient place for road excursions, while pedestrians will find the greater part of the southern division of the district within a day's march there and back. Coniston, the Langdales, Rydal, Grasmere, Easedale Tarn, Ullswater, and Troutbeck ; the Old Man, Wetherlam, Bowfell, the Langdale Pikes, Fairfield, and High Street, all come under this category.

At Waterhead, in Borrans Field, between the Rothay Bridge road and the lake, is the site of the Roman Camp, *Galava*, now under the care of the National Trust. It has been thoroughly excavated, and the remains are exposed for the interest of visitors.

The most attractive **Walks from Ambleside** are as follows :—

1. Stock Gill Force ($\frac{1}{2}$ *m.*).—Admission free. The walks are well kept. The daffodils in Spring are a wonderful sight.

The way is by the lane behind the *White Lion* or *Salutation Hotel*. The water comes down in two channels, separated by an intervening rock, and each broken by a cross ledge. The entire fall is about 60 feet, and, after rain, the scene is very charming. A feature is the distant fells seen through the trees.

2. Wansfell Pike and Troutbeck. *Ambleside to top of Wansfell, 1 hr. ; Troutbeck, 2 hrs. ; Low Wood, 3 hrs. ; Ambleside, 3½ hrs. Distance of the road part of this walk, from Troutbeck to Ambleside, 4½ m. Total distance, 8 m.*

The lovely ramble up **Wansfell Pike** is especially to be recommended to those who wish for typical views from easily-accessible heights. Of course the descent may be made by the same route as the ascent, but the charm of variety at the expense of slight extra toil is obtained by combining with Wansfell a visit to the quaint, straggling village and green pastoral valley of Troutbeck. The return route from Troutbeck keeps well up the south slope of Wansfell and presents almost all the way a splendid panorama of Windermere, its islands and mountain background.

The way up, clearly marked, is past the entrance to Stock Gill

(*see above*), 500 yards beyond which, at a direction-post, pass over
a stile on the right and cross a field to another stile.   Here the
stiff part of the climb begins, winding up a steep grass slope;
then through a gateway in front and an opening on the left, and
so to the top.   This route has the advantages of a *coup*.   You
gain the top and the whole scene, beautiful beyond expression,
bursts on the eye.   The full length of Windermere, with its winding wood-fringed shores and its finely-timbered islands, presents
itself.   From no other point of the compass does the beautiful
bend which so thoroughly individualises the lake appear to such
advantage.

We are generally much more alive to the beauties of art than
to those of nature.   The curve of the " High " at Oxford is
famous ; but one seldom hears the key-note of Windermere's
beauty struck even by those who are sensible of its full charm.
That long-drawn curve of unspeakable grace, which has neither
the monotony of the circle, like Geneva, nor the rigidness of the
corner, like Lucerne, is very inadequately expressed in the term
" river-lake " so frequently employed to sum up the beauty of
Windermere.

View from Wansfell Pike.—From the lake itself the eye wanders
on to the blue fells beyond, separated from it by a belt of rich
valley and undulating wood.   To the north and east the view is
abruptly closed by mountains of greater height, with most of which
the tourist will have become familiar while staying at Ambleside.
The circular depression almost due north is the Kirkstone Pass,
filled in by the Pikes, over Patterdale, and the white building at
the bottom of it, the *Kirkstone Inn*.   The three ridges descending
into the Rothay valley from Fairfield, Hart Crag, and Red Screes,
appear to great advantage.   Eastwards and north-eastwards on
the far side of the Troutbeck valley is the High Street range, the
southern peak of High Street itself, Thornthwaite Crag, being
marked by a columnar pile of stones, while Ill Bell is conspicuous
by its cone-shaped summit.   The somewhat similar intervening
peak is Froswick.   The village of Troutbeck lies to the south-east,
but is hidden by a ridge of the fell on which we stand, and which
somewhat mars the view in this direction.   Southward the Troutbeck valley opens on to Windermere.   Blelham Tarn is seen over
the upper reach of the lake, but Latterbarrow, the flat-topped,
uninteresting hill, rising south of the tarn, hides Esthwaite.   Hawkshead appears to the right of Latterbarrow, and beyond it, a little
to the right again, in the far distance, the whaleback of Black Combe
brings to an abrupt end the range which separates the Duddon
valley from the Irish Sea.   Then comes the weather-beaten Old
Man, the southern buttress of that range so familiar to the Windermere sojourner, which, with the single depression of Wrynose,
seems to extend in rugged but unbroken line all the way round to
the Kirkstone Pass again.   Scafell Pike is just visible over the right
shoulder of Bowfell, almost due west, and Scafell itself beyond the
abrupt southern dip of the same mountain.   Even on a clear day
the unmistakable dome of Great Gable now becomes visible.   Rydal
Water and Grasmere are both in sight, to the right of Loughrigg Fell.

A round-backed strip of fell in the far distance, just over Rydal, is Eel Crag, between Derwentwater and Crummock. In this direction, a little south of Eel Crag, just the crest of Dalehead may be seen,

It may be remarked that the actual summit of Wansfell Pike is not at the point marked on the map but is where the Ambleside–Troutbeck path crosses the ridge at a height of 1,587 feet above sea level.

If it be desired to return to Ambleside by a different route, but without visiting Troutbeck, an easy descent may be made by Skelgill to the *Low Wood Hotel*, 1¾ m. from Ambleside, the general direction to be followed being a little to the left of a line drawn to Wray Castle on the other side of Windermere : or, on reaching Skelgill Farm, a lane (*below*) will conduct one back through Skelgill Wood in about two miles, the latter route being of exquisite beauty.

The descent to **Troutbeck** (*see p.* 90) is marked by a series of cairns as far as *Nanny Lane*, which drops into the road from Kirkstone to Low Wood at a point a little south of the *Mortal Man Inn*, from which, by the way, there is a charming peep down the dale and over a portion of Windermere. On reaching the road walk southwards down the village as far as the Institute.

A return to Ambleside may be made either by Low Wood (*see p.* 82) or Skelgill Farm (*p.* 112) and Jenkin Crag (*p.* 111). The route branches to the right by Robin Lane, just beyond the Institute. Follow this, where it bends sharply to the right. A gate is seen on the left marked " Skelgill and Ambleside." Pass through this and, leaving a ruined barn on the right, take the track which crosses the Holbeck and leads up to High Skelgill Farm.

The direct road from Troutbeck to Ambleside leaves the village at Town End and joins the main Windermere and Ambleside road near Low Wood Hotel.

Another way back is by the *Kirkstone Inn* on Kirkstone top, 3½ miles north of Troutbeck, and thence down to Ambleside, 3 miles more. Beautiful views of the Upper Troutbeck valley are obtained from this route. A *footpath* with fine view starts ¾ miles short of the inn. (Walk 3 reversed.)

3. To the Kirkstone Pass by Stock Gill and the Grove Farm. Continue along the Stock Gill road (*p.* 107) which, after passing some farm buildings, becomes first a rough track, and then a field-path. The route emerges on the Windermere–Patterdale road ¾ mile short of the *Kirkstone Inn.* The shortest alternative return route is by the Ambleside–Patterdale road, the longest and more pleasing by Troutbeck and Skelgill.

4. The Rothay Valley. *To Pelter Bridge,* 1¾ m. ; *Ambleside,* 3.

The Rothay valley is remarkable for its verdant pastures and the size and abundance of its timber, the two features together giving it the appearance of a nobleman's park set in a framework of mountains.

Leave Ambleside by the archway on the west side of the market place, or by a path out of the main road, $\frac{1}{4}$ mile north towards Rydal. Leave St. Mary's Church on the left, and traverse the meadows by a public footpath which crosses the Rothay at Miller Bridge. Here turn to the right and keep along the road skirting the eastern slopes of Loughrigg, and past Fox How and the Stepping Stones, to *Pelter Bridge*, on the other side of which the main road from Ambleside is entered.

By crossing the Stepping Stones a short cut will be found leading into the Rydal and Ambleside road.

The walk may be extended by continuing on the cart-track along the west side of the Rothay, instead of crossing that stream at Pelter Bridge. This road skirts the south side of Rydal Water to *Loughrigg Terrace* and *Red Bank*, fully described on *p.* 148. From Red Bank the circuit of *Grasmere Lake* may be made, and Ambleside regained by the main road, the entire round being one of from 9 to 10 miles (buses connect Grasmere and Ambleside); or by turning sharp to the left from Red Bank, where the track joins the road from Grasmere to Skelwith Bridge, one may return to Ambleside by Loughrigg Tarn and the Brathay valley, after a beautiful walk of 8 miles, comprising the circuit of Loughrigg Fell.

A pleasing and shorter extension of the excursion is the circuit of Rydal Water. The path along the south side connects with the main road at the east end by a footbridge opposite the *Glen Rothay Hotel*, at the west by the Shepherds' Bridge crossing the Rothay between Rydal and Grasmere Lakes.

5. **Loughrigg Fell** (pron. *Luffrigg*), 1,101 *ft.* ; *time, anything from 2 hrs. to a day.* Loughrigg Fell occupies almost the entire space between Windermere, Rydal Water, and Grasmere. Westward it descends steeply to the lower undulating slopes of the Langdale valley. It commands an uninterrupted view southward, and, in other directions, a grand amphitheatrical display of mountains, its many peaks and the wide area over which they extend render a great variety of prospect. Though its highest point is less than 1,000 feet above Ambleside, it affords, in miniature, all the delight of mountain climbing—crag, soft turf, and freedom unalloyed. There are two pleasant routes up from Ambleside :—

(*a*) Follow Skelwith Bridge road for nearly a mile, then at telephone kiosk at *Clappersgate*, take a path that ascends steeply up to *Todd Crag* (695 ft.), as the highest southern eminence of the fell is called. This overlooks Windermere, but does not show off the peculiar beauties of the lake. Hence for the highest points, which overlook Grasmere and Rydal and are nearly 2 miles north-west of Todd Crag, it is best to keep along the right-hand side of a wall.

(b) Proceed as in walk (4) as far as Miller Bridge, after crossing which on to the road and going through a gate on the right, turn up a steep lane that leads to a farm called *Brow Head*. Pass round to the left of this and you will soon come to the open fell whence, over broken and undulating ground, you reach the two highest peaks in 1½ miles.

View from Loughrigg Fell.—This comprises the upper end of Grasmere Lake, while the more easterly peak looks down on Rydal. The depression beyond Grasmere is Dunmail Raise, the highest point on the road from Windermere to Keswick, and the hill which fills it up is part of Skiddaw. The fell to the right of the Raise is Seat Sandal, immediately above which appears the sharply-toothed ridge of Helvellyn. Westward the familiar range reaching from Coniston Old Man to the Langdale Pikes appears, the principal dip being the Wrynose gap between Carrs and Pike o' Blisco. Loughrigg Tarn and Elterwater lie close beneath to the south-west, and Esthwaite Water, with its wooded shores, is seen almost due south, to the right of Windermere, which is visible from Low Wood to Belle Isle. If the weather is clear, the flat top of the Yorkshire fell, Ingleborough, is visible just over the *Low Wood Hotel*. Eastward we have the higher part of Ambleside, backed by Wansfell, and beyond the latter to the left, Ill Bell and Froswick, part of the High Street range. Nab Scar, Fairfield, Hart Crag, and Red Screes are already well-known objects to the viewer from Ambleside. From the southernmost point of the highest part there is a fine view of Loughrigg Tarn.

A fairly steep but easy descent may be made on to *Loughrigg Terrace* and *Red Bank* (for *Grasmere*). The best general direction is to keep as nearly as possible in a line with the west shore of Grasmere Lake. This course will lead to a little footpath, which drops into Loughrigg Terrace at its western extremity. Thence the village of Grasmere may be reached in half an hour (*see p.* 148).

If you have come up by Brow Head and wish to descend by the Clappersgate route (a), recollect that on reaching the end of the wall you must wind down to the *right* of Todd Crag. The path is steep but plain.

6. Jenkin Crag, 1½ m. No one staying at Ambleside should omit this walk. It may be taken by itself, or made part of the ascent or descent of Wansfell.

Follow the Waterhead road for nearly half a mile, and then turn to the left at a cluster of houses (*Low Fold*), at the Car Park opposite the telephone exchange, crossing the old road immediately afterwards. (Two other paths, both with direction-posts, lead up to this route from nearly opposite Waterhead Pier or 250 paces beyond it.) In about five minutes, where the road forks, take the lower branch to the right. The upper one leads on to Wansfell. In another seven or eight minutes cross a beck, avoiding a track up the left-hand side of it. Hence the road is unmistakable. It threads its way through a wood well up on the side of Wansfell. Kelsick Scar (National Trust) is now on the left. A little beyond this, a stile on the right leads to **Jenkin Crag**, whence from a natural platform of rock is an exquisite view of the lake, with the verdant Brathay and Rothay vales seen in detail at its head, and the Coniston mountains in the background.

A little farther on, the lane reaches (2 *m.* from Ambleside) *High Skelgill Farm*, whence *Low Wood Hotel* may be reached in ¾ mile, or a track pursued into the Low Wood and Troutbeck road, and so on to Windermere, as described the reverse way on *p.* 82.

7. Scandale (Sweden Bridge) and back, or on to Patterdale.

High Sweden Bridge, 1¾ m. ; Low Sweden (Nook End) Bridge, 3½ ; Ambleside, 4. Over Scandale Head (1,700 ft.) to Brothers' Water Inn (Kirkstone Foot), 2½–3 hrs.

Scandale is the middle glen of the three which sink into the Rothay valley from the north-east. A spur of the Red Screes mountain separates it from the Stock Gill valley, and Scandale Fell from Rydal. The Sweden Bridge walk is very interesting, alternating richness and cultivation with wildness and sterility with a rapidity uncommon even in this region of quick transitions. The tourist who prefers grass and moorland to hard high road will also find in this route a pleasant substitute for the ordinary Kirkstone Pass road to Patterdale.

Turn to the left out of the Kirkstone road at a guide-post just before the old church. Avoid a divergence to the left and two turns to the right along wider roads. The track rapidly ascends between hedges and walls, and reveals a charming prospect of the Rothay valley, with Rydal Water reposing under Nab Scar at its extremity. The Langdale Pikes and other western fells appear over Loughrigg. The valley below narrows into a glen, down which the beck rattles merrily along, forming a multitude of little falls. The banks on both sides are pleasantly wooded almost as far as **High Sweden Bridge**, a primitive and picturesque little stone arch. The bridge may be crossed and a return made by the other side of the stream or the ridge climbed until a view into the next valley (Rydal) is obtained. In either case recross the stream at Low Sweden Bridge, close to a farm called *Nook End*, whence a few minutes' walk will take you on to the Kirkstone road again at Ambleside.

Those who intend to cross the *col* at the head of the dale will continue from High Sweden Bridge for more than a mile along a cart-track, and then bear slightly right-handed, leaving the two rocky knobs called Little Hart Crag on the left. A stone wall crosses the head of the pass. Hence a track will be found descending into a wide combe from which **Caiston Beck flows** down to Brothers' Water. Descend the combe with the beck on the right till the foot of the combe is reached. Here cross the beck where convenient, a little above some cascades, and continue down its right bank to the junction of the Caiston and Kirkstone Becks. There is no bridge. From this point the path continues at the foot of the fall on the left and across several fields to Hartsop Hall, whence there is another path to the *Brothers' Water Inn* at Kirkstone Foot. From Hartsop Hall direct to the *Patterdale Hotel* is 3 m., **Ullswater**, 4 (*p.* 212).

8. Nab Scar, 2½ m., and **Grasmere**, 5 m. Turn to the right out of the high road at Rydal village (1⅓ m.), ascend the steep wide road between the church and Rydal Mount on the left and Rydal Hall on the right, and after passing through a gateway turn up, left, through a gate to a path that ascends steeply between two straggling walls. A step-stile (15 *min.* from high road) leads on to the open fell, up which the path proceeds staircase-fashion. At the top of the steepest part a square block of stonework indicates the position of the Manchester Waterworks tunnel below. From the top of the Scar there is a lovely view. Rydal is at one's very feet ; the Rothay valley looks its best behind, and soon Grasmere comes into sight. Beyond these, to the west, is the glorious array of fells extending northward from Coniston Old Man. · Another step-stile close to the corner of the wall, and then the track, fainter, is alongside the remains of a fallen wall.

For *Grasmere*, go down to the left a few minutes after crossing the stile, in the direction of Alcock Tarn, which, however, must be left some way on the right. Then cross *Dunney Beck* above the point at which it begins to descend rapidly with steep banks. The way down the ridge beyond the beck is beside the remains of a watercourse. A track winding down is soon traceable as far as a high wall, on reaching which it bends to the left and skirts the wall round, or partly round, three sides of an enclosure. From the third side it drops into a rough lane that leads through a fir-planting down to the old Rydal and Grasmere road, at an open green, whence it is three minutes' walk to the *Prince of Wales* and ten into Grasmere village.

Another way to Grasmere is down Greenhead Gill (*see Map*) which brings one into the main road at the *Swan Hotel*.

9. Skelwith Bridge. It is a short 3 miles to Skelwith by the direct road that turns down at the *Royal Oak*. For an enjoyable walk, however, leave this road at a stone footbridge (1¼ m., crossing the *Brathay* to Brathay Church (ascend to the church-yard for the view) and up to *Skelwith Fold* (2½ m.), whence from a knoll called *Spy Hill*, a little to the right, there is a splendid view over the Langdales, the mountain amphitheatre appearing to great advantage. ¾ m. farther you recross the Brathay at Skelwith Bridge close to the hotel.

As an alternative to the main road there is a pleasant route over the corner of Loughrigg Fell and across the old Ambleside Golf Course. *Length of Walk*, 6 or 6½ m. (*Buses between Ambleside and Skelwith Bridge.*)

The Round of the Langdales. (*Map at end of the book.*)

Ambleside to Rothay Bridge, ½ m.; *Skelwith Bridge*, 2¾; *Colwith Force*, 4½; *Little Langdale*, 5½; *Blea Tarn Farm*, 8; *Dungeon Ghyll (Old Hotel)*, 9½; *(New Hotel)*, 10¼; *Chapel Stile*, 12½; *High Close*, 14; *Grasmere Church*, 15½; *Ambleside*, 19½.

This is the favourite circular route of the southern part of the Lake District, just as the Buttermere excursion is of the northern. It is not equal to the latter in richness and grandeur of separate views, but in variety and rapid change of scene it is unsurpassed. Cyclists will find it of the switchback order, especially on the crossing from Little Langdale to Great Langdale. The latter valley—which has, perhaps, the finest head in the Lake District— loses much by being almost always traversed in the wrong direction : down instead of up.

The route admits of numerous variations, some of which we shall describe *en passant*, but the only one to be specially recommended for its own sake is the walk from Red Bank, ¼ m. beyond High Close, along Loughrigg Terrace and the south side of Rydal Water to Pelter Bridge, which crosses the Rothay at Rydal village, and places the traveller on the high road a little over a mile from Ambleside ; or, better, keep the west side of the Rothay.

We leave Ambleside by the road which strikes down to the level of the Rothay valley at the *Royal Oak Inn* and, after crossing Rothay Bridge, skirts the southern slopes of Loughrigg for about 2 miles. The colouring and vegetation along this side of the fell are very rich. The village of **Clappersgate**, flowery and picturesque, is passed about ¼ mile from Ambleside, and at its farther end the road to Coniston branches off to the left across Brathay Bridge.

Here pedestrians may, at the cost of an additional half-mile, follow the Skelwith Fold route (*No.* 9, *above*) to Skelwith Bridge.

The main route, after leaving Clappersgate, skirts the north bank of the stream, making a couple of bends round the slopes of Loughrigg, which command excellent views, that from the latter enhanced by the two arches of Skelwith Bridge. The Lancashire fell, Wetherlam, is monarch of the scene, and his fine crest, massive and rounded, is a really grand feature. At 2½ m. the Grasmere road (*see p.* 121) strikes up Eller Brow to the right.

The hamlet of **Skelwith** [1] (*Hotel*), with its picturesque bridge and saw-mills, terminates the level part of the Brathay valley.

(*a*) An **alternative route** through Elterwater village, good for cyclists, and affording beautiful views, is the road to Great Langdale, and turn left at **Elterwater village** (*see p.* 130). Walkers may cut a corner of this route by crossing some meadows by a track to the right of Elterwater.

(*b*) Most tourists will be glad to halt for a few minutes here, and if they chance to drop upon **Skelwith Force** without having had their expectations raised by reading of it as one of the forces of the district, they will not regret the delay. It lies just to the left of the road a few hundred yards up-stream, beyond the hamlet. A new path along the river bank allows the pedestrian to approach the force unworried by traffic. After rain there is a considerable volume of water, but the height is only about 15 feet.

Our road after crossing Skelwith Bridge turns sharply to the right, and climbs for a mile round the north side of Black Fell, being thus far the same as the Oxenfell route to Coniston. Notice the pretty vista filled in by the Langdale Pikes.

Footpath from Skelwith to Colwith, ½ *m. shorter, and more interesting.* Cross stile on right 100 yards beyond the turn. (Diverge for a couple of minutes to Skelwith Force on this side.) Path crosses field and ascends through hazel-wood into (4 *min.*) open field, whence the Langdale Pikes are a conspicuous feature : then past two cottages. Where cart-track descends through gate on right, keep to left and very soon Seat Sandal, the shoulder of Helvellyn, and Fairfield come into view. After passing Park Farm and yard continue as much as possible in direction of Wetherlam. Beyond another farm, passed on right, path drops very steeply down cliff to meadow by river-side and re-enters road a little short of Colwith Bridge.

As we ascend, fresh views open up to the north and north-east. Elterwater Lake appears below us on the right, and over its western end the village of the same name, marking the commencement of Great Langdale. The conspicuous house well up in the dip north of Loughrigg Fell and over the lake is *High Close,* and the round-shouldered mountain beyond it Helvellyn, easily distinguishable by its succession of little crests, which suggests to the experienced eye the precipitous character of the eastern side. The Langdale Pikes over Great Langdale, and the long straight back of Fairfield lying south of Helvellyn, will easily be recognised, as well as the cone of Ill Bell to the north-east on the far side of the Troutbeck valley. The depression in front, to the right of Wetherlam, is the Wrynose Pass, traversed by the road to the Duddon and Esk Dales. Northward to the pass appear the

---

[1] Properly Skelwith Bridge. For our purposes, however, confusion is avoided by describing the hamlet as Skelwith, and the bridge as **Skelwith** Bridge.

short level top of Pike o' Blisco, the three humps called Crinkle Crags, and the clear-cut peak of Bowfell, sloping steeply south.

A mile beyond Skelwith Bridge we leave the main road to Coniston, and turning sharply to the right descend a steep pitch to *Colwith Bridge*. A few yards farther, the road forks, the right-hand prong leading to Elterwater village, and the left, by which we shall shortly continue our journey, to Wrynose and Blea Tarn. Near at hand is **Colwith Force**, a waterfall at all times worth seeing, and after a good downpour one of the finest in the district. Direct access is not possible. To obtain a view, a fine sight when the fall is in full spate, leave footpath from Skelwith where it meets road coming down from the main Coniston to Skelwith Bridge road, and walk a few hundred yards along this road to a National Trust sign. Climb stone stile and proceed up incline through wood till we arrive at corner of high stone wall. Take right fork downwards through wood. At old wall proceed along path bearing right and downwards. Colwith Force consists of several falls, accomplishing in all a descent of about 60 feet into a picturesque little glen. The upper portion is an irregular cascade, and the lower is broken into two, like Stock Gill, by a massive abutment of rock.

On leaving Colwith, we enter **Little Langdale**, a valley which is separated from Great Langdale by Lingmoor Fell, a longitudinal ridge attaining a height of nearly 1,500 feet. Wetherlam still reigns supreme on the left, with the more pointed Carrs behind it. In about a mile we pass the village of **Little Langdale** (the *Tourist's Rest*). The road hence to the left leads to Tilberthwaite and Coniston (but is inaccessible to cars), and that to the right, farther, to Elterwater. Then comes **Little Langdale Tarn.**

A short distance below the tarn is a picturesque little stone bridge over the Brathay, called **Slater's Bridge**, best reached from the road on the other side of the stream. To reverse route take field-path with wall on right hand.

Half a mile farther the open fell is gained, and our road ascends steeply to the right out of the Fell Foot and Wrynose road. The climb is continuous and increasingly steep for over a mile.

After a minute's climb a huge thimble-shaped rock pops up over the hollow in front. This is **Pike o' Stickle**, and soon its companion height, **Harrison Stickle**, appears—the two forming the lions of Langdale. The prominent crag between the two is **Loft Crag**. Gimmer Crag is the precipitous buttress of this point.

In the way of surprises there is, perhaps, nothing equal to this in the district, unless it be Honister Crag from the top of Honister Hause. Swiss travellers may possibly be reminded of the double-crested Mythen above Schwyz, as seen from the Lake of Lucerne on rounding the sharp bend into the bay of Uri. The **Langdale Pikes** are, to be sure, not half the height of those two wondrous limestone crags, but for all that they will hold their own in any company. Where else, it may well be asked, do 2,400 feet create such an impression on the mind of the beholder ? The rocky projection of Lingmoor in front of us is Side Pike. The hill-sides are sprinkled with juniper and bracken. The road is steep and winding but is well surfaced.

We are now on classic ground. From the gate at the top of the first brow we look down on **Blea Tarn**, fringed by a few Scots pine and other conifers on the far bank. Photographs have magnified it, and made it a worthy foreground to the twin peaks which rise so maesjtically behind. Photographs are right, of course, but the human eye fails to grasp foreground and background simultaneously, when presented to it on the large scale of nature, in the same way as it grasps them on the small area of a photograph, and therefore does not obtain that exactness of perspective which the photograph presents to it. Passing the tarn Bowfell reappears, followed at once by Crinkle Crags and Pike o' Blisco. This portion of the drive affords a sort of natural switchback. Hereabouts is a notable echo.

The cottage of the Solitary,[1] the " one bare dwelling, one abode, no more," now a farm-house, is beyond the tarn, and the top of the pass, a gateway some 700 feet above sea-level, about half a mile farther. As we approach, the mountains which form the head of **Great Langdale** come into prominent view, but not till the actual summit is reached does the full force of the prospect strike us. We then feel that we are looking down into one of those recesses which Nature has carved out for herself, and which the hand of man can only spoil. There is nothing in the district, except the head of Ennerdale, which surpasses this view for silent and solemn grandeur. The one or two farmsteads in the valley scarcely diminish the sense of isolation inspired by the scene, and it is comforting to know that most of the foreground belongs to the National Trust. Crinkle Crags, Bowfell, and the Langdale Pikes, all displaying their full stature to the greatest advantage, form an effectual barrier to the west and north, and the lower part of the valley is shut out by higher ground on the right. The winding track to the left of the Langdale Pikes is the Stake Pass into Borrowdale. A steep crag, Rossett Crag, rises between it and the deep gulley of Rossett Gill. The *Band*, as the green tongue projecting towards us from Bowfell is called, splits the valley into two—Mickleden to the right, and Oxendale, fed by Browney Gill, Crinkle Gill, and Hell Gill, to the left.

Hence to the bottom of the valley we have a steep winding descent of a good half-mile. The *Old Dungeon Ghyll Hotel* (*bus terminus*) is half a mile farther, across the flat ; the *New Dungeon Ghyll Hotel*, farther down the valley.

By road the distance between the two hotels is nearly a mile, by footpath (direct) $\frac{3}{4}$ mile.

---

[1] See Wordsworth's *Excursion*, Book II.

The approach to Dungeon Ghyll is somewhat shorter and better from the New Hotel, but a good plan is to get out at the Old and walk to the New, taking the ghyll on the way.

1. From the Old Hotel to Dungeon Ghyll, ⅓ *m.* The ghyll is so situated as not to be visible from this direction until you are almost in it. The route is along a steep lane skirting the slopes of the Langdale Pikes.

To reach this lane, pass through the gate which appears close to the hotel on the right hand as you approach it. Cross the field diagonally to the wall at the top and then go to the right along the green track on the other side of the wall until another green path diverges obliquely to the left. Ascend by this, and cross the stream at the end of it (this is the Dungeon Ghyll stream). Work round a little rock on the left, and recross the Dungeon Ghyll stream. The path climbs steeply for a few yards, and then ends where the bottom of the ghyll and force are in full view. The inner chamber of the ravine can only be reached by the agile.

2. From the New Hotel to Dungeon Ghyll, ⅓ *m.* Go through two gates beyond the hotel stables, and, leaving the side of *Mill Gill*, take the path to the left that crosses a field and goes through a gate in a wall. Turn at once to the right alongside the wall, and a few minutes will bring you to the Dungeon Ghyll stream as in (1).

Mill Gill is itself very beautiful, and well repays a walk some way up it. It descends from Stickle Tarn in a succession of falls which in the lower part are beautifully overshadowed by rowan and other trees, and fringed with ferns and mosses. For the upper part of the gill an alternative route is by the foot of Dungeon Ghyll, turning up to the right from slab bridge.

Stickle Tarn, 1,540 feet above sea-level, is one of the most attractive upland tarns and combines with the precipices of Pavey Ark, than which there are few finer in the district, to form a very impressive picture.

Dungeon Ghyll Force is the most remarkable water-fall in the Lake District, and is by no means dependent for its attraction on the volume of the stream. Perhaps it shows to best advantage when little more than a silver thread. The name is appropriate. Perpendicular cliffs, 100 feet high, and not more than two or three yards apart, enclose the basin into which it makes an unbroken plunge of 60 feet. Two rocks have wedged themselves into the top of this ravine, and form a natural bridge. There is a character about the scene which will prevent those who have once visited it from ever confusing it in afterthought with any other fall.

In descending to the Old Hotel, you turn to the right and recross the beck after going through the highest gate ; for the New Hotel you go through the second gate on the left, below the highest gate.

Excursions from Dungeon Ghyll Hotels

1. Ascent of Langdale Pikes, *see p.* 251.

2. **Hell ("clear") Gill, Crinkle Gill, Browney Gill,** etc. These gills, amongst the wildest and finest scenes of their kind in the District, are deep clefts in the steep sides of Bowfell, Crinkle Crags, and Pike o' Blisco, and are situated from 2 to 3 miles beyond the *Old Dungeon Ghyll Hotel,* whence recross the bridge, and turn to the right along the cart-road that leads to *Stool End,* the highest farm in the valley. Beyond this farm the valley is split into two by a projecting spur of Bowfell, called the Band. The left branch is **Oxendale,** and this we must follow by a track along the north bank of its stream.

A bit of a winding track may be noticed ascending the green breast between *Hell Gill* and *Crinkle Gill.* By this track, after crossing a footbridge, you may examine either gill, or climb to the Three Tarns, in the dip between Bowfell and Crinkle Crags, and thence drop into Eskdale by Ling Cove and Esk Falls (*p.* 126). Another way is along the north side of Hell Gill. These routes are very rough, but safe enough in clear weather. In bad weather they need knowledge of map and compass reading to negotiate safely. **Browney Gill** is almost inaccessible except after a drought. From the head of the gill you can either ascend Pike o' Blisco or follow a cairned track by Red Tarn to the top of Wrynose Pass.

To Grasmere by Codale and Easedale Tarns, 6 *m.* The map and the description of the route taken the reverse way (*p.* 155) will be sufficient direction. Care must be taken to cross the stream descending from Low White Stones and get nearly west of Codale Tarn as there is a great deal of crag on the Easedale side of Blea Rigg. From Codale Tarn the best descent to Easedale Tarn is not by the connecting beck, but by a path which goes south and then east. By this route, too, a pleasant ascent of **Sergeant Man** (a conspicuous knob with a cairn) and **High Raise** may be made, by bending to the left where the descent to Codale Tarn begins. From High Raise—in itself little more than an elevated plateau— there is, perhaps, the most comprehensive and, in the opinion of many, the finest panoramic view in the Lake District (*see pp.* 252 and 253).

The return journey to Ambleside is made by **Great Langdale,** a green and well-defined valley, by which the waters gathering on the slopes of Bowfell, Crinkle Crags, Pike o' Blisco, and the Langdale Pikes make their way into Elterwater and the Brathay valley. It is, however, seen to great disadvantage in this direction. The shape of the valley is that of a modified S, and the feature of it the back views of the two peaks which owe their name to it. They rise full-length from the level strath, and convey to the mind as powerful an impression of bold and rugged grandeur as any mountain in Great Britain. The cause of this impression is two-fold—first, the striking contour of their skyline; and secondly, their continuous steepness. The Lake mountains, from top to toe, have probably a greater mean steepness than any other mountains in the kingdom, except the Cuillins of Skye; but even in Lakeland an average slope of 40 degrees continued for 1,800 feet—as it is in the case of Pike o' Stickle—is unique. Honister Crag and Wastwater Screes are both rather steeper, but in actual height, from the point where their steepness begins, they fall short of Pike o' Stickle by several hundred feet, nor is their skyline so boldly marked.

Two miles lower down the valley than the *New Dungeon Ghyll Hotel*, we reach the hamlet of **Chapel Stile**, with *Langdale Church* conspicuous in its midst. All about here the beauty of the fell-sides is marred by slate-quarries.

Near the church the road forks, the left-hand branch leading to Grasmere, the right to Elterwater village and Ambleside.

The latter route must be taken by those who wish to return **direct to Ambleside,** a good five-mile walk. First of all the *Langdales Hotel* is passed on the right.   At Elterwater village, nearly a mile on the way, the road from Grasmere to Little Langdale is crossed. (On it there is a small inn, the *Britannia*, about 100 yards to the right of the crossing, whence the field-route, starting a few yards short of the bridge over the Langdale Beck, and already mentioned on *p.* 115, may be taken.) The road then climbs the open fell for a short distance and proceeds with Elterwater on the right to Skelwith Bridge (1¼ *m.*, *see p.* 115) and Ambleside (4¼ *m.*). The old road passes within a field of the west shore of Loughrigg Tarn, and then by a steep descent to the left (the right-hand route leads down to Skelwith Bridge) joins the main road by which we started out, **at a** turn about ⅓ mile from Skelwith Bridge, and 2½ miles from **Ambleside.**

Taking the left-hand, or upper road at Langdale Church, **we** skirt the southern side of Silver How, and soon emerge upon an open common, where a road from Elterwater village joins us on the right. Hence, by a steep, zigzaggy ascent, the top of **the** depression (520 ft.) between Loughrigg Fell and Silver How is soon gained.   On the summit is a seat bearing the inscription " Rest and be thankful," followed by a vexatiously long and high garden wall and a large house, built on to an old farm, called *High Close* (*Youth Hostel*).

Walkers may shorten the way to Grasmere by about half a mile by taking a track to the left from a short distance beyond the junction of the roads from Elterwater village and Chapel Stile. The path is easily discernible, alongside or near the telegraph-wire passing under a projecting spur of Silver How. From its highest point a lovely view is obtained both before and behind, but that of Grasmere in front is not nearly so complete or characteristic as the one from Loughrigg Terrace. The path then descends, and, after becoming a lane at *Hunting Stile*, where a path from the top of Red Bank comes in, rejoins the road about half-way between High Close and Grasmere village. (For other routes between Langdale and Grasmere, *see pp.* 150 and 155.)

The view, looking back from High Close, is very grand. The Lancashire fells rise beyond Elterwater Lake, and, to the right of them, Pike o' Blisco, Crinkle Crags, Bowfell, and the Langdale Pikes maintain their usual solemn and uncompromising attitude, and form a striking contrast to the leafy luxuriance and the perennial verdure of the intervening landscape. But fresh fields are in store for us. In ten yards all the back view is lost and we are descending to Grasmere. Our road is joined in 300 yards by one from Ambleside and Skelwith Bridge.

After descending for 150 yards we reach **Red Bank** and on the right a rough lane drops at once to **Loughrigg Terrace,** whence the whole lake, village, and valley of Grasmere burst upon the view with magical effect. (*For a description, see p.* 148.) A footpath strikes off to the left, and is an immense improvement on the road. It joins the Elterwater and Grasmere path at *Hunting Stile* (*see above*). For Grasmere continue along the road almost to the church, and then turn to the left—the first turn leads through the village on to the Keswick main road, the second to the *Rothay, Dale Lodge, Moss Grove,* and the *Red Lion Hotels.*

The **shortest way** back to **Ambleside** from Red Bank is by the above terrace-route. Rydal Water comes into view towards the other end of it, and then a sharp short descent leads to a track skirting its southern shore. When the other end of the lake is reached, there are two ways of proceeding—one by crossing the Rothay either by the footbridge just below the lake or by Pelter Bridge a little farther on and joining the high road at Rydal village, 1¼ miles from Ambleside ; the other by keeping the river on the left, and following the road past Fox How as far as Miller Bridge, just opposite the town. The latter (¼ *m.* longer) is much the pleasanter of the two.

Ambleside to Coniston, *viâ* Barn Gates. *Map at end of the book.*

Ambleside to Rothay Bridge, ½ *m.*; *Brathay Bridge,* 1 ; *Barn Gates Inn,* 3 ; *High Cross,* 5 ; *Coniston,* 7½.

The following excursion may be extended by continuing by road from Coniston to Furness Abbey, whence the return *viâ* Ulverston and Lake Side, and by steamer on Windermere, completes a very pleasant circular tour, easily accomplished in one day.

The outward portion of this route, though presenting beautiful distant views, has not the absorbing interest of journeys through the heart of the district.

The route as far as *Brathay Bridge* has been described in the Langdale Round (*p.* 114). After crossing the bridge the way proceeds, through pleasant woods and meadows of the *Brathay Hall* estate, for about 1¼ miles, and then diverging to the right (the road straight on is the main one to Hawkshead and along the west side of Windermere) a few hundred yards after crossing the beck which flows into Pull Wyke Bay, climbs a steep hill to a roadside inn, called *Barn Gates* (locally *The Drunken Duck*). Hence a fine prospect is obtained to the north and north-east, Helvellyn and Fairfield over Loughrigg, and Red Screes over Ambleside, being prominent, as also the High Street Range over Wansfell Pike.

Hawkshead (*see p.* 79) may be reached in 2½ miles from Barn Gates by taking the cross-road opposite the inn, which joins the main road from Ambleside in about a mile at Outgate (*inn*).

Hence there is a gradual ascent through comparatively open country, with views of Hawkshead and Esthwaite Water, till a height of about 600 feet above sea-level is attained at **High Cross.** Here the road from Hawkshead and the Ferry on Windermere converges.

Notwithstanding the beauty of the direct descent from High Cross to Coniston, pedestrians, but not motorists, should certainly adopt the route *viâ* **Tarn Hows,** which strikes up to the right 1¾ miles beyond Barn Gates, and ¼ mile short of High Cross, opposite a lane also coming up from Hawkshead. The route is described on pp. 90 and 91 and Tarn Hows itself on *p.* 136.

From High Cross there is a more or less steep descent for nearly 2 miles with lovely peeps at **Coniston Lake** through the woods. The Old Manasserts himself with immense dignity in front, but the depth and wealth of foliage is the striking feature of the scene. Nowhere in the district does that variety of sylvan beauty which is so characteristic of the shores of its principal lakes impress itself more strongly on the traveller. The shore-line of Coniston is comparatively tame, nor are its encircling hills marked by so much gracefulness of outline as those of Windermere, but it is difficult to imagine anything much finer than the glorious coronal of wood which surrounds its head, and is so nobly supported by the richly-tinted crags of Yewdale and the weather-beaten brow of the Old Man.

For Coniston, see p. 134 ; *the return route by Oxenfell, p.* 140.

Those who are not making Coniston their headquarters for any time but who have three or four hours at their disposal may devote them to climbing the Old Man (*p.* 281) or making the tour of the lake (*p.* 135) ; or, if ruins be preferred to either climbing or sailing, there is the excursion to Furness Abbey (*p.* 98).

Ambleside to Patterdale (Ullswater).   *Map at end of the book.*

Ambleside to Kirkstone Inn, 3 m.; Brothers' Water Inn, 5½; Patterdale Hotel, 8½; Ullswater Hotel, 9½.

We have chosen to describe this route *in extenso* from Bowness and Windermere rather than from Ambleside, because the valley of Troutbeck and the grand views of Windermere obtainable from it are missed by starting from Ambleside.

By returning through the village of Troutbeck, however, and along the road to Low Wood, one obtains very fine views of Windermere (*see p.* 81). The three-mile ascent between Ambleside and the Kirkstone Inn is tremendously steep. The rise is nearly 1,300 feet, and, like most Lake District roads which follow the course of the old pack-horse roads, is so badly engineered as to be rather a succession of jerks than a steep hill in the ordinary sense of the word. It is appropriately called the " **Struggle** " out of Ambleside.

A waggish entry in a visitors' book of the horse-coach era ran :—

> " He surely is an arrant ass,
> Who pays to ride up Kirkstone Pass
> He'll find in spite of all their talking,
> He'll have to walk, and pay for walking."

The road leaves the main highway to Keswick just beyond Stock Gill Bridge, to which, however, there is no need to descend, as the street starting from below the *Salutation Hotel* joins the route some way up the hill. The " Struggle " commences almost immediately. The *old church* is passed on the right, and the rest of the route lies between a spur of Red Screes and Wansfell Pike, Stock Gill Beck being some way below it on the right all the way. The retrospect consists of the head of Windermere, robbed of all its river charm ; then Wray Castle, Blelham Tarn, the familiar Old Man, and the other Lancashire fells. After a while comes a comparatively level stretch of road, to be paid for at compound interest by the last half-mile or so up to the *Kirkstone Inn,* " one of the highest inhabited houses in England," *see p.* 89   There, within a few yards of the inn, we join the Windermere and Patterdale route (*p.* 89). Excursion 3 (*p.* 109) is commended as an alternative to the " Struggle."

Ambleside to Wasdale Head by Eskdale and Strands.

Ambleside to Fell Foot, 7 m.; Three Shire Stone (top of Wrynose Pass), 8¾; Cockley Beck, 11¼; top of Hardknott Pass, 12½; Woolpack Inn (Eskdale), 15; Beckfoot Station and Stanley Ghyll, 16¼; Santon Bridge (inn), 21½; Strands (inns), 24; Wasdale Head, 30.
Height of Passes :—Wrynose, 1,270 ft.; Hardknott, 1,290 ft.

This route affords the opportunity of visiting Dalegarth Force (Stanley Ghyll), the finest waterfall in the District, and of seeing its wildest lake, Wastwater, to the greatest advantage.

The road from Fell Foot to the far side of the Hardknott Pass (7 miles) is mostly steep and narrow. There is one house about half-way, the farm at *Cockley Beck.*

The first 7 miles of the route, to within a few hundred yards of **Fell Foot,** have been described in the Langdale Round (*p.* 114). Fell Foot is a farm-house, almost surrounded by yews, reached by a left-hand turning out of the Blea Tarn road about ¼ mile beyond Little Langdale Tarn. The Eskdale road swerves to the right past the front of the house at the fork about ¼ mile from the above-mentioned turning.

Lying as it does on the main Roman road from the Roman camp at Ambleside to those of Hardknott and Ravenglass, this old farm at the foot of the pass has always held an important position. According to Swainson Cowper, we may find in the strangely terraced mound behind the building an ancient place of meeting for the gathering of the Thing, or judicial assembly ordered by King Ethelred in all Danish districts; it would thus compare with the Tynwald Hill in Man. On the front gable of the house there still remain in oak the arms of the le Fleming family of Rydal Hall (a *fret* below a *serpent mowed*). Fletcher Fleming resided here 1707–1735.

From Fell Foot to the **Three Shire Stone** (where Lancashire, Westmorland, and Cumberland met) is 1¾ miles of steep ascent through the **Wrynose Pass.** The main length of the pass road is excellent, surface concreted over its steepest parts to the summit, and is now used by many as a touring road. Wetherlam and Carrs occupy the space to the left ; Blake Rigg, overlooking Blea Tarn, and Pike o' Blisco to the right. There is a good retrospect over Little Langdale Tarn and the Brathay valley to Wansfell Pike, Ill Bell, the latter always recognisable by its conical shape, with Ingleborough, flat-topped, beyond.

About a mile from Fell Foot, where the road bends to the left, a bridge is crossed. Here on the right is the starting-place for the ascent of the **Pike o' Blisco** (*see p.* 277).

The Three Shire Stone is an upright pillar inscribed " Lancashire, W.F. 1816." There was nothing to mark Cumberland and Westmorland. Just beyond it we reach the summit of the pass, **Wrynose Gap,** whence, by the side of the infant Duddon, we descend for 2 miles or more through a wild, bare valley, without any feature of interest except the little patch of verdure at Cockley Beck and the craggy top of Hardknott beyond it. Wrynose (locally *Raynus*) may possibly be a corruption of Raven Hause. Cars are often taken over the Pass, and it is now a road much improved for motoring.

[A little short of the Three Shire Stone a line of cairns will be seen running away to the right. These are useful in putting you on the way to Crinkle Crags and Bowfell. Beyond Red Tarn they derogate into a somewhat dangerous trap, as they come to an end at the head of Browney Gill, a rough and intricate descent, not to be recommended.]

From *Cockley Beck* there is a peep of the Scafell Pikes over the Mosedale valley—a name, by the way, which is of frequent occurrence in the Lake District, and may generally be accepted as an index to dreariness, the only exception being that from Wasdale Head to Black Sail and the Pillar, which is redeemed by grandeur. From Cockley Beck a horse-track runs for some way up the aforementioned Mosedale in the direction of Scafell.

From Cockley Beck the road down the **Duddon valley** strikes off to the left. There are several gates. As it descends the scenery becomes more varied and beautiful. The distances from Cockley Beck are :—to *Seathwaite*, 4 m. (p. 141); Ulpha, 7 Broughton-in-Furness, 12.

There is a farm-house at Cockley Beck, where refreshments may be obtained preparatory to the ascent of **Hardknott Pass**, which is short but steep in places. The pass is nearly 1,300 feet high, but owing to the elevated position of Cockley Beck itself, only involves an ascent of about 600 feet. It is the watershed between the Duddon and Esk valleys.

As the road ascends Hardknott, the view down the Duddon valley expands. From the top of the pass the sea is visible, and the prospect of the rich sylvan beauty of Eskdale is most refreshing after the treeless wilderness we have been confined to for the last hour or so. The Scafell group rises majestically on the right. About 100 yards to the right of the road, and a short distance before enclosed ground is again reached, are the remains of a **Roman Camp**, now called *Hardknott Castle*.

The camp was partly excavated by the Cumberland & Westmorland Antiquarian and Archæological Society in 1889–94, and the stone buildings have since been consolidated by the Department of the Environment. The principal discoveries have been south of the main camp and consisted of a circular building 15 feet in internal diameter, with walls 4 or 5 feet high, which, when complete, would have had a beehive roof of stone. To the south was a three-roomed bathhouse and an elaborate system of hypocausts. These lie very near the road. The main camp is an enclosure of about 250 feet square. Not far away is a levelled space supposed to have been the parade ground.

The *Esk* is first reached and crossed a little more than a mile beyond Hardknott Castle, and a mile farther we reach the *Woolpack Inn*. On the way the gracefully tapering peak of Bowfell, heading the valley on the right, may remind the passer-by of Snowdon from Porthmadog or Schiehallion from almost anywhere.

1. Those who wish to explore the beauties of **Upper Eskdale** *en route* should take a track to the right, just short of a wood and about 100 yards before reaching the cattle grid at the bottom of the Hardknott Pass. Thence they pass a farm-house, **Butterilket,**[1] about ¼ mile after leaving the road, and continue along the eastern bank of the river to the **Esk Falls,** on the main stream, 2 miles farther. These falls lie on the main river just beyond the junction with the Lingcove Beck which descends from Bowfell. They are as perfect little pictures of wild mountain-torrents as can be imagined. By following the Esk towards Scafell, keeping to the right of the stream, **Esk Hause** may be reached in from 1½ to 2 hours, or by following Lingcove Beck towards Bowfell, the depression south of Bowfell may be crossed at the **Three Tarns,** and a descent made into Great Langdale ; but neither of these trackless wildernesses should be traversed except in perfectly clear weather.

Note. There is a bridge across Lingcove Beck close to Esk Falls but no bridge across the Esk, so it is impossible except in dry weather to return down the west (Taw House) side of the valley.

2. For **Dalegarth Force (Stanley Ghyll),** the finest scene of its kind in the district, continue from the *Woolpack* along the road for 1¼ miles, passing a little to the south of **Boot** village (*see below*), and noting on the opposite side of the valley *Low Birker Force,* a long and conspicuous fall. Then, opposite the schoolhouse, turn to the left, and cross **Dalegarth Bridge** (note the flood levels on the side of the bridge).

From the other side of the bridge bear left, leaving Dalegarth Hall on the right. **Dalegarth Hall,** with its many round chimneys and air of antiquity, is mainly 14th-century. A little farther is the entrance-gate beyond which cross a field and to the foot of wooded ghyll, which is private but open to the public.

The route of access may vary, but if it is remembered that the fall is part of the stream, vain digression may be avoided. Unless familiar with the way, it is well to reserve the upper gate on the south side of the Ghyll for an exit. From this point you gain a fine view of the force from the cliff overlooking it.

On the way to the Ghyll a superb prospect of the Eskdale fells opens up and within the ravine the beauty of the scene gradually develops till it finds its climax at the last bridge (there are three in all) beneath the force.

Stanley Ghyll.—The height of Dalegarth Force at the head of the Ghyll is 60 feet, less than that of many other well-known forces in the district ; but here again it is neither the height nor the volume of water which constitutes the attraction, but the setting, and in this respect the scene is justly regarded as the finest of its kind in Lakeland. The cliffs on either side are precipitous, the foliage rich and varied, and greatly enhanced by the variety of exquisitely fresh and luxuriant ferns which drape the purple crags from head to foot. It is not desirable to proceed beyond the third bridge, *as the path becomes dangerous.*

[1] Also known as Brotherilkeld. The names are of equal standing.

In returning ascend the steep path and steps between the second and third bridges, near a tributary rill, turn to the left, climb up some steps, turn left again at the top across a small beck, and follow path through shrubbery to reach the cliff overlooking Dalegarth Force. There is a grand view over Boot to Scafell. Cross the wooden stile, keep right to join a rough road which leads down the hill back to Dalegarth Hall.

3. From the *Woolpack* the walker may cut off the Boot corner, on the way to **Wasdale Head** *via* Burnmoor Tarn, by climbing behind the house to a peat-track leading up to **Eel Tarn** (route marked as far as Burnmoor Tarn by white crosses on the rocks) a reedy little sheet of water. Leaving this on the right, make for the Burnmoor beck on the left hand, across which you will find a footbridge in less than 1½ miles from the tarn, and a little distance short of Burnmoor Tarn. For rest of the route see description from Boot (*see below*).

A mile beyond the *Woolpack* is the village of **Boot**, lying a little to the right of the main road, on a beck which descends from Scafell and Burnmoor Tarn. Here is another inn, the *Burnmoor*, and within a quarter of a mile is Dalegarth Station, the terminus of the Ravenglass & Eskdale miniature Railway.

Pony-track to Wasdale Head, 6 *m.* Starting this journey from Boot, cross the beck, climb the hill for 150 yards, and then pass through a gate on the right into a field-track. The cart-road is simply a peat-track and works away to the left. After this you keep Whillan beck at a distance of from 50 to 300 yards on your right the whole way to **Burnmoor Tarn**, where you cross it just as it issues from the tarn. On your way you leave a keeper's house some way on the left, beyond which the path is rather inter-mittent, but occasional piles of stones mark the doubtful places. The route is dreary at first, but as it advances the Pillar range in front breaks the monotony, and when the highest point of the journey is reached, a little way beyond the tarn, and the fells sur-rounding Wasdale Head, including Great Gable and Kirkfell, come into full view on one side, and Wastwater and the Screes on the other, ample atonement is made for the previous dullness. The track leads down to the right past some ruined huts, and at the foot of the slope through a gap in a wall on the left, where it again bends slightly to right across a field. Next it crosses a bridge over the Lingmell Gill, passing the camping site, then another bridge, the work of the same hands, and a little farther on comes out through a gate on to the main road rather less than a mile below Wasdale Head.

Quitting Boot, we follow the main road down the valley, and arrive in a couple of miles or more at the *George IV Inn*, close to which the road from the Duddon valley across Birker Moor converges on the left.

We now cross the railway and proceed past a few scattered cottages and villas called **Eskdale Green**. The road turns sharply to the left then bears right, and crosses the low ridge separating Eskdale from Miterdale. The high ground to the left between the two valleys is **Muncaster Fell** (757 *ft.*). From a point near the tarn on Muncaster Fell it is possible, given the right atmospheric conditions, to see Criffel, the Isle of Man, the mountains of Mourne, and the Welsh mountains. The *Mite* is crossed about half a mile beyond Irton Road Station, just before reaching the *Bower House Inn*, about 1½ miles beyond the *George IV*.

The road now crosses the side of Irton Fell, and descends to **Santon Bridge** where we find the River Irt, flowing out of Wastwater. Here is another small inn, and the convergence of the road from Drigg. To reach Wastwater, however, we turn right just short of the bridge.

A steep hill is now ascended, from the top of which almost everything connected with Wastwater is visible except the lake itself, which is hidden by an intervening belt of trees. Two miles beyond Santon Bridge the road crosses the river Irt, and the village of **Strands** (*p.* 47) or Nether Wasdale is reached by bearing back to the left for a quarter of a mile. To reach Wasdale Head, however, without visiting Strands, turn to the right immediately after crossing the bridge, and keep straight on. The road soon enters the woods of Wasdale Hall (Youth Hostel).

Those who are not in a hurry to reach Wasdale Head should unquestionably make the following detour. Opposite the farm on the left about 200 yards before the entrance to Wasdale Hall, a signposted footpath goes down a field to a gate which gives access to the bridge over the river Irt. Then turn left and follow up the stream to the actual outlet of the Lake, where there is a modern pumping station. The view up the lake is very fine. Great Gable is superb, with Kirkfell and Yewbarrow conspicuous on the left. A very rough path continues along the slope of the Screes, and it is possible to reach Wasdale Head by this route ; but the adventure is tiring and troublesome and nothing is to be gained by it. It is worth while, however, to walk along it for a short distance, if only to obtain a just appreciation of the deeply riven crags which hang over the Screes along which the path passes. A return should be made by the route of approach.

Those who anticipate finding nothing but wildness in **Wastwater** will be astonished at the extent and luxuriance of the woods which surround its lower end. Not only do all kinds of native British trees elbow one another in every direction, but many of the favourite flower-garden shrubs grow with remarkable vigour. For all that, there can be no doubt that wildness is the pervading feature of Wastwater. The woods only form a foreground ; the middle and far distance is the quintessence of wildness, and it is perhaps the only scene of like character in Great Britain, if we except Loch Coruisk. The lake itself bursts suddenly into view where the road emerges from the wood and descends in a few yards to its margin. Whether its surface be unruffled as a pond, as often is the case, or lashed into storm so violent that the spray, flung up from its mid-waters, is felt hundreds of feet above their level, the scene is most impressive. There are a unity of spirit in the whole and a beauty and grandeur of outline in the surrounding fells which are seldom if ever found in combination elsewhere. The **Screes**, with their perpendicular crags towering above them, add greatly to the scene. The variety of colour for which they are celebrated is best seen in the winter time, when russet tint of the dead bracken contrasts with the red streaks of iron-ore, the dark umber of the crags, and the patches of verdure in their interstices.

Hence, the road skirts the north-western shore of the lake all the way up it. Here and there a few patches of cultivation diversify the general wildness. The most remarkable feature, however, is the razor-like edge of **Yewbarrow**, which becomes more and more marked as we advance across the mouth of the side valley, Bowderdale. At the head of the lake we enter Upper Wasdale, a narrow tract of green fields and stone walls, in the midst of an amphitheatre of steep and lofty fells. Scafell Pike and its northern spur, Lingmell, are on the rght, Great Gable in front and Kirkfell and Yewbarrow on the left. The effect is striking and one feels at once what an effective feature the lake itself is.

The *Wastwater Hotel* is a mile beyond the head of the lake. Just before reaching it the road forks, the right branch leading past the church to the upper part of the valley, and the left past the hotel to Row Head. For a full description of Wasdale *see p. 204*.

Ambleside to Keswick, by Great or Little Langdale and the Stake Pass (1,576 ft.).   *Map at end of the book.*

Ambleside to Dungeon Ghyll Old Hotel (by motor-road through Great Langdale), 8 m.; Dungeon Ghyll to Rosthwaite, 8 m.; 4–5 hrs. (bridle-path). Rosthwaite to Keswick (bus-services), 6½ m.

This route is to be commended to those going to Keswick, but desirous of gaining a fair insight into the *arcana* of the district on the way. The Stake Pass is less interesting than Esk Hause, but the Langstrath valley is excessively wild though somewhat monotonous from its straightness and length.

Of the two routes to Dungeon Ghyll, the longer one, by Little Langdale (*p.* 109), includes the greater variety of scenery, but with the Stake to follow, the Blea Tarn road is for strong walkers only ; we shall therefore start *via* Great Langdale.

For the first 2¾ miles the road is identical with that described in the *Round of the Langdales* (*p.* 114). Then, just short of Skelwith Bridge, the beautiful newer road to Elterwater strikes off to the right.

The old road, much more hilly, climbs a very steep pitch called **Eller Brow**, from about ⅓ mile short of Skelwith Bridge, and passes Loughrigg Tarn, ⅓ mile beyond which a branch goes off to Red Bank and **Grasmere**, distant from Ambleside by this route 5 miles. **Loughrigg Tarn** is a calm, unassuming sheet of water, which adds its own soft charm to many a bright scene of Lakeland. This tarn, Lily Tarn, and Tewfit Tarn near Naddle, are among the first tarns to bear in the skating season.

After passing Skelwith Force (*p.* 115) we have lovely views over **Elterwater**, ragged and ill-defined in itself, but nobly backed by Wetherlam and others of the Lancashire fells, while in front the Langdale Pikes grow more and more impressive as they are approached. **Elterwater village**, where there is a small inn (*The Britannia*), is passed a little on the left, and half a mile farther the *Landgales Hotel*. Then come Langdale Church and the village of Chapel Stile, with Thrang slate-quarries close at hand. Once past these quarries the full beauty of **Great Langdale** reveals itself " unmixed with baser matter "—a green flat strath, gracefully curved, with the rugged Pikes in their full glory in the background. A finer scene of its kind can hardly be imagined. Beyond Harry Place, Bowfell appears, and, a mile farther, the *New Dungeon Ghyll Hotel* is close by on the right.

For Dungeon Ghyll, *see p.* 118. It is the next ghyll beyond Millbeck, and those wishing to visit it on this journey should ascend to it from the *New*, and descend from it to the *Old Hotel*.

The road continues across flat meadows to the *Old Dungeon Ghyll Hotel*. The scenery is most impressive. The skyline of encircling fells—Crinkle Crags on the left, Bowfell in front and the Langdale Pikes on the right—is remarkable for its boldness, and the rugged fell sides shoot down with striking precipitancy to the wild dalehead.

A short distance beyond the *Old Dungeon Ghyll Hotel* the valley is cut in two by the *Band*, a long projecting spur of Bowfell. The route from Ambleside to Keswick is up the right-hand and larger branch, called *Mickleden*. The track starts between the Hotel and *Middlefell Farm*, and after following the strath of the valley for a couple of miles commences the ascent of the **Stake Pass** at a sheepfold. The pass is the depression on the right hand, between Pike o' Stickle and Rossett Crag, the comparatively low but precipitous cliff rising exactly *vis-à-vis* to the traveller as he ascends the dale. The ravine on the left, between Rossett Crag and Bowfell, is Rossett Gill, close to which the track to Esk Hause and Wasdale Head struggles up.

The Stake path zigzags up by the side of a beck, after crossing which at the top of the steep part it bears slightly to the right, and in ½ mile (mostly over moraine heaps) reaches a cairn which marks the summit of the pass (1,576 *ft.* ; Skiddaw well seen in front). Hence, after a comparatively level half-mile or so, it reaches the side of another beck, which descends by a series of falls into Langstrath, the eastern arm of Borrowdale. Proceeding down the slope, with the beck on our right, we cross it in about half a mile, at the same time entering the main valley, whose stream descends from Angle Tarn.

From the foot of the Stake pedestrians can follow whichever bank of the stream they prefer. In dry weather it is better to cross the stream at once. Bull Crag and Eagle Crag are fine cliffs on the right, and where the two stream-side routes join, the beck sliding and leaping over a rocky bed is very charming. There are two bridges across Langstrath Beck, one at the top of the valley and another at the bottom, not far from Eagle Crag. Where the valley opens, the track turns sharp to the left round a precipitous crag. A smooth, short, and pleasant variation is to cross a stone stepstile a little short of a barn and take a grass path that leads direct to **Stonethwaite**.[1] This is a charming part of the valley, and the rambling hamlet is a welcome sight. The track on the other side of the stream is the Easedale route from Grasmere, which joins our present one at Stonethwaite. Then, leaving Borrowdale church on the left hand, saving, if we like, 100 yards or so by crossing a couple of fields, we enter the main Borrowdale Road about half a mile above **Rosthwaite** (*see p.* 180). The road between *Rosthwaite* and *Keswick* (*bus route*) is described on *pp.* 177–80, etc.

Ambleside to Wasdale Head, by Dungeon Ghyll and Esk Hause (2,370 ft.). *Map at end of the book.*

Ambleside to Dungeon Ghyll Old Hotel, 8 m. (*end of road*). *Dungeon Ghyll to Wasdale Head,* 8–9 m. (4½–5½ hrs. ; *bridle-path*).

This is the roughest and grandest of all the Lake District passes. There is no habitation between Dungeon Ghyll and Wasdale.

The route is the same as that over the Stake Pass (*p.* 130), until the latter begins to climb to the right, two miles beyond the *Old Hotel,* and at the sheepfold. On the way up the valley a steep rock is seen in front, breaking the depression between the Langdale Pikes on the right and Bowfell on the left. This is Rossett Crag. The Stake Pass ascends by the stream to the right of it, and is clearly marked ; the Wasdale route by the stream to the left, and is quite unmistakable. Where the steep part begins an alternative route avoids the bed of the ghyll and makes a zigzag with the old pony-track, which ascended under Bowfell all the way. Walkers may take which route they like, but they will find the gill extremely rough and exasperatingly steep.

---

[1] This hamlet does not see the sun from early November till early February.

For the alternative route cross the Stake Pass branch of the stream just beyond the sheepfold and keep the Rossett Gill Beck on your left, and ascend gradually till you reach the steep part of the gill, where another runnel from Bowfell joins it. The crags of Bowfell look very grand in front. At the runnel the path crosses the gill and winds up over the steep grass humps, making a bend to the left and back again to ease the ascent. Then, instead of entering the bed of the gill (usually dry), the path strikes off square to the left, and in ¼ mile joins the old pony-track under Bowfell, which fronts us most imposingly during this part of the ascent, some huge slabs of rock (Flat Crags) at a sharp angle being specially noteworthy.

This stiff climb lands us at the top of **Rossett Gill**, about 2,000 feet above sea-level. Esk Hause, separated by two minor depressions, is now directly in front. Beyond it, on the left, is Great End, the northern buttress of the Scafell group. Saddleback appears far away to the right, and the Helvellyn range south of it. A few steps farther, and **Angle Tarn** is seen, deep and lonely, under the craggy scarp of Hanging Knott, the northern spur of Bowfell. The stream flowing out of it threads the Langstrath branch of Borrowdale. Descend for a short distance and then cross the stream below the tarn, and climb the boggy ground on the other side. The track's general course is easily discerned striking straight ahead. When the atmosphere is thick the tourist should never lose sight of it for many seconds together, and he must be careful not to descend into the Langstrath valley, which defiles off to the right again at the second depression beyond the top of Rossett Gill. From this depression ten minutes' steepish ascent brings you to the " Shelter " (a rough stone shelter being provided amongst its piled stones by each of the arms built out from the centre) on **Esk Hause** (*see p.* 206). The path passes a few yards to the right of this shelter, and the actual top of the hause, whence there is a prospect down Eskdale, is a few hundred yards to the left of them. In foggy weather care must be taken to keep to the track here, neither ascending southward from the shelter to the top of the hause, nor getting down into Grain Gill, which drops into Borrowdale on the right a little farther on. In short, the correct direction from Angle Tarn to the Sty Head is, generally, north-west by compass—and a compass should invariably be taken.

Those who are likely to revisit Esk Hause—and it is quite an important cross-roads—should take the first opportunity of noting its shape and plan. Such knowledge would be invaluable should one be caught here in mist, when it is fatally easy to descend into Borrowdale instead of into Langdale or vice versa.

In the Eskdale direction there is a sort of track and a succession of small stone heaps which mark the ascent of Scafell Pike. Esk Hause itself is the depression between the Bowfell and Scafell groups, both of which rise on the left of our present track.

From the vicinity of the shelter there is a grand view of Great Gable in front, with the Pillar in the dip between it and the nearer crags of Great End. The fells between Crummock and Derwentwater are visible to the right of Great Gable, and there is a retrospect of part of Windermere between Bowfell and Rossett Crag. Allen Crags shut out the view northward, but after a few minutes' descent by the side of a streamlet, Derwentwater, Skiddaw, and Saddleback come into sight in that direction. Between us and the lake is the beautiful little pyramid of Castle Crag in Borrowdale. The vista thus obtained is one of singular richness and beauty.

Very shortly the streamlet which has accompanied our path disappears down a ravine on the right, well named (from the colour of the soil) Ruddy Gill, an arm of Grain Gill, leading down (*p.* 205) to Seathwaite in Borrowdale, which may be reached from here in about an hour. The Wasdale track goes straight on to **Sprinkling Tarn**, skirting its western side, and crossing the beck which connects it with Sty Head Tarn. Shortly after leaving Sprinkling Tarn we recross the beck, and, half a mile farther, traversing some very boggy ground to the south of Sty Head Tarn, join the Borrowdale and Wasdale track 2½ miles short of Wasdale Head,[1] at the cairn (1,600 *ft.*) on the top of **Sty Head Pass.**[2] Hence a steep and very stony track obliquely descends the southern slope of Great Gable into the green valley of Wasdale. The mountain to the left during the descent is Lingmell, and the deep ravine between it and Great End, Piers Gill (*see p.* 264), perhaps the finest chasm in Lakeland. It may be reached by descending to the bottom of the valley from near the top of the pass, and climbing up by the stream on the other side. Exploration of this ravine is unwise.

The first house reached in the valley is a farm called *Burn-thwaite*. Passing through the farmyard to the left of the house, we follow the road onward as far as the church, whence a field-track at right-angles brings us to the *Wastwater Hotel*, or an alternative footpath may be followed to the right of the farm at Burnthwaite which leads by the beckside to *Wastwater Head Hotel*.

A strip of the upper end of Wastwater is seen during the descent of the pass, but that is all (*see p.* 44).

[1] From the top of Sty Head you may drop into the valley at once. The right bank may be followed or the stream crossed and recrossed according to inclination, which is sometimes regulated by the amount of water in the channel.

[2] Sty Head Pass is a misnomer. Sty Head is merely the head of the Sty (*stee,* "ladder") Pass.

CONISTON

Angling.—*See p.* 26.
Banks.—*Barclays, National Westminster.*
Boats can be hired at moderate charges by the day or week.
Buses, etc., to Ambleside and to Torver, Barrow, etc., Lake Bank, Greenodd and Ulverston.
Church.—Sunday Services, 8, 11, 6. *Methodist,* 11 a.m. and 6 p.m. R.C. Church, Torver Road.
Distances.—By road—Ambleside, 8 *m.*; Bowness, 10; Dungeon Ghyll, 9; Grasmere, 10; Hawkshead, 4; Keswick, 23; Windermere, 11½.
Hotels.—*Crown,* in the village; *Sun; Black Bull; Ship.*
Institute and Library, Yewdale Road.
Population, about 1,000.
Ruskin Museum, Yewdale Road.
Tennis, Bowls and Putting Green, Yewdale Road.

Coniston village is beautifully placed at the foot of the Old Man and Yewdale Crags, and about half a mile from the head of the lake. The mines and quarries, which abound almost the whole way up the Old Man, considerably mar the prospect from what would otherwise be the best points of view, but the scene, as a whole, is very impressive. The height of the village above sea-level varies from 160–250 feet.

Coniston Lake is a little over 5 miles long, and not more than ½ mile wide. Its characteristic beauty is of the Windermere type, but its inferior size and the greater regularity of its shores prevent it from exhibiting that variety and grandeur of prospect which its big Westmorland brother possesses in such an eminent degree. At the same time, it may be said that while all views with the lake in the foreground, backed by the Old Man *massif,* especially that from Brantwood, are grand in their simplicity, no purely lake view in the District is more charming than that straight down Coniston from the heights which crown its upper end. For the latter a view-point near Hollin Bank on the road to Hawkeshead is the best vantage ground, and for the former the walk along the east side of the lake should be taken.

Coniston is the best headquarters for the Lancashire fells.

Coniston will for all time be the place most closely associated with **John Ruskin.** His residence, *Brantwood,* where he died, is on the east side of the lake, a mile from the pier by water; 2½ by road from the " Waterhead." Brantwood was bought by Mr. J. Howard Whitehouse as a Ruskin Memorial in 1933. It is now used as an Adult Education Centre. *Daily, Feb.–Nov., fee. Refreshments and car park.*

Ruskin was buried in the corner of Coniston churchyard. A Runic cross 9 feet high, covered with symbolic representations of his principal works, bears the simple inscription—John Ruskin, 1819–1900.

In the village is a **Ruskin Museum.** It is about 100 yards from the church, on the Yewdale road. " The contents include numerous interesting and valuable articles—drawings by Ruskin, representative of his style at different periods, from maps drawn in early boyhood down to his latest sketches of sunset as seen from his study window at Brantwood. There is also a valuable and varied collection of minerals and other relics, including many manuscripts written by Ruskin at periods covering the greater part of his life, with notes on architectural and mountain subjects. Conspicuously placed are copies after Tintoretto, Prout, Turner, and other artists whom Ruskin admired. There is a set of photographs from the Sheffield Ruskin Museum, and the nucleus of a Ruskin reference library."

On 14th May, 1959, Mr. Donald Campbell set up on Coniston Lake in *Bluebird* the world water speed record of 260·35 miles per hour. He died in 1967 while attempting a further bid.

On Coniston Lake.—The boats are reached by a turning off the Ulverston road near a garage. From this point, setting aside the presiding genius of the scene, the Old Man,[1] the most noticeable feature at first is the head of the lake, which is most beautiful. As we proceed down, the distant fells rise behind us, over the lower hills on the northern shores. On the right the grouping of the Coniston fells open up. First Great How Crags and then Wetherlam come into sight, the spurs of the latter seeming to merge into the rich crags of Holm Fell. In the north Helvellyn, Fairfield and Red Screes show themselves. A little way down the lake on the west side, easily recognisable by its quaint chimneys. is *Coniston Old Hall,* once the seat of the ancient le Fleming family, now a farm-house. Farther down, the precipice of Dow Crags stands up boldly over the shoulder of the Old Man. Beyond this point the scenery deteriorates,and is more in consonance with that of the east shore, which, backed by the uninteresting Coniston Moor, is tame throughout. On that side the most noteworthy objects are *Tent Lodge,* where Tennyson once lived, and a mile lower down, *Brantwood,* boasting a succession of distinguished occupants culminating in Ruskin (*see p. 134*). At the foot of the lake are some pretty bays and islets (*see also* excursions). The mansion on the west shore is *Brown How,* that on the east shore *Water Park.* The voyage up the lake is more attractive than the voyage down, the fells being in front all the way.

Excursions from Coniston

(1) **Tarn Hows** (2½ *m.*).—This is the most attractive short walk near Coniston, and should be *separately* taken by all who do not

[1] Old Man, Alt Maen, " High Crag." This derivation has been challenged.

make a special detour for it, either in coming from or going to other places.[1]

Follow the Barn Gates road as far as the second turn (1½ m. from village) to the left beyond the *Waterhead Hotel*, and nearly opposite the entrance gate to Monk Coniston Hall. Take this turn, and ascend an enclosed road till *Tarn Hows Farm* (2¼ m.) is passed on the left. Here the road emerges into the open and, still ascending, leads up to **Tarn Hows** or " the Tarns." The scene is one of the most lovely in the District. The tarn itself, once a medley of small pools and marsh, was converted some years ago into a graceful lakelet. This has strictly no name. Tarn Hows is properly the farm just passed on the *how* (hill) overlooking Yewdale. From the slopes above the tarn charming prospects are obtained in the direction of the Langdale Pikes with many other fells all around.

Tarn Hows was presented by Sir S. H. Scott to the National Trust and the public are specially asked *not* to leave litter and *not* to light fires.

In returning, you may either descend by a steep cart-track from **Tarn Hows Farm** into **Yewdale**, the main road through which is reached near Yew Tree Farm, or you may bear to the right, and passing between two plantations, and leaving the tarn some distance on the left, regain the Barn Gates road at nearly its highest point, about 1½ miles beyond where you left it. This is the motor road. The particular view-point upon it, reached through a gate on the left, is described on *p.* 91. There is hardly a more beautiful one in the district. There is also a path, **Glen Mary** or **Tom Gill**, descending from the artificial outlet of the tarn, at its south-west corner, to the Coniston–Skelwith road close to Yew Tree Farm. This is the shortest route from the tarn to the Tilberthwaite glen. From near the head of Tom Gill is a striking view of the Langdale Pikes. By turning to the right at the foot of the Gill *Yew Tree Tarn* (National Trust) will be found close to the side of the road ; it was formed artificially for fishing.

(2) A visit is recommended to **Beacon Crag**, a low rocky eminence close to the foot of the lake, overlooking Lake Bank Lodge. It commands a full-length panorama of the lake, with the Westmorland hills forming a noble background, while the Coniston group rises finely to the left. This is the best view up the lake. From Coniston, Lake Bank may be reached by bus. If one part of the journey is to be made afoot, it is preferable to ride *from* Coniston and to walk back—and by the road along the eastern shore of the lake (*see* 5, *p.* 138). The bus route is by Torver.

The more effective plan is to reverse the following route. Follow the Ambleside road (*p.* 139) either afoot or by bus to the cross-road beyond High Cross, and then proceed as directed on *p.* 90.

(3) **Tilberthwaite Gill** (2½ *m.*).—Landslips have robbed the gill

of some of its charm, but it is still one of the most striking rock-ravines in the Lake District, though in grandeur and impressiveness it cannot compare with Piers Gill at Wasdale Head. There used to be a succession of ladders, bridges, steps, and planks, the bed of the stream being too rough and the rock too steep to admit of an ordinary path. The bridges have been partly restored by the Lake District Planning Board, and although it is possible to reach the foot and top of the Gill, the route through the Gill is inaccessible.

Follow the Oxenfell road for about 1½ miles from Coniston, and then take the narrow lane on the left, which runs high above the Yewdale beck. About a mile from the main road the lane arrives at a heap of slate slag. Here is the foot of the gill and here cars must be left.

The scenery about here is almost unique for the Lake District. **Tilberthwaite** is more of a Scottish glen than an English dale. The eastern and northern sides belong to the National Trust.

The rule in English Lakeland is for the transition from the wild to the cultivated part of a valley to be rapid. Where the rough, craggy upper reach, untouched by the ploughshare and affording pasturage for sheep only, comes to an end, the strath itself, rich in meadow and pasture and woodland, begins. The Scottish glen is as rare in England as the English dale is in Scotland. Tilberthwaite, the Watendlath valley, and parts of Borrowdale, are the chief exceptions to this rule. Hence, though Tilberthwaite cannot vie with the magnificent glens for which Scotland is so justly famous, it presents that charm of freshness and variety which is ever grateful to people who are not biased in their appreciation of nature. Its becks run riot at the bottom of deep rocky gills, from whose smallest nooks and crannies spring the freshest and greenest of ferns. The dale has been sadly shorn of timber, but on every side crags, purple and picturesque, diversify the verdure of the grassy slopes. Climb a few yards on the eastern side of the gill, and you see the noble crest of Wetherlam. The glen is sparsely studded with farmsteads, and the patches of cultivated ground about them keep up the memory of the patient toilers who, in days gone by, cleared and tilled the unwilling soil (" thwaite " signifies a " clearing ").

For **Tilberthwaite Gill** the track climbs over the slate refuse at the foot of the gill, and in a few hundred yards drops again to the bend of the stream at which the water issues from the ravine and the steps and bridges begin.

The ravine itself is about two hundred yards long. Its sides, rough and sheer, but of no great height, support a partial vegetation, the yew being conspicuous amongst the trees. Pending the restoration of artificial aids, only the most venturesome can get up the bottom of the gill. Where the gorge ends, just beyond a small fork, a lofty and picturesque waterfall is crossed by a plank bridge. To the left of it is a hole in the rock nearly a hundred yards in length, with a bend in the middle. A descent may be made by a track along the left side of the ravine, to the houses at Tilberthwaite. The view from the higher part of this road commands the Fairfield *massif*, extends far away into Yorkshire, and is altogether very beautiful. Walkers may also continue their journey from the ravine to the top of Wetherlam (*p.* 299).

(4) **The Eastern Shore.** Take bus to Water Yeat on the Greenodd road and take turning to the left that leads across the *Crake.* Immediately beyond the bridge cross a stile on the left and take a field-path which runs by the river for a short distance. From this point the Coniston fells present a most artistic outline. The main road is rejoined and continues past Nibthwaite along the shore, affording alluring views first of the Coniston fells and later of the Helvellyn range. After 4 miles Brantwood (*p.* 134) is passed close at hand on the right. From near Bank Ground there is a charming vista of Tilberthwaite, backed by Lingmoor and Blea Rigg. The village is regained round the head of the lake. (Distance, about 8 *m.*)

(5) **Grizedale.** From the fort of Coniston Lake, and returning along the east shore through Low and High Nibthwaite to Parkamoor, the hills may be crossed through afforested plantations to Grizedale, from which proceed as directed on *p.* 78, re-entering Coniston by the head of the lake.

(6) **By High Cross, Borwick, and Oxenfell.** Take the Ambleside road *viâ* High Cross (*see p.* 139) as far as **Borwick Fold** (3¼ *m.*). Opposite Borwick Lodge a rough lane will be seen ascending on the left. Follow this. The earlier stage is between walls. On the right fine views are obtainable towards Fairfield and Windermere. After a while wire fences take the place of walls. As the lane approaches its summit, glimpses appear of the Langdale Pikes and Bowfell range, and soon after, a magnificent prospect opens of the mountains surrounding the Langdales with Wetherlam on the left. During the descent between Tarn Hows on the left and Arnside Tarn on the right the high character of the scenery is maintained. The main road (for the return to Coniston) is reached at Oxenfell. At the expense of about an extra half-hour an alternative return may be made by *Hodge Close Quarries* and Tilberthwaite. For this cross the road at Oxenfell and pass through a gate almost opposite. From this a rough lane contours round to the Quarries and reaches the main road by the left bank of Tilberthwaite Beck. The views during the earlier part of this route are extensive and of a high order. Time, 3-4 hours.

Coniston to Bowness, by Hawkshead and the Ferry

For *walk* between Coniston and Bowness by Grizedale, *see p.* 71.

Coniston village to Hawkshead, 4 m. ; *the Ferry,* 8 ; *Bowness,* 9½.

This route is fully described the reverse way on *pp.* 77–80. We will therefore now confine ourselves to a mere indication of points at which the tourist may feel uncertainty as to the road to be pursued.

The beginning of the route is past the *Waterhead Hotel* and Monk Coniston Hall to (2½ *m.*) **High Cross,** where the Barngates road diverges to the left, and our road begins almost immediately the long descent of Hawkshead Hill. During the ascent from Coniston beautiful views may be obtained by looking back.

Pedestrians who wish to include **Tarn Hows** (*p.* 135) in the expedition may easily do so by leaving the main road a short mile beyond the *Waterhead Hotel,* on the way, and rejoining it close to the Baptist Chapel at the hamlet of Hawkshead Hill, a little below High Cross.

From High Cross to Hawkshead the footpath (*p.* 79), which strikes out to the right 250 yards beyond the Baptist Chapel, should undoubtedly be preferred to the road. It not only shortens the distance by a quarter of a mile, but is a delightful field-walk. The mountain prospect from it is very beautiful.

After descending Hawkshead Hill, the road turns sharp to the right at *Hawkshead Hall* (*p.* 80), and reaches **Hawkshead** (*p.* 78) in half a mile. Beyond Hawkshead it branches left again with equal abruptness, and works round Esthwaite Water to *Near* and *Far Sawrey,* whence it drops round the southern slope of the Claife Heights to the *Ferry.* (For the Ferry details, *see p.* 57.) Two hundred and fifty yards beyond the other side of the Ferry a footpath diverges to the left, and leads straight to Bowness.

Coniston to Ambleside.

Route (a) viâ **Barn Gates,** 8 *m.*

Fully described the reverse way on *pp.* 121 and 122. The route is usually taken on the outward journey, *from* Ambleside. As far as *High Cross* (2½ *m.*) it is identical with the Bowness route (*above*). Then it affords fine and wide views as it descends to *Barn Gates Inn* (5 *m.*) and *Brathay Bridge* (7 *m.*), where it joins the Langdale route (*p.* 114).

It is a delightful walk from Barn Gates to **Skelwith Bridge** (2 *m.*). Lovely view from *Spy Hill* which is somewhat to the right of the road (*p.* 114).

Route (b) viâ **Oxenfell** (500 ft.) and **Skelwith Bridge,** 8½ *m.* *Buses to Ambleside, Windermere and Bowness.*

From Coniston village the route is northward, with the Yewdale

Beck on the right of the road and the precipitous crags of Yewdale on the left.   There is a footpath as far as the Tilberthwaite Road.

The road bends to the right about 1½ miles from Coniston, leaving the opening into Tilberthwaite (*p.* 137) on the left ; and passing *High Yewdale Farm*, makes a gradual ascent to the top of the pass, 526 ft. above sea-level.   All round here is National Trust property.   The particular yew from which the valley took its name stood in a field close to Yew Tree Farm, but was ruined in a storm in 1894.   Raven Crag and Holme Fell are fine objects on the left, and their appearance is, if anything, enhanced by the artificially-formed *Yew Tree Tarn*.   When the descent into the *Brathay Valley* is commenced, nearly 4 miles from Coniston, the fells surrounding the heads of the Langdales suddenly break upon the vision with telling effect.

Wetherlam is to the immediate left, and very soon we shall recognise the Wrynose depression to the north of it.   Pike o' Blisco, the mountain with the short flat top, Crinkle Crags, three rounded humps, and Bowfell, sloping majestically to the south, succeed ; then, over the intervening height of Lingmoor, which separates Great from Little Langdale, the unmistakable Langdale Pikes are prominent.   In front of us, over Elterwater, is the dip between Loughrigg and the Langdale range.   Farther north Helvellyn and Fairfield are seen with the Grisedale Pass between them.   Red Screes lies north-east ; and then, as the road veers to the right round the copsy slope of Skelwith Brow, the Brathay valley is revealed in front, backed by Wansfell and the High Street range, with the pyramidal Ill Bell for its most conspicuous peak.

Nearly a mile beyond the top of the pass a road branches off at right-angles to the left and descends a steep pitch to **Colwith Bridge** and *Waterfall* (6½ miles, *p.* 116).

The level of the Brathay valley is reached at **Skelwith Bridge** (*p.* 115), by crossing which the traveller enters Westmorland. Skelwith Force is a short distance on the left.

For the remaining three miles see *p.* 115.   The backward views are charming, especially from two bends of the road, but the valley is better seen in ascending than in descending it.   Passing Clappersgate and crossing Rothay Bridge, we then enter Ambleside (*p.* 106).

Coniston to the Langdales, by Tilberthwaite

Coniston to High Tilberthwaite Farm, 3 *m.* ; *Fell Foot,* 5 ; *Blea Tarn Farm,* 6½ ; *Dungeon Ghyll (Old Hotel),* 8.

The route as far as the entrance to Tilberthwaite Gill has been described on *pp.* 136 and 137.

At *High Tilberthwaite Farm,* just beyond the slate refuse at the entrance to the gill, the road forks, the direct route to Dungeon Ghyll passing through the left gate, and that to Little Langdale and Elterwater the right-hand gate.

Dungeon Ghyll may also be reached by the latter route at the expense of an additional mile. The track runs along by Pierce How Beck into Little Langdale, crossing the Brathay a few hundred yards below a most picturesque little stone bridge, called *Slater's Bridge*. For the route onward, *see p.* 116.

The direct road climbs the fell-side to the left of the digression just described, and passing some slate-quarries soon descends into the upper part of *Little Langdale*, branching to the left about a mile after leaving the farm ; and then crossing the valley nearly to **Fell Foot** (*see p.* 124), the farm almost hidden by yew-trees, behind which is Pike o' Blisco. Crossing the Brathay short of Fell Foot, the route turns to the right for three hundred yards, and then, bending sharply to the left, climbs the open moor for *Blea Tarn* by a road which has been for some time visible, and is fully described on *p.* 117. There is a bus service down Great Langdale from the *Old Hotel*.

Coniston to Wasdale Head by Walna Scar (1,990 ft.); Birker Moor (850 ft.), and Eskdale.

Coniston to Seathwaite, 5 *m.* ; *Ulpha,* 8 ; *Stanley Ghyll,* 13½ ; *King George Inn* (*Eskdale*), 15½ ; *Santon Bridge,* 18½ ; *Strands,* 21 ; *Wasdale Head,* 27.

This route crosses the southern spur of the Lancashire fells to the Duddon valley, passes thence over a bleak moor, from which are fine mountain views, and enables the tourist, by making a few digressions, to see the best part of Eskdale. It comprises the most beautiful portion of the Duddon valley, Dalegarth Force (Stanley Ghyll), the finest waterfall in the district, and the view of Wastwater from its foot. It is from the foot the lake is seen to advantage. Walna Scar may be avoided by taking bus to **Broughton** (*Old King's Head* ; *Manor*), and driving thence. The drive from Broughton to Ulpha (5 *m.*), where the pony-route over Walna Scar converges, is one of great and increasing interest. Motorists should take the east side of the Duddon, walkers may take either side.

The **Logan Beck**, which is crossed on the west side about half-way between Broughton and Ulpha, is a stream of great beauty, though almost unknown. A road, winding high up on the south side of it, crosses the fells to Bootle. About half a mile to the right of the highest part of this road (about 1 hr. from the Duddon valley) is a wild rocky height, locally known as *Worm* or *Buckbarrow Crag*. The rocks which comprise it are thrown about in chaotic confusion—all the more striking from the generally uninteresting character of the adjacent fells.

The *Walna Scar* track passes out of Coniston under the railway bridge, leaving the old station on the left, and thence ascends through a wooded dingle, with a beck on the same side. About

½ m. from the station it takes a sharp turn to the left, and immediately afterwards another to the right. The open fell is reached at
Fell Gate, near which four tracks diverge. The one most to the
right is a good cart-load, leading up to the slate-quarries on the
Old Man. The next to it, almost in a line with the previous part of
our route is the Walna Scar track. Follow this [the retrospective
view hereabouts is glorious (*see* p. 281)], avoiding a track to the
left, about 300 yards farther, and passing Boo Tarn, the smallest
in the district. All by-tracks to the right must be disregarded ;
that to the quarries by Goats Water is most misleading. The
true route skirts the southern shoulder of the Old Man, and crosses,
by a bridge, *Torver Beck*, the stream which descends from *Goats
Water* (*Gaits Water*), a wild and lonely tarn in the hollow between
the Old Man and the screes and precipices of Dow Crag. After
crossing the beck, the track, alternately stony and grassy, is seen
zigzagging up to the summit ridge of Walna Scar. During the
ascent the retrospect is equal to that from above Fell Gate ;
and when the top of the pass is reached at **Walna Scar,** the whole
line of fells from Black Combe to Scafell Pike breaks upon the
view with almost startling effect.

Bowfell just peers over the high ground to the right. Black
Combe is the whale-backed mountain terminating the southern spur
of the long range which extends as far northward as the Whinlatter
Fells on the west of Bassenthwaite lake. It strongly resembles the
Wrekin. In front of Black Combe almost the whole of the lower
Duddon valley is visible ; and for that short period of the day during
which the tide is fully up, the view over Duddon sands is a smiling
relief to the frowning fell-scenery northward. Westward of the
Scafell group are the mountains between Wasdale and Ennerdale,
the Steeple and Haycock being prominent.

From the summit of the pass an unmistakable track leads first
obliquely down the fell-side and then straight down. Soon it
becomes a road to the side of a beck called *Longhouse Gill*, which is
visible all the way down, and beside which it keeps till the first
house in the valley is reached ; after which it turns left, and soon
joins the Wrynose road, rather more than half a mile north of
Seathwaite Church and the *Newfield Hotel.* At the junction a
guide-post directs to Langdale, Broughton, and Coniston. This
Seathwaite, by the way, must not be confused with the hamlet of
the same name in Borrowdale.

The shortest and best (though bad at its best) walking route from
Seathwaite to **Eskdale** is :—
From the guide-post follow the Langdale route northward, for
about ½ m., first crossing the Seathwaite Tarn beck, and then
climbing the ridge which separates it from the main Duddon valley.
Then, beyond a cattle grid, descend by a grass pathway to the
Duddon itself, which may be crossed by stepping-stones. (Should
the Duddon be in flood, instead of following the Langdale road, turn
down the valley as far as Seathwaite Church and cross a stile on
the right. The path leads across a footbridge to Wallowbarrow

Gorge (*National Trust*), where the Duddon is crossed by another foot-bridge. The track leads through a wood and then joins a cart-road which runs up a steep hill-side and across some fields to Grass Guards.) During the descent a fine waterfall, **Gill Spout**, is seen across the valley. This the tourist will probably turn aside to visit as he climbs the fell on the other side. At the head of the valley, northward, the graceful peak of Bowfell stands out with telling effect ; and southward, the deep gorge of the Duddon stream reminds one of the Devil's Bridge scenery near Aberystwyth. About ½ m. beyond the stepping-stones the track reaches a farm-house called **Grass Guards**, the only dwelling between the Duddon valley and Eskdale. Here the stream is crossed by stepping-stones. Hence there is a road up to a peat-bog, when the track practically ceases. Keep well to the right under the southern slope of Harter Fell, which may be easily ascended *en route* if desired. At the highest part of the moor, about half an hour's walk beyond Grass Guards, and close to a worked peat-bog, a wall descending from Harter Fell is crossed. At length a clearly marked track descends to the Eskdale end of the Hardknott Pass, crossing a stream by means of stepping-stones, about half an hour's walk from the *Woolpack Inn*. During the descent, Haycock, the Steeple, and the Pillar come into view over the dip between Wasdale Screes and Scafell. Also in view is the peak of Bowfell in front, between which and the Burnmoor Tarn depression are the wild precipices of Scafell Pike and Scafell.

Those who wish to reach the inns in Eskdale by the shortest route should leave the track at a point where it is nearest to the beck and the wall bends to the left. By a sharp descent they will reach *Penny Hill Farm* in the valley and the " Doctor's Bridge," close to the *Woolpack*.

Proceeding down the Duddon valley by the main road we pass, in half a mile, **Seathwaite Church.**

Nothing but the venerable yews around the former serve to remind the passer-by of the days when that model Jack-of-all-trades, the " **Wonderful Walker**," amassed a fortune out of a variety of occupations, the profits of any single one of which would not have sufficed to keep him from beggary. His nest-egg was his stipend as vicar of the parish, amounting at first to five pounds; but this, as time wore on, increased to £50, and to it he added the fruits of his casual labours, becoming, as occasion required, teacher, lawyer, doctor, woodcutter, wool-spinner, day-labourer, and beer-seller. In the last-named capacity, we are told, he dispensed excellent home-brewed to his congregation on Sunday afternoons. Having educated his children and exercised what must be regarded as a bountiful hospitality and charity to all, he closed his long-suffering and self-denying life, after being Vicar for 66 years, at the age of ninety-two, leaving a fortune of £2,000. His grave—covered by a flat slab—is on the south side of the church and the right-hand side of the walk. Seldom, if we may believe local tradition, has a poet's fancy needed to exaggerate fact so little as did Wordsworth's when he sang the praises of Robert Walker (1709–1802).

Opposite the church a rough footpath strikes off, crossing the stream at once and reaching in ½ mile Wordsworth's **Stepping-stones** across the River Duddon, at a point quite close to the deep rocky gorge mentioned above. The stones are covered after a slight freshet, and impassable dry-footed. The path continues to the farms of Wallowbarrow, where it becomes a road, rejoining the main road at the next-mentioned bridge.

One and a half miles beyond the church Dunnerdale Bridge is crossed, and at a like distance farther on we reach the *Traveller's Rest* at **Ulpha.** For notes on the neighbourhood, *see* p. 210. This is the southernmost point on the road, for from Ulpha the road zigzags up through coppice woods to the right, and soon gains the open fell—**Birker Moor,** to the north-west. In a little over a mile the farmhouse of *Crosbythwaite* is passed on the right, and at about the same distance beyond, a track skirting the south shore of *Devoke Water* (good fishing) branches off to the left.

Walkers who wish to visit **Dalegarth Force** (*Stanley Ghyll*) on the way to Boot and Wasdale Head should diverge from the road north-ward, about ¾ m. after passing the farm-house, and a few hundred yards beyond a gateway, following an ill-defined cart-track, which leads to a cluster of farm-buildings called *Birkerthwaite.* The exact track is difficult to discover at times, but the Pillar mountain, which rises in the distance over the brow of the moor, is a good guide. Birkerthwaite is a full two miles beyond Crosbythwaite, and from it an obvious road runs to the bottom of Eskdale, passing another farmstead called *Low Ground* about ½ m. beyond Birker-thwaite, whence it drops steeply and tortuously into **Eskdale,** crossing the Esk and then entering the main road of the valley. This can be reached by turning right at the cross roads near Devoke Water, then follow the road past *Low Ground,* and half a mile beyond, just before a plantation on the right, leave road to enter plantation by a wooden stile about ¼ mile to right of road. Descend by path through plantation, bear right at beck, down some steps which lead in to Stanley Ghyll.

The *Burnmoor Inn* at **Boot** is about ½ m. up the valley, and is reached by taking the first turn to the left in that direction. The *Woolpack* is only a short mile higher up.

After passing the turn to Devoke Water, the road traverses the bleak moor for a couple of miles. The nearer eminences are tame to a degree ; but the fells northward beyond Wastwater present a striking contour. The chief heights are Haycock, the Steeple, and the Pillar. To the right of the latter Kirk Fell is soon seen ; and still farther in the same direction, and nearer at hand, the towering heights of Scafell, between which and Kirk Fell appears Great Gable. The road to Dalegarth Force (Stanley Ghyll, *p.* 126) strikes off ¼ mile short of a farm-house called *High Ground,* through the yard of which it passes. The direct one to Strands and Wasdale Head turns sharply to the left soon after commenc-ing the steep part of the descent, and for a while seems to be going right away from the district towards the flats of Lower Eskdale and the sea. On reaching the valley, however, it sweeps round to the north again, and, after crossing the Esk, joins the Ambleside and Wastwater road close to the *George IV Inn.* For the rest of the route, *see pp.* 128 and 129.

GRASMERE

Angling.—*See p. 26.*
Banks.—*Barclays, National Westminster,* Mondays and Fridays.
Boats on the lake.
Buses, etc., to and from Ambleside, Waterhead, Windermere–Bowness, Keswick, etc.
Church.—Sunday services, 8, 10.30, 6. Also Methodist and Roman Catholic.
Distances.—(*By road*) Ambleside, 4 *m.*; Windermere, 9; Bowness, 10; Coniston, 10; Keswick, 12½; Ullswater, 14.
Hotels.—*Prince of Wales,* on the lake; *Rothay,* close by the church; *Moss Grove* (unl.) near the church; *Red Lion,* in the village; *Swan,* on main road, ½ *m.* from village; *Dale Lodge,* in village.
Population, about 1,000.
Postal Address.—" Grasmere, Cumbria." *Tel.*—" Grasmere."
Public Hall, where there are annual picture exhibitions by local artists.
Sports (*see p.* 147).
Tennis Courts, Keswick Road.
Youth Hostels.—*High Close, Butharlyp How, Thorney How.*

The aggregation of lake, village, church, valley and mountain forms a scene which can hardly fail to hold a lasting place in the memory of even the most casual of sightseers; while those who love Nature for herself will never, after once seeing it, wonder why one of the truest of Nature's poets chose it as his resting-place in life and death.

The first thing one does in Grasmere is to visit **Wordsworth's Grave.** It is in the far (south) corner of the churchyard, beside the murmuring Rothay. A simple upright slate slab bears the inscription, "William Wordsworth, 1850." "Mary Wordsworth, 1859." Behind is the more elaborate tombstone of Hartley Coleridge (*d.* 1849). The yews were planted by Wordsworth himself. Other members of the Wordsworth family are buried in the churchyard, and among the more noteworthy tombs is that of Sir John Richardson, the discoverer of the remains of Franklin. There is an inscription on his mother's tomb to Arthur Clough, the Rugby poet who died in Florence in 1861.

Dove Cottage, the residence of Wordsworth from 1799 to 1808, stands at Town End on the Old (Wishing Gate) road, half a mile from the church and on the far side of the Keswick–Ambleside main road. To it he brought his wife, Mary Hutchinson, in 1802. It was afterwards inhabited for many years by de Quincey. The house and an adjacent Museum are a repository for relics of the poet and of ancient Grasmere. (*Combined ticket for admission to the Cottage and Museum available. Closed Sundays.*) After leaving Dove Cottage Wordsworth lived at Allan Bank (1808–11) and the Rectory (1811–13) where two of his children died.

Grasmere Church (St. Oswald's) is a massive but barnlike structure, which no one with an eye to the picturesque would wish to see altered.

It may be that, as tradition says, Oswald, King of Northumbria in the 7th century, gave his name to the old well here, and founded the church ; but the earliest existing record of Grasmere states that when the Conqueror gave the Barony of Kendal to Ivo de Talebois, "Gris-mere" had a chapel, which then passed with Kendal over to St. Mary's, York. It came into the hands of the Bellinghams, and afterwards to the le Fleming family. The registers date back as far as 1570, and in Kendal Museum are some bits of ancient carving taken from the church.

It seems pretty certain that the earliest church stood on the foundations of the present nave. The lower tower may, together with the lower walls of the nave, perhaps be as old as the 13th century. To these was added the north aisle, with a separate roof ; and later, at a date unknown, the two parts were covered under one wide roof by raising an ugly skeleton wall to bear it above the present nave arches : hence the curious appearance of the central wall. In 1851 the east walls were rebuilt, in 1893 new windows were put in the south aisle and in 1937 the east window was renewed.

It is, indeed, as Wordsworth said, "for duration built," rather than "raised in nice proportion." Before entering the quaint south porch note, just to the left of the porch, the oldest window, which may date perhaps from the 13th century.

The most noticeable features within are the central wall explained above, and the forest of "naked rafters intricately crossed." The font, at the west end, has an ancient top, said to have come from Furness Abbey. In the choir is a piscina. The poor box dates from 1648. The two alms-dishes (south wall, near door) were found a few years ago in the old tithe barn, now the Rectory Room. On the north side of the nave is the tablet to Wordsworth (1851), bearing a portrait by Woolner, with an inscription telling how the poet—

> " Whether he discoursed on men or nature,
>   Failed not to lift up the heart
>   To holy things."

In rather different vein is the inscription on a wall tablet almost opposite that to Wordsworth, and beginning :—

> " These vales were saddened with no common gloom
>   When good Jemima perished in her bloom."

In the chancel is a tablet by Chantry to Mrs. Quillinan (1822). The chancel doorway, from the mason's mark, was, it seems certain, brought from Furness Abbey. At the west end a tablet recalls that Frank Bramley, R.A. (d. 1915), lived at Tongue Gill.

Two ancient local customs deserve mention. By an ancient religious regulation the men and women sat apart here until as late a date as 1861. The "men's door" was the old one at the west end.

Grasmere is one of the few northern villages where a **Rush Bearing** is still held. This takes place here on the Saturday nearest August 5th (St. Oswald's Day); and records exist of its annual observance at least as far back as 1682. The custom, which was a common one in the churches of London and elsewhere up to the 15th and 16th centuries, originated in the strewing of the floors with rushes in lieu of carpets. The fact that for the " ale bestowed on ye rush-bearers " in the 17th century was substituted " gingerbread for rush-bearers " in the registers of 1830, is, perhaps, a sign of the times. In the Public Hall is a celebrated picture of the ceremony, by the late Frank Bramley. It is vested in the National Trust. A similar rush-bearing takes place at Ambleside (*see p.* 107), where the festival is practically a flower service, and also at Musgrave, and Warcop and Urswick-in-Furness, but nowhere else in the diocese of Carlisle.

Grasmere is the most central of all the so-called tourist centres of the Lake District, yet its attractiveness results rather from its own intrinsic merits than from its position with regard to other places. Situated as it is, in the midst of the mountains, it has not so many road outlets as either Ambleside or Keswick. Northward the high road passes over Dunmail Raise, but does not admit of any divergence till the road along the west side of Thirlmere (*p.* 85) strikes off. Southward, Ambleside is reached in four miles, and there is also a good but forbiddingly steep road leading into Langdale, by Red Bank, and so on to Coniston.

The pedestrian, however, in search of good headquarters will find in Grasmere a veritable Paradise. From it he may radiate in as many directions as he pleases. Windermere, Coniston, Ullswater, Derwentwater, and Thirlmere are all within a day's march there and back. Helvellyn, Fairfield, the Langdale Pikes, and Coniston Old Man may each be climbed between sunrise and sunset ; and, at the expense of one night out, any other lake in the district may be visited, or almost any other mountain climbed.

The principal part of the village is situated at the north end of the lake, and some way to the left of the direct road from Windermere to Keswick. Two of the hotels, however—the *Prince of Wales* and the *Swan*—and the part of the parish called Town End, as well as a goodly number of modern villas, are on, or close to, the direct highway. A large proportion of the houses in the parish cater for visitors.

The **Grasmere Sports** are an important event. They are held annually on the Thursday nearest the 20th of August (the " Derby day " of the district), and include the guides' race up and down Grey Crag, immediately above the arena, wrestling, hound trails, etc. Over 10,000 people usually attend. The centenary of this famous Lakeland meeting was celebrated in 1952.

Excursions from Grasmere

Distances reckoned from the church.

The country about Grasmere is full of pleasant little walks. The favourite ones are round the lake by Loughrigg Terrace (4 m.) ; Easedale Tarn (5 m. there and back) ; Tongue Gill (3½ m. there and back) ; Helm Crag (4 m. up and down) ; Silver How (3½ m. up and down) ; the Wishing Gate (2 m. there and back).

1. **Loughrigg Terrace (round Grasmere Lake).** *Loughrigg Terrace*, 1½ m. ; *Grasmere*, 4 m.

In making this round you return by a footbridge (Shepherds' Bridge) across the Rothay between Grasmere and Rydal Lakes. The walk may be extended to six miles by including the circuit of the latter. In so doing you cross the Rothay, either by Pelter Bridge close to Rydal village or by the plank bridge opposite the *Glen Rothay Hotel*, and return to Grasmere by the high road (*bus route*) or by the path described on p. 110.

Take the Skelwith road from Grasmere, bending round the west side of the lake. It is preferable, about a mile beyond the church, to take an alternative road, with telegraph-posts, on the right, which contours along the hill-side at a higher level than the main road. Before long the road becomes a track. At a point where it ascends more steeply and directly upwards, go through a gate on the left, whence a path commanding views through the trees of Grasmere Lake leads out on the main road close to the summit of **Red Bank** (523 ft.). Shortly turn down a rough lane to the left and you will, in 300 yards, reach the west end of **Loughrigg Terrace.**

If you do not intend on another occasion to take the drive or walk from Grasmere to Langdale or Skelwith Bridge, you should continue along the road 100 yards farther and turn to the right. After passing *High Close* (300 yds.), the youth hostel on the highest point of the road, you will obtain a splendid view over the Langdales and Elterwater to the Old Man, Wetherlam, Bowfell, and the Langdale Pikes. A return is then made to the rough lane to Loughrigg Terrace.

Beyond the gate through which the path proceeds on to the open fell-side, a narrow grass-path winds steeply up. This is the best way up **Loughrigg** from Grasmere. The top (1,100 ft.) is not visible from Red Bank, but it may be reached in less than half an hour by following this path and continuing as straight forward as possible after it has ceased. There are two summits, a very short distance from one another, each boasting its cairn, and the tourist should go from one to the other for the sake of the difference in the near views. In descending to Grasmere keep as much as possible in a line with the western shore of the lake. For the view from Loughrigg Fell, *see* p. 110.

View from Loughrigg Terrace.—From this point the view— lake, vale, and village—breaks upon the eye with magical effect.

The lake lies nearly 300 feet below, and the steep, green slope descending to it is covered with bracken, whereby the prospect is greatly enhanced in the late autumn. To the left the steep western slope is beautifully timbered with a variety of trees, till it sinks down to a level greensward on the north. There, at the far end of the lake, is the village, with squat church tower, very picturesque in its relation to the surrounding scene. All round, and beyond, for several miles, the valley extends, studded with villas and farmsteads, and remarkable for its verdure even among the green valleys of Westmorland. The high road to Keswick may be seen climbing its eastern side, as far as the semicircular dip of Dunmail Raise, formed by Seat Sandal on the right hand and Steel Fell on the left. The mountain in the rear, filling up the gap, is the eastern spur of Skiddaw, Lonscale Fell. Beyond Seat Sandal, Helvellyn appears on the left, and Dollywaggon Pike on the right, and, to the right of the latter, the Grisedale Pass, leading to Ullswater. Nearer at hand on the same side, an arm of Fairfield stretches southward to Nab Scar, whence it descends abruptly to Rydal Water. The stream connecting Grasmere with Rydal is seen winding its way, through a grove of varied foliage to the east, but the latter lake is not visible from our present standpoint. Turning northwards again, we see between us and Steel Fell, Helm Crag, and to the left of it the commencement of the Easedale valley. Loughrigg Fell shuts out all view to the south, and Silver How is the prominent feature to the west.

The path descends slightly, traversing the steep northern slope of Loughrigg, but keeping over two hundred feet above the lake. When the track passes beyond the side of the lake it mounts a low ridge from the crest of which an exquisite surprise view of Rydal Water, backed by Nab Scar, delights the eye. From this point a short, steep descent to Rydal Water commences, having a wall and a wood on the left. Go through a wicket-gate in this wall, and drop down for about five minutes through the wood till you reach Shepherds' Bridge (*see above*). The high road is just on the other side of this, and you may either follow it round the sharp turn which brings Grasmere into sudden view, or you may cross the low, rocky hillock in front by the old and more direct thoroughfare which re-enters the modern road 200 yards beyond Wordsworth's Cottage. This saves a quarter of a mile. At a turn half a mile along this old road is the *Wishing Gate* (renewed 1948) into a field on the left, and the least superstitious will not begrudge a few minutes' halt for the sake of the beautiful view.

2. Easedale Tarn (2½ *m.*, 1¼ *hr.*).

Easedale Tarn is situated in a wild upland valley north-west of Grasmere. It is 915 ft. above sea-level. The walk up to it is the favourite short excursion from Grasmere, and owes its attraction almost entirely to its immediate surroundings, there being no distant views except the retrospective one over

Grasmere Lake, which is very charming. There is a good though roughish pony-track all the way, and an old stone hut close to the tarn. Walkers may continue over the fells into Langdale or Borrowdale, climbing *en route*, if so disposed, the Langdale Pikes, Sergeant Man, and High White Stones.

The position of the tarn is easily discovered from Grasmere by the stream which flows out of it. A long and broken streak of white foam, called Sour Milk Force, forms part of this stream, and is conspicuous from almost all parts of the valley. The tarn lies above it about half a mile beyond.

The Easedale Road is indicated by a stone slab in the wall as one leaves the village in the direction of the *Swan Hotel*. Avoid a turn to the right, and half a mile from the village cross the Easedale beck by a bridge of stone slabs and continue through the meadow beyond.

From the footbridge up to the tarn the track keeps the stream on the right. After crossing Blindtarn Gill, which flows from Blindtarn Moss, keep straight ahead in the direction of **Sour Milk Force**, which forms a striking feature in the whole scene. Looking back, you see the lower portion of the Grasmere valley and part of the lake, backed by Nab Scar and Loughrigg Fell, between which Wansfell Pike (beyond Ambleside) fills up the distance. Silver How is on the left as you advance, and Helm Crag, with its rocky summit-ridge, on your right. The main Easedale valley, of which the basin containing Easedale Tarn is only a branch ("a vale within a vale"), stretches upwards a little to the right; and over the depression to the west of Helm Crag, parts of Seat Sandal and Fairfield, with the Grisedale Pass to Patterdale between them, are visible.

Easedale Tarn presents itself very suddenly, just as you breast the steepish pitch beyond Sour Milk Gill. The fells drop into it from all sides, except the one from which we have approached, more or less steeply, and to the north precipitously. The scene is wild without being in any way bare, the abundant heather and fern growth, as well as the craggy character of the ground, giving it an appearance of velvety luxuriance. The water is generally still and dark, but at times, when the storm rushes down the narrow ravines, and expands itself over the wider surface of the lake, the spray is apt to be flung up mountains high. Altogether, it is, perhaps, the best scene of its kind in the district.

For the way on to Dungeon Ghyll, *see p.* 155.

3. Ascent of Helm Crag.—*An hour's steep climb.* 1,300 *ft. above sea-level,* 1,100 *ft. above the lake.*

No one walking from Grasmere should omit this climb. The view from the top is far inferior to that from many equal or even less elevations—notably to those from Loughrigg and Silver How —but the weird and chaotic nature of the summit-ridge gives it a character of its own. For rocks and boulders,

" Confusedly hurl'd
The fragments of an earlier world,"

nothing can, on a small scale, surpass it in the district. It is an excellent spot for a picnic.

The ascent is best made from the Easedale valley. Follow the track to Easedale Tarn (*p.* 150) as far as the footbridge, instead of crossing which keep on the road for about a third of a mile, and then ascend to the right between some houses. Passing through a gate, you leave the track for Far Easedale on the left, and then turn sharp to the right up an old quarry road with a wall on the right, leaving it in a couple of minutes, and ascending by a fair track that zigzags up the green slope with a wall first on the left and then on the right hand. When you reach the highest point of the latter wall and look over into the vale of Grasmere, turn to the left along a narrow grass-path which traverses the eastern slope of the fell, and in a few hundred yards rises to the ridge by another sharp bend to the left. Hence the top is reached in a few minutes. The curiously poised crags which have given to **Helm Crag** its notoriety are about 250 yards apart. The first group is the *Lion and the Lamb,* the second the *Lady at the Organ* (*see p.* 84), etc. Just underneath the first is a deep hole paved with boulders of every shape and size, and scattered about in the most promiscuous fashion. Herein, should a storm come on, no matter from what point of the compass, there is shelter both from rain and wind but local opinion maintains that the place is not very safe.

View from Helm Crag.—The view northward and westward extends only as far as the loftier heights of High Raise and Steel Fell : southward, Windermere and one of its islands appears over Loughrigg, and Esthwaite Water over the north end of Grasmere Lake. Farther west than Esthwaite are the Lancashire fells, the most prominent of them being Wetherlam ; then Pike o' Blisco and Crinkle Crags, the continuation of the range being lost behind the nearer height of Harrison Stickle, one of the Langdale Pikes. To the right of the latter Easedale Tarn and Sour Milk Gill are seen. Northward the gap between Steel Fell and Seat Sandal is filled by Saddleback ; and eastwards, Helvellyn and Fairfield bound the prospect.

In returning, leave the lane by a small gate and some steps on the left, and proceed by a very pretty footpath that goes behind Lancrigg into the Easedale road again.

[The walk may be continued along the ridge from **Helm Crag,** round the head of **Greenburn Bottom,** and over **Steel Fell** down into the Grasmere valley again. There is no big dip, but a constant succession of small ones which make the journey tedious : and having regard to the many superior walks of the same kind in all parts of the district, it is doubtful whether the expedition is to be recommended.]

4. Silver How and over the Fells to Langdale. (*See also p.* 154.)

The long and broken range of hills that separates Grasmere from Langdale affords a great variety of easy and delightful excursions. For a moderately short walk the tour of Silver How is admirable. The view is comprehensive and charming, the great feature of it being the number of lakes. The short velvety grass, too, is an attraction.

The shortest way to Great Langdale is by the route that passes at its highest point (about 1,320 feet) under Yew Crag. This, too, is the first part of a very interesting walk to Sergeant Man and High Raise, whence the return is best made by Greenup Edge and Far Easedale.

The Meg's Gill route to Chapel Stile in Great Langdale may be recommended with or without the ascent of Silver How.

Silver How, *about* 1,300 *feet* ; 1¼–2 *hours* (3½ *m.*) *up and down.* From the village take the road that leads through the Allan Bank property to two small farm-houses called Score Crag. These you leave below on the right, and proceed alongside a rough enclosed track which, beyond a second gate (1 *m.*), comes out on to open ground.

Hence for **Great Langdale** (4 *m.* from Grasmere ; 1½ *hrs.*) or **High Raise** (6 *m.* ; 2¼ *hrs.*) continue up between the crags that face you. The path becomes intermittent, and then ceases. A square-topped castle-like hill seen in the right front over an intervening ridge is *Blea* (*Castle*) *Rigg.*

It is pleasant going over short grass, thick with juniper bushes, as we approach the *col,* looking down into *Blindtarn Moss,* as an old lake-bed on the right is called. This *col* is just beyond the rocky slope by Yew Crag. From it a splendid view up Great Langdale bursts on the eye, terminating in the Oxendale branch, with Crinkle Gill, Crinkle Crags, Pike o' Blisco, Bowfell, and the Pikes in their full glory. It is well to add that in misty weather this route is exceedingly puzzling.

The descent into Langdale, a mile short of the *New Dungeon Ghyll Hotel,* Langdale, is obvious—a steep, grassy slope.

For **High Raise,** bending to the right from the *col* round Yew Crag, you will in about a mile come to *Blea Rigg* beyond which the Grasmere and Langdale route by Codale Tarn is crossed. On the left is the fine precipice of Pavey Ark, with Stickle Tarn at its foot, and right ahead **Sergeant Man** (2,414 *ft.*)—a knob with an obelisk-like cairn—has long been conspicuous, and a stiff climb lands us upon it. Hence to High Raise the ascent is gentle, over long grass. For **High Raise** (2,500 *ft.*) and the view there from, *see p* 252.

For **Silver How** turn up to the left after reaching the open ground, and climb by a track that leaves an intake on the left, followed, after a bend to the right, by a shallow gill on the right and a deeper one on the left. Crossing the latter at a bend near its head, you reach the summit, which is marked by a cairn, in 8 to 10 minutes.

View from Silver How.—The features of the view are the charming foreground of greensward, wood, and water, the grand array of mountains, and the number of lakes. Grasmere—village and lake —Rydal, Windermere, Elterwater, and Loughrigg Tarn are seen to perfection. To the left of the Old Man group there is a glimpse of Coniston. The mountain environment extends from Wetherlam to the Langdale Pikes on one side ; from Wansfell Pike to Helvellyn on the other. Over the gap of Dunmail Raise, Saddleback appears. Scafell Pike is hidden by Bowfell.

It is worth while to descend in a direction some way to the right of the old rifle-butts, till you look down **Meg's Gill** into the opening of Great Langdale at Elterwater village. Then return and keep between the crags on your left and a large plantation on the right. The path enters a lane which comes out into the Red Bank road opposite the boat-landings, five minutes short of the church. The commencement of the path for the descent is not quite easy to find.

Grasmere to Langdale by Meg's Gill, $4\frac{1}{2}$ m. ; **2 hrs.** ($5\frac{1}{2}$ m., $2\frac{1}{2}$ hrs., including *Silver How*). A very interesting walk. Leave the Red Bank road by a lane opposite the boat-landings (5 *min.* from the church). The lane leads to a field up which you continue to the left and soon find yourself between crags on the right and a large plantation on the left. Keep under the crags and you will soon look down *Meg's Gill* on to Elterwater. The gill is wild and beautiful, making a pretty cascade or two. A narrow path crosses it above the bend, and drops into Langdale half a mile north-west of the church.

5. The Walk to Rydal, $2\frac{1}{2}$ m. From Town End (at the junction of the Keswick–Ambleside road with that south-eastward from the church) take the lane past Dove Cottage (*p.* 145). At the top of the succeeding hill, however, instead of the Wishing Gate road take the still higher one, passing on the left White Moss Tarn, and avoiding the steep descent by White Moss to Rydal Water on the right. After that the path is unmistakable. It is described the reverse way, *p.* 83.

6. Nab Scar and the Fairfield Ridge. The best way of ascending Nab Scar from Grasmere is by the path starting from beyond Wordsworth's Cottage at Town End. Another route starts at the *Swan Hotel*. *Time,* $1–1\frac{1}{4}$ hr. from Grasmere to top of ridge (Lord's Crag) ; $\frac{3}{4}–1$ hr. thence to Rydal ; $\frac{3}{4}$ hr. back to Grasmere.

From Wordsworth's Cottage follow the old road up the hill and at the far end of the open green turn sharp left. In a few yards the road becomes a rough lane ascending through a fir plantation. Where the lane ceases just above a gateway and the wall on the left strikes away, bear slightly to the left (avoid plainer path), but not alongside the wall. Almost at once another wall fronts you, and the path, now easily followed, keeps ascending round two sides of a rough and steep enclosure, looking down into *Dunney Beck* and the spot where the Manchester Waterworks tunnel under Nab Scar begins. Then, after bending back for a few yards round the third side of the enclosure, it winds up towards the ridge, and soon vanishes. If bound for *Nab Scar* bear a little to the right in climbing to the ridge ; if for *Fairfield*, to the left, past Alcock Tarn—an old reservoir.

An *alternative route* to **Rydal Fell** and **Nab Scar** is from the *Swan Hotel* by Greenhead Gill, crossing the gill at Greenhead and leaving it soon after by a fairly marked steep zigzag path to **Butter Crags** near Alcock Tarn, whence there is a fine view up the valley and of the upper part of Greenhead Gill. From **Alcock Tarn** there is a magnificent panorama including Windermere, Rydal, and Coniston.

For the descent to Rydal from Nab Scar, *see* p. 276 and for footpath Rydal to Grasmere, *p.* 83.

7. The Wishing Gate (1 *m.*). From Town End follow the old road, past Wordsworth's Cottage (*p.* 145). The gate is at a bend of the road (*see Map and p.* 148). The view over the lake, up Easedale, and as far as the Langdale chain, is very charming.

The walk may be continued down to the new road again as shown in map.

8. Tongue Gill (1¾ *m.*).—One of the most refreshing small-scale pictures even round Grasmere, and as pretty a waterfall as any in the district. It is about a quarter of a mile from the commencement of the Grisedale Pass route (*p.* 160) at the foot of a steep, bracken-covered slope on the right.

9. Fairfield direct, 4 *m.* to top ; 4 to 4½ hours up and down. Take the road that goes north-eastward from the south side of the *Swan*, and becomes a lane at cross-roads, continuing up a shady gill. In one-third mile it bends to the left, leaving the beck, and then zigzags through the bracken up a very steep slope over Greenhead Gill, between two walls crossing the pipe-track of the waterworks and then bending to the right on to the open fell, where, after doubling the shoulder of Stone Arthur, it continues northward and joins the route described on *p.* 276 on Great Rigg, a good mile short of Fairfield top.

Grasmere to Langdale. *See also p. 152.*

(*a*) By **Easedale Tarn**, 6–7 *m.* ; 3 to 4 *hrs.* A rough path between Easedale and Stickle Tarns, but a very interesting one. An extra hour will bring the Langdale Pikes (*p.* 250) within the scope of the excursions, and High Raise (*p.* 252) and Sergeant Man (*p.* 119) are equally accessible.

For the route as far as Easedale Tarn, see p. 150.

From the old stone hut, coast along the south side of the tarn, do not cross its main feeder but continue up a steep pitch some way to the left of the course of the stream. This brings you to

Codale Tarn, a deeply nestled sheet of water. Passing along the south side of this also, you may either ascend Sergeant Man, or soon bear away to the left across the ridge for Stickle Tarn. On gaining the top of the ridge, a splendid view opens up before you across Great Langdale to Crinkle Crags, Pike o' Blisco, and Wetherlam. **Stickle Tarn** lies a few hundred feet below, and frowning over its northern shore are the precipices of Pavey Ark, backed by Harrison Stickle, the chief of the Pikes of Langdale. The descent is accomplished by a path, steep and very rough at first, from the dam at the south of the tarn, that goes pretty direct, with Mill Gill on the left, to the *New Dungeon Ghyll Hotel*. An alternative route is to strike up the fell-side from the old stone hut at Easedale Tarn to the ridge line with Blea Rigg crags on the right. This avoids Codale, which is swampy, and stuffy. A middle course, leaving Blea Rigg on the left and Codale on the right, is partly marked by small cairns.

If you go on over Pavey Ark to the top of the Pikes, care must be taken in selecting the route of descent to Langdale (*see* p. 252).

(*b*) By **Road,** 6 *m.*; described the reverse way, on p. 114. Take the right turn at the top of Red Bank (2 *m.*), passing High Close—splendid view of Langdales, Bowfell, etc.—and descending by upper road (*see Map*) past Langdale Church (3½ *m.*; *inn*), where route described on *p.* 120 is joined.

A charming variation with a saving of half a mile may be enjoyed by diverging ¾ mile on the way to the right by a narrow road. This soon, at Hunting Stile—whence diverges the beautiful path to the top of Red Bank (*p.* 115)—becomes a track, crosses a lovely *col*, and then drops down by the telegraph-posts to the road as shown on the map.

Grasmere to Keswick.   *Map at end of the book.*

By **main road** (*east or west side of Thirlmere*), *see pp.* 85–6.
Foot Routes (*by the fells*).

There are three ordinary fell-routes from Grasmere to Borrowdale—by Far Easedale, Harrop Tarn, and Armboth Fell respectively. The first-named reaches Rosthwaite by Greenup Edge and the Stonethwaite valley, climbing about 2,000 ft. on the way; the two latter by Watendlath, whence there is a direct road to Keswick, should the tourist be minded to put off Borrowdale to another day. In that case he would be well advised to leave the carriage-track about 1½ miles beyond Watendlath, and explore the magnificent scenery of High Lodore (*see p.* 178), which for rich blending of crag, water, and foliage is unsurpassed in the kingdom. We must in fairness add that the fell portion of these walks is hardly up to the general standard of the mountain-passes of the district except perhaps the Easedale route and that is wearisomely boggy in parts. The high level of the fells which extend north and south from Derwentwater to Langdale Pikes, and east and west from Thirlmere to Borrowdale, is perhaps the least interesting in Lakeland. Splendid panoramic views are, however, afforded, and what dreariness there is lasts a very short time.

1. By Far Easedale and Greenup. *Map at end of the book.*

To Rosthwaite, 4–5 hrs. (about 8 m.). Top of Pass, 1,995 ft. Rosthwaite to Keswick (road), 6½ m.

Leave Grasmere by the Easedale Tarn route (*p.* 150), and instead of crossing the footbridge, keep the road for a third of a mile farther, crossing a meadow, and then turn up to the right between a group of 3 or 4 houses. Beyond these are a gate and a choice of tracks. That dropping to the left at once is the proper one. The rough lane soon becomes a bridle-path, which in another mile crosses the beck by some stepping-stones called *Stythwaite Steps.* The track leads along the main rill of the beck to the top of the grassy slope which forms the head of the Easedale valley, about 2 miles beyond Stythwaite Steps. Experienced mountain walkers will not be surprised to discover that this is not the top of *their* pass. A second ridge appears nearly a mile in front, and about 350 ft. higher than their present standpoint. The intervening depression, winding down to the right, is the *Wythburn valley*, descending to Thirlmere. Be careful not to be misled into following the Wythburn stream, which is most beguiling, especially in misty weather. From the wire fence look ahead for small cairns trending down to the stream, and a bigger cairn and indicator beyond. At this cairn a change of direction is necessary to the left to the guide-post which marks the top of the rise above Borrowdale. This ridge is **Greenup Edge.**

From it a splendid panorama of hill-tops suddenly breaks upon the eye. To the right and left the higher parts of the ridge on which you are standing limit the prospect, Ullscarf being the eminence on the former side, and High Raise on the latter. In front the view extends from the fells on the far side of Derwentwater to those of Buttermere, while the retrospect includes stretches of the Helvellyn and Fairfield range. Glaramara rises due west, on the far side of the Langstrath branch of Borrowdale and to the right of it the precipice of Honister Crag, almost in a line with and below the Buttermere Fells of High Crag and High Stile. Over a dip of Glaramara the Pillar is seen, and Scafell Pike rises to the left of the same mountain.

Several small heaps of stones, placed on big boulders, mark the route across the Edge, and when Skiddaw and Bassenthwaite come into view on the right the track takes that direction, descending very little, until it reaches a crag called *Lining Crag,* down the right-hand side of which flows a small runnel. Descend as near as may be to the runnel, and then thread the numerous moraine heaps which appear at the bottom of the valley. The path soon recommences, and crossing several lateral streamlets keeps the main stream of the valley on the left during the whole

distance to the hamlet of Stonethwaite, *Eagle Crag* bringing to
an abrupt end the ridge which separates it from the Langstrath.
Beyond Eagle Crag we join the latter valley, down which comes
the long rough path from Dungeon Ghyll over the Stake Pass.
As we descend, the front view into Borrowdale, the level of which
is broken by Castle Crag, is very charming. The path becomes a
cart-track where the Greenup Gill enters Langstrath (notice the
charming waters-meet) and opposite **Stonethwaite** (*refreshments,*
etc.) crosses the beck, which has now become a considerable
stream, by a cart bridge.[1] A short distance farther, the road,
after leaving on the left Borrowdale church—opposite to which
a corner may be cut off by taking a self-evident footpath across
two fields—joins the main Borrowdale road about half a mile to
the left of **Rosthwaite** village. For the remaining 6½ miles to
Keswick, *see pp.* 177–83.

2. By Dunmail Raise, Harrop Tarn and Watendlath. *Map at end of the book.*

*To Watendlath, 3–4 hrs. Watendlath to Keswick, 5 m. Highest
point,* 1,750 *ft.*

Either afoot or by motor proceed along the Keswick road
(*pp.* 84–5) for 3½ miles, and then take the west Thirlmere road for
a mile.

A field or so beyond the third farm—*West Head*—strike up to
the left, and pass below some crags, close to which a bridle-path
will be found leading up by the side of *Dob Gill* to **Harrop Tarn.**
This path crosses the beck close to the outlet of the tarn, and
continues for some little way along the north side of it. Above
the level of the plantations the view looking back over the tarn
and the white cottages of Wythburn, on to the sturdy shoulders
of Helvellyn, is good.

Thence keep up well to the right of the main feeder of the tarns
in a line with your previous course and with some craggy heights,
on your right, till you reach the summit of the ridge about a mile
beyond the tarn. Hence is a fine mountain-view to the north
and west. Saddleback, Skiddaw, and Bassenthwaite Lake appear
in the north ; then, westward, comes Grisedale Pike, recognisable
by its gracefully tapering summit, succeeded by the Newlands and
Buttermere Fells, Honister Crag just peeping up below the
latter, south of which the bold contours of the Pillar and Great
Gable close the distant view. *Per contra,* the foreground is
dreary in the extreme. Just below us is one of the several Blea
Tarns of the district, a most dreary sheet of water. Between
us and the tarn lies a sort of moss-hag, which, however, is not
so bad as it looks but requires care of negotiation in mist. The
tarn forms the head-waters of the Watendlath valley. Hence the
best direction is to make for a cairn lying north-west, about half

---

[1] Or you may keep to the lane along the north side and cross a stone bridge
near Rosthwaite.

a mile off, in the direction of Bassenthwaite Lake, and not approaching any nearer to the tarn. The Watendlath valley gradually deepens on the left, but do not be in any hurry to descend into it; rather continue along the ridge with a slight inclination to the north, in the direction of Skiddaw, for upwards of a mile, having a wall on your left during the latter part, and looking down on to Watendlath Tarn, until you strike at right angles the zigzag pony-track, which climbs eastward from Watendlath hamlet, and crosses Armboth Fell to Thirlmere. A five minutes' descent leads into the hamlet of **Watendlath**, where accommodation and " teas " can be obtained. Hence you may continue your journey either over the fell (a climb of only a few hundred feet) to *Rosthwaite* (2 *m.*) by a regular bridle-path, or proceed by a narrow road to Keswick (5 *m.*). As the Rosthwaite track forms part of the next walk (*p.* 159), we shall here adopt the direct Keswick route. For the " *Churn*," see p. 173.

The Watendlath depression is one of the few upland valleys of the district, being from 700 to 800 ft. above sea-level—narrow, beautiful, and secluded.

Proceed by a footpath which starts to the right from across the bridge from Watendlath, rises over a small hill at first, then later drops to the banks of Watendlath Beck. Continue down the valley until you reach a wooden footbridge, cross the bridge, and a few yards up the hill, cross a wooden stile on your left, and proceed to the next wooden stile, continue over this and in the same direction until you reach the road, turn left along here past the view point and down to Ashness Bridge, and on to Keswick. There is a footpath on the left hand side of the road, behind a hedge for much of the last two miles into Keswick. The distance from Watendlath to Keswick is 5 miles.

From the wooden footbridge about a mile below Watendlath, you can also descend to Borrowdale by turning left before crossing the bridge, the path passes through a gateway on the right to enter a wood. The track reaches a stream, but before this, turn left down another path and cross a ladder stile. From here, of all the " Little bits " of Lakeland scenery there are few places to equal this. Crag, water, and foliage of every sort and shade combine to form a series of exquisite pictures, equal to anything of the same kind in Britain. One of the most beautiful is the vista of Derwentwater and Skiddaw, seen through the two precipitous crags which beetle over the famous **Lodore Falls.**

From the stile, follow the winding path down the steep slope (Ladder Brow) from where it commands a splendid view of the **Shepherd's Crag** to the right. This is a favourite place for rock climbers, many of which can frequently be seen in action at week-ends. At the bottom of the slope, you join the Keswick-Borrowdale road at *High Borrowdale Farm*, between the Borrowdale and Lodore hotels. It is about 3½ miles from Keswick. There is a bus service along the road and in the summer season, a launch can be caught at the Lodore landing for a pleasant sail back to Keswick.

3. By Armboth Fell to Rosthwaite.   *Map at end of the book.*
Grasmere to Armboth, west side of Thirlmere, 6½ *m.* (*bus to near Wythburn*).   *Armboth to Watendlath* 1½ *hrs.* ;   *Rosthwaite* 2¼ *hrs.* 5½ *m. Highest point* (High Tove), 1,665 ft.   Route marked by cairns.

This is a more circuitous route than either of the two last described, but the walk or drive along the west side of Thirlmere is fair compensation.   The main Keswick road must be followed to within one-third mile of Wythburn, at which point the west coast route of Thirlmere strikes off, and is followed for 3 miles of hard road to Fisher Gill (6¼ m.).   A few yards farther, passing through a gate (guide-post), you enter a steep path through an enclosed plantation.   This path bends left and then right.   In ¼ m. from the bottom gate you come to a narrow gate, looking through which you will see right ahead the cairn—**High Tove**— which marks the highest point of the fell.   The path continues a little farther, as far as some stones by which Fisher Gill is crossed.   Between this and the cairn is one of the boggiest bits in Lakeland.   The line to be taken passes a little south of High Tove (1,665 *ft.*), beyond which it crosses a wire fence. Hence there is a striking panorama of fells.   Immediately to the right, and forming part of the moorland on which we are standing, is High Seat, only a few hundred feet above us, and hiding Skiddaw, but not Saddleback, which bounds the view to the right of it.   In front, from the south-west to the north-west, are the fells on the other side of Borrowdale and Derwentwater, from Great Gable to the cone of Grisedale Pike.   Southward, Coldbarrow Fell, just beyond Blea Tarn, closes the prospect ; and between it and Great Gable appear Crinkle Crags, Bow Fell, Scafell Pike and Great End.   Glaramara lies between us and the latter.   The Helvellyn range and Fairfield form the eastern distance.

Hence to the few cottages and the tarn of Watendlath is about a mile, still in the same direction, and in a line with the Watendlath and Rosthwaite track, which soon becomes visible in front, the latter part of the descent being by a steep zigzag bridle-path. At **Watendlath** (*p.* 171) refreshments may be had, but there is no inn.   The distance to Keswick is 5 miles down the valley (*pp.* 172-3) by a narrow road.   To Rosthwaite there is a pony-track (*p.* 173) ascending for a few hundred feet, and then rapidly falling into Borrowdale, which is entered just below Rosthwaite, the Stonethwaite beck being crossed in the last few hundred yards. The very finest views of Borrowdale are obtained during the descent.   From **Rosthwaite** to Keswick is 6½ miles (*pp.* 177-9).

Grasmere to Patterdale, by Grisedale Pass. *Map at end of the book.*

Grasmere to Patterdale, 8–9 m. Time, 3–4 hrs. Top of Pass (3½ *m.*), 1,929 *ft.*

This pony-track is not characterised by that wild prodigality of ruggedness which marks the famous passes in the western part of the Lake District ; nevertheless it is strikingly beautiful and very wild. Further, it is eminently practicable. Man, woman, or child possessed of ordinary lung-power may tackle it with confidence. Strong walkers may take either Fairfield or St. Sunday Crag, or both (crossing the narrow ridge between them, *p.* 291), on the outward journey, and return by the pass, or they may climb Helvellyn by Dollywaggon Pike and Grisedale Tarn, and descend from it to Patterdale.

For ordinary walkers the most enjoyable way of taking the Grisedale Pass from Grasmere is to drive to Patterdale by the Kirkstone Pass and walk back (*see p.* 219).

From Grasmere, follow the Keswick road for 1¼ miles, and crossing Tongue Gill by a bridge, just beyond the *Travellers' Rest*, pass through a gate beyond it (notice-board : " To Helvellyn and Patterdale "). A cart-track leads up to another gate, Tongue Gill Force being on the right. Next the Tongue itself blocks the way. More than one track is in evidence, but that to the left should be taken.

After following this for a short distance the route bears up a steepish slope to the right, with lovely views backward of Grasmere, with Silver How and the Coniston Fells behind it. To the right of them is Helm Crag, almost in front of the chief Langdale Pike and Crinkle Crags. After a time our track approaches some small crags. The top of these must be gained by diverging sharply to the left, after which we skirt their ridge, the path being again perfectly plain. Then comes a slight depression in order to cross a beck. The big, green fell on the left is Seat Sandal. Soon a track from the right joins our well-beaten one. Then the top of the pass appears in front, concave and distinguishable by a transverse wall with a horse-gap, through which lies our route. Coniston Lake with one of its islands now comes into view behind. Some ten minutes before reaching the wall, the pony-track descends to what appears to be the bed of an old tarn. A rough track on the left, along the slope of **Seat Sandal**, avoids the dip.

The summit is now gained, and a fresh view, striking, but limited, is opened up. **Grisedale Tarn** (1,768 *ft.*), deep-set among the steep bare hills, with the most pellucid of water and singularly free from rushes and reeds, lies directly below. Beyond it is the steep shoulder of Dollywaggon Pike, with the Helvellyn track conspicuously zigzagging to its highest ridge, between which and Seat Sandal, set in a natural frame, appears the range of fells from Derwentwater to Crummock, with Grisedale Pike prominent on the right, and below it Causey Pike.

Fairfield may be gained from this point in about half an hour by keeping the side of the wall to the top of the ridge.

Seat Sandal (2,415 *ft.*), a mountain seldom ascended, is easily climbed from a little beyond the same spot. It commands a glorious view—Grasmere, Coniston, Esthwaite, peeps of Ullswater, Windermere and Thirlmere, and mountains innumerable.

The journey from the high road to the "Gap in the Wall" has taken 1¼ hours (more or less), and now begins our descent. In another seven or eight minutes we have dropped to the outlet of the tarn, for a few yards beyond which boggy ground is crossed and the path is vague. It rises slightly to a stone indicator, which marks the divergence for Helvellyn (left) and the Patterdale track (right).

A sharp ascent of 20 minutes from here leads to the top of the *col* between Fairfield and **St. Sunday Crag** (*p.* 260).

Just below Grisedale Tarn stands, "sacred as a shrine," a stone called the **Brothers' Parting**—the spot where William Wordsworth bade farewell to his brother John, commander of the East Indiaman *Earl of Abergavenny*, who shortly after perished in the wreck of that ship.

The descent is at first rather steep and rough, and does not allow the eye much leisure to admire the stupendous escarpments of Helvellyn and St. Sunday Crag, which grow more and more impressive as we get lower. We see little of Ullswater during our descent, the far-reaching shoulder of Helvellyn first hiding it, and then the high ground south-west of the lake.

In about 25 minutes after leaving the tarn *Ruthwaite Lodge*, a disused shooting-box, is reached, just beyond which a beck descends from *Ruthwaite Cove* on the left. Descend to the right and, a little farther on, cross the main stream by a bridge to the other side of the dale. Twenty minutes more brings us to the farm-buildings of *Elm How*, whence to the Grisedale Bridge at Patterdale is half an hour's walk along a cart-road, still on the right of the stream. The scenery during the last mile or so becomes sylvan and cultivated. Ten minutes before reaching the bridge the path from Helvellyn comes in at right angles on the left. Turning to the right at the bridge, and passing by the church, we have five minutes' walk to the *Patterdale Hotel*. To the left the steamer pier, on the lake, and the village of Glenridding are ten minutes distant (*see p.* 212).

Ascent of Helvellyn from Grasmere, *p.* 240.

KESWICK

Angling.—*See p. 26.*
Banks.—*National Westminster, Lloyds, Barclays* and *Midland.*
Bathing Place on lake, by footpath off road to boat-landings. Day, weekly ,
and season tickets are issued. Mixed bathing.
Boat-landings, ⅓ m. from centre of town. For note on boating *see p. 28.*
Motor launches make trips up and down the lake.
Buses, etc., to Grasmere, Ambleside, Waterhead, Windermere, Bowness,
Borrowdale, Patterdale, Penrith, Cockermouth, Buttermere (summer only), etc.
Churches.—*Crosthwaite (Parish Church),* ¾ m. from centre of town. Sun-
day services, 8, 10.45, 6 ; *St. John's* (in the town), services, 10.45, 6.30
etc. *Congregational, Methodist, Roman Catholic,* etc.
Distances.—(*By road*) Grasmere, 12½ m. ; Ambleside, 16¼ ; Waterhead
(Windermere), 17 ; Windermere Station, 21 Bowness, 22 ; Rosthwaite, 6¼ ;
Buttermere (by Honister), 14, (by Newlands), 9 ; Scale Hill, 10 ; Ullswater,
by Troutbeck, 16.
Early Closing.—Wednesday.
Entertainments in Pavilion, Station Road. *Cinema,* St. John's Street.
Height above the sea, about 280 feet.
Hotels.—At the station, *Keswick* ; in the town, *Royal Oak, Queen's, George.
Lake. King's Arms. County,* between station and town.
Unlicensed—*Blencathra, Skiddaw.* Numerous private hotels and boarding
houses.
In the neighbourhood :—
At PORTINSCALE (1½ m.) : *Derwentwater.*
On the BORROWDALE ROAD : *Lodore,* 3½ m. ; *Borrowdale,* 3¾ m.
On the road to Cockermouth, *Swan.* At north end of Bassenthwaite lake,
Armathwaite Hall, Castle Inn.
Library (*St. John Street*). Open daily, except Sunday and Thursday, p.m.
Market-day.—*Saturday.*
Museum, Station Road, open 10-7 ; winter, 10-5 (*fee*), contains Flintoft's
Model of the Lake District, and many objects of local interest including MSS
of letters of Wordsworth, Southey and Ruskin.
Population.—4,800.
Post Office in main street.
Publicity Office at Council Chambers and at Moot Hall, Market Place, in
summer months.
Sports.—Tennis courts and bowling and putting greens in Fitz Park, and
putting greens also beside Lake Road.

From a picturesque point of view, Keswick itself has not the
attractiveness of any of its southern rivals. It consists of one
wide street, and a good many narrow ones. It reveals the growth
of a country town into a popular holiday resort.

Reversing the usual order, the most picturesque part of Keswick itself is immediately outside the station, where the *Greta*
winds past **Fitz Park,** with its sheltered lawns and tennis courts.
The rest of the town has the plain appearance common to so
many stone-built places—though the Moot Hall, in the Market
Place, strikes a note that is rather interestingly reminiscent of
German Switzerland. One of the curious features of Keswick

is the very slight indication from its interior of the glorious scenery by which it is immediately encompassed. Derwentwater, only a few hundred yards distant, is not seen until one has walked to the far end of Lake Road and stands almost on its shores.

The road descending the Market Place from the Moot Hall reaches in ¼ mile **Greta Bridge**, close to which are the *School of Industrial Arts* (metal work and wood-carving) and the *Pencil Works.* Beyond the bridge the road leads directly to **Crosthwaite,** and by looking back one sees *Greta Hall,* the residence of Southey from 1803 to 1843, the year of his death. It stands on a slight eminence and is not shown to the public.

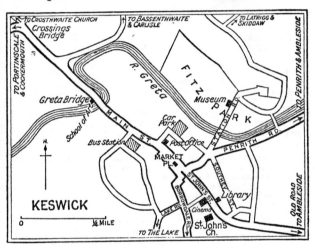

Keswick is not a parish of itself, but a part of Crosthwaite. The **Parish Church** (St. Kentigern) is one of the most interesting churches of the Lake District—quiet in style, and in harmony with the surrounding scenery.

Though, generally speaking, it is a Perpendicular church, there is evidence that a church existed here before the Conquest. It is also certain that it once belonged to the diocese of Glasgow, and it claims a very ancient foundation from its dedication to St. Kentigern (or Mungo), the 6th-century Bishop of Glasgow. The building was restored by Sir Gilbert Scott in 1845.

Inside is a recumbent monument to Southey, with an inscription written by Wordsworth; and in the chancel is an altar tomb to Sir John Radcliffe and his wife, ancestors of the Earls of Derwentwater.

A more recent memorial of note is the *Baptistry*, which commemorates Canon and Mrs. Rawnsley, whose great work for the preservation of Lakeland scenery has already been referred to (*see p. 13*). Canon Rawnsley was Vicar of the Parish for 34 years. The organ, with the restored tower and west window, form the 1914–18 war memorial. Note the glass case, on a pillar of the baptistry, containing the old pitch pipe and baton—relics of pre-organ days. The windows of the church are interesting. Most of them still retain on the left sides the "chrisms," or consecration crosses. The oldest bit of glass represents St. Anthony with a "tau" cross (*above*). The font—a century older than the building—dates from 1390, and bears the arms of Edward the Third. It also bears signs of inscriptions, some still decipherable, in each of its eight faces.

DERWENTWATER

Derwentwater is three miles long and a little more than a mile wide. Like Windermere, it is unique, but the two lakes have nothing in common. While the scenery of Windermere owes a great deal of its effectiveness to its mountain background, the charm of Derwentwater hangs chiefly on the rich blending of the steep crags, green fells, and feathery woods which sink almost directly into its waters. In breadth and grandeur of prospect, untainted by any tricks of sensation, Windermere is as supreme as Derwentwater is without a rival in complete and compact loveliness. In a word, if Windermere is the Apollo, Derwentwater is the Venus of the district.

In finding his way about Keswick, the tourist must be careful not to confuse Castle Head, Castle Rigg, and Castle Crag.

The first-named is the famous view-point which we are about to describe ; the second is on the Ambleside road (a mile away from the town); and the last is a rock which rises in the middle of Borrowdale near its entrance.

1. Castle Head.—From no point is the essence of Derwentwater scenery so well grasped as from here. The position is high up but very easily accessible. The view corresponds to that of Windermere from Miller Brow. The Head (*National Trust*) is a wooded height, half a mile from Keswick, on the left of the Borrowdale road, which leaves the town by the narrow street striking to the south-east from the Market Place and Town Hall. From the road to the top is a few minutes' walk up a winding path, entered by some stone steps into the wood.

View from Castle Head.—From the summit the whole expanse of the lake is visible, including its beautifully wooded islands, whose trim oval shapes are perhaps more accordant with the general character of the surrounding scenery than less regular outlines would be. A too scrupulous trimness is probably the only fault which the most implacable of critics could find in Derwentwater. In fact, it is almost too faultless, though exception may possibly be taken to the overwhelming and unrelieved massiveness of Skiddaw.

The features of the favourite Derwentwater views are the entrance to Borrowdale and the crags clustering round it at the southern end of the lake.   Here is a wonderful richness of rock-colouring, at no time of the year so striking as in mid-winter, when the combined tints of the dead bracken, the oak-coppices, and the lofty crags diffuse a strange, rich glow through the atmosphere.

This entrance is called the **Jaws of Borrowdale**, and is apparently filled up by a steep pyramidal rock called **Castle Crag**, nearly 1,000 feet high.   How the valley escapes being thus locked in you will find out when you pass through the Jaws on your way to the farther recesses of the western lakes and fells.   The prominent bold-crested fell just over Castle Crag is Great End, the northern buttress of the Scafell group, and to the right of it, a little farther back, appear Scafell Pike itself and Scafell.   Then the nearer fells to the west of Borrowdale, Gate Crag, and Maiden Moor, close the prospect in the direction of Great Gable.   The downward slope of Maiden Moor to the ridge of Catbells, descending at a steep angle into the lake, reveals a view of part of Hindscarth and Robinson, which lie on the near side of the Honister Pass and Buttermere.   Robinson descends sharply to an arm of the Newlands valley and Buttermere Hause, over which appear High Stile and Red Pike, the latter recognisable by its tapering summit, and the two together forming the south-western defence of Buttermere lake.   Then come the hump of Causey, with Sail, Eel Crag, and a portion of Grasmoor beyond, and the cone of Grisedale Pike, and farther north, the Whinlatter Fells, Lord's Seat and Barf, overlooking the west shore of Bassenthwaite.   Beyond the latter lake, Criffel in Kirkcudbrightshire may be visible.   Skiddaw is dominant to the north, Saddleback is hidden by the trees, but a portion of the north part of the Helvellyn range peers over the high ground to the east.   The sylvan-footed precipice hanging over the east shore of the lake is Walla Crag, beyond which are Falcon Crag and the deep recess of Lodore.   The rough rocky ridge of Glaramara tops the crags on the east side of Borrowdale, with Esk Pike just peeping up to the right.

Castle Head itself is said to be the plug of a mighty volcano " to whose eruptions the formation of the Lake District is primarily traced."   In 1925 it was given to the National Trust by Sir John and Lady Randles.

2. Friar's Crag commands the best marginal view of Derwentwater.   The crag does not rise more than a few yards above the surface of the lake, and the prospect is therefore more circumscribed than that from Castle Head, but it is almost equally beautiful.   To reach it, start as before by the Borrowdale road, taking the first turn to the right—Lake Road—about 150 yards from the Moot Hall.   Lake Road leads to the Landings and a path continues to the Crag.   The distance from the centre of the town is about three-quarters of a mile.   The features of the surrounding scene appear in the same order and direction as from Castle Head.

Near the end of the promontory is a rough-hewn memorial of John Ruskin, with a bronze medallion portrait and the words—

"JOHN RUSKIN, MDCCCXIX–MDCCCC.

"The first thing which I remember as an event in life was being taken by my nurse to the brow of Friar's Crag on Derwentwater." On the reverse side is a beautiful and appropriate quotation from Ruskin's *Deucalion*.

The National Trust hold, as a memorial of Canon Rawnsley, Friar's Crag, Lord's Island, and eight acres of Calf Close Bay.

3. Along the Shore of Derwentwater. Start off as in foregoing walk. Just before reaching Friar's Crag leave the main path and go through a wicket gate on left to a path skirting the shore of the bay, at the far end of which enter Ings Woods by a wicket gate. A well-defined path leads through the wood and over a bridge across the Brockle Beck. On the far side of the wood disregard the lane leading to the main road and keep on towards Stable Hills House. Go through the wicket here, and then through the wicket immediately on the right and cross a meadow to the lakeside, opposite Lord's Island. Hence keep along the shore of the lake as far as a spinney on **Broomhill Point,** a headland similar to Friar's Crag, and a fine view-point. From the spinney continue to follow the shore of the lake to Calf Close Bay and through Great Wood, which extends between the Lake and the road to the Barrow Landing, opposite the beginning of the road to Watendlath. The whole of this walk is over National Trust property acquired in 1929.

The walk may be extended to Borrowdale, or the return to Keswick made afoot or by bus along the main road.

4. Applethwaite. 2¼ *m. (by road) from Keswick.*
"From the terrace between Applethwaite and Millbeck is the best general view of Derwentwater"; such was Southey's opinion, and though one may be disposed to dispute it, on the plea that the lake is too far off, and the foreground not strong enough to support the exceptional beauty of the other parts of the picture, there can be no doubt that the walk is very attractive.

To reach Applethwaite, proceed down the main street as far as Greta Bridge, beyond which turn to the right along the Bassenthwaite road, cross the railway, and then turn up the first lane—again to the right—which, after an almost straight course of half a mile, curves to the left past *Ormathwaite* to **Applethwaite.** *Millbeck* is nearly a mile farther on, and between the two are the view-points which are the main object of the excursion. The strength of the position lies in its being in a line with the greatest length of Derwentwater and Borrowdale. The panorama on pages 316–17 and the description of the prospect from Castle Head (*pp.* 164–5) will enable the spectator to identify all the principal features of the scene.

The **Vale of Keswick,** so conspicuous during this walk, is not seen to the same advantage as from Castle Rigg and similar elevations. It is frankly a little disappointing.

In returning to Keswick, the main road may be regained in a

quarter of a mile by taking a lane to the left at Millbeck, or one may continue for nearly a mile farther along the terrace-road, and then join the main road about three miles from Keswick. There are other obvious footpaths marked on the map, which diversify the return to Keswick.

Skiddaw Dodd (1,612 *ft.*) may be easily climbed from several points near the last-named junction of the main and terrace roads, close to which are one or two farm-houses. The lower slopes are planted with trees but there is a fine view from the top, with the principal features of which the tourist will already have become familiar.

For routes over Latrigg, *see p.* 169.

Boat trips on Derwentwater (*boats for hire by hour or day, with boatman, if required. There are also motor launches, etc.*). We make no attempt to direct the tourist to particular spots. Once embarked, he cannot go wrong. Everything around is beautiful ; so much so, that to particularise would be invidious. The Landings are about half a mile from the centre of the town, at the end of Lake Road—the street which strikes out of the Borrowdale road on the right about 150 yards from the Moot Hall. There is fishing, of course (*see p.* 26), but few bent solely on fishing go to the Lakes ; and in Derwentwater, as in all the other lakes, it may be regarded as a supplementary occupation.

There are three larger **Islands** on Derwentwater, all abundantly clothed with wood, the foliage of which drops down almost to the water's edge. They are also remarkable for the regularity of their shape as contrasted with those on other lakes. They are by name **Derwent Isle** (*private property*) near the Landings, and to the west of Friar's Crag ; **Lord's Island** (*National Trust*) in the recess formed by Friar's Crag and the eastern shore, almost within a stone's throw of the latter ; and **St. Herbert's Island,** in the middle of the lake. A human interest, ancient or modern, attaches to all three. Beginning as far back as the 7th century, we find St. Herbert (*Herebert*), the *fidus Achates* of the venerable St. Cuthbert, domiciled on the island which now bears his name. The remains of a cell in the middle of the island are evidence of the fact. A thousand years elapse, and Lady Derwentwater issues from the family mansion on Lord's Island, traces of which are still to be seen, and flying up by the " Lady's Rake," the great fissure in Walla Crag, speeds on her way to London, bent, womanlike, on purchasing with her tears and the family jewels the life of her rebel lord, who perished on the scaffold for participating in the rebellion of 1715.

Derwent Isle has had a house upon it for about 150 years.

A fourth island, considerably smaller, is **Rampsholme** (*National Trust*) between St. Herbert's Island and the eastern shore of the lake. The **Floating Island,** near Lodore, appears very occasionally. It is due to the buoying effect of marsh gas evolved in a mass of vegetation, and by the growth of the plants.

The Barrow and Lodore falls (*see p.* 178) on the east side of the lake may be easily visited by boat. There is a landing-stage for each, that for the latter being at the south-east corner of the lake.

In crossing the lake the projecting knob of **Causey Pike,** visible over the ridge of Catbells on the western side, is a singular feature. On the west side of the lake is **Derwent Bay,** a beautiful, wood-fringed recess, from which the ascent of Catbells, or the walk to Buttermere by Newlands, may be advantageously commenced. The names of the near and distant fells will be gathered from our description of the scene from Castle Head (*p.* 164). From a considerable part of it Scafell Pike is visible just to the right of Castle Crag, the pyramidal hill which seems to stop up the Jaws of Borrowdale. Skiddaw, however, is, of course, the mountain monarch of Derwentwater.

Note.—The regular launch service goes round the lake clockwise calling at Barrow, Lodore and the two Brandelhow Landings. Very few launches go the other way round.

Round Derwentwater by Road. Derwentwater is certainly the most charming of the lakes to travel round. The views are varied, rich, and beautiful, and the whole distance is only 12 miles.

The route along the eastern shore—which is decidedly the best to begin with—is described in the Buttermere excursion (*p.* 177). The pedestrian may shorten the distance by leaving the road a little beyond Lodore, crossing a footbridge over the Derwent, and walking through Manesty Wood (*National Trust*) to the road again. At *Grange* the bridge over the Derwent must be crossed, and a straight course pursued past the church ; after which the road bends sharp to the right. **Peace How,** on the left, was given to the nation by Canon Rawnsley. In three-quarters of a mile the farm-house of *Manesty* is reached, and just beyond it an old upper road commences, which is pleasanter going for the walker, and commands better views.

A few hundred yards up this old road another track branches up the fell-side to the left. This is the path over Catbells into New-lands, and by reason of the narrowness of the summit ridge intro-duces the walker to a beautiful panorama at the cost of very little extra exertion.

Lovely views over Derwentwater, with Skiddaw and Saddle-back as a background, now present themselves. The upper track is still the better, as the prospect from the lower is often hidden by trees. At the end of the Catbells ridge, about 1½ miles beyond Manesty, the two roads reunite, and half a mile further the Newlands road from Buttermere to Keswick is joined. Hence most of way to Portinscale is through woods which hide the lake.

A considerable strip of Catbells slope, partly wooded and partly bare, between the road and the lake about here—**Brandelhow Park**—was purchased at the instance of the National Trust. It was the Trust's first property in the Lake District and comprises 108 acres.

From just beyond the cattle grid at the northern end of Catbells a footpath leads almost direct to Portinscale, the last half-mile of the route being along the Newlands road. The footpath starts by an iron kissing gate, descends to cross a narrow road where it is signposted, passes through a wood, a meadow and another wood to join the main road next to Derwent Bank Guest House. The road is still farther to the left—that is, still farther from the lake-side.

OTHER WALKS ABOUT KESWICK

1. **Ascent of Latrigg**, 1,203 *ft.*; 2¼ *m.*; 2 *hrs. up and down.*
Latrigg is the " cub " of Skiddaw. It rises north-east of Keswick, beyond the railway station. It commands, of course, a comparatively limited view, but in real beauty of prospect it not only surpasses the parent mountain, but can vie with any other hill of its height in the district. Derwentwater, which is too far removed from the highest ridge of Skiddaw to play its proper part in the panorama, holds the pride of place in the view from Latrigg, and appears to its greatest advantage.

The ascent is by the Skiddaw track, which passes under the railway to the right of the station, and then takes the second turn to the right, ascending a long straight lane, called *Spoony-Green Lane.*

The Skiddaw track must be followed for 1¾ miles from the station, almost as far as the dip between that mountain and Latrigg (up to this point the hill-side is jealously guarded by wire fencing). The view in ascending—Skiddaw, Underscar, the Vale of Keswick, Bassenthwaite, and Derwentwater—is very attractive. Then we bend back at an opening in the fence, and after one sharp zigzag reach the top.

The return may be agreeably varied by continuing a little farther up the Skiddaw track, and, after passing through a gate turning down the lane that leads past the mansion of *Underscar* on to the Applethwaite road (*see Map and p.* 166).

The view is similar to that from Castle Head, but more extensive, the most notable additions being the Helvellyn range to the south-east and Pillar, overtopping the Buttermere fells a little west of south. Almost at our feet is the bosky Greta valley with its winding stream and the town of Keswick. A little of Bassenthwaite is visible, but the hills beyond it lack that rugged beauty of outline which we have learnt to associate with other lakes. Castlerigg Stone Circle (*p.* 170) is conspicuous to the south-east.

2. **Walla Crag.**—This is a very refreshing walk. From the Moot Hall follow St. John Street and the old Ambleside road to about 350 yards beyond the church, then take the Springs Road on the right, passing Springs Farm and the pretty dingle of *Brockle Beck.* Or about a quarter of a mile beyond the toll-house at the junction of the new and old Ambleside roads take a lane

on the right (this point, about 300 feet above Keswick, may be reached by bus) leading down past *Castle Rigg*.

The two routes unite at *Rakefoot*. At Rakefoot the track crosses the beck and becomes unenclosed. For a time it keeps close by the beck, ascending to a wide stretch of heathery moor. Bending to the right it then crosses to the wall enclosing *Great Wood*. Almost opposite the gamekeeper's cottage is a wicket gate by which one can enter the wood and cross it to the edge of the precipice. For the Lady's Rake, *see p*. 167. The view is very fine. It is usual to return as far as Rakefoot, whence a descent may be made through Great Wood, but those who wish to continue farther may go over the top of Falcon Crag by a path to Ashness Bridge on the Watendlath road, or descend a steep path by Cat Gill (between Walla Crag and Falcon Crag) to the Borrowdale road (*see Map*).

3. Another pleasant walk is along the Borrowdale road for 1¼ miles, and then over stile and up wood-path through **Great Wood**. Issuing from wood, either turn down from top of field (*see Map*) by *Brockle Beck*, or take stile on right and enter lane at Rakefoot.

4. Castlerigg Stone Circle, 1¾ m.

Leave Keswick by Penrith road—turn to right from Station Road and just short of river. For some way Greta runs close by on left. The road goes under railway and then over it. Beyond latter crossing take second divergence to right (first is the " new " Ambleside road)—the old Keswick and Penrith road.

The Circle is in the field beyond Castle Lane, the first turning on the right along the road. It forms rather an oval than a circle with a maximum diameter of some 35 yards. Apart from the archæological interest attaching to such circles, the notable features are the extraordinary bleakness of the situation on the threshold of the most beautiful scenery in England and the extent of the prospect in a hill country from an elevation relatively low. It is interesting to know that a line drawn from the summit of Skiddaw to the summit of Helvellyn passes through the circle and the two highest stones are exactly sited upon it. Also another line from the outlier stone, 200 ft. to the south-west, drawn through the centre of the circle and continued to the horizon ends in Fiends' Fell in the Pennines and coincides with the line of sunrise on May 1st. This line of sunrise also passes through the circle of Long Meg (p. 51), a fact suggesting some relationship between the two. The date of the Circle is calculated as about 1400 B.C. The stones are in the ownership of the National Trust and are scheduled as an ancient monument.

A return may be made by Castle Lane—which in ⅔ of a mile joins the Windermere high road, 1¾ m. from Keswick Town Hall, and just opposite the farm-road to Rakefoot (*see above*) ; or the excursion may be continued through the Vale of St. John to Thirlspot, Thirlmere, etc., as below.

5. To the Vale of St. John, Thirlspot, Thirlmere, and back.
Castlerigg Circle, 1¾ m. ; *Wanthwaite Bridge (Vale of St. John)*, 4 ; *Thirlspot*, 7½ ; *Wythburn*, 10½ ; *leave main road*, 11 ; *rejoin main road*, 16½ ; *Keswick*, 20½. **Shorter round** (*by Dam*), 13 m.

Every visitor to Keswick should take one or other of these rounds. The longer one—round the lake—is, of course, to be preferred, but the shorter—by the Dam—gives a very fair idea of the beauties of Thirlmere, especially if it be extended to the foot of Raven Crag, an additional mile. Walkers should bear in mind that there are no facilities for refreshment at Wythburn.

Follow the Penrith road as above to Castlerigg Stone Circle and thence descend to *Naddle Bridge*, where the new and old Penrith roads reunite. A third of a mile farther our road strikes off to the right, and in another mile crosses *Wanthwaite Bridge.*

A pleasant little detour may be made by turning down a footpath (signpost) on the right, about ½ m. after entering this road, and proceeding almost past *St. John's in the Vale Church*, which stands high up, yet secluded, on the road from St. John's Vale to Naddle Vale. Thence a cart-track may be followed along the west side of St. John's Vale to *Sosgill Farm* (1¼ miles beyond the church), where the stream is crossed by a stone bridge, and the main road of the valley joined. The crags on the opposite side of the valley are very fine.

On the far side of Wanthwaite Bridge our route ascends a short distance to its junction with the main road of St. John's Vale, the whole length of which is traversed. The ravines of the *Wanthwaite Crags*, high up on the left, are very wild and picturesque.

For the **short round** we leave the Vale of St. John's road 6½ miles from Keswick (1¼ short of Thirlspot), and, crossing the main—Windermere and Keswick—road, reach the **Dam** in half a mile. Thence the return journey is described on *p.* 191.

For the longer—all-round route—we keep southward from the Vale of St. John and past Thirlspot (*King's Head*). The Vale of St. John is narrow and beautiful, and its best is seen looking back from the Windermere and Keswick road, whence the deep-cleft Saddleback forms such an effective background to the view. Hence, too, the famous **Castle Rock of Triermain** looks its most castellated. It rises from the steep slopes of the Helvellyn Dodds, which flank the whole length of the valley. The low range on the west is Naddle Fell (or High Rigg).

For the route on from Thirlspot to Wythburn, *see p.* 192, and from Wythburn along the west side back to Keswick, *pp.* 84–7.

6. Keswick to Watendlath ; returning by Rosthwaite and Borrowdale.
To Watendlath, 5 m. ; *Rosthwaite*, 7 ; *Keswick*, 13½.

This walk is one of the easiest in the district, and certainly not surpassed by any other in richness and variety of scenery. The upland vale of Watendlath has a quiet and secluded beauty of its own, but the charm of the excursion lies in the exquisite views as we climb the hill from Derwentwater, in the sylvan magnificence of the region above Lodore, and in the prospect of Borrowdale from the fell-track between Watendlath and Rosthwaite—perhaps the most glorious valley-view in Britain.

(The Borrowdale road (p. 177) or the lake-side path (3, p. 166) should be followed for the first two miles, at the end of which a divergence must be made through a gate on the left (sign-post).)

The road to Watendlath rises behind Barrow House and Barrow Cascade (p. 177) crossing the stream which forms the latter in about half a mile at **Ashness Bridge,** a very ancient structure. The view down-stream from this point is remarkably beautiful, having for its foreground all that richness of wood and water which the artist revels in. Derwentwater and Bassenthwaite, the latter stretching far away seawards, and Falcon Crag to the right, with the massive bulk of Skiddaw in the background, contribute to the formation of a picture as rich as it is compact.

From the far side of the bridge a pleasant path leads up by the stream to the heights of **High Seat** and **Bleaberry Fell** or back to **Falcon Crag** and **Walla Crag.**

Just beyond the bridge the road passes into a wood and through two gateways. After crossing a tiny rill, just beyond the second, a grand view may be obtained by striking up to a shelf about 250 yards from the road. The rich Trossach-like cliffs, which stand upright as sentinels over Lodore, look remarkably fine from here, and the bold phalanx of the Borrowdale mountains constitutes a worthy background.

Scafell Pike is distinguishable by its cairn and bracket-shaped summit. Scafell itself forms the right of the ridge, and the long, dashing sweep of Great Gable is conspicuous still more to the right. The whole of Derwentwater and Bassenthwaite are visible, but Catbells abruptly closes the prospect in front, Causey Pike and Grisedale Pike appearing to the right of it. A footpath takes us into the road again a little higher up. Very much the same view, only more extensive in front and less so over Borrowdale, may be obtained by a slighter deviation, about half a mile higher up, where the road, after crossing a meadow and entering another wood, approaches very near to the headlong, giddy cliffs which beetle over Lodore. Two points of view are unmistakable, lying only a few yards from the road.

The region which we are now traversing affords the finest combination of wood and rock to be found in the Lake District. The walker who is not in hot haste to scale some mighty fell, or to accomplish an unheard-of number of miles in his day's round, will linger long in this Paradise within a Paradise, where he may wander at will.

Those who wish to shorten their walk without losing the best part of the scenery should turn down a grass lane a short distance beyond the viewpoint, cross the first ladder stile on the left, continue along a fenced track to a second wooden stile, then turn right down to the footbridge. Working round a wood, they may descend by a winding path, "Ladder Brow," to the *Borrowdale Hotel* (3¾ *m.* from Keswick). By climbing Shepherd's Crag to the right of this track after it has left the side of the wood, a splendid view of Derwentwater and Bassenthwaite and their surroundings may be obtained. The falls of High Lodore, near the same spot, are very beautiful (*see p.* 178). Halfway between Ashness Gate and Watendlath there is an old hill-fort, called Reecastle, up the fell-side to the left.

For Watendlath, from the aforementioned footbridge, a well-defined footpath to the right of the stream leads up the valley to the hamlet, consisting of a sprinkling of farmsteads, at which light refreshments can be had.

About 100 yards short of Watendlath is the Churn, or Devil's Punchbowl, which is reached through a gate on the right of road from Keswick. The beck, with the aid of stones, has scooped out a real bowl—small but exceedingly pretty, with the pure water splashing into it, and escaping, not over the brim but through a leakage below, into a pool, whence in a few yards it takes another headlong plunge. Another feature of Watendlath is its rustic bridge.

The name is pronounced Wat*e*ndlath—furnishing an exception to the local habit of emphasising the first syllable. As a rule, this habit is etymologically correct, for the same reason that justifies the accentuation of the last syllable farther north—namely, that the particular and not the generic portion of the name should have the accent. The Scot says Brae*mar*, and the Cumbrian " *Scaw*fle," on the same principle. With the one the question is, *What brae ?* with the other, *What fell ?*

The track for Borrowdale crosses the beck by the bridge, just below Watendlath Tarn (avoid a turn left)—a sheet of water about ¼ mile in diameter—and climbs the low ridge which separates Watendlath valley from Borrowdale. Just beyond a plantation there is a momentary glimpse of the peak of Bowfell on the left, and from the highest part of the track a magnificent panorama— best seen 50 yards after passing through a gate—bursts upon the eye. Looking directly up the Seathwaite branch of Borrowdale, at the head of which is the silvery streak of Taylor Gill Force, backed by Lingmell, we see, to the *left* of that mountain, Scafell Pike, Great End, and, nearer, Glaramara, in the order named ; the *right*, Great Gable—over Green Gable and Base Brown— Brandreth, and Grey Knotts, a commonplace ridge ; then the road winding up Honister Pass, and, to the right again, Dale Head, with a long slope to the left and a more abrupt one to the right.

Descending, we soon look down upon the village and green strath of Rosthwaite, with Castle Crag and the other crags that flank Borrowdale more to the right.

Those who wish to go straight to the **Bowder Stone** without calling at Rosthwaite can do so by diverging through a wall by the second gap on the right, about half-way down the hill, 120 yards short of the point at which the main track crosses a rill.

The track proceeds (*a*) with a wall first on the right and then on the left, and, skirting the upper side of a wood, drops into the main road a long half-mile short of the Bowder Stone ; (*b*) through the wood, entered by a stile.

The whole descent to Rosthwaite village is very delightful, the grass being soft and velvety, and heather and wild-flowers growing in abundance. For Rosthwaite *see p.* 180.

7. **To Barf** (1,536 *ft.*) and **Lord's Seat** (1,811 *ft.*). These two heights afford a pleasant and easy walk from Keswick, though, neither in respect of themselves nor of the views they command, can they be ranked as first-class. Barf is the more interesting of the two. The length of the walk is about 12 miles, of which 2½ can be saved each way by taking bus to the foot of Barf.

After viewing the " Bishop " (*see below*) from the road, ascend the gully to the south of the screes of **Barf**, and, on reaching the top of the steep part, double round to the right. The summit is soon reached. It commands the whole of Bassenthwaite Lake and a large part of Derwentwater ; Skiddaw in all its glory, the Helvellyn range, the fells south of Borrowdale, with Criffel and other heights across the Solway. The thimble, a little east of south, is the Pike o' Stickle, Langdale. The wide, treeless marsh at the head of Bassenthwaite disfigures the foreground, but the green shoots of the bilberry, with which the hill itself is carpeted, are a delight to the eye.

From Barf, we make our way westward to Lord's Seat. After a short descent there is a lovely peep across the valley, the marshland being hidden. Then comes a somewhat tedious trudge through heather. The top of **Lord's Seat** is at a junction of wire-fences. The view includes a long stretch of the low-lying west coast of Cumberland, and the lower end of Bassenthwaite. The "Seat " is formed in the rock 20 yards north-west of the summit.

In descending follow the wire-fence to the top of the gully, and then pursue the route by which you came up from the road.

8. **Round Bassenthwaite Lake**, 18 *m.* ; *Portinscale*, 1¼ *m. Barf*, 4 ; *Pheasant Inn*, 8 ; *Castle Inn*, 10 ; *Keswick*, 18.

This is a very pleasant circular drive over good roads and affording beautiful views, though, being through the outer circle of the district, it lacks the powerful interest of the inner routes.

The route as far as the foot of Barf is noted above. As we raise our eyes to the steep screes of Barf, we see some way up, a singular bit of rock, called from its sacerdotal appearance the **Bishop of Barf**. From time to time it is zealously whitewashed.

Hence the road runs within a few yards of the old railway and the shore of the lake.

Castle How, between the *Pheasant Inn* and the lake, 8 *m.* from Keswick, is wooded and shows traces of an ancient fort.

Beyond the old Bassenthwaite Lake Station bear to the right, avoiding the Cockermouth road (left). After crossing Ouse Bridge over the Derwent the road passes between the lake and *Armathwaite Hall Hotel.*

A little farther we reach the cross-roads at the *Castle Inn* ; the road straight ahead is the way to Caldbeck and the " John Peel " country (*see below*).

Five miles north of this point is the small village of Torpenhow— locally *Trepenna*—(*inn*). The road—a good one—gradually ascends for half the distance, and then descends, affording fine views across the Solway to the Scottish hills. Torpenhow church is extremely interesting, being untouched Norman and Early English, but the interior is dark and difficult to see.

The Keswick road is that to the right at the *Castle.* It runs at some distance from the lake. About 3 miles on, a glimpse may be caught of the little, isolated church of St. Bridget, near the water-side, and then the road enters *Mirehouse Woods*, which clothe the steep slope of Skiddaw Dodd (*p.* 167). A variation, adding about ½ mile to the distance, may be made by Millbeck and Applethwaite Terrace—one of the finest view-points in the neighbourhood (*see p.* 166). Keswick is entered by Crosthwaite and Greta Bridge.

9. Keswick to Caldbeck (the home of John Peel), 18 *m.*; Threlkeld, about 31 ; and back, 35 (round Skiddaw and Saddleback).

This makes a fair motor round from Keswick, but is not to be commended to the cyclist or walker. It presents a somewhat sombre back view of the Lake District, but the interest of John Peel is a powerful magnet, and the first and last parts of the route are very interesting.

The first eight miles, from Keswick to the *Castle Inn* at the northern end of Bassenthwaite, have already been described in the reverse direction (*see above*). Hence the road ascends for a mile or so and thence undulates sharply all the way to Caldbeck.

The village of Caldbeck is chiefly of interest through its association with John Peel, the renowned huntsman, whose gravestone, appropriately carved, is to be seen in the churchyard. The church is large and ancient and has been well restored.

" D'ye ken John Peel ? " the famous Cumberland hunting-song, is known and sung in every quarter of the globe, but so few people know its history that a few notes here may be of interest. Despite the common notion—arising from the erroneous alteration of the original in the later editions—it was not " at Troutbeck once on a day," but at Caldbeck, in Cumberland, that Peel was born and died.

Here, at Greenrigg Farm, " back o' Skidda'," was the home of the immortal huntsman. His appearance was striking, for he stood six feet high and more, and with a form and gait quite surprising ; " terble lang in th' leg and lish (nimble), w' a fine girt neb (nose), and gray eyes that could see for iver." The sport was a passion with him, and for it, we are told, he would at any time neglect any serious business or household cares. He passed to " the happy hunting fields " in 1854, aged 78.

John Woodcock Graves, the woollen weaver of Caldbeck, stated that he composed the words of the song in 1832, whilst he was sitting by the fire with John ; and that the tune which inspired their rhythm was an old rant called " Bonnie Annie," which was being sung at the time by an old woman as she crooned to sleep one of Graves's own children. The room in which they are said to have been sitting is marked by a plaque in a house near to the *Oddfellows' Inn.* To the choirmaster of Carlisle Cathedral (Mr. Metcalf) is due the setting of this old melody.

The return from Caldbeck to Keswick should be made by Hesket Newmarket, Mungrisedale, and Threlkeld. There are romantic glimpses of the small valleys running up into the fells on the right-hand side of the road.

10. **King's How** (*Grange Fell*), 4½ to 5¼ miles. Grange Fell and the Borrowdale Birches, 310 acres, were purchased in 1910 as a memorial to King Edward VII, and the fell was named King's How. It is a delightful walk, and those who find ten or eleven miles, exclusive of the ascent of the *How*, too much for them may be sure of picking up a public conveyance on the way there or the way back, without tedious waiting. A further advantage is that either route of ascent is as good as the other. By that nearer Keswick there awaits you on reaching the summit a lovely surprise view of Borrowdale ; by the further ascent, a lovely surprise view of Derwentwater. It is a pleasant afternoon expedition.

From Keswick to Grange go either by the main road (*see p.* 177) or by the lakeside walk described on *p.* 166. About a hundred yards beyond Grange bridge a stile on the left guards a path leading to King's How. This ascent winds up round the head of Troutdale and conducts one easily to the summit, whence a steepish descent leads down to the main road a short distance beyond the Bowder Stone. Many prefer to use this as the ascent, returning comfortably to Grange. The craggy western part of the Fell is precipitous.

On a slab of Borrowdale slate near the summit and facing Derwentwater is the inscription :

> "In loving memory of
> King Edward VII
> Grange Fell is dedicated by his sister
> Louise
> As a sanctuary of rest and peace.
> Here may all beings gather strength and
> Find in scenes of beautiful nature a cause
> For gratitude and love to God giving them
> Courage and vigour to carry on His will."

The view from the summit comprises Derwentwater in all its loveliness, with the surrounding fells, Skiddaw dominant beyond. To the east is the smooth outline of the Helvellyn range as far as Fairfield. Southward the prospect is equal as a dale view to Derwentwater as a lake view, which is praise indeed. There are the waters-meet of the Derwent and the Stonethwaite Beck, Castle Crag, Gate Crag, Scawdell Fell, Dale Head, the fells leading up to Great Gable, Lingmell, Scafell Pikes, Great End, Glaramara, Eagle Crag, High Raise, Pike o' Stickle and Bowfell.

KESWICK TO BUTTERMERE BY BORROWDALE

Distances.—*Keswick to Barrow Falls*, 2 m.; *Lodore Hotel*, 3¼; *Grange Bridge*, 4; *Bowder Stone*, 5, *Rosthwaite*, 6½; *Seatoller*, 8; *Honister Hause*, 9½; *Gatesgarth*, 12; *Buttermere*, 14; *Buttermere Hause*, 15½; *Newlands* 18¾; *Portinscale*, 21½; *Keswick*, 23.

Height of Passes. Honister, 1,190 *ft.*; Buttermere Hause, 1,096 *ft.*

Motoring.—*Honister Pass*, after being for many years one of the worst roads in the district, is now quite practicable for cars. It should be borne in mind, however, that although the surface is good the gradients are very steep and need great care.

This excursion—through the loveliest valley, under the steepest crag, and past three of the most beautiful lakes in the District— is indeed one of the finest drives in Britain. That exquisite regard for proportion which Nature has observed in the Lake District is nowhere more strikingly exemplified. Mountains, which in point of height are mole-hills, lakes which are ponds, and valleys which are scarcely noticeable depressions, in comparison with natural features of similar kind in other parts of the world, are here blended in such wonderful harmony as to upset all judgment which is based on mere size, and to produce a succession of scenes which are not only thoroughly beautiful, but fall little, if at all, short of being sublime.

Leaving Keswick by the Borrowdale road, we can soon look across Derwentwater to where High Stile occupies the gap between Robinson and Causey Pike, and Hindscarth fills the depression of Catbells. A fine view through the Newlands valley is obtained across the lake, the Buttermere Red Pike forming its limit. Then we enter *Great Wood*. Catbells and Causey Pike are across the lake. Walla Crag towers above the road on the left, and on emerging from the wood Falcon Crag forms a striking feature on the same side.

Two miles from Keswick the Watendlath road diverges to the left, and just beyond it are the private grounds into which an entrance has to be obtained by application at Barrow House Youth Hostel, to see *Barrow Waterfalls*.

The **Barrow Falls** are better described by the word cascade than by the expressive force, which is the local term for nearly all the other waterfalls in the district ; and the visitor will not be surprised to hear that their present appearance is, to some extent, the result of artificial means. The paths, however, through the woods, which fence the fall in on every side, present many a pretty peep and bit of sylvan sweetness. The total height of the two falls is over 120 ft.

From hereabout the knob of Causey Pike, peering over Catbells, is curious rather than picturesque. Another mile brings us to the famous **Lodore Falls** (*small fee for admission*). Visitors who expect to find a mighty torrent are doomed to disappointment unless they come just after a storm. In dry weather there is often nothing visible but a steep, rough channel of boulder and rock, threaded by a countless number of petty rills, which do little more than trickle their way down the craggy bed. After heavy rain it is different ; then the rills swell into torrents, which tumble against and jostle one another in all directions, keeping up a real roar which may be heard far away. However, at all times the scene is very beautiful in the eyes of all who can bear without chagrin to be cheated of the special attraction they have come to see. On both sides of the fall, perpendicular cliffs—*Gowder Crag* on the left, and *Shepherd's Crag* on the right—rise to a considerable height, feathered with wood to their summits, and the whole scene is very lovely. The path from the road is through the garden of the hotel and across a wooden bridge, beyond which are several attractive pathways on the fell-side.

Behind the *Borrowdale Hotel*, ¼ mile beyond Lodore, is **Troutdale**, a beautiful little valley, so called from an old fish-hatchery now in ruins.

We are now beyond the upper end of the lake, and passing a level tract of swampy ground. This is the worst view-point of Derwentwater, which is dwarfed by the foreground.

Approaching the Derwent, the road enters Borrowdale. On the left rises Grange Fell, which, with the Borrowdale Birches, 310 acres, were purchased in 1910 by the National Trust as a memorial to King Edward VII and named **King's How** (*see p. 176*). At the foot of the rock a picturesque stone bridge of two arches, crossing two separate channels of the Derwent, leads to the village of **Grange**. There are several boarding and apartment houses in and about the village. On the far side of the stream, just south of the bridge, the geologist will notice with interest the smooth-worn and striated boulders, showing the marks of glacial action.

Alternative Route : Grange to Honister. Those who have already walked by the Bowder Stone and through Rosthwaite (a part to be on no account missed), may agreeably vary their present route by crossing the bridge and taking a rough cart-track which strikes out to the left a little short of the church. This track passes between *Gate Crag* on the right, and the beautiful little **Castle Crag** (*900 ft.*)

on the left. The latter may be climbed from it, and the detour is worth making for the exquisite views up Borrowdale and down Derwentwater from the top. It is crowned by the site of an ancient British hill-fort, often but probably wrongly attributed to the Romans. Castle Crag and adjoining woods were presented to the National Trust by Sir William and Lady Hamer and their family.

Shortly after passing Castle Crag, the cart-track climbs the fell on the right to a slate-quarry. Leave it at the turn ; cross the stream, the wall, and the track from Rosthwaite to the quarry, by which a pleasant descent may be made to Rosthwaite, and proceed along a footpath which crosses the depression between High Scawdel on the right and a wooded tongue called " High Doat " on the left. Then the path veers to the right, and rejoins the old Honister toll-road on a steep ascent, about half a mile above Seatoller.

A short half-mile beyond Grange the Bowder Stone track mounts a short pitch to the left, leaving the main route to thread its way alongside the stream, through the narrowest part of the ravine ; so sweet a passage that one is loath to leave it, even when such a powerful magnet as the Bowder Stone draws us away. Here trees now grow to soften the harsh outlines left by the huge slate quarry which at one time threatened to consume the beauty of this incomparable scene—the " Jaws of Borrowdale," as it is called. However, we need not miss anything, for the Bowder Stone is easily reached by a path from the road. There can be no doubt that, regardless of its size and weight (its dimensions are 30 feet high by 60 long, and its weight is computed at 1,900 tons), it is the most marvellously poised piece of rock in the country. So sharp is it in its beam ends that two people lying down on opposite sides of it may shake hands beneath it ; the top, with plenty of standing room, may be reached by a flight of steps.

The stone rests on a velvety patch of greensward, which commands lovely views over the lower half of the valley. Whatever difference of opinion there may be as to the relative merit of the principal lakes of the District, there can be no doubt that Borrowdale holds the first position amongst its valleys ; and that is no mean praise, when we recollect that its rivals include Patterdale, Grasmere, Langdale, and Troutbeck. The witchery of Borrowdale is the splendid contrast between its rugged shapely hills and its perfectly level green strath.

The mountain which rises just behind Rosthwaite and cuts the valley in two is Glaramara. A fantastic rock on one of its highest ridges brings to mind Helm Crag at Grasmere. Then, as we proceed on our way, Lingmell comes into view, beyond the head of the valley, followed in turn by Great Gable, and a glimpse of Scafell Pike. A wooded tongue (High Doat) beyond Castle Crag shuts out the upper part of the main valley, the ramifying character of which makes it very difficult for a stranger to guess his way out. Let him know, then, that the eastern branch of it, passing to the left of Rosthwaite, is Langstrath, leading up to the Stake Pass into Langdale ; and that the branch still farther to the east, divided from Langstrath by the noble Eagle Crag, is the route to Grasmere by Greenup (*p.* 196). Beyond the wooded tongue already mentioned, to the right of Glaramara and in the direction of Lingmell, is the Sty Head Pass to Wastwater ; while a fourth exit—the one we are about to use—strikes out to the right just beyond the tongue, and begins at once the climb of Honister Hause.

As we approach Rosthwaite, the beautiful eastern arm of Borrowdale, leading to Langstrath and Greenup (for Langdale and Grasmere respectively), reveals itself. Eagle Crag, between the two, is a fine feature. **Rosthwaite** [Hotels : *Scafell, Royal Oak (Temp.*), good farmhouse accommodation. *Post and Telegraph* office.] This small and comely village is as charmingly situated as any in Britain. It is a very handy and popular centre with walkers.

Half a mile beyond Rosthwaite the road to Stonethwaite, beyond which Eagle Crag stands up grandly, and the Stake Pass strikes off to the left, near the church which supplies the spiritual wants of the four " thwaites," and in less than another mile on the same side of the road is the lane leading up the main valley to Seathwaite and Sty Head. The Buttermere road sweeps round to the right, through **Seatoller,** another excellent centre for mountain excursions.

At Seatoller begins the modern road over Honister Hause to Buttermere. For more than half a mile it climbs through trees, with a beck, *Horse (Hause) Gill,* descending in a succession of cataracts on the left, and the ascent continues to the quarry buildings at the top of the Hause, rather less than two miles from Seatoller.

At the top of the Hause (1,176 *ft.*) the full downward sweep of **Honister Crag** bursts suddenly into view. Though not maintaining so great a degree of steepness to so great a height as Pike o' Stickle in Langdale, it is decidedly the most striking crag in the ordinary tracks of the Lake District. Its maximum height above sea-level (Black Star) is 2,070 ft., and in its steepest part there is something like 1,000 or 1,200 ft. from base to summit, at an average angle of nearly 45 degrees. The upper part is sheer precipice, down the side of which quarry tracks have been blasted or hewn out of the rock ; the lower, screes of a most formidable appearance, when looked at face-to-face, but in reality making rather an agreeable descent than otherwise. Motorists should bear in mind that the road they are now going down is quite as steep as the one they have just come up.

A mine-track, striking to the right from the exact top of the pass, makes a terrace from which a beautiful view (singularly enhanced by a fine sunset after a day's rain) is obtained of Buttermere and Crummock and the fells beyond them—High Crag, High Stile,

Red Pike, and Melbreak. By following the fence posts on the right from the summit of the hause you will soon gain the ridge of the Newlands Fells, and, if so inclined, may continue your walk over **Dale Head**, Hindscarth, and Robinson, descending on to the Buttermere and Newlands road near the village of Buttermere (*see p. 183*). Rosthwaite may also be reached in slightly over an hour. The route passes Dale Head Tarn, whence make for a gap in the fells (Rigg Head), and descend by quarry-path.

The top of **Honister Crag** may also be easily reached from the summit of the pass, by climbing the fell to the left, and working round the ridge. From the summit a descent of the precipice may be made by following the quarrymen's track which connects the different workings, and taking to the screes half-way down ; but those who prefer scenery to athletics will continue along the ridge in the direction of Buttermere to the top of **Fleetwith** (about 20 minutes' walk), which is the real name of the mountain of which Honister Crag only forms a part. Hence the view of the three lakes, Buttermere, Crummock, and Loweswater, with High Stile, Red Pike, and Melbreak on the left, and Robinson and Grasmoor on the right, is very fine. Great Gable and the Pillar are prominent to the south and south-west. A descent may be made—with care— almost straight down the ridge in a line with the right-hand shore of Buttermere, the road to which will be regained at Gatesgarth, two miles from the village.

Those who knew the Honister road of old will hardly fail to notice the transformation in the road as it leads down towards Buttermere. Once notoriously dangerous, it is now despite severe gradients nearly as safe as any road in the District.

As the road descends on the western side of the Hause, Buttermere and part of Crummock Water and the surrounding fells— High Crag, High Stile, and Red Pike, in the order named—appear on the left ; Melbreak and Hen Comb, beyond Crummock, in front and Robinson to the right, come into view, the route skirting the base of the last-named all the way to Buttermere.

At the foot of the pass the farm-house of **Gatesgarth** is reached, whence starts the bridle-path over Scarth Gap, the depression between Hay Stacks and High Crag. Then come two miles of mingled fell and park-like scenery, with the lake of Buttermere on the left. About half-way is the promontory and house of *Hassness* on the left and on the right the picturesque ravine of *Gaits Gill*, overlooked by the crags of Robinson. Just beyond the far end of the lake a short, steep descent leads into **Buttermere village**, consisting of a church, hotels, youth hostel (*Fish, The Bridge*), half a dozen houses, a shop and a Post Office.

Buttermere Lake is $1\frac{1}{4}$ miles long, and nearly half a mile wide. It is very shallow at its lower end (by remembering this bathers will avoid disappointment), and nowhere as much as 100 feet in depth. Its angularity and the sombre character of the massive mountains which descend almost sheer into it, relieved by little foliage except that of fir and larch, make it more imposing than picturesque. Its mountain outlines are not so graceful as those of Wastwater, nor is its general scenery so wild ; yet; not only when taken in conjunction with Crummock, which enhances the whole picture enormously, but even by itself, it leaves a strong and lasting impression on the beholder. It is gratifying to know that the National Trust now guards much of the Butter-mere district.

The conspicuous stream which rushes in a succession of little cataracts down the fells into the north-west corner of the lake is *Sour Milk Gill*, descending from Bleaberry Tarn, an upland sheet of water lying in the deep hollow between High Stile and Red Pike.

As Crummock Water should undoubtedly be approached from the northern or Scale Hill end, we shall describe it in the route from Keswick *viâ* Whinlatter (*p.* 185). The most popular short excursion from Buttermere is to **Scale Force.** There are two routes—one the water-route, by the right side of the *Fish Hotel* (as you approach it), and the other the land-route, by the left. The latter is circuitous, and often very sloppy, though by keeping a little up the fell-side the water may generally be avoided. It strikes sharply to the left to begin with ; and then, turning right again along a cart-track through the nearest of three gates, goes straight across the " strath " till the stream connecting Butter-mere and Crummock is reached, after crossing which it turns to the right ; and, skirting the beck and the lake for about three-quarters of a mile, bends to the left just beyond a small islet and joins the water-route about quarter of a mile from the landing-place at the second beck—the one descending from the force itself. A short cut may be made athwart the fell-slope as soon as the shore of the lake is reached. The entire distance from the village is two miles.

The regular track after leaving the *Fish Hotel* crosses some pleasant meadows by the side of a beck, and reaches a wood—in which is the Crummock boat-landing—in about half a mile. The distance to be rowed is three-quarters of a mile (*if a boat is available*). The mountains seen in crossing are Melbreak, the fell dropping to the western margin of the lake, and on the opposite side Grasmoor, huge, red, and long-backed ; Whiteless Pike, considerably lower and nearer to Buttermere, and, between them and the lake, the low and isolated Rannerdale Knotts.

On landing, another $\frac{3}{4}$ mile of rough fell has to be travelled over to reach the force, which will be seen in a ravine to the left after a few minutes' walking. It is unwise to proceed far into the gorge owing to risk from falling stones.

Scale Force is certainly one of the finest waterfalls in the Dis-trict. It has a sheer leap of over 100 feet—so deep that in ordinary times the sheets of water are, before reaching the bottom, almost converted into spray, and, as such, held suspended in the air. This effect is nowhere in the Lake District so noticeable as at Scale Force. The aspect of the fall, being north, is not favourable for the iris display one expects under such circumstances. It is well set in a rocky frame, abounding with copse and fern, though in this respect it is far inferior to Dalegarth Force in Eskdale.

There is a delightful bathing-place with a shingly bottom at the little promontory, about a quarter of a mile north of the landing-place, called Ling Crag. There is also a very fine view-point a couple of hundred yards or so lower down the lake.

The neighbourhood of Buttermere abounds in pleasant short walks through the woods and fields, and beautiful views are also obtained from the fell-side to the right of the Scale Hill road, a few minutes' walk from Buttermere village. To reach them proceed along Scale Hill road, for about 300 yards, then climb open fell on right, where it comes down to road beyond first farm-house.

Rannerdale.—A very pleasant little ramble, starting from the Scale Hill main road near Hause Point and skirting the Knotts. Buttermere may be regained by walking up from the Dale on to Blake Rigg and following the ridge down to the Post Office.

Buttermere to Keswick *vid* **Newlands.**—The road begins to climb at once, and in 1¼ miles mounts to 750 feet above Buttermere village. Robinson is the fell on the right, and Whiteless and Wandhope Fells on the left. The range of which the latter forms a part, and of which Grasmoor (2,791 *ft.*) is the crowning ridge, is a strong contrast to the rough, craggy contour of the more southern peaks. Its sides are of smooth green turf or ruddy screes. At the fall of the year, when the bracken turns to gold on the fells, the walk up **Buttermere Hause** is particularly fine.

Walkers may vary the route by following the course of *Sail Beck* instead of breasting Buttermere Hause, and descending by *Rigg Beck* into the main road again at Newlands. This means 600 feet extra. Except that it is off the main road, the walk has not much to recommend it. The best starting-point is from the Post Office, keeping the beck on the right at first. The latter part of the course is rough. An alternative is to quit the Pass close to the hause and walk to the left over Knott Rigg, descending to Keskadale by Addicombe, the open gully shown on the map (*p.* 163). This gully is extremely rough and will involve some scrambling. It is definitely *not* a route to be taken lightly.

The scenery after passing the summit-level of the hause is for a time desolate and barren, the road traversing the high-level *Keskadale Valley.*

The descent then commences through Keskadale into the green **Newlands Valley,** far inferior to Borrowdale, to be sure, but possessed of a soothing pastoral beauty which suffices to keep alive without overstraining the interest of the traveller, who, possibly, is beginning to feel that he has had enough of fine scenery for one day. The distant mountain in front beyond Keswick is Saddleback, and Hindscarth, Eel Crags, Maiden Moor, and Catbells—the last three on a declining scale—appear close at hand to the right of it. The main Newlands Valley comes down on our right, and is brought to an imposing end by Dale Head. Then, crossing Rigg Beck, the road passes a few buildings, and *Newlands* hamlet, and skirting the slope of Causey Pike, descends to right through a gate, nearly ¾ mile farther, to *Stair*, where an old mill, now a guest house, shows the former occupation of the people. General Fairfax lived in a house on the Keswick side of Stair marked " F. F. 1647." The Newlands valley continues north to Bassenthwaite.

From Stair, after crossing the Newlands beck, the road passes the hamlet of **Swinside** (*Inn*), and leaving Swinside Fell on the left soon reaches Portinscale. Hence walkers may save ½ mile by turning right to pass the Derwentwater Hotel, cross footbridge over river, turn right again along footpath crossing a meadow to join main road near Keswick Pencil Shop at Greta Bridge.

Keswick to Buttermere, by the Coledale Pass (*see p.* 202). *Time* 4 *hrs.*

Proceed as in the following excursion to Braithwaite where instead of following the Whinlatter road a track to the left should be taken up Coledale to Force Crag Mine. Keep south of Force Crag and climb to the *col* between Eel Crag and Grisedale Pike. The descent is by Gaskell Gill to Lanthwaite Green on the Cockermouth–Buttermere road.

Keswick to Buttermere, by Whinlatter Pass and Scale Hill ; also to Calder Abbey and Wasdale Head by Egremont or Ennerdale Bridge.

Distances.—*Keswick to Braithwaite* (*inns*), 2½ m. ; *Whinlatter Pass,* 4½ ; *Scale Hill Hotel,* 10 ; *Buttermere,* 14.

Scale Hill to Loweswater, 1½ m. ; *Lamplugh,* 6½ m. ; *Egremont,* 15 ; *Calder Bridge Hotel,* 19 ; *Strands* (*inns*), 25½ ; *Wasdale Head,* 31½.

Lamplugh Cross Inn to Ennerdale Bridge (*inn*), 3 m. ; *Ennerdale Lake,* 5.

Height of Whinlatter Pass, 1,043 *ft.* ; *Ennerdale Lake,* 368 *ft.*

The Whinlatter Pass offers a pleasant alternative route to Buttermere, or Ennerdale and Wastwater, for those who have already made the Buttermere excursion by Honister and Newlands. Beyond Loweswater the road passes the confines of the Lake District, and does not enter them again till the foot of Ennerdale or Wastwater, as the case may be, is reached. Walkers will prefer to cross the fells from Scale Hill to Ennerdale (*p.* 199).

From Keswick the road is that crossing the Greta Bridge, on the far side of which is a footpath cutting directly across the fields to Portinscale. The road bears sharp to the left a few hundred yards beyond the Greta Bridge. 1½ miles farther, after crossing the Newlands Beck and leaving the Bassenthwaite road on the right, we reach **Braithwaite,** after passing which the ascent of the **Whinlatter Pass** begins. During the ascent fine views are obtained across the vale of Keswick, over Bassenthwaite, and part of Derwentwater. The road then passes between Hob-carton End, the northern shoulder of Grisedale Pike, on the left, and Whinlatter Crag on the right and past one of the afforestation areas. A quarter of a mile beyond the sixth milestone (direction sign) walkers may take a short cut to the left and join the road again near Scale Hill. The main route descends steeply to Lorton.

Lorton Vale, with the river Cocker winding through it, is seen below. Beyond it, in the far distance, appear the Solway Firth and the Scottish hills, while the prospect southward gradually unfolds itself. Whiteside Dodd, and then Whiteside itself, rise close at hand, on the left, as we descend farther into the valley. Melbreak, with sides sloping as regularly as the roof of a house, Red Pike, recognisable alike from its colour and its shape, and High Stile successively appear on the farther side of Crummock and Buttermere ; and then the red, torrent-scarred Grasmoor presents itself. The fells which surround **Crummock Water** are much less wild and rugged in their contour than the other groups of Lake mountains. They are almost like so many vast heaps, and yet so graceful, and at the same time impressive, are they in their groupings, and so effectively is the shore of the lake indented, that Crummock justly challenges admiration as one of the most beautiful of our lakes. Few will deny that superiority which its comparative lightness gives it over Buttermere, and many prefer it even to Wastwater, for, though it shows less boldness of outline and unity of composition, it possesses a more varied picturesqueness.

From Lorton village the road runs west and then south for two miles through pleasant country which slowly increases in beauty and grandeur. At a fork, the left-hand branch leads direct to Buttermere (4 *m.*), and the right-hand branch to *Scale Hill Hotel,* which is reached in another mile.

The drive to Buttermere along the eastern shore of Crummock Water is very charming, especially on the terrace between Ran-nerdale Knott and the lake. It may also be commenced at Scale Hill, by a foot-road through Lanthwaite Wood (*National Trust*), joining the main one in just over a mile. The latter is decidedly the preferable route. In any case a digression should be made to **Lanthwaite Hill** (674 *ft.*), for the sake of the beautiful views of the lake and surrounding fells.

The hill is reached (*a*) by the right-hand branch by entering the road through the wood opposite the *Scale Hill Hotel* and diverging from it a few yards up a footpath on the left ; (*b*) by the left-hand branch, by crossing a wall on the right of the road, about ¼ of a mile short of Lanthwaite Green, once a British settlement. The nearer fells will be recognised from the previous description given of them in this route. The low crag descending into the lake at the far end on the left is **Rannerdale Knotts,** a little to the left of whose summit

Great Gable holds the pride of place in the distance. Green Gable is the lower and more pointed peak to the left of the latter, and Ill Crag, Scafell Pike, appears in the slight depression immediately on its right, between it and Kirkfell.

The **Circuit of Crummock** (9 *m.*) may be made on foot—a delightful walk, except the spongy bit, *Scale Bottom*, between Buttermere village and the Scale Force boat-landing. (There is a pleasant *alternative route* along the lake-side which avoids two miles of main road : a little below the *Scale Hill Hotel* a path leads through a wood to the lake near its outlet. The track continues above the lake side to the boat landings, through the wood to a stile, then along open fell land for about half a mile until a wooden ladder stile leads to the road near Cinderdale car park.)

Walkers can also go from Scale Hill to Buttermere by way of **Melbreak**, a very steep fell. From Loweswater village take the Mosedale track and turn up the green slope to scree close to crags. The top may also be reached from the shore of Crummock by the Pillar Rake, an interesting scramble to the depression between the two summits. The view includes Criffel, the Solway, Steeple, a bit of Pillar, Gable, Helvellyn, and Catchedicam.

Beyond the *Scale Hill Hotel* the road crosses the Cocker and, leaving the church and the village of Loweswater on the left, gradually ascends to High Cross and descends again to Loweswater, which is more than 100 feet higher than Crummock.

Loweswater Village (Inn) is half-way between Loweswater and Crummock lakes. On the old church land is **St. Ringan's** (= Ninian's) Well.

The two lakes are connected by a stream called Park Beck. A good view of Crummock and the surrounding fells is obtained during the ascent, Melbreak being prominent on the west side of the lake.

Loweswater is about 1¼ miles long by ⅓ mile broad. Its southern shore is gracefully fringed with wood, but it is almost entirely dependent for its attractiveness on the back views over Crummock and Buttermere, which are very beautiful, Grasmoor and Melbreak looking their best. For the lake walkers should turn down the first lane on the left after leaving Kirk Stile, then at first fork turn right through gate to Waterhead Farm. Continue through woods (Holme Woods) noticing Holme Force on left, turn right at Hudson Place to rejoin road at Grange Hotel.

The Ennerdale road passes Waterend and climbs Fangs Brow. On reaching the open fell (680 *ft.*), about a mile beyond the lake, and within a short distance of the top of the ridge, a sharp turn to the left must be taken. A wide view opens up to the right, including the sea and the Kirkcudbright hills of Criffel and Bengairn. The road crosses a shoulder of **Blake Fell**, whose summit (1,877 *ft.*) appears on the left, and two miles farther passes through the district of *Lamplugh* (formerly *Glanplugh*), between the church on the right and the hall on the left. There is a crusader's grave on the west side of the churchyard.

To reach Ennerdale Lake (2 *m.* from Ennerdale Bridge), walkers should take the turn to the left ⅓ mile beyond Lamplugh Church. Hence the distance is from 3½ to 4 miles. The road twists a good deal, but there is no difficulty until the farm-houses at *Croasdale*, about 2½ miles on the way, are reached. Turn right on joining a road near Croasdale, and after about 2 miles, turn up the second road on left, passing How Hall farm, then descend to the lake.

A mile beyond the church are **Lamplugh Cross** and the *Lamplugh Arms Inn.* Hence the nearest way to Calder Abbey is by the road which turns to the left half a mile beyond the inn, after crossing a small beck, and goes due south to **Ennerdale Bridge** (*inn*), three miles from Lamplugh Cross, and 1½ west of Ennerdale Lake. Ennerdale Bridge is the scene of Wordsworth's pastoral poem, "The Brothers." Hence to Calder Bridge is seven miles, by a hilly road, partly over the fells, and attaining a height of nearly 1,000 *ft.* From portions of the road the mountains flanking the Ennerdale depression are well seen—the Pillar conspicuous amongst them—and at one point the lake comes into view. Scafell Pike itself and Scafell, with the ravine of Mickledore between them, appear for a short time during the latter part of the drive, when the side of Cold Fell is being traversed. There are also wide views over the lowlands to the sea and the Isle of Man. The reactors at the Calder Hall atomic power station are a conspicuous landmark. For *Calder Abbey* and the road to Wasdale Head *see p. 47.*

The main road from Lamplugh to Egremont (9 *m.* ; *Globe Inn*) and Calder Bridge (13 *m.*) is 2 miles farther round, and passes through a good deal of the mining district.

Keswick to Patterdale (Ullswater). *Map at end of the book.*

The routes between these places may be summarised as follows:

	Motor. m.	Steamer. m.	Foot. m.	Total m.
(1) By *Troutbeck and Dockray* .	16	—	—	**16**
(2) ,, *Penrith and Pooley Bridge* .	23½	7½	—	31
(3) ,, *St. John's Vale and Dockray*	4	—	10	14½
(4) ,, *Sticks Pass (Helvellyn range)*	5	—	6	14
(5) ,, *Thirlspot, and over Helvellyn*	—	—	5½–6½ *hrs.*	

Distances in every case reckoned to Glenridding. For the village of Patterdale, at the entrance to the valley, one mile must be added.

Bus services between Keswick and Patterdale *via* Troutbeck station and also between Penrith and Patterdale, *via* Pooley Bridge and *via* Troutbeck. Buses to Ambleside connect Keswick with the western end of Sticks Pass and with Thirlspot. Times, etc., are prominently advertised in the town. There is a small hotel at

Troutbeck ; which, by the way, must not be confused with the Troutbeck near Windermere. No two places could be more different.

The last few miles of the Troutbeck route are very beautiful, but as the first half of the way from Troutbeck station lies through a remarkably bleak and uninteresting country (*see below*), those who have only one day to give to Ullswater will derive compensation for the extra time and expense of the journey by adopting route (2), by Penrith, for their journey to Ullswater, returning by Troutbeck. They will thus add to the day's enjoyment a pleasant drive from Penrith to Pooley Bridge and a beautiful sail along the whole length of Ullswater.

The St. John's Vale and Dockray track attains a summit-level of nearly 1,500 feet, and the immediate prospect, during a great part of it, is dreary—a high-level version of the Troutbeck route. It presents, however, fine views of the many-ridged Saddleback and of the Pennine chain on the far side of the Eden valley. Aira Force, too, may be visited *en route*, and the best of Ullswater seen in descending thence to Patterdale.

Of the remaining two routes, the shortest is the " Sticks," but the most interesting is the one over the top of Helvellyn, and as the Sticks mounts to within a few hundred feet of the summit of the mountain itself, few will grudge the extra toil and time which the latter exacts.

1. By Troutbeck and Dockray.—The Penrith road runs first through the romantic glen of the *Greta* and keeps south of the railway as far as Threlkeld Bridge, where it crosses to the north, when fine views are obtained of Saddleback on the left. **Threl-keld** (*Inns, Horse and Farrier* and *Salutation*) is an active little village. The church is old and not without interest. The *Hunters' Stone* in the churchyard, with its quaint inscription, is worth inspection. At **Troutbeck** station, situated on a dreary wilderness at a height of nearly 1,000 feet above sea-level, the Patterdale road branches off almost due south. Mell Fell rises on the left. The scenery becomes gradually more attractive, Matterdale Church is passed on the left, then **Dockray** (*Royal*) is reached, and the road crosses the stream which contributes Aira Force to the attractions of Lakeland. Thence the descent to Ullswater is very beautiful. *Gowbarrow Park* is on the left, and *Glencoyne* on the right—both rich in woodland scenery of the highest order.

Aira Force (*p.* 213) lies in **Gowbarrow Park**, a couple of hundred yards off the road, to the left, nearly a mile from Dockray. The footpaths to it are clearly marked. The road is rejoined on the lake-side near Lyulph's Tower. The Force and Gowbarrow Park are vested in the National Trust.

The uppermost and by far the finest reach of Ullswater is now in full view. On the left Place Fell rises abrupt and rocky. The western margin is beautifully wooded. The Patterdale valley rising to Kirkstone Pass, with Red Screes on the right and Caudale

Moor on the left, makes a fine perspective background ; and St.
Sunday Crag, which, by the by, has a great deal more to do in
forming the Ullswater scenery than Helvellyn, towers over the
woods on the right. This is one of the most impressive views in
the district, and has caused many visitors to form the idea that
Ullswater is the finest of the English Lakes. *For a full description, see pp. 52–3 and 212–13.*

The rest of the way along the margin of the lake is a delightful
drive or walk through the most varied of woods, interspersed
with the purplest of crags, and along a pebbly shore. The property
on both sides of the road belongs to the National Trust. Stybarrow Crag, once a feature of this part of the route, has been
much disfigured by blasting to widen the road.

2. By Penrith and Pooley Bridge.—The route to Troutbeck is
described in the foregoing, and the approaches *viâ* Pooley Bridge
on *pp.* 52–3. In the descent from Troutbeck to Penrith there is
nothing particular to arrest the traveller's eye, unless he is a
geologist : in which case he will mark with interest the transition
from the Skiddaw slate to the limestone, and from the limestone
to the red sandstone, which last contributes so greatly to the
beauty and fertility of the Eden valley. The Pooley Bridge
buses start from Penrith station.

3. By St. John's Vale and Dockray.—The first four miles of this
route, as far as *Wanthwaite Bridge*, by which the road crosses the
St. John's Beck, are described on *pp.* 170–1. Beyond that point
the road degenerates into a cart-track, which may be seen rounding
the northern shoulder of the Helvellyn Dodds, during the descent
into St. John's Vale.

From the bridge over the beck (4 *m.* from Keswick) the lane
ascends for a couple of hundred yards to the principal road
through St. John's Vale. Turn to the right along this for a
hundred yards, and then to the left up to some farm-buildings.
After a zigzag to the left, the road forks. Take the left-hand
branch, which leads between two walls on to the open fell, skirting for some distance farther the left-hand wall. On leaving the
wall, the track veers round to the right, and a long, up-and-down
stretch of some four miles commences. The first part of the road
is rough, but after crossing the Mosedale beck (a name indicative
of dreariness in these parts), nearly half-way between St. John's
Vale and Dockray, it greatly improves, and is for the rest of the
distance good going. During our long moorland trudge, the sharp
ridges of Saddleback and the distant prospect over the Eden valley
have been redeeming features in what must otherwise be described
as one of the dullest walks in the district ; nor has the monotony
been greatly relieved by our having as a constant *vis-à-vis* the
round Mell Fell. After passing some farm-houses the road

descends to **Dockray** (*Royal Hotel*) having, during the latter part of the descent, the dingle of the Aira Beck on the right. The remaining five miles to Patterdale are described in Route (1), *p.* 188.

4. **By the Sticks Pass.**—The existence of a tolerable bridle-path across this wild upland waste is to be attributed rather to the requirements of the natives than to the ardour of the tourist, though as a *tertium quid* between the labour of Helvellyn and the long monotony of the Dockray track the route is not to be despised. It is especially useful to Patterdale-bound tourists who, after getting well away from Keswick on the Ambleside road, are prevented going the " whole hog " of Helvellyn by the sudden on-comings of mist and other meteorological surprises, by no means unusual in the district.

Follow the Ambleside road (*p.* 191) as far as the head of St. John's Vale, where, after crossing at Smeathwaite Bridge, the stream which issues from Thirlmere, continue for half a mile to where a guide-post directs to Threlkeld, etc. Go through a gate to the white farm-house above, called *Stanah*. Beyond this farm you will have noticed a track zigzagging up the fell on the right of a gill.[1] This is your route, and, to reach it, you must cross the beck at the end of the field beyond the farm. After a steep rise of 700 or 800 feet a sheepfold is reached, and here the path bends slightly to the right, leaving the gill and ascending the shoulder of the fell at a more gradual slope, until it approaches and looks down upon another gill, at the top of which (2,420 feet above sea-level) the summit-ridge of the Helvellyn range is crossed. This point may also be easily reached from the *King's Head* at Thirlspot, by following the Helvellyn pony-track (*p.* 241) until it bends to the right on approaching **Fisher Gill**, which contains several very pretty falls, and then crossing the beck, and continuing along the left-hand side of its most northerly branch.

The highest part of the pass is appropriately marked by a number of sticks stuck into the ground at intervals. During the latter part of the ascent there is a fine retrospect of the northern and western fells, extending from Skiddaw to Bowfell. Underneath Skiddaw, Bassenthwaite Lake appears. At the summit a strip of Ullswater, backed by Place Fell and the High Street range, comes into view.

The descent, which is tedious in the extreme, is by *Greenside Reservoir* and *Lead Mine,* the former being kept on the right hand. From it there are two tracks—one leading straight on and crossing another ridge into *Glencoyne*, and the other, a good cart-track, passing between the reservoir and the huts, and joining the Glenridding descent of Helvellyn (*p.* 243), less than a mile lower down.

[1] This gill has, with others, been laid under contribution for Thirlmere by Manchester.

Hence the ordinary road descends on the left-hand side of the beck to the shores of the lake close to the *Ullswater Hotel.* The pleasantest route, however, is to cross a footbridge at the Mill, and, following a green path on the other side of the beck, descend after about a mile to a cart-track, which recrosses the beck and joins the regular road half a mile short of the hotel. If, instead of dropping into the cart-track at once, you climb the ridge which separates Glenridding from Grisedale for a little distance, you will be rewarded by a beautiful view down Ullswater, and you may without much trouble make your way down into Grisedale close to Patterdale Hall.

5. By Thirlspot, and over Helvellyn.—The route as far as Thirlspot is described below and thence in the ascents of Helvellyn in the Fell Section (*pp.* 239–44).

Keswick to Windermere and Bowness.   By Road.

Keswick to Thirlspot (inn), 5½ m. ; *Wythburn,* 8½ ; *Grasmere* (hotels), 12¼ ; *Ambleside* (hotels), 16½ ; *Waterhead* (hotel), 17¼ ; *Windermere Village,* 21¼ ; *Bowness,* 22¾.

Bus services between Keswick, Grasmere and Ambleside. Change at Windermere for Bowness. In summer buses and coaches make the through trip.
Route more fully described the reverse way, pp. 81–7.
The west-side Thirlmere road is to be preferred on account of the splendid views, though trees are screening these ever more completely. The greater part of the east-side road is entirely hemmed in by trees, which cut off all views across the lake. Those who are making the round of Thirlmere from Keswick (18–19 m.) will do best to take the east (main road) side on the outward journey, and the west on the return.

Leaving Keswick (by the Penrith road for nearly a mile), we ascend steeply for half a mile to *Castlerigg,* 700 ft. above sea-level. Hence very beautiful views are obtained over Derwent-water and Bassenthwaite (*see p.* 87). Saddleback is a striking object on the left.

At 2 miles from Keswick a path (finger-post) strikes off for St. John's-in-the-Vale Church (1¼ m.; *p.* 171), whence by either of two very pleasant tracks you may descend into St. John's Vale.

For the next two miles the route is comparatively dull, being neither valley nor mountain-pass. Helvellyn Low Man comes into view in front, and for some little distance remains visible at the same time as the summits of Skiddaw and Saddleback. Then (3 m.) we bend to the left and have a good view up *Shoulthwaite*

Gill (right), which after heavy rain presents a succession of foaming cascades.

West side of Thirlmere.—All those who have already travelled along the east side of Thirlmere should certainly sample the west side. The road, a grand one, is fully described on *pp.* 85–6.

It strikes off 4¼ miles from Keswick. Taken in this (the southward) direction the first ¾ mile is dull. Then comes, on the left, the Dam, and all the rest of the way is fair as fair can be. The chief points of interest are **Raven Crag** and the view up the lake, with Helvellyn Low Man occupying the pride of place. Then we pass (2 *m.*) the site of Armboth House, now demolished in connection with the raised level of Thirlmere, the Armboth Fell route (*p.* 159), and in another mile the foot of **Launchy Gill.** Another half-mile places us under Rough Crag—one of the gems of the route. Then after going through " New Nick " we skirt the lake and gradually drop till we cross the valley and re-enter the main road ¼ mile beyond **Wythburn Church.**

Nearly 4½ miles along the main road from Keswick the stream which issues from Thirlmere and threads the valley of St. John is crossed by *Smeathwaite Bridge.* The **Castle Rock of Triermain** presents an imposing front on the left, and soon a vista of the narrow valley of St. John, brought to a fine termination by sharp ridges of Saddleback, forms a pleasing retrospect northward. The road up the valley converges just short of the fifth milestone. The zigzag path, climbing the ravine from a white farm-house on the left, is the Sticks Pass to Patterdale.

In another half-mile we reach **Thirlspot** (*King's Head Inn*), near which is the start of the shortest ascent of Helvellyn from Keswick. Breasting the hill south of Thirlspot, the road suddenly reveals a splendid view across Thirlmere to the Armboth Fells—a view which is worth a halt, as here is almost the only break in the thick screen of trees between the road and the eastern shore of the lake. The huge bulk of Helvellyn rises on the left all the way, but only the lower skirts of the mountain are visible. Near the end of the lake is the hamlet of **Wythburn** (*see p.* 86). Wythburn is the handiest place for commencing the ascent of Helvellyn. The track is seen winding up the fell on the left.

Half a mile beyond Wythburn the west-side Thirlmere road comes in on the right, and then we begin the ascent of **Dunmail Raise,** the top of which (783 *ft.* above sea, *p.* 84) is rather more than a mile beyond Wythburn. The raise is between Steel Fell on the right and Seat Sandal on the left, and is the lowest depression in a chain of fells which extends west to east, from Wastwater and Ennerdale to the North Riding of Yorkshire. There is nothing particularly wild or grand about it, but the backward view of Thirlmere from shortly below the summit and, later, the view southward of the Vale and Lake of Grasmere are both very charming.

From Dunmail Raise the road makes a long descent to Grasmere. *Helm Crag* is conspicuous on the right and looked at from this direction, one of the famous rocks on its top certainly presents a grotesque appearance. First, it looks like a real " Lion " *minus* the " Lamb " ; then it changes to " a lady playing the organ." From the Grasmere side are seen the " Lion and Lamb."

After passing Helm Crag *Easedale* opens very beautifully on the right, and Sour Milk Gill is seen leaping down from the mountain recess in which lies Easedale Tarn. Loughrigg Fell is at the south end of the lake, and Silver How between it and Easedale.

The direct road goes straight on to Rydal and Ambleside ; but for **Grasmere** (*see p.* 145) turn off on the right at the *Swan Hotel.* The road through the village rejoins the main road near Wordsworth's Cottage and the head of Grasmere lake.

Alternative routes from Grasmere :

(1.) Pedestrians who are not paying a special visit to Grasmere on another occasion should take the right-hand road from the church, ascending by the western side of the lake, and then either regain the main road by **Loughrigg Terrace** and the western side of **Rydal Water** (*p.* 83), or keep straight along the road by the west slope of Loughrigg Fell, till they join the Ambleside and Langdale road about 2½ miles from Ambleside. In the latter case, when you have reached the highest point in the road—the depression between Loughrigg Fell and Silver How—go 300 yards up the road to the right, till you pass the large house called *High Close* (Y.H.). From here is a splendid view up the Langdales, and over Elterwater to Wetherlam and the other Lancashire fells.

(2.) The Keswick and Ambleside **old road** branches off to the left at the point, about a mile below the *Swan Hotel,* where the Grasmere village road rejoins the main route. It ascends past Wordsworth's Cottage (*see p.* 145) and crosses the rocky knoll which lies at the foot of Nab Scar, between Rydal and Grasmere, descending again into the present main road just as the former lake is reached This route is about a quarter of a mile shorter than that by the road alongside Grasmere Lake. It is hillier, but the views are excellent (*see pp.* 154–5).

(3.) Or starting from the same point, the footpath by White Moss Tarn and below Nab Scar to Rydal may be taken.

The main road, after skirting Grasmere Lake almost to its end, bends sharp to the left, and passes through the wooded dale along which the Rothay rattles in its sparkling course from Grasmere to Rydal Water. Some little way along the side of Rydal Water, in a short " bypassed " section of the old road, is *Nab Farm,* with memories of Hartley Coleridge and de Quincey (*see p.* 83). Then comes *Wordsworth's Seat* on the right, his house hidden behind Rydal Church on the left, the pretty village of **Rydal,** and the richly-timbered Rothay valley. For **Ambleside** (note the quaint *Bridge House* on right as the village is entered) *see* *p.* 107. Three-quarters of a mile farther on, the road reaches Windermere Lake at the **Waterhead** pier, whence one may continue to Bowness and Lake Side by boat. The head of Windermere is now in view. Wansfell shoots down its side to the left of the road, and for the next mile or so we have an excellent view across Windermere.

Beyond Low Wood the road leaves the lake, and for pedestrians it is for a couple of miles rather tiresome, chiefly between high walls and veils of trees. Beyond Troutbeck Bridge there is a fine view across the lake. Motorists and others not concerned with taking the most direct route into Windermere should turn off on the right, by the Bowness road, at the cross-roads about a mile beyond Troutbeck Bridge. This road is well worth following for the sake of the views across the Lake, especially that from Miller Brow (*see* p. 63).

For **Bowness and Windermere** *see pp.* 57–61.

Keswick to Ambleside, by the Stake Pass and Great Langdale.   *Map at end of the book.*

To Rosthwaite (road—bus services), 6½ m.   Rosthwaite to Great Langdale (bridle-path), 3 to 3½ hrs. (8 m.).   Dungeon Ghyll to Ambleside (road—bus services), by Great Langdale, 7½ m.   (Total mileage, 22 ; by Little Langdale, 24.)

Route described reverse way, pp. 129–31.

For the route as far as Rosthwaite, see p. 177. Hence take the first lane to the left, about half a mile beyond the village. In another 200 yards, when the road turns at right angles for the church, make a short cut straight ahead across two fields. Then pass as direct as possible through the hamlet of *Stonethwaite*, and, at the last house, take to the fields again, thus avoiding the rough cart-road above. The path, keeping the stream on the left, turns in about another mile sharp to the right round the base of a steep crag. There is a bridge about half a mile farther on and another bridge will be found nearly 3 miles higher up the valley.

The **Langstrath valley**, which the path now enters, is perhaps the most desolate in the Lake District in spite of the relief afforded by its delightful pools and cascades. Either bank of the beck may be followed, both are rough, but the right bank a little easier. The rugged slope of Glaramara, which separates Langstrath from the main Borrowdale valley, flanks the former throughout its entire course. The main valley veers to the right and ascends to Angle Tarn under Bowfell (*p.* 132). Avoid this, and the beck crossed, if still necessary, by a foot bridge about 100 yards below the confluence with Stake Ghyll. The pass itself is unmistakable, **zigzagging** up a steep slope with a tributary beck on the left

The top of the **Stake Pass** is soon reached, and then comes a mile or so of moraine-heaps, the highest point (1,576 *ft.*) marked by a cairn, after which the path crosses a beck which descends into Langdale. The fells surrounding the head of Langdale are now in view. Just in front, across the valley, is the peaked summit of Bowfell, lord of the scene ; beyond it, on the left, Crinkle Crags and the comparatively isolated Pike o' Blisco. Immediately on our left, and rising from the ridge over which we are travelling, is Pike o' Stickle, looking like a huge thimble.

As we zigzag downwards, with the beck on our left, the Langdale valley opens up, and the " Pikes " on the left of it begin to show their Windermere side. Strange as it may seem, they literally have no other, being quite lost to the north and west in long stretches of moorland of equal, or almost equal, height. From Scafell or Bowfell they are veritable pigmies.

At the bottom of the pass a sheepfold is reached, and here the track down Rossett Gill from Wasdale Head converges. Hence a pleasant grassy walk of about two miles leads to the *Old Dungeon Ghyll Hotel.* The *New Hotel* is nearly a mile farther down by road, ⅝ *m.* across the fields : Dungeon Ghyll itself may be visited *en route* (*see p.* 118). For the rest of the route to Ambleside, *see pp.* 129–30.

Keswick to Grasmere over the Fells. *Map at end of the book.*

There are three ordinary routes by which walkers can cross the fells between Keswick and Grasmere. Of these the finest and most laborious is through Borrowdale, Greenup, and Far Easedale ; the easiest by Watendlath and Harrop Tarn. The fell part of all these excursions is of little interest in itself, being across the somewhat featureless range which extends northwards from the Langdale Pikes to the neighbourhood of Keswick. As compensation, however, they disclose, one and all, a succession of very fine panoramic prospects. As they have all been fully described the reverse way in the Grasmere section (*pp.* 155–60), we shall content ourselves here with giving such bare instructions as are necessary.

1. By Borrowdale, Greenup, and Far Easedale.

Keswick to Rosthwaite, 6½ *m.* (*bus route as far as this*). *Stonethwaite*, 7½ ; *Stonethwaite to Grasmere village*, 3 to 4 *hrs.* ; *distance, about* 7 *m.* ; *pony-track. Top of Greenup Edge*, 1,995 *ft.*

The road as far as Rosthwaite is fully described on *pp.* 177–184.

Either leave Rosthwaite by the path behind the Scawfell Hotel, or, taking the main road, turn to the left along the road leading *vid* Stonethwaite to the Stake Pass and Langdale. (Time may be saved by crossing a couple of fields where the road turns sharp to the right in the direction of the little church.)

At Stonethwaite cross the beck by a cart bridge on the left, and join the track which runs alongside the stream. In about a mile the Langstrath opening, leading to Langdale, diverges between two finely-cut crags on the right. The Greenup track goes straight on up the valley in front. In about a quarter of an hour, when you have passed through a gate with a sheepfold on the far side of it, keep near the left-hand branch of the gill for a while. Numerous moraine-heaps now appear, and the path is very intermittent. The landmark to make for is a prominent rock, called Lining Crag, some way higher up the valley. Climb near the runnel on the left of this crag. At the top of the steep part a succession of small cairns begins, turning sharp to the left on reaching the summit of the pass, Greenup Edge, which is the depression between Ullscarf and High Raise. From the summit you look over the upper part of the Wythburn valley and a small ridge beyond, down to Helm Crag and Grasmere, getting also a glimpse of Rydal Water. Looking back westwards, Honister Crag presents a striking appearance over the northern slope of Glaramara.

From the top of the pass *Great Langdale* may be easily reached by bearing to the right and crossing High Raise (2,500 *ft.*), whence there is perhaps the finest panoramic mountain-view in the district (*p.* 252). Thence you may proceed either direct to the Langdale Pikes, or south-east to *Sergeant Man*, a rocky excrescence crowned by an obelisk-like cairn. Descend thence to *Stickle Tarn*, leaving the prominent height of Harrison Stickle on the right, and thence follow a track to the foot of Dungeon Ghyll (*see Map*). From Sergeant Man, too, you may easily descend to *Grasmere* by Codale and Easedale Tarns (*pp.* 154–5).

From the top of Greenup, be careful not to descend the Wythburn valley on the left, but cross the little ridge beyond it, and then you can have no further difficulty in reaching Grasmere, which is visible at the bottom of the Easedale valley. The path reappears some way down the latter depression, and crosses the beck at *Stythwaite Steps*, 2 miles short of the village.

2. By Watendlath, Harrop Tarn, and Dunmail Raise.

Keswick to Watendlath, 5 m. (*road*). *Watendlath to Grasmere*, 3 to 3½ *hrs*. (*about* 8 *m.*). *Highest point, about* 1,700 *ft*.

The route, as far as Watendlath, is described on *pp.* 172–4.

The Bowder Stone and Borrowdale may be included in the excursion at the cost of an extra hour, by keeping to the Borrowdale road as far as Rosthwaite and returning thence to Watendlath by the pony-track (*p.* 174) or by turning up the fell-side about half a mile short of Rosthwaite almost opposite Castle Crag, and picking up the pony-track higher up.

From Watendlath hamlet, climb the zigzag path up the fell to the left. The route is very easy to see. Where the ascent becomes more gradual, turn sharp to the right and keep along the upper side of the highest wall, where a finger-post shows the way. Hence there is no trustworthy path until you reach Harrop Tarn. Go on, in a south-easterly direction, till you see a dismal sheet of water in the midst of a peat bog. This is another *Blea Tarn*, and must be left considerably on the right hand.

A fine variation is to follow this track nearly to Blea Tarn, then bearing right by iron fence, with tarn on left, over *Coldbarrow Fell* and *Ullscarf* to Greenup Edge (p. 196).

Climb slightly beyond it, and you will soon look down upon *Harrop Tarn* with Wythburn beyond, a little to the left of your previous course. Pass close by the northern shore of the tarn, and cross the stream close to where it starts. Thence, skirting the craggy ground on the right, you will soon reach a cart-track, which leads to the Thirlmere west road and so to the top of *Dunmail Raise*. This means ending the walk with 4¼ miles of road work.

3. By Watendlath and Armboth Fell.

Keswick to Watendlath (road), 5 m. ; Watendlath to Wythburn, 2 to 3 hrs ; Wythburn to Grasmere (road—bus route), 4 m. Total distance, 14 m. Time, 4½ to 5¼ hrs. Highest point, 1,665 ft. It is well to bear in mind that with the closing of the Nag's Head at Wythburn there is no inn on this route.

For views this route is best taken the reverse way (p. 159).

The road to Watendlath is described on page 173. Thence the track zigzags up the steep fell-side, disappearing when it gains the grassy moorland above. Keep straight on in a line with the track from Rosthwaite to Watendlath, visible behind. Very well built cairns, the second on the highest point of the fell—*High Tove*—mark the way. It is better, however, to pass 100 yards or so south of the latter ; beyond it the ground is dreadfully boggy. Make straight for a little gate and in the direction of the foot of Helvellyn Gill, visible on the far side of Thirlmere. Before reaching the gate you cross *Fisher Gill*, and the track begins again. It passes through the gate and outside a walled-in wood all the way down to the west side of Thirlmere, 6¼ miles from Grasmere. The rest of this route is all road work.

Keswick to Wasdale Head.

For the *road route vid* Calder Abbey, *see p. 47.*

The two principal walking routes between Keswick and Wasdale Head pass through the heart of the grandest scenery in the district—the region of Scafell, as it is appropriately called. The direct route is by Sty Head Pass, 14 miles ; the other includes three passes—Honister, Scarth Gap and Black Sail, and the distance is nearly 20 miles. Vehicles can proceed as far as Seathwaite, 9¼ miles, on the Sty Head route ; or one can get to Buttermere by bus from Keswick *vid* Crummock and then walk to Gatesgarth at the beginning of the Scarth Gap route.

1. By Sty Head.

Keswick to Seatoller, 8 m. ; Seathwaite, 9¼ ; Sty Head Tarn, 11½ ; Wasdale Head, 14.

Height of Sty Head Pass, 1,600 ft. Time from Seathwaite to Wasdale Head, 2 to 3 hrs. Sty means "ladder"; from stigan, to rise.

The route has already been described as far as Seatoller (*p.* 180), to which point it is identical with the Buttermere excursion.

At a bend in the road a hundred yards or so before the village is reached (1½ *m.* beyond Rosthwaite), there is a lane on the left, which passes between a wood and the main stream of the Derwent to Seathwaite, crossing it about half-way.

A gateway on the right, just before the lane crosses the river, leads to the site of the famous yews, Wordsworth's "fraternal four of Borrowdale." They flourished on the near side of the beck, about ¼ mile from the bridge. Though destroyed by storms, up to quite recently their decayed trunks were to be seen. The girth of the largest was 22 feet. That of the famous yew in Darley Dale, Derbyshire, is 32 feet.

The main route may be regained by proceeding on along the track by the old plumbago mines, to which the Keswick pencils owed their fame, and recrossing the stream just opposite the hamlet of Sea-thwaite by a footbridge. Close to the crossing, one of the numerous Sour Milk Gills of the district descends by a series of small cataracts into the main stream from the wild upland valley of **Gillercombe,** which lies between Base Brown, Brandreth and Green Gable. (Those who adopt Gillercombe as an approach to Green Gable may be warned that it is a very monotonous route once the scramble up beside the Gill has been accomplished.)

Seathwaite is principally remarkable for rain (its average annual rainfall is 125 inches—London's average being 23 inches per annum). It is the wettest inhabited place in England. Cars may be left here, and refreshments obtained.

As we leave the houses, we are closely hemmed in by the steep slopes of Glaramara on the left and Base Brown on the right. The precipices of Great End, the northern buttress of Scafell, fill up the valley in front. Some distance ahead *Taylor Gill Force* descends between our track and Base Brown. Two hundred yards after its waters join the main stream, our path crosses **Stockley Bridge** (the valley straight ahead is *Grain Gill,* the shortest way up to Esk Hause and Scafell Pike, *p.* 262), and passing through a gate pursues a tortuous course up the fell on the right, drawing gradually nearer to Taylor Gill. When it has reached the level of the top of the force it becomes comparatively flat ; Lingmell appears in front, and Scafell Pike to the left of it. After crossing the beck, we pass **Sty Head Tarn** on the left. The streamlet which crosses our path just before reaching the tarn comes down the depression (Aaron Slack) between Green Gable and Great Gable.

Some little distance to the left of the track hereabouts is a small Bowder Stone. It rolled down Green Gable many years ago.

Soon after passing the tarn, the track over Esk Hause to Rossett Gill and Langdale strikes off on the left. (The boggy character of the ground makes it inadvisable to attempt short cuts.) Then a pile of stones marks the top of **Sty Head Pass** (1,600 *ft.*), and the path, sweeping round the side of Great Gable to the right, commences the steep, stony descent to Wasdale Head. It affords curious views of the **Napes Rocks**.

We are now in the very heart of the wildest scenery of England. There is an almost savage grandeur in the prospect all round, such as few who have not experienced it could imagine to exist at so small an elevation as 1,500 feet above sea-level.

A descent may be made from near the top of the pass into the valley in front, and then the course of the stream followed to Wasdale Head. The stream can be crossed by the new footbridge erected in 1973. The imposing fissure running down east of Lingmell is **Piers Gill**, the deepest, narrowest, and most striking ravine in the district (*but see p.* 264).

From the top of the pass to the first house in Wasdale (*Burnthwaite*) is 1¾ miles. Go to left of the house, whence a cart-road leads to the church, which, if not the smallest, is certainly the least pretentious ecclesiastical edifice in England. From it a path to the right, across a field, leads straight to the *Wastwater Hotel*.

2. By Honister, Scarf Gap, etc. To *Gatesgarth, see p.* 181; *thence to Wasdale Head, p.* 203.

Buttermere or Scale Hill to the Anglers' Hotel, Ennerdale, by Floutern Tarn. *Map at end of the book.*

Distance, 6 *m. Time,* 3 *to* 3½ *hrs. Foot-track. Height of Pass,* 1,300 *ft.*

Each of these routes is rather tiresome—the Buttermere one especially—in consequence of the quantity of bog to be crossed. The scenery is not of a high order, but tourists who wish to see Ennerdale will find these the most convenient approaches from the Keswick part of the district, and they may obtain ample amends for any temporary disappointment by following up with the glorious walk from the foot of Ennerdale Lake over the Pillar (*p.* 255), or the Wastwater Red Pike to Wasdale Head.

The two routes converge a little more than half-way, and shortly before reaching Floutern (pronounced Flootern) Tarn.

1. From Buttermere.—Follow either of the Scale Force routes (*p.* 182) as far as the force itself. Thence travel westward, keeping well up on the fell-side to avoid the boggy ground on the right. The cart-track from the Scale Hill is seen coming up on the right between Melbreak and Hen Comb. In front is the low ridge which you have to surmount. Cross the bog as near to its upper end as possible, and join the Scale Hill track at a gate in a wire fence.

2. From Scale Hill.—Take the road to *Loweswater* village, which diverges from the main road to Loweswater Lake by the second turn to the left after crossing the Cocker. Leave Loweswater Church and Inn on the right, cross the beck which connects Loweswater and Crummock, and proceed by the cart-track between Melbreak on the left and Hen Comb on the right, keeping the Mosedale Beck on the right for about two miles, and then crossing it. Loweswater is pleasing during the ascent from the bridge. Soon after crossing the beck the track winds round to the right and passes through a gate in a wire fence, at which point it is joined by the Buttermere route.

From the point of convergence the track becomes indefinite, but by climbing the fell with the fence a little to the left you will soon come in sight of **Floutern Tarn** on the same side. It is a dreary sheet of water, with but little of the picturesque about it, except the craggy slope of Herdhouse on its southern side. During the ascent there is a pleasant retrospect over Buttermere Hause, with Robinson and Whiteless Pike on its right and left hand respectively, and part of the Helvellyn range forming the distant skyline.

On reaching the watershed just beyond the tarn, the scene opens westward, but, until Ennerdale Lake appears in the foreground, it has anything but an inviting appearance.

The track, faintly marked, proceeds past remains of three iron gates, the first of which is about 50 yards to the right of a square corner in the fence. For a mile or so it keeps a short distance on the left a beck descending into Ennerdale. In descending keep it slightly left of the line of your course, and pass from the open fell through a gate which brings you on to a green cart-track and footpath. Avoid a lane on the left, and about 200 yards farther, when you come to cross-roads, enter a field by the first gate on the left beyond the cottage at the corner. The conspicuous crags on the left are Bowness Knotts. Hence descend to the lake-side.

Reverse Route, Lake Ennerdale to Scale Hill or Buttermere by Floutern Tarn.

Time, 3 to 3½ hrs. Distance, 6 m. Foot-track all the way. Height of Pass, 1,300 ft.
The Scale Hill route is by far the better going of these two, and affords the tourist the opportunity of continuing his journey to Buttermere by the beautiful walk along the eastern shore of Crummock Water.

From the lake-side car park proceed along the lake shore road eastward, keeping left after passing through the second gate. Pass a farmhouse and continue along lane until a narrow made-up road is reached. Turn left up the hill and at top turn right through a gate on to open fell towards Banna Fell. Bear right and follow well-worn footpath to the left of Roughten Gill to Floutern Tarn which is just over the rise. Keep the beck, which you will shortly see, well on your right hand, and proceed along the faintly-marked path which passes through three iron gates, the last one being near the highest point of the walk, and about 50 yards to the left of a square corner in a wire fence. A green hump, Floutern Kop, is noticeable in front ; this should be kept well on the left. Near the summit **Floutern Tarn** comes into view, with the pyramid of Red Pike rising over the ridge beyond it. Then, as you descend, keeping the wire fence above mentioned about 50 yards to the right, the depression of Buttermere Hause appears in front, with Robinson on its right hand and Whiteless Pike and Grasmoor on the left, the Helvellyn range cutting the far horizon. You will shortly reach a gate in the fence, after passing through which walkers to (*a*) **Scale Hill** will find no difficulty in tracing the cart-track, which works round to the left, and after crossing the Mosedale Beck descends between Melbreak and Hen Comb to **Loweswater** village. Here there is a snug little inn, beyond which you leave the church on the left, and turn to the right a short distance farther down the road which, after crossing the Cocker, ascends in 300 yards to *Scale Hill Hotel.*

(*b*) For **Buttermere** cross the bog to the opposite fell-side, as soon as you can after passing the last-mentioned gate, and proceed along it past the gorge in which lies Scale Force—only a few yards from the track (*p.* 182). Hence proceed to the south-west corner of Crummock Water, and follow a sloppy track alongside the stream connecting Buttermere and Crummock Water, till you come to a stone bridge, which takes you on a cart-track leading across the meadows to *Buttermere Village* (*p.* 181).

Buttermere to Keswick, by Honister Pass. *Map at end of the book.*

To Gatesgarth (farm-house), 2 m. ; Top of Honister Hause (1,190 ft.), 4½ ; Seatoller, 6 ; Rosthwaite (hotels), 7½ ; Bowder Stone, 9 ; Keswick, 14.

The route from Keswick to Buttermere has been fully described (*p.* 177), and as there is no fear of losing the way we shall merely give the barest details of the reverse route.

Leave Buttermere village by the right-hand road, which soon runs along the north-east side of Buttermere Lake. The promontory of *Hassness* is passed in about 1½ miles, and the farm-house of *Gatesgarth* in two miles. Beyond the farm the scenery changes from green pastures to stern and sterile rocks. Just beyond the top of the hause Glaramara comes into view in front, and beyond it the Helvellyn range.

An alternative and slightly shorter route to Grange—and one which is entirely free from motor and other traffic—begins at a stile in the fence on the left of the old toll road, a few hundred yards below point where it finally parts company with main road. The path leads across to a gap in a wall, beyond which and parallel to our route is another wall, which should be kept on the *right* hand. The path soon becomes well marked, and leads very pleasantly along the slope of the western fells of Borrowdale between Scawdel Fell on the left and a wooded knoll, followed by Castle Crag, to *Grange*, where the river may be crossed, and the regular road, along the east side of Derwentwater, resumed ; or the route along the west side of the same lake under Catbells taken, for a description of which *see p.* 168.

On leaving the open fell about a mile beyond the hause, a steep descent is made to *Seatoller* whence the route to Keswick has been fully described in the reverse direction on *p.* 177.

Buttermere to Keswick by the Coledale Pass. (*Time* 4 hrs.)

Take the Cockermouth road to Lanthwaite Green and thence turn up by Gaskell Gill, which runs down the ravine between Grasmoor and Whiteside. The beck at the bottom can be crossed by a bridge a short distance downstream at Lanthwaite Green, then keep the beck on right all the way to the summit. The path is very narrow. Farther up the pass are some pretty falls and on the left, on Whiteside, is a fine craggy combe. From the top of the *col* the track is to the northwards directions ; in descending take the right-hand track round Force Crag and cross the valley depression ; do not take the quarry ropeway from the top of the *col*. An easy alternative lies down the lower slopes of Eel Crag. Coledale Beck is now crossed and a green track taken which leads along the slopes of Grisedale Pike to Braithwaite, 2½ miles from Keswick.

Buttermere to Wasdale Head, by Scarth Gap and Black Sail. *Map at end of the book.*

Road to Gatesgarth, 2 m. Bridle-path from Gatesgarth to Wasdale Head, 3 to 4 hrs. Total Distance, 9 m. Height of Passes—Scarth Gap, 1,400 *ft. ; Black Sail,* 1,800 *ft.*

From no other trodden path in the district is the rugged grandeur of the wildest of the Lake mountains so fully revealed. Scafell, the Pillar, and Great Gable appear to the greatest advantage, and the dip down into **Ennerdale**—the wildest, loneliest, and yet by no means the gloomiest, of English valleys—is full of delight.

From Buttermere the walker may take which side of the lake he chooses. As a variety, we recommend the path along the southern side which starts from the village by the lane on the left (Buttermere) side of the *Fish Hotel*. A track traverses the meadows and crosses the beck which connects Buttermere and Crummock. Cross the stone wall by a wooden ladder stile and turn left along the southern shore of the lake. Red Pike, High Stile, and High Crag tower above the lake very imposingly, and there are fine views. Scarth Gap lies immediately beyond High Crag.

The northern route follows the Honister road as far as the farm-house of **Gatesgarth**, two miles from the village, whence, passing through the gate, it traverses a couple of fields which form part of the strath at the head of the lake, and, after converging with the southern track just beyond another bridge, commences the steep ascent of **Scarth Gap**. The passage into Ennerdale is made over the dip between High Crag on the right and Hay-stacks on the left. Some of the way is very rough. Descending into the valley, we have Kirkfell just opposite to us, with Great Gable forming a fine headpiece on its left, and the massive front of the Pillar farther down the valley to the right. The famous Pillar Rock, a few hundred feet below the summit on the Enner-dale face of the mountain, shows up grandly from near the foot of the pass.

As we descend, the most natural outlet on the other side of the valley appears to be the dip between Great Gable and Kirkfell—that is, on the left of Kirkfell; the real one is on the right between Kirkfell and the Pillar, but the pass is hidden by a pro-jecting spur of Lookingstead. This should be remembered in ascending on the other side. The head of Ennerdale is afforested, and enormous numbers of young trees are springing up to the right of the path. After affording a view of Ennerdale Lake, far down the valley to the right, the path descends to the bottom of the valley, along which it proceeds till, leaving the Youth Hostel on the left, it turns down to a footbridge right opposite the foot of Black Sail. Then it climbs again with a beck on the left-hand side and a fence on the right.

When the summit of **Black Sail** is gained, Kirkfell Crags rise boldly on the left. On the right is the south side of the Pillar, and across the Mosedale valley in front a fine view of Red Pike and Yewbarrow opens up.

As the path works round to the left into *Mosedale*, the precipices of **Scafell** itself tower like a huge castellated fortress over the Wasdale valley. There are few grander prospects anywhere than this sudden vision of England's greatest mountain.

The *Wastwater Hotel* soon appears below, and the path leads down the valley straight to it, keeping the Mosedale Beck on the right hand all the way.

Wasdale [1] **Head** (Telephone Kiosk outside the *Wastwater Hotel*. Postal address : Wasdale Head, Holmrook, Cumbria). Approaches from Seascale and Drigg, *pp.* 46, 47.

As it is only from its lower end that the lake of **Wastwater** can be seen with advantage, we have described it in the first route approaching it from that direction—that from Ambleside to Wasdale Head (*p.* 128).

It now only remains for us to say a few words about **Wasdale Head** itself. Situated in a deep depression formed by the loftiest and steepest mountains in England, and with no natural outlet except the narrow one along which the lake leaves little more room than is sufficient for the road to pass, Wasdale Head is perhaps the wildest of all the inhabited spots in our country. The green patches of cultivation, intersected by stone walls, and the few farmsteads, each claiming by name and position its individuality, are scarcely strong enough features in the scene to relieve it of its pervading severity of aspect, caused by the mass and close proximity of the mountains ; and it is only when the lake itself comes into prominent play, or the fell-sides are exceptionally chequered with light and shade, that the prospect can be called strictly beautiful. The *maximum* population of Wasdale Head during a long period has been little more than fifty. It boasts a church which, if not positively the smallest in England, is certainly the quaintest. Externally the building measures 42 by 16 feet.

There can be but little doubt that human association has materially assisted Nature in establishing the renown of Wasdale Head, The name of William Ritson, who was for many years prior to 1879 landlord of the *Wastwater Hotel*, was known in every county, probably in every town in England. He was the " Cumberland 'statesman " to the marrow of the backbone. An intercourse with almost every class of society, extending over two generations of men, had not the slightest perceptible influence in changing either his manners or his dialect. An inveterate and at the same time consistent foe to modern luxury—this " old man eloquent," seated on a rude wooden bench in his own unevenly paved kitchen, held forth to visitors of every degree. His tales were as varied as they were numerous, and it was seldom that a topic could be introduced upon which he would not have some original opinion to offer. The stories of the wrestling match with Professor Wilson, of the miserly Eskdale parson, and the famous pony-race down Sty Head, are only a few of a host of Cumbrian " epics," which will, we hope. be preserved, though they can never be seasoned by a copyist with the " salt " imparted to them by their author.

A charming little force, ⅓ mile above the inn, was named " Ritson Force " by the late Mr. Baddeley.

---

[1] The name is sometimes, but less correctly, spelt Wastdale.

Will Ritson died at Strands in 1890, at the venerable age of eighty-three. He was one of the very last representatives of a type of Englishman which has, alas, been "civilised" out of the country—the "Cumberland 'statesman."

The lake itself is about a mile from the hamlet, and a walk to its head is very well worth while. The view down Wastwater is impressive and singular—there is nothing like it in Britain, at any rate south of the Border. On the left the lake is walled in by the long parti-coloured slopes of the Screes. On the right are Yew-barrow, Middle Fell, and beyond the foot, Buckbarrow. The conspicuous little eminence at the foot of the lake is Irton Pike, Wasdale Head is the best rock-climbing centre in the district. most of the famous climbs being on either Great Gable or Scafell.

Wasdale Head to Ambleside, by Esk Hause (2,370 ft.) and Langdale. *Map at end of the book.*

Wasdale Head to Dungeon Ghyll Hotels, 4½ to 5½ hrs., 8 to 9 m. (bridle-path). Dungeon Ghyll to Ambleside, 7 to 8 m. (road).

This is considerably the shortest route from Wastwater to the Windermere and Grasmere district, and one of the finest walks.

As far as the top of Sty Head (1,600 *ft.*) the route is the same as to Borrowdale (*p.* 211). A few yards beyond the cairn at the top of the pass, the path, such as it is, for Esk Hause bends away to the right, crossing some boggy ground, which makes the first part of it difficult to trace. It then climbs a small depression in the fells, from which the principal feeder of the tarn descends. Crossing this beck in about ¼ hour, keep it close on the right till you recross it at the point of its outflow from *Sprinkling Tarn* (*p.* 133). The precipices and gullies of Great End on the right are very fine. From Sprinkling Tarn the path goes on ascending, and very soon passes a ravine on the left, down which one of the tributary becks of Borrowdale flows. This is *Ruddy Gill*, and is so called from the red colour of the rock exposed to view. Down it a glorious view now opens over the lower end of Borrowdale and Derwentwater to Skiddaw and Saddleback, with the beautiful little Castle Crag popping up in the midst of the valley. The path continues upwards, with the beck on the left hand, to the summit of our pass on the *Esk Hause* ridge. Everything is perfectly plain in clear weather ; but if clouds are about the tourist will do well to remember the following facts :—

Esk Hause is the depression between Great End and Esk Pike (this is the correct name for the 2,903-feet peak which is popularly but incorrectly termed Hanging Knott : Hanging Knott is the shoulder of Bowfell above Angle Tarn), portions of the Scafell and Bowfell groups of mountains respectively, both of which are kept on the right during the whole of the present route. The summit (2,490 *ft.*) of the hause is the watershed of Borrowdale to the north, and Eskdale to the south. Consequently the track from Wasdale to Langdale, which bears from north-west to south-east, does not actually cross the main ridge, but runs parallel to it, a few hundred yards on the Borrowdale side, and about 100 feet below the level of the hause itself. Oddly enough, the waters from both sides of the lateral ridge which our present route crosses, though starting in exactly opposite directions, find their way into the same valley—Borrowdale— and it is probably ignorance or disregard of this fact which has caused so many people to go wrong at or about this particular spot, when from bad weather or other causes they have lost sight of the path. Hence it will be seen that the points to be avoided are—first, descending into Eskdale on the right; secondly, dropping down to Borrowdale on the left. The first danger may be avoided if it is remembered that the cairn and shelter are *below* and to the north of the actual summit of the hause.

The cairn and the shelter erected by the Lake District Association are some few yards to the right of the track, so far from it that in thick weather it is possible for people to pass by without noticing it. Windermere is visible in front on reaching the summit. Just past the cairn the path becomes rather indistinct, but is soon met with again. After about 10 minutes' descent, the first beck descending to Langstrath (the eastern arm of Borrowdale) is passed. Then a slight ascent, and another drop to the second beck, flowing into the same valley. This stream issues from **Angle Tarn,** just below the margin of which the path crosses it. Hence is a short steep rise to the top of **Rossett Gill.** The sharp peak of Pike o' Blisco and Wetherlam, filling up the gap between it and Bowfell, here come into view on the right. In front a portion of the upper reach of Windermere reappears. The old track straight down the gill is rather rough, though with a good deal of stumbling about it may be practicable. It is preferable to descend for ¼ mile or so by the old pony-track considerably to the right of the gill, till you come to a new bit which diverges sharp to the left. Very little further direction is needed. The path zigzags down to the bottom of the steep part, where it crosses the bed of the stream, and then, keeping to the left of it, joins the Stake Pass (*p.* 195) at a sheepfold. All the way down, the green pastures of Great Langdale are spread before the eye, and exactly in front the road from Dungeon Ghyll to Blea Tarn and Little Langdale is seen winding up the depression between Pike o' Blisco and Lingmoor.

The route from the sheepfold to the *Dungeon Ghyll Hotels* (2 and 2¾ *m.* respectively) is quite plain (*see p.* 195). The Langdale Pikes rise grandly on the left hand.

Wasdale Head to Buttermere, over Black Sail (1,800 ft.) and Scarth Gap (1,400 ft.), 3 *to* 4 *hrs.*, 9 *m. Map at end of the book.*

For those who have reached Wasdale Head from Strands, Eskdale, or by the Sty Head Pass from Langdale or Borrowdale, this is the most remunerative route to Keswick. It is described, the reverse way, on *pp.* 202–3.

Starting from Wasdale Head the path ascends by the Mosedale valley, which separates Kirkfell from Yewbarrow, and the Wastwater Red Pike. Keep the stream on the left for a few hundred yards, avoiding a route on the right to Burnthwaite. Passing through a gate and along the upper side of a wall, the track runs along the open fell-side. Where it forks, take the upper branch. From this point the way can hardly be mistaken during the rest of the journey. At first the Pillar rises directly in front, the slight depression to the left of it being Windy Gap. So far, Black Sail is hidden by the steep slope of Kirkfell, whose base we are skirting. Presently the path crosses Gatherstone Beck, and winds steeply up *Gatherstone Head*, a glacier mound, some three-quarters of a mile short of the head of the Pass. During the ascent the retrospect of the magnificent cliffs of Scafell itself (not Scafell Pike) are very striking.

At the summit of Black Sail, rather more than an hour's walk from Wasdale Head, Great Gable reasserts itself on the right, beyond Kirkfell, and the range of which it is monarch is continued northwards by Green Gable, Brandreth, and Grey Knotts. In front the prospect is bounded by Dale Head and the other heights between Honister Pass and Newlands. Scarth Gap is the lowest part of the depression between the Haystacks and the heights of High Crag, High Stile, and Red Pike, which separate Ennerdale from the Buttermere valley. Beyond it is the red broadside of Grasmoor.

The descent into Ennerdale is clearly marked. It keeps a beck close on the right-hand side nearly the whole way, and crosses the Ennerdale stream (the *Liza*, locally " Leeza ") at the bottom by a footbridge opposite the Youth Hostel, where it bears to the left. After about half a mile, the track climbs up to the right, over Scarth Gap. As we climb there is a fine view down Ennerdale. The Pillar to the left and Great Gable at the head of the valley present their boldest front ; and after reaching the summit-level between High Crag on the left and Haystacks on the right, the valley of Buttermere, with Robinson straight in front, and the Fleetwith ridge separating the head of the dale from the Honister Pass, disclose themselves with telling effect. The descent is rough and steep, the lower part, however, zigzagging over a smooth grass slope, at the bottom of which is a bridge over the beck, which leads on to the level strath and the head of the lake. Cross this to the farm-house of *Gatesgarth* where the path joins the Honister road, just two miles from Buttermere village (*p.* 181).

There is also a path along the south side of the lake at the bottom of High Stile and Red Pike, affording fine views of the twin waters of Buttermere and Crummock. It turns sharply to the right immediately beyond the lower end of the Buttermere lake, and, crossing a footbridge and some meadows, enters the village at the back of the *Fish Hotel*.

Wasdale Head to Coniston, by Eskdale, Birker Moor, and Walna Scar.   *Map at end of the book.*

Wasdale Head to Strands, 6 m. ; *George IV Inn,* 11½ ; *Travellers' Rest* (*Ulpha*), 17½ ; *Coniston,* 25½.

This route is practicable for vehicles as far as the foot of Walna Scar, 3¼ miles beyond Ulpha, and half a mile past Seathwaite. The path over Walna Scar (2,035 *ft.*) is a pony-track leading out of the Duddon valley, whence the ascent commences. Those who drive must go round by Broughton.

The walker can choose from a variety of routes, but the one by Burnmoor Tarn will probably be preferred, as being considerably shorter than that by Strands, and passing Stanley Ghyll on the way. From Wasdale Head to Boot, in Eskdale, is a two-hours' walk ; thence to Stanley Ghyll, half an hour ; from Stanley Ghyll to Ulpha, 2 hours, allowing time to see the force ; and from Ulpha to Coniston, over Walna Scar, 3 hours—the whole forming a long summer-day's expedition. In clear weather it is not difficult to save an hour or so by cutting off the Ulpha corner, as will be seen from the description.

The road route in this direction is seldom used, and the descriptions of it . taken the reverse way, on *pp.* 141–4, from Coniston to the *George IV Inn,* and on *pp.* 127–8 from the *George IV* to Wasdale Head, will afford sufficient information on the subject. At the same time it is really a fine drive, especially as it shows off Wastwater to advantage.

Walking route.—From Wasdale Head, take the road to the lak for about ¾ mile, as far as a large white gate on the left. Pass through this and then cross two bridges. Do not turn off in the direction of Wasdale Hall farm, but go through a gap in the wall on the left. Thence there is but little difficulty as far as Boot. The path, a horse-track, works up to the right, for the depression between Scafell itself and the Screes. During the ascent there is a good view down Wastwater, and the Pillar at the head of the Mosedale valley soon becomes conspicuous in the rear.

From hereabouts the broken skyline (Green Crag, etc.) beyond Boot on the far side of Eskdale assumes the appearance of a colossal recumbent figure, lying on its back with its head towards the sea.

The top of the pass is on the Wasdale side of **Burnmoor Tarn,** the stream issuing from which is forded close to its eastern shore. After this the path is in places indistinct, but cannot be lost for many steps as long as you keep parallel to the stream at from

100 to 200 yards' distance from it, giving it a wider berth when it diverges slightly to the left.

A short cut to the *Woolpack Inn* in Eskdale, and thence round the western base of Harter Fell into the **Duddon valley,** may be made by crossing the stream by a little bridge about half a mile from where it leaves Burnmoor Tarn. Thence follow a line of whitened stones. A peat-track winds down from near **Eel Tarn** in the direction of the inn, which may be recognised by a short avenue in front of it. From the inn turn right down the road for about 100 yards then left down a lane to the river which is crossed by Penny, or Doctor's, Bridge. Continue to Penny Hill Farm and, beyond, take second cart track on the right which rises and follows the line of a wall part way up the fell side until it joins a track near a stream which comes in from the foot of Hard Knott. Turn right up this path and, for *Harter Fell,* leave it a little higher up to the left on the fell side. For the *Duddon Valley* keep to right of Harter Fell until you look down into the valley. A farm-house—**Grass Guards**—is visible some way down the slope, and the Walna Scar route rises in front on the opposite side of the river. At Grass Guards the stream may be crossed by a bridge and thence a track descends to some stepping-stones (there is a bridge ¾ mile down stream as an alternative should the Duddon be in flood *(see p. 143)*), beyond which it rises quickly into the valley road. Ten minutes' walk along this road to the right brings you to the junction of the Walna Scar track (sign-post). (For alternative route, *see p. 143.*)

Before commencing the steeper part of the descent from Burnmoor Tarn into Eskdale you leave a keeper's house—the second during the journey across the moor—a short distance to the right. The main route descends to the bridge and the *Burnmoor Inn* at **Boot** *(p. 127).* During the descent Harter Fell and the other rocky heights rising to the right of it look their best.

From Boot enter the main road leading down Eskdale, and follow it as far as the first turn to the left, opposite the old school. Take this turn, cross the river, and, immediately beyond the bridge, if you want to see Dalegarth Force (Stanley Ghyll), turn up through a gate (signposted) about 200 yards beyond Dalegarth Hall. The route to the force is described on *p. 126.*

After emerging from the wood in which the force lies on to the road again, you will pass, in less than a mile, a farm-house called *Low Ground.* Avoid a cart-track to the right, a little way beyond this, and proceed to another and more extensive group of farm-buildings called **Birkerthwaite.**

After passing Birkerthwaite, there is little or no track, and nothing much in the way of a landmark in front. The direction is a little west of south; in the rear, the Pillar mountain, when visible, is a good guide, and by holding on with it directly behind you, and in the direction of your previous course, you will soon enter the road from Eskdale *(p. 142)* to the Duddon valley. For an alternative and unmistakable route by a cart road see the Map. Hence to the comfortable little *Travellers' Rest* at **Ulpha** the route is clear.

Holehouse Gill is a charming little ravine, a mile south of the inn. Take the road to Broughton, but, instead of crossing the bridge, continue past the mill, where the gill is crossed, and ascend the hill to the old smithy, whence drop again to the waterside by a woodpath. The **Lady's Dub**, ¼ mile higher up the stream, is a waterfall where tradition avers the Lady of Ulpha to have been worried by a wolf. Near at hand are the remains of the *Old Hall*.

Fine views of the **Duddon valley** may be obtained with little exertion from **Pike Hill** (1,214 *ft.*), just above the Lady's Dub; also from **Mount Kingdom**, the **Penn** (near Frith Hall) and from **Hesk Fell** (1,566 *ft.*).

From Ulpha on to Broughton is 5 miles (*p.* 141).

From Ulpha it is 3½ miles up the valley to the point of divergence of the Walna Scar track, marked by a finger-post. The main road crosses the river at *Hall Dunnerdale* (1½ *m.*).

Without crossing the river here you may continue along its west side to Wallowbarrow and reach **Seathwaite** (*inn*; *p.* 142) by a footbridge just above Wordsworth's "Stepping-stones."

Beyond the finger-post the route is approximately eastwards (avoid tracks northward to Seathwaite Tarn) in the direction of a disused quarry. The track climbs the hill to the right, scales Walna Scar at a height of nearly 2,000 *ft.*, and then, crossing the stream which flows from Goats Water on the left by a rude stone bridge, skirts the steep part of the south shoulder of the Old Man and, joining an excellent cart-road leading up to the quarries on that mountain, drops down to Coniston by the old railway station.

(The Walna Scar route is described in the reverse direction on *pp.* 141–2.)

Wasdale Head to Keswick, by Sty Head Pass.

To Seathwaite, 2½ hrs. ; Rosthwaite, 3½ hrs. Rosthwaite to Keswick, 6½ m. ; 14 m. in all. (Road from Seathwaite to Keswick ; buses from Seatoller or Rosthwaite.)

This is the best return route to Keswick for walkers who have come to Wasdale by Buttermere and the Scarf Gap and Black Sail passes. Those who have approached from Langdale and over Esk Hause are advised to make the detour of Black Sail, Scarf Gap, and Honister, which affords ample compensation in the way of beauty and scenery for the extra distance and labour—viz., 5 miles and two passes.

On leaving the hotel either cross the field to the church, and there take the lane to the left, or cut the corner by a footpath in the direction of Burnthwaite, the highest house in the valley. Hence, after passing between the buildings, the track at once begins to rise along the steep southern slope of Great Gable. It is stony and fatiguing, and nearly two miles long. Just before reaching the summit, it turns sharply to the left, and Sty Head

Tarn appears in front. A more interesting alternative is to take the right-hand track at the junction where the pony track begins to rise sharply. Cross Lingmell Beck by a footbridge and follow zig-zag track with the beck on the left to the summit where the old pony track is joined. The route to Langdale over Esk Hause strikes off on the right, and then *Sty Head Tarn* is skirted. (A pleasing and more picturesque variation is to follow the Esk Hause track to Ruddy Gill, just beyond Sprinkling Tarn, and then descend to Stockley Bridge by Grain Gill, keeping on the Glaramara side at first and crossing the gill about half-way down (*see p.* 267)). *Aaron Slack*, the gulley on the left after passing Sty Head Tarn, separates Great Gable from Green Gable, and a little farther, on the opposite side of the stream, is a remarkable piece of rock, which became detached from Green Gable during last century, and, bounding across the valley, finally deposited itself on its beam ends very much in the same position as the famous Bowder Stone at the other end of Borrowdale.

Our track now crosses the Sty Head Beck, and keeping it henceforth on the left, soon commences a sharp descent to *Stockley Bridge*, where it enters the main Borrowdale valley, which descends on the right from Esk Hause. *Taylor Gill*, a fine cataract after heavy rain, shows itself on the left, and the hamlet of **Seathwaite** (*see p.* 198) is reached in less than another mile.

Hence to *Seatoller*, where we join the Honister Pass road and whence buses run to Keswick, is 1¼ miles. **Rosthwaite** (*p.* 180) is 1¼ miles farther. Glaramara forms a striking feature on the right all the way from Stockley Bridge. Half a mile before reaching Rosthwaite, the routes from Langdale over the Stake and from Grasmere over Greenup strike in on the right.

The 6¼ miles between Rosthwaite and Keswick are fully described, the reverse way, on *pp.* 177-80. A mile beyond Rosthwaite a road (walkers only) strikes up the hill-side to the right, and passes by the *Bowder Stone*, rejoining the lower road a few hundred yards farther. Immediately above is the *King's How*. Then comes *Grange*, on the other side of the river.

Walkers will do well to make a detour up the hill on the right by a footpath called Ladder Brow from the *Borrowdale Hotel*, for the purpose of seeing the beauties of *High Lodore* (*p.* 178), continuing the walk by the Watendlath road over Ashness Bridge, rejoining the Borrowdale road just beyond Barrow House.

PATTERDALE (ULLSWATER)

Approaches.—By motor from Penrith to Pooley Bridge, thence by boat up Ullswater. There is also a direct bus service from Penrith to Patterdale. Summer bus services from Keswick and from Windermere.

Bank (Glenridding), *Barclays.*

Boats and Motor Launch at the boat-landing.

Church.—Sunday Services, 8, 10.30, 6.30.

Distances, from Glenridding.—(*By water*)—Howtown, 5 *m.* ; Pooley Bridge, 7½. (*By road*)—*Brackenrigg Hotel*, 6½ *m.* ; Pooley Bridge, 8½ ; Penrith, 14 ; Troutbeck (Cumberland), 8½ ; Ambleside, 9½ ; Troutbeck (Windermere), 10 ; Windermere, 14 ; Bowness, 15 ; Grasmere (*pony-track*), 9, (*road*), 15.

Hotels.—*Ullswater*, on the lake-side ; *Glenridding* ; *Patterdale*, at the foot of the dale, ½ *m.* from lake ; also a small one, the *White Lion.* Numerous Apartment Houses.

Population : about 600.

Post Office in village ; also at Glenridding. *Postal Address.*—" Glenridding, Penrith " ; " Patterdale, Penrith." *Telegraph*, " Patterdale."

Motor Yachts ply regularly up and down the Lake during Summer.

The village of Patterdale (500 *ft.* above sea-level) is one of the most charmingly situated in Britain, and in itself clean and comely. In the church (modern), which is unpretentious and not remarkable, is an ancient font, and the churchyard contains several yews.

" Patterdale was formerly *Patrick*-dale. The church is dedicated to St. Patrick, and there is a St. Patrick's Well near the church."

Ullswater.—This lake disputes with Windermere and Derwentwater the sovereignty of the English Lakes, and those who find the nearest approach to their ideal of what a lake should be in the lakes of Switzerland, or even in the most famous of the lochs of Scotland, will probably give their vote for Ullswater. Not that it is in any way a servile copy of its larger sisters at home and abroad. It has a beauty of its own which will not suffer from comparison with any of them, but in its essential features it is cast in the same mould. As we sail up one after another of its three reaches we receive a distinct impression of the individual beauty of each, and feel that we are working up to a climax ; but there is always something which suggests to the experienced tourist a recollection of what he has seen before. Windermere and Derwentwater, on the contrary, whatever be their actual merits, are unique. There is no other lake in Europe which the most superficial admirer of Nature could mistake for either of them.

Further, it may be remarked that though the three reaches of Ullswater possess entirely distinct characteristics—the first being pastoral, the second picturesque, and the third grand—it is, as a whole, much more quickly comprehended than either of its two rivals. The hills and woods to which it owes so much of its attractiveness crowd closely round it, and, with the exception of Patterdale, there is no long valley sinking gradually to its shores and disclosing such a vista of woodland, hill, and distant fell as the valleys of Borrowdale and Newlands reveal in connection with Derwentwater, and those of Troutbeck, Rydal, and the two Langdales with Windermere. Place Fell, a fine mountain in itself, sinks abruptly into the waters on the eastern side, and opposite to it St. Sunday Crag and the Helvellyn range with its projecting spurs leave but little room for effective distances. Singularly enough there is only one important mountain which really commands Ullswater, and that is St. Sunday Crag. In a word, its scenery may be summed up as being much more impressive than diversified. The length of the lake is some 7½ miles, and its greatest breadth—that of its middle reach—little more than half a mile. For a description of the sail, *see pp.* 52–3. From May to September motor yachts, connecting with buses, sail between Pooley Bridge and Glenridding, calling at Howtown.

Patterdale to Glencoyne Wood, Aira Force and Gowbarrow.

4 m. by road from Patterdale ; 3 m. from Ullswater Hotel. A boat may be taken to within ¼ hour's walk of the Force.

The journey to Aira Force (sometimes pron. *Airy*), whether by land or by water, is very beautiful. The water-route has the advantage in point of views, as by keeping well out in the lake the traveller can look up at the Valleys of Glenridding and Glencoyne, which descend to the lake-side from the main ridge of Helvellyn, more easily than from the road, which is overhung the greater part of the way by the richly-wooded crags of Glenridding and Stybarrow.

A considerable stretch of land northward of Glenridding is in the care of the National Trust, including the lovely Glencoyne Wood, with many fine old oaks and a most interesting bird-population, which is fortunately protected. Below the wood Stybarrow Crag overhangs the highway.

The entrance to Aira Force is at the point where the Dockray and Troutbeck road leaves the lakeside. The square tower seen from the road is Lyulph's Tower, an 18th-century shooting-box possibly standing on the site of one built by Lyulph, first Baron of Greystoke. The reputed origin of the word " Lyulph " is Ulf, or l'Ulf, a former Baron of Greystoke, who would seem also to have bequeathed his name to Ullswater. " Till Ulfo's lake beneath him lay " (Scott, " Bridal of Triermain ").

The fall is about half a mile up the beck and the path to it unmistakable. There is a bridge at the bottom and another at the top, so that the visitor may make the entire tour of it. Taken in conjunction with its surroundings, it forms a lovely scene, though in itself it will probably be thought less beautiful than Dalegarth, as it is certainly less individualised than Dungeon Ghyll. The height of the fall is about 60 feet. The dell scenery is very charming. Aira Force is the scene of the tragedy recorded in Wordsworth's "Somnambulist." **Gowbarrow Park**, some 750 acres in all, contains red-deer (one of the two wild herds in the north of England) and fallow-deer, and commands most charming views of Ullswater and the adjacent fells. A full afternoon may be spent wandering over it. The main road may be reached in 250 yards by a path from the top of the fall. Gowbarrow Park and Aira Force are now vested in the National Trust.

Patterdale to Howtown, returning by Boardale. *To Howtown,* 2½ hrs. ; *Patterdale,* 4½ hrs. , *about* 12 *m. Pony-route.*

This is a most enjoyable walk, and should be taken either one way or the other by everyone staying at Patterdale. By far the most beautiful portion of it is alongside the lake. A couple of miles may be saved by rowing across the lake to *Bleawick Woods* (N. T.).

From Patterdale take the lane across the valley, which starts at the far end of the village, and follow the track which bends round to the south-east corner of the lake. Hence the walk along the foot of Place Fell, by the higher of the two paths, discloses views of the various glens on the other side of the water, which are not obtainable from the road on their own side, and only in a modified degree from the surface of the lake itself. There is a beautiful retrospect over Brothers' Water to Kirkstone and the Red Screes, as well as up the Deepdale arm of Patterdale, with Fairfield at its head. St. Sunday Crag separates Deepdale from Grisedale, whose lower part is hidden by the wooded and hilly grounds of Patterdale Hall, forming a continuation of the sharp, lateral ridge of Helvellyn called Striding Edge. Glenridding and Glencoyne, the latter remarkable for the almost perfect semicircle described by the fells at its head, follow in rapid succession ; and then the path, descending to the shore, coasts along under Birk Fell for a mile, after which it retires behind a plantation, and does not reach the water's edge again until it has passed the hamlet of *Sandwick* and crossed the beck descending from Boardale and other remote valleys generally included in the one name of Martindale. Southward, at the head of these valleys, the High Street range has come into prominent view.

From Sandwick we may either follow the footpath round the lake-side of Hallin Fell, or turn inland (*see Map*). In either case we soon have a full-length view of the lower, or tame end of Ullswater, with Pooley Bridge and the wooded hill of Dunmallet at its foot, after which we quickly reach **Howtown**.

On our return journey, we first climb the hause between Hallin Fell on the right and Steel Knotts on the left, passing on our way the modern Martindale church at **Cowgarth.** From top of the hause we descend to and recross one arm of the beck which we first crossed on our outward journey at Sandwick. The depression in front of us, watered by this stream, is *Rampsgill*, a long valley with a characteristically fine head. It is important to get into the correct valley. **Boardale** is the next parallel valley, and the road to it climbs for a short distance from the bridge, by the side of the stream, and then turns straight up the dale, keeping its beck some way on the right hand for about a mile, after which it crosses it, and continues past a farm-house called *Boardale Head* (3 m.), where the cart-road ceases, to the foot of *Boardale Hause*, which is climbed by a gentle zigzag. From the summit the lakes, valleys, and fells which we lingered to admire on our outward journey again break upon our vision with remarkable suddenness, and with that change of aspect which is the natural result of their being seen from a much greater elevation. The height of Boardale Hause is 1,260 feet. Hence the descent to Patterdale is short, fairly steep, and unmistakable.

An alternative route from Howtown to Patterdale—longer but more interesting—is past the old Martindale Church (interesting interior) to Dalehead Farm, 3 miles south of Howtown, then by a good grass road to Boardale Hause, leaving Beda Fell on the right.

Ascent of Place Fell (2,154 ft.). *2 to 3 hrs. up and down. Map at end of the book.*

An excursion delightful in itself, and still more so if it be extended to Howtown, whence the return to Patterdale may be made either by boat (*pp.* 52-3), or along the shore of the lake by the route described the reverse way above.

The Route.—Cross Goldrill Beck as in the shore route to Howtown, and turn to the right. Thence climb by the conspicuous green path to within a few yards of the top of *Boardale Hause.* The view during the ascent, especially across Patterdale into the emerald-green glens of Grisedale and Deepdale, are very beautiful. In the background the crags of Fairfield and Helvellyn rise with striking effect.

From the Hause a path, at first very indistinct, strikes away to the left and ascends to the top of the ridge. On the highest part of the fell are a succession of small cairns. The route presents no difficulty. Besides the fine mountain and valley view south and westward, the prospect from the summit extends over the rich Eden valley to the Pennine range. Penrith is easily recognised in the north-east.

To descend to Howtown, which lies just beyond the union of the two valleys of Boardale and Rampsgill, make for the cairn in the direction of Penrith, and continue beyond it to the edge of the steep lower part of the slope. Here you will find a narrow path, commencing close to a small gully, and descending obliquely through the bracken. Follow this track, and enter the Boardale road at the bottom of the valley, a few yards short of a farm-house. The road crosses the beck at once. Where it forks, $\frac{1}{4}$ mile farther, take the right-hand branch, and, after crossing the Rampsgill Beck, cross the hause between Hallin Fell and Steel Knotts to Howtown. From the top of Place Fell to How-town is from 1 to $1\frac{1}{2}$ hours' walk.

Patterdale to Angle Tarn ($2\frac{1}{2}$ to 3 hrs. up and down ; a delightful expedition).—Follow the foregoing route as far as the finger-post on Boardale Hause. Then take a well-marked track to the right (hereabouts there is a peep of the head and foot of Ullswater, the remainder of the lake being shut by Place Fell) through a miniature pass between two grassy elevations. Beyond this a magnificent view opens and expands to the right to Dovedale and Deepdale, backed by the crags of Fairfield. Continuing along the side of the highest point of the Pikes, you come suddenly on the tarn. It is very attractive, and is remarkable among Lakeland tarns for the indented character of its shores. In front is a fine panorama of the High Street range, of which perhaps the most conspicuous feature is Rampsgill Head.

For Ascent of Helvellyn, *see p.* 239.

Patterdale to Ambleside or Windermere. *Map at end of the book.*

Brothers' Water Inn, 4 m. ; *Kirkstone Pass* (inn), $6\frac{1}{2}$; (—*Ambleside*, $9\frac{1}{2}$) ; *Troutbeck*, 10 ; *Windermere Village*, $13\frac{1}{4}$.

Bus service in summer only.

Route more fully described reverse way, pp. 89–90.
Walkers who have already been over Kirkstone may agreeably vary the journey to Windermere by striking off to the left at Low Hartsop, and crossing the Threshthwaite Hause or *Mouth* into Trout-beck for Windermere. In so doing they will not increase the distance at all, and the time by not much more than half an hour. The views obtained from the summit of the pass, including the upper reach of Ullswater to the north and a great part of Windermere to the south, are very beautiful.

Three-quarters of a mile beyond the *Patterdale Hotel*, a fine view up Deepdale opens on the right, the crags of **Fairfield** at its head being the most conspicuous feature. No mountain in the district combines to so great an extent the lion and the lamb. The " dear old Fairfield " of Harriet Martineau's yearning aspirations from Ambleside, it frowns on the traveller through Patterdale with a severity almost equal to that of Scafell in its sternest mood. In front, Caudale Moor thrusts out its pyramidal shoulder, Low Hartsop Dodd, separating Pasture Beck from the Kirkstone Pass.

After passing Deepdale the road proceeds between wooded hills on the right and the Goldrill Beck and green meadows of Patterdale on the left. The main beck is crossed, and, soon after, a tributary descending through a deep valley on the left from Hayeswater and High Street. Then we skirt the shores of **Brothers' Water** and look up a second lateral valley to the crags of Dovedale on the right.

The **Thresthwaite** route leaves the main road at a sign-post just before the second, or Hayeswater, beck is crossed. It passes through the hamlet of **Low Hartsop,** and then crosses the beck at once. The Pasture Beck Glen runs parallel to the Kirkstone Pass, between Caudale Moor and Low Hartsop Dodd on the right and Gray Crag on the left. The walking here is very rough, and the final ascent to the top of the hause is a sharp rise of nearly a thousand feet. A wall connecting High Street on the left with Caudale Moor on the right crosses the top of the hause. **Thornthwaite Crag,** marked by a cairn, the Windermere extremity of High Street, may be ascended by keeping the side of the wall, a steep climb, and the walk extended over the top of Ill Bell, or down the slope north of Froswick to Troutbeck. The latter route is to be preferred to the direct one from the hause. An alternative route is by the wall to the right over **Caudale Moor** (*see p. 247*) to the *Kirkstone Inn*. It is quite a little scramble to begin with. Then comes the almost level summit of the moor, aggravated by stone walls. Fine views of Ullswater on the right, and of Windermere, Blelham Tarn, and the Coniston range on the left, are obtained by a little irregular wandering. The summit of Red Screes is an excellent guide (*see also p. 275*). From nowhere does Red Screes present a finer aspect than from the dip to the Kirkstone Pass ; and, beyond, the Helvellyn and Fairfield ridges are seen to advantage. The descent is then diagonally to the left across some roughish slopes to the *Kirkstone Inn*. Unless one keeps high up until the inn is almost reached, this is apt to be tiresome.

The view from the hause is very beautiful. Windermere is seen trailing away to its extreme end, and the upper reach of Ullswater is a worthy companion picture northwards.

In descending, keep the beck for some time on the left. The bottom is very boggy. In a couple of miles **Troutbeck Tongue is** reached, a tract of rising ground in the midst of the valley, with streams on both sides of it. Either course may be taken. A little way down the west side you find a track that crosses the beck *Hird Gill,* which is very pretty lower down. If you cross to the east side of the Tongue, you will find a good cart-road beginning between it and Ill Bell and descending *Hag Gill.* The two meet beyond a farm, called Troutbeck Park. Then a lane leads into Troutbeck either close to the *Queen's Head* (by first turn up beyond second bridge) or a few hundred yards nearer the church. By the latter route there is no inn till you reach Windermere.

A little beyond Brothers' Water is an inn, called the *Brothers' Water Hotel,* whence a third valley, called Caiston Glen, is seen diverging to the right.

Brothers' Water to Ambleside.—From this inn it is a 2–2½ hours' walk to Ambleside by an almost direct course, commencing with the Caiston depression and continuing over *Scandale Rigg* into

Scandale itself. The **Caiston Glen,** as it is called, lies between Middle Dodd, Red Screes and High Hartsop Dodd. The route is as follows (be careful to get into the right glen):—

Cross the fields to the farm called *Hartsop Hall,* then turn left (leaving Dovedale well on the right) by a path which skirts the bottom of the fell till it reaches the Caiston Beck. Continue up a fair track with the stream on the left. Alternatively ascend with the Caiston Beck on the right until a wide combe is reached. Here cross the stream as soon as convenient, above some cascades, and continue by an intermittent track to the skyline. Cross the summit-level (1,700 *ft.*) near its lowest point, where there is a high wall descending from Red Screes on the left, and rising to the Fairfield range on the right. The upper part of Windermere and the Coniston Fells come into view at the top, and the track down *Scandale* is seen to the left of Scandale Beck all the way. At the end of it is Ambleside. *High Sweden Bridge* is a picturesque object rather more than half-way down.

Soon after leaving the *Brothers' Water Hotel* the steep part of the Kirkstone Pass commences. Then comes a struggle of some 700 or 800 feet up to the *Kirkstone Inn* (p. 89). Red Screes on the right and Caudale Moor on the left, flank the pass.

To the right of the road, a little short of the summit-level, is the *Kirkstone* itself, which poetically, according to Wordsworth, " gives to the savage Pass its name."

Here the Ambleside road diverges to the right, descending in a rough-and-ready sort of way, by a succession of break-neck pitches, 1,300 feet in three miles (*see* p. 123). A pleasing alternative route to Ambleside is down Stockdale by a track on the right of the Windermere road about ⅔ mile from the inn (*see also* p. 109).

From the inn the Windermere road passes along the ridge which separates Stockdale from Troutbeck, the latter valley very shortly appearing on the left. Looking down Stockdale, part of the head of Windermere is seen and Blelham Tarn beyond it, but the lake does not appear to advantage. As the road descends into the valley, Thornthwaite Crag, the southern arm of High Street, marked by a columnar cairn, rises at the head of Troutbeck, and the range is continued by the tapering heights of Froswick and Ill Bell, the latter an especially fine feature. Troutbeck is fully described on *p.* 89.

The Windermere road diverges to the left at the commencement of the village and crosses the Trout Beck near the church. Presently it rises again to the Borrans, on the top of a hill, after passing which a very fine **Troutbeck** view of Windermere suddenly presents itself.

Three-quarters of a mile beyond the Borrans (*see Map*), pedestrians should take the Elleray footpath (*p.* 88), entered by a drive-gate facing them.

Patterdale to Grasmere, by Grisedale Pass. *Map at end of the book.*

From Patterdale to Grasmere, 8 to 9 m. Time, 3 to 4 hrs. Height of Pass, 1,929 ft.

This route is described the reverse way on *p.* 160. We shall therefore limit our present description to a bare indication of the points at which there is any possibility of deviating from the right path. These points are few, as the route is closely hemmed in for nearly the whole distance by Helvellyn and Seat Sandal on the right hand, and by St. Sunday Crag and the Fairfield range on the left.

Leave the main road by the lane which strikes up into the Grisedale valley on the south side of the bridge over Grisedale Beck, about ⅓ mile from the *Patterdale Hotel*, and ⅜ from the *Ullswater*. Follow this lane for about half an hour, keeping the beck on the right hand. Beyond the farm-buildings of *Elm How* the road becomes a mere track. A short distance farther on the old track crosses the stream by a bridge. Disregard this, and continue till another bridge is reached. Here cross, and ascend by Ruthwaite Lodge, a stone hut overlooked by Eagle Crag. In front on the right Dollywaggon Pike throws out a striking buttress, Tarn Crag. Leave Grisedale Tarn on your right, and when you reach the top of the pass at a horse-gap just beyond it, do not drop to the bottom of the hollow, as the pony-route does, but take a roughly-marked, stony track along the slope of Seat Sandal. The view from about here is described on *p.* 160. The pony-route is soon rejoined, and doubling round to the right and left in turn it descends by the side of a green tongue of the mountain into a cart-track which strikes the Grasmere and Keswick road about 1½ miles from Grasmere church. A quarter of a mile before the converging point is *Tongue Gill Force*, a small but very picturesque waterfall (*p.* 154). To reach Grasmere village, diverge to the right ⅔ of a mile after entering the main road, and just before reaching the *Swan Hotel*. There is also a wayside house, the *Traveller's Rest*, 300 yds., after entering the road. For *Grasmere, see p.* 145.

Patterdale to Keswick. *Map at end of the book.*

	Water M.	Road. M.	Foot. M.	Total M.
Route.				
(1) *By Dockray and Troutbeck*	—	16	—	16
(2) ,, *Pooley Bridge and Penrith*	7½	23½	—	31
(3) ,, *Dockray and Matterdale*.	—	4	10	14
(4) ,, *Sticks Pass*	—	5	6	11
(5) ,, *Top of Helvellyn and Thirlspot*	—	—	5½–6½	hrs.

Bus services between Patterdale, Pooley Bridge, and Penrith; between Patterdale, Troutbeck, and Penrith, and between Patterdale, Troutbeck, and Keswick. For times, etc., see local announcements.

Distances calculated from Glenridding, whence the boats start. From Patterdale add another mile.

The various routes having been fully compared and described in the Keswick section (*pp.* 187–91), we shall only give such directions here as are called for by the fact that the journeys are made the reverse way.

Motorists will take the Troutbeck route. " Assisted " pedestrians who are making the round should bus to Keswick, returning by Penrith (road), Pooley Bridge (road), Ullswater (boat).

For walkers the Helvellyn route is immeasurably the best, the roundabout by Dockray and Matterdale being very dreary for a great part of the way, and the ascent of the Sticks Pass almost as toilsome as that of Helvellyn itself, with no compensating advantage. The last few miles, from Thirlspot to Keswick, are on a bus route.

1. **By Troutbeck.**—To avoid possible disappointment, let us again remind the tourist that this Troutbeck has no connection with the beautiful green valley which adds so much to the interest of the Windermere scenery. On the contrary, it is situated on a bleak moorland outside the limits of the Lake District. There is a very fair inn near the disused station.

The route for the first few miles, up to the point where it leaves the Pooley Bridge road just before reaching Lyulph's Tower and Aira Force, skirts the lake, across which it discloses a striking view of Place Fell and the Patterdale valley. Before the road leaves the water's edge, the middle reach of the lake opens up. The Lyulph's Tower corner may be cut off by a footpath leaving the road nearly half a mile beyond the bend of the lake.

An ascent is then made to the village of **Dockray** (*Royal Hotel*). A splendid retrospective view is obtained during the ascent, but afterwards there is nothing calling for remark, unless it be the sharp spurs of Saddleback in the left front, and the ugliness of Mell Fell on the right, during the whole distance to Troutbeck station. (Thence to Keswick, *see p.* 188.)

2. **By Pooley Bridge and Penrith.**—The features of this route are described in the Approaches from Penrith to Patterdale and Keswick (*pp.* 51–2).

3. **By Dockray and Matterdale.**—Leave the Troutbeck road at *Dockray*, taking the left turn and ascending with a stream on your left for about half a mile. After leaving the stream the road continues uphill till it attains the extensive and monotonous moor called *Matterdale Common*. Then you have a long up-and-down trudge, the road—a very fair one as far as the Mosedale Beck, more than half-way over—crossing the northern slope of the Helvellyn Dodds. The only interesting feature in the view is Saddleback, which rises in front. Beyond the Mosedale Beck the road becomes rougher, but when it has reached its

highest point, 1,410 feet, the fells between Derwentwater and Crummock come into view with fine effect. Then, sweeping round to the left, you descend into the *Vale of St. John*, and cross its beck by *Wanthwaite Bridge*, after a walk of nearly two hours from Dockray. To reach the bridge, take the right turn when you descend into the St. John's valley road ; keep the latter for 100 yards, and then turn left. After crossing the bridge, the first road on the right will lead you, in about a mile, on to the Keswick and Penrith highway close to the third milestone from Keswick. By again diverging to the left, in less than another half-mile, soon after crossing *Naddle Beck*, you may shorten the distance (note also short footpath) and pass by *Castlerigg Stone Circle* (*p.* 170), which lies in a field on the left-hand side of the road, just past a bend to the right. The main road is again joined about a mile from Keswick.

4. **By the Sticks Pass** (2,420 *ft.*) —Leave the Patterdale and Pooley Bridge highway by the road opposite the *Ullswater Hotel*. Follow it for nearly half a mile past some cottages, and then take a sharp turn to the right and another to the left immediately after. Ascend for a mile, with the beck on the left, to the former *Mill*. Cross a tributary beck which descends from the right, and in another ¼ mile leave the Helvellyn pony-track and climb the steep zigzag to the right up to the reservoir, being careful not to cross the beck till you get close to the lead-mine.

Pass the north bank of the reservoir, and then keep due west to the top of the ridge. The western and northern fells from Great Gable to Skiddaw here come in view. A number of up-right sticks are placed alongside the track at the top of the pass. Continue straight on for a few hundred yards till you have a beck descending in a westerly direction on the left. Gradually leave this, bending very slightly to the right. Here the track is not so well marked, but in about twenty minutes from the summit-ridge you reach a sheepfold some 1,000 feet below, beyond which it is again distinct. Descend steeply with a beck on the right to a white farm-house below, called *Stanah*, whence you drop into the Windermere and Keswick high road, about 4¾ miles from Keswick. For the rest of the route to Keswick, *see pp.* 87–8. From the top of the pass you may make straight for the *King's Head* at Thirlspot which lies rather to the left. In misty weather this route is not recommended to strangers to the neighbourhood

5. **Over Helvellyn.**—This route is fully described in the ascents and descents of Helvellyn (*p.* 239 *et seq.*).

Patterdale to Mardale (Haweswater).

There are numerous ways of reaching Haweswater from Patterdale, and it is very difficult to gauge their relative merits.

The tourist, however, will probably have one of two special objects in view—to see Haweswater properly, or to cross the highest part of High Street. To attain the former of these objects he must descend to Haweswater itself not higher up the lake than Measand Beck, the pleasantest though not the shortest route to which is by Howtown and Fusedale. If the boat is taken as far as Howtown, the walking distance becomes also less than by any other route. If High Street be our aim, our best route will be by Hartsop and Hayeswater, though we may also reach it by Boardale Hause and Angle Tarn, a rough but easy walk.

Distances by motor road : to Pooley Bridge, 8½ m. ; to Bampton Grange, *vid* Askham, a charming village, 16½ ; Haweswater Hotel, 22 m. From Pooley Bridge pedestrians may save 2 miles by crossing Moor Divock, whence are lovely views up Ullswater. Scattered hereabout are many Druidical remains.

1. By Howtown, Fusedale, and Measand Beck.

Patterdale to Howtown, 2 hrs. (6 m.) ; Measand, 5 hrs. ; Mardale, 6 hrs. Highest point, 2,100 ft. Total distance about 14 m.

The route as far as Howtown, which may be reached on foot or by boat, is described on p. 214.

Pass through a gate between the *Howtown Hotel* and lodging-house, and the Fusedale glen, running due south, appears almost immediately. Keep its beck on the left hand for a short distance, and then cross it. There is a farm-track for some way up it. In about half an hour from the hotel pass to the left of a stone shieling, and then turn up the fell-side to the left, crossing a beck in a few minutes. As you climb, Saddleback comes into view behind, and Helvellyn on the right, while the summit of High Street appears some distance beyond the head of the valley you have just ascended, rather to the right of the line of a stone wall. The deep valley on the right, divided near its head by a conspicuous spur, the Nab, is a deer forest. Keep the stream on the left hand, and then cross the ridge in a direction rather more east than south. From the summit a strip of Ullswater is visible on both sides of Hallin Fell, and the mountain panorama south and west is very fine. Far away to the south-west the Coniston Old Man rises over the depression between Fairfield and Red Screes. A wide extent of comparatively flat country appears in the opposite direction, reaching over Penrith and the Eden valley to the Pennine chain, in which the flat-topped Crossfell is the most prominent height. Here you will also cross the Roman Road, of which the traces are very slight ; and in a few minutes more *Measand Beck (p. 224)* appears at the bottom of a steep pitch in front. Veer to the left and skirt the edge of the ridge till you find a convenient descent. Cross the beck by a footbridge visible from above, and descend to the Ramblers' Path, round the base of the fell on the right. During the descent Haweswater, backed by Harter Fell and Branstree, looks its best. For a description of **Haweswater**, *see pp. 55 and 53.*

2. By Hayeswater and High Street or Kidsty Pike.

The whole of this route is fully described in the ascents and descents of High Street (*pp.* 244–8). Those who wish to keep the direct route over Kidsty Pike without diverging to High Street, must, on reaching the top of the ridge, go on in their previous direction through a gate in the wall which runs along it, and avoid diverging to the right over the narrow *col* which separates the Hayeswater valley from Riggindale.

Mardale to Ullswater.

1. By Kidsty Pike.

The favourite route for this journey is over Kidsty Pike or High Street, and down by Hayeswater and Hartsop, into the upper end of Patterdale, all of which will be found fully described in the ascents and descents of High Street (*pp.* 244–8). Agreeable variations may be made in the descent by continuing northwards from Kidsty Pike along the main ridge by the Roman Road, and dropping into Fusedale, on the left-hand side, care being taken not to get so much to the right in starting as to have the Measand Beck also on the left hand. **Rampsgill,** the long and deep valley extending from the western summit of the Kidsty Pike ridge to the middle reach of Ullswater, should be visited. The view down it from that summit is very fine, and strikingly exemplifies the fact to which we have already drawn attention, that the general abruptness of the mountains of the English Lake District gives the scenery an impressiveness which far outstrips expectations formed from a mere knowledge of their actual height.

To reach **Howtown** or **Patterdale,** follow the course of the High Street range northward from the top of the Kidsty Pike ridge for about 2½ *m.* and then descend. The first part of the route climbs another height of the same range—*High Raise*—about 70 feet higher than Kidsty, beyond which a gate is passed through at the top of a steep gully on the left, and at the recommencement of the wall, which should be kept on the right. Continue along the ridge until the valley of Fusedale also appears on the left between you and Rampsgill. Howtown is at the foot of this valley. This route is not to be recommended in misty weather, as the ridge line of High Street is wellnigh featureless.

Instead of dropping into Fusedale you may take a good peattrack that descends to Martindale old church, about half a mile south of the new church on the north side of Rampsgill. This is a better descent than to Fusedale.

Howtown to Patterdale, *see p.* 214.

2. By Measand Beck and Fusedale.

Mardale to Measand (on Haweswater), 1 *hr.* ; *Howtown,* 3½ *hrs.* ; *Patterdale,* 5½ *hrs. Highest point,* 2,100 *ft. Total distance, about* 14 *m.*

Those who have reached Mardale by the Nan Bield or High Street route, and who wish to see Haweswater on their way to Patterdale, should adopt this route.

From Mardale (Gatescarth Foot) at the end of the road follow the path down the western side of the lake for nearly 3 miles. Riggindale is on the left, succeeded by Whelter Knotts. At Measand climb round the base of the fell on the left till you reach the *Measand Beck*, some little way above the series of cataracts— very fine in appropriate weather—which it forms in its final leap down towards the lake. Hence the retrospect of Haweswater is very fine. Cross the beck by a little bridge, and then climb the ridge on the left between the courses of the Measand Beck and a small tributary stream. A peat-track near the top of the ridge may be followed for a short distance, but its general direction is too much to the left. The top-level of the ridge consists of peat-bog and long grass. Cross it in a direction rather north of due west. From the summit a splendid mountain-view breaks upon the eye to the west and south. Saddleback, too, is a striking feature in the north-west. Westwards Helvellyn is monarch of the scene, and on its left rise the crags of Fairfield, between which and the Red Screes the Coniston Old Man fills up the dip. A strip of Ullswater is visible on both sides of Hallin Fell.

To reach *Fusedale*, which is the first valley in front of you, drop down its head in a north-westerly direction. The stream (*p. 222*), which is not far down, is a good guide. The bottom of the valley is reached not far from a shieling, and by descending it along the beck-side you will reach Howtown in another half-hour.

Hence the best route is to climb to the depression south of Hallin Fell, and cross the *How Grain* and *Boardale Becks*, taking care to avoid the valleys down which they flow. A good road takes you to the hamlet of *Sandwick*, a few yards short of which the path to Patterdale along the lake-side strikes off on the left. For a description of it, *see pp. 214–15*.

3. By High Street and Hayeswater.

See Ascents and Descents of High Street, *pp. 244–8*.

Mardale to Windermere, by Nan Bield, Kentmere, and Garburn Pass.

Top of Nan Bield, 2½ m.; Kentmere Village, 6½; Windermere, 12¼. Time, 5 to 6 hrs.

Height of Passes:—Nan Bield, 2,100 ft.; Garburn, 1,450 ft.

The descent from the Garburn Pass into Troutbeck by this route is very fine. Still finer ,however, is that from Ill Bell to Troutbeck village, and as the valley of Kentmere is not seen to advantage in descending it, we are inclined to advise tourists to avoid the unnecessary dip into it, and to make their way either from the near side of Small Water or the top of Nan Bield over High Street (not necessarily turning aside to its highest plateau) and Ill Bell. Full directions will be found on *pp.* 246–7.

There is no inn in Kentmere village. The two Troutbeck inns —*Queen's Head* and *Mortal Man*—are at the north end of Troutbeck village.

The walk up Nan Bield from Mardale is very fine, after the new road has been left behind. Harter Fell towers grandly in front, and the spurs of High Street shoot out on the right hand. Almost immediately beyond where the new road ends—the main route diverges to the left of Harter Fell on its way to Long Sleddale and Kendal over the *Gatescarth Pass* (*p.* 94). The divergence of the Nan Bield track is not very clearly marked, but after crossing a beck it becomes plainer, and there can be no further fear of missing it. It rises to the right of Harter Fell, and, after skirting the north and west sides of *Small Water*, climbs steeply to the top of the pass, descending with almost equal abruptness on the opposite side, and, about a mile beyond the summit, leaving the *Kentmere Reservoir* some distance on the right (or a descent may be made into the valley a little below the reservoir, and a fair road on the far side of the stream followed all the way to Kentmere village). The steep slope of Ill Bell overlooking the reservoir, and the cliffs of Rainsborrow Crag beyond it, are fine ; but the view straight down the valley is dull and featureless. Just above Kentmere village the valley is broken in two by a sudden drop which the stream descends in a pair of picturesque cascades. At the foot of the slope turn sharp to the right and cross the bridge.

Hence the ascent of the Garburn Pass bends to the right past the church ; then left again at two gates, and to the right at the last farm. *Kentmere Hall* (*p.* 92), with its sycamore-girdled tower, is some way below on the left. The cart-track now rises more or less steeply to the top of the pass, on reaching which a grand view opens up in front, the mountain chain from the Old Man to the Langdale Pikes being visible. Great Gable, square-shaped, is specially prominent. Bowfell, too, is conspicuous in front, and Red Screes on the right. Beyond the gate the road turns to the left. A little farther on, the road gradually drops, leaving some disused quarries on the left. At the first fork bear right and at the second bear left. Continuing along a comparative level, we turn abruptly in another mile to the right by a road which descends to the Patterdale and Windermere road, joining it nearly two miles from Windermere Station, at Borrans (*p.* 88).

The track down the Garburn Pass may also be continued to the bottom of Troutbeck by the Howe, where it strikes the Windermere and Patterdale road a short distance from the bridge and church. Hence Ambleside or Windermere is easily reached.

Mardale to Shap, 12 m., *see p. 54.* Along the east side of Hawes-water to **Bampton** (*Crown and Mitre*), 6 m. ; whence a path, first by the river-side, then ascending through *Rosgill* (8¼ m.), may be taken all the way to the north end of Shap village, 1 m. from the station. A shorter route, but much more hilly, goes over the fell to Swindale and then by Tailbert and Keld direct to Shap.

Patterdale to Patterdale, by Deepdale and St. Sunday Crag.

Patterdale to head of Deepdale, 2½ hrs. ; Deepdale Hause, 3¼ hrs. ; Patterdale, 5½ hrs.

A grand walk. From Patterdale village follow the Kirkstone road for ¼ hour, till Deepdale opens on the right. Here pass through a gate, and up the valley by a cart-track, past a farm and through several gates. High up on the right Arnison Crag is conspicuous ; and in front, at first, the precipices of Fairfield form an imposing background, but as you advance they are hidden from sight by Greenhow End, a rocky spur of the mountain. Towards the head of the valley the cart-track becomes merely a rough path, and eventually disappears. Here the dale is broken up by moraine heaps, and numerous streams converge. Amongst these the pedestrian must pick his own way, eventually coasting along upwards to the right to Deepdale Hause, between Cofa Pike and St. Sunday Crag, returning to Patterdale over St. Sunday Crag (*see p. 260*).

Patterdale to Dovedale, returning by Hartsop above How.

Distances :—Patterdale Hotel to Hartsop Hall, 4 m. ; Dovedale Falls, 5½ ; Hartsop above How, 6½ ; Patterdale, 4. Time, 4½–5 hrs.

From the village of Patterdale follow the Kirkstone road for nearly 3 miles to a gate on the right, just to the right of the new bridge over the Goldrill. Pass through the gate, and follow a shady road by Brothers' Water till **Hartsop Hall**, a National Trust farm, is reached.

The Hall and Manor of Hartsop (Hertshope) were held in the 17th century by a family of the name of Lancaster. Towards the end of that century they passed to Sir John Lowther (afterwards first Viscount Lonsdale). There is a public right of way through part of the house, owing to an extension having been built on the south side over a bridle-path which ran close on that side of the building.

A few hundred yards to the south of the Hall are the remains of what may have been a prehistoric village.

Passing the Hall, the track leads by some sheepfolds along the side of the valley and round a low mound to a point where two streams unite. The stream in front descends a very steep slope from Sales, a deep recess in the fells; that on the right from Huntsett Cove, a similar recess, of striking formation. Between the two, the Stangs, a curious spur, knotted with rocky excrescences, projects into the valley. Above these Dove Crag towers grandly. Turn to the right, and, keeping the stream on the left, follow its course past a series of delightful cascades up the steep, wooded fell-side till a wall is encountered. Here the track lies between the wall and the stream, and the walker must edge his way around it. Continue for about 400 yards, and then climb up on the right, keeping the crags below Hartsop above How on the right. No track is marked here and the walker must pick his way, but except for a little occasional scrambling, the going is quite easy. Once on the crest of the fell, there are impressive views of Dovedale, Deepdale, Fairfield and St. Sunday Crag.

The return journey is made along the crest of the fell, passing through woods at the lower levels, before regaining the road at Bridgend.

THE FELLS

For descriptions and notes respecting each Fell consult Index at end of book.

Hints to Climbers and Others.—In the first place, however promising the weather, and however early in the day the climber may expect to get down again, he should never begin the ascent without such provision as will enable him to endure delay and exposure on the higher parts of the mountain. When mists unexpectedly come on, the difficulty of descending is aggravated by the exceptional steepness of the Lake mountains, and by the fact that they are so closely packed together that a traveller, when his vision is limited to a radius of 20 or 30 yards, may wander on from height to height for many hours without hitting upon a convenient place of descent. Consequently, it is always sound practice to keep an " emergency ration "—be it merely a slab of chocolate; indeed, for all but the most frequented routes and during the most popular seasons, such a ration forms as essential a part of the climber's equipment as a stout pair of boots, properly soled, a map, and a compass.

At the first sign of mist it is important to take one's bearings. Many hill-walkers wait till the mist comes on before consulting the compass, which is then almost useless. If without a compass, it is useful to remember which way the wind was blowing before the mist came down.

It is a good plan to read up the expedition on the previous evening, and study it with the map. The time thus occupied will be found to have been well spent.

It should be noted that a route marked with a red dotted line on the maps does not necessarily mean that a path exists.

When a difficulty occurs in the descent of a mountain, the safest plan is generally to keep along one of its shoulders, either to the end, or until the way down one side or the other is seen to be quite practicable. This calls for a good deal of patience, as the descent is often very gradual at first, and in places level ground has to be traversed, or even a slight ascent made. Generally speaking, though it may prove a longer route, it is a good tip to follow running water—not necessarily the stream bed, which may be rough, but the general direction as indicated by the sound.

Another fact which mountain climbers learn by experience is that in ascending a slope, the eye has a tendency to *underrate*, and in descending to *overrate* its steepness, especially if it is a grass slope.

Lastly, speaking generally, there is no danger in descending loose screes, provided one knows that they are not succeeded by crags at the bottom. Such screes will only rest at an angle which admits of a secure footing. Still, under all circumstances and everywhere, safety first is the maxim :—safety not only for oneself but for others. Rolling stones down hill is criminal—the word is not one whit too strong.

Likewise it is undesirable, except in emergency, to indulge in shouting on the fells, because shouting is normally taken to be a sign of distress and should be used only as such. A good hint is to carry a whistle to attract attention in case of accident.

For Emergency Descents, *see pp.* 294–305.

A simple but often neglected precaution in a fog is worthy of passing mention. It is to *lay one's stick on the ground*, point forwards, in the direct line of march, whenever a halt is made for reconnoitring or other purposes. Through neglecting this precaution we have known people, after a halt, while intending to go straight on, start back in the direction from which they have come.

Again, direction-posts are not infrequently blown down or turned in the *wrong* direction by tourists with a perverted sense of "humour." If you find a prostrate or misguiding sign, put it right *at once*, which you can do by setting the proper finger to the direction from which you have come.

Choice of Ascents.—The tourist influenced only by height and notoriety in choosing ascents will make Scafell Pike, Helvellyn, and Skiddaw the first objects of his climbing ambition. For the benefit of those who care first for views, we prefix to our description of the various ascents a few words regarding their comparative merits.

There is no more attractive feature in a mountain prospect than the full-length view of a lake more or less at hand. Such a view of one single lake is worth strips of twenty. For this reason the ascent of those fells which lie north, or nearly north, of Windermere is especially to be recommended. *High Street, Ill Bell, Red Screes, Fairfield,* and *Wansfell Pike* come under this category. Rydal Water and Grasmere give an additional charm to the prospect from the last-named height. From a like cause, *St. Sunday Crag* is worthy of special notice for its view of Ullswater ; *Saddleback* for Thirlmere—an exquisite vista ; *Fleetwith* (the mountain of which Honister Crag forms a part) and *Grasmoor* for Buttermere, Crummock, and Loweswater ; *Glaramara* and *Great End* for Derwentwater, with the beautiful foreground of Borrowdale ; and *Great Gable* for Wastwater. The ascent of Great Gable is also worthy of a special effort, if it be only for the sake of the mountain itself, and the general prospect from its summit. For a *lake* view, however, no mountain in the district is equal to the *Buttermere Red Pike*, From its summit, Buttermere and Crummock Lakes lie mapped out immediately below; considerable portions of Ennerdale Lake and Loweswater are visible, and a strip of Derwentwater.

The *Pillar* deserves special attention for the glorious crags which descend from it almost sheer into the Ennerdale valley. *Bowfell* is in itself a splendid mountain; and *Coniston Old Man* is, perhaps, unique in the happy blending of mountain, sea, inland lake, and rich lowland visible from its summit.

It will be noticed that, so far, we have said nothing of the three first favourites of Lakeland—Scafell Pike, Helvellyn, and Skiddaw—and here, we fear, we must lay ourselves open to a charge of heresy. Scafell Pike challenges admiration for the grandeur of the climb itself, which is undoubtedly the roughest and most exhilarating in the district. The prospect from the top is very fine, but hardly equal to that from several others already mentioned. Helvellyn, from its height and central position, commands a more extensive panoramic view of the Lake District than any other mountain in it, but the ascent, except from Patterdale by Striding Edge, is rather tedious. The ascent of Skiddaw is long, and affords none of the excitement of mountain-climbing. The view falls off in quality as the summit is approached, by reason of its comparative remoteness from the best part of the landscape and the extensive sweep of dull moorland which forms the far side of the mountain itself. In fact, a more beautiful view is obtained, at a cost of a fourth part of the exertion, from its " cub," Latrigg, and from its eastern shoulder, Lonscale Fell. Skiddaw, however, is a prince of mountains for nervous people who do not like precipices.

BLACK COMBE, 1,969 ft.

Coniston to Broughton or Silecroft by road, 10 and 20 miles respectively. Silecroft to top of Black Combe, 1½ to 2 hrs. Black Combe to Broughton, 2½ to 3½ hrs.

Black Combe, recognisable by its whale-back outline and isolated position, rises from the extreme south-west corner of the Lake District, between the Irish Sea and the Duddon estuary. Being thus situated on a promontory, and separated by a long range of inferior elevation from the great mass of the Lake mountains, it commands a much wider prospect than would be inferred from its actual height, and in clear weather well repays the climber for his exertions.

Ascent.—Starting from Silecroft, the tourist will notice a grass-path winding through the bracken up the nearest hollow of the mountain, and just behind a modern-looking farm-house.   To reach this, turn to the left where the road from the station strikes the main road at right angles, and a hundred yards farther take the path across the field on the right.   Entering another road (the old highway from Broughton to Bootle and the West Coast), turn to the right.   In half a mile Whicham Church and

School are reached on the left. Cross the schoolyard, and follow a lane to the left till, passing through a gate beyond the farm-house before mentioned, you reach the open fell just where the grass-path strikes up it. Follow this path, avoiding turns to the left, and later keeping a beck close on the right. The path soon becomes very intermittent. By bearing slightly to the right, however, where the boggy ground whence the beck issues is reached, and keeping well up on the ridge, the summit will be gained after a long but gradual climb. The view thence is certainly one of the most extensive in Britain, scarcely, if at all, falling short of Wordsworth's often-quoted description. The dark heather which clothes the combes on the western side of the hill is a more popular derivation of the name than the poet's " clouds and storms," but there is no need to invent a fancy origin. The title is taken from the black combe near the summit on the south-east side, *the* feature of the fell.

The View.—The sea-view reaches to the Isle of Man and the Scottish and Welsh coasts. Beyond the last Snowdon is, in clear weather, conspicuous. At times, when the mist hangs over the sea, but has been dissipated from the higher strata of the atmo-sphere, extraordinary appearances are presented. The peak of Snowdon has been seen suspended, as it were, in mid-air, the inter-vening space of sea being quite invisible. Landwards there is a wide view over the Furness and Mid-Lancashire districts, the York-shire fells, with the flat-topped Ingleborough, closing in the view.

The Coniston range appears close at hand, to the north-east, with Ill Bell to the right of it, and Helvellyn filling up the gap between it and the Scafell group on the left. Bowfell, Scafell Pike, and Scafell are prominent among the latter, and to the left of them Skiddaw appears in the far distance. Then the Pillar and Haycock shut out further view northward.

Descents.—Those desirous of proceeding along the west coast, so as to travel up Eskdale, or approach Wastwater from its foot, should descend in a north-westerly direction to *Bootle* (a very different Bootle from that beside the Mersey !), and take train or bus, remembering that the station is about 1½ miles beyond the town. To return to *Broughton*, keep along in a north-easterly direction over a wide stretch of tiresome and often boggy ground, leaving White Combe on the right, and descending to the farm *Swinside*, near which is a prehistoric circle (*Sunkenkirk*) nearly 100 yards in circumference. The steep declivity above Swinside is turned on the left. Thence a road leads in a south-easterly direction to a cluster of houses called *Broadgate* (1½ m.), from which Broughton is reached in less than an hour by the regular road over Duddon Bridge. The Broadgate angle may be avoided by crossing the stream below the Swinside Stone Circle and taking a steep path over the wood-covered fell between Swinside and Duddon Bridge. The route, however, is intricate, and the stream, unless very low, impracticable.

FLEETWITH, 2,126 ft., AND HONISTER CRAG, 2,070 ft.

Emergency Descent, see p. 301.

Ascent from Buttermere or Rosthwaite, 2½ to 3 *hrs.*—The ascent of Fleetwith Pike has two particular features—the exquisite vista of the lakes of Buttermere, Crummock, and Loweswater from the summit, and the look down Honister Crag during the walk along the ridge. Fleetwith, in fact, is simply the highest point of the comparatively low ridge which is so well known from the part of it called Honister Crag. Those who cannot afford the time for a special ascent may take it in the route from Keswick to Buttermere at the cost of about an extra hour's exertion.

The nicest method of climbing the mountain is undoubtedly to begin at the top of the Honister Pass, whether one has set out from Borrowdale or from Buttermere. The spur which descends steeply, but regularly, in the direction of the three lakes should be made use of for the descent, the prospect being delightful the whole way. The only necessary direction is to continue in the line of the road from Borrowdale when the sharp corner at the top of the Honister Pass is reached, and, when the ridge is attained, to proceed all the way with the precipice and steep slope as near as may be on the right-hand side. Beyond the top of the crag and a little to the north of the summit of Fleetwith a natural rock gateway affords a charming vista of Buttermere, Crummock Water, and Loweswater.

The View.—From the summit of Fleetwith the prospect is beautiful but circumscribed. Robinson and Dale Head close it in to the north and north-east, except that in the dip between them a portion of Skiddaw is seen ; but eastward the view extends as far as the Helvellyn range. Great Gable is dominant to the south ; Scafell itself peers over its western shoulder, and Bowfell rises on its left. South of Buttermere Lake appear High Stile and Red Pike, and beyond it, to the right, the red broadside of Grasmoor. The Pillar, on the far side of Ennerdale, is the chief height between the Buttermere Fells and Great Gable.

In **descending**, be careful to keep, as nearly as possible, the summit of the ridge in the direction of Buttermere, joining the Honister road at Gatesgarth, 2 miles short of Buttermere village.

GLARAMARA, 2,560 ft.

Emergency Descent, see p. 296.

Ascent from Rosthwaite, 2 to 2½ *hrs.*—The ascent of Glaramara forms a beautiful summer excursion, owing its charm to the lovely views of Borrowdale and Derwentwater obtained during the climb. These views are unfortunately retrospective ; but they may be made prospective by striking northward from the top of Esk Hause (*see p.* 205), which is the point where the bulky mass going by the general name of Glaramara strikes out of the main Scafell and Bowfell range. It should be said, however, that Glaramara is an exasperating mountain along which to walk, especially in bad weather—being by no means as smooth and level as it appears to be when viewed from Esk Hause.

From Rosthwaite the ascent is almost due south. The best route is through a gate opening on to a cart-track, about half a mile beyond the church on the Seatoller road, and a short distance after crossing the beck, Combe Gill, which flows from the mountain itself. The cart-road passes an old mill, beyond which cross the beck and climb the wooded slope on the western side of it. There is a track for some distance. On attaining the top of the ridge the rocky summit, or rather double summit, of the mountain is seen some way ahead, and there can be no difficulty in reaching it beyond that of traversing ground of rather more than average roughness.

The View from the top is very fine, the proximity of Borrowdale and Derwentwater relieving the almost universal aspect of wildness which would otherwise characterise it. To the left of these rise Grisedale Pike, Grasmoor, and the other fells between Derwentwater and the Buttermere valley, Dale Head being the nearest conspicuous height in that direction. Westward, Great Gable, close at hand, with the Pillar and the High Stile range on its right, is the prominent feature. Farther south the Scafell heights and Bowfell, the latter backed by the Coniston range, cut the horizon. The thimble-shaped Pike o' Stickle is conspicuous in the south-east, and the far side of Windermere in the same direction. The Helvellyn range and Fairfield close the prospect due eastward. The cluster of houses to the north-east is Watendlath.

The walk may be continued along the rough, broken ridge to *Esk Hause*, and so back by Grain Gill or Sty Head, or a descent made by the route of ascent to *Rosthwaite*.

GREAT GABLE, 2,949 ft.

Emergency Descent, see p. 297.

No mountain in the Lake District is better worth ascending than Great Gable, whether it be for the grandeur of the fell itself, or the magnificent prospect from its summit. There are various ways of climbing it, the simplest being from the higher part of the Sty Head Pass, whence those staying at Keswick, Rosthwaite, or Wasdale Head may reach the top in considerably less time and with less exertion than Scafell Pike demands. The Honister Pass route involves spending the greater part of a day on the fells, but the walk is from end to end one of unflagging interest and it has the advantage that except for the final stage from Wind Gap to the summit there is nothing steeper than—or so steep as—the old mine tramway by which one climbs from the hause. Although three other lesser heights—Grey Knotts, Brandreth, and Green Gable—are scaled, or nearly scaled, before the Gable itself is reached, the walk is by no means a tiring one for its length, the intervening depressions being very slight. Tourists lose very little (except time) and gain a great deal by substituting this route for the stereotyped Sty Head one from Keswick to Wasdale Head.

The main tracks up Great Gable are well cairned. In descending, however, especially in a mist (*see* emergency descent), it is well to remember that there is more than one line of cairns. It should also be remembered that there is a precipice overlooking Ennerdale on the north-west, and another overlooking Wasdale on the south.

1. **By Sty Head.**—*From Seatoller (p. 180) to Sty Head*, 1½ *to* 2 *hrs. ; from Wasdale Head (p. 205)*, 1 *hr. From Sty Head to the top*, 1 *to* 1¼ *hrs.*

From Seatoller *via* Seathwaite as described on *p.* 198 ; from Wasdale Head as described on *pp.* 210–11.

The ascent by **Aaron Slack,** the gully between Green Gable and Great Gable, is not recommended. From Sty Head Tarn to Wind Gap is a long, uninteresting grind up a stony gully with practically no compensatory views. As a *descent*, especially in mist, Aaron Slack has its uses.

From the highest point on the Sty Head Pass, a rough track zigzags up the south-eastern flank of Great Gable. About half-way up the path forks ; the two branches re-uniting a short distance from the top. The general direction is in a line with the path, which you will easily trace behind you, ascending Esk Hause on its way to Langdale. There is a series of guiding cairns. Take care to keep well to the right of the crags which we have already mentioned as overlooking Wasdale. The climb is steep and continuous, but a trial of lungs rather than nerves.

The ascent by Gavel Neese, the long spur which runs down from Great Gable to Wasdale Head, is perhaps the most trying in the District. About half-way up, just about the level of the depression between Great Gable and Kirkfell, a prominent splinter of rock indicates where a track bears away to the north and, passing below Gable Crag and along the breast of Green Gable and Brandreth, ends above Seatoller. It is known as "Moses's Sledgate," and is popularly attributed to an old smuggler.

2. **From Rosthwaite by Honister Pass, or from Buttermere.**— *Rosthwaite to Honister,* 3 *m. Honister to top of Great Gable,* 2 *to* 3 *hrs.*

Leave the Buttermere road just at the top of the pass, and follow the track of the disused cable tramway up to the drumhouse (a very useful landmark). From this point ascend southward to the rocky summit of Grey Knotts, whence to Great Gable the direction is to keep the top of the ridge the whole way, only diverging a little now and then to the right to avoid craggy ground. There is a somewhat indistinct track along the western side of Brandreth which may be of use in thick weather, but the ridge line is preferable on account of the views to the east which are otherwise lost. In clear weather there is no possibility of a mistake after this. Great Gable itself rears its precipitous front straight ahead, and the route to it is plain. When mists are about, however, even one who knows the district well may be baffled by the spasmodic appearances of valleys and hills, that present to him no recognisable feature during the few seconds which the breaking cloud allows for observation. Our route leaves on the left *Gillercombe*, a desolate upland valley whose waters descend by Sour Milk Gill into Borrowdale, near Seathwaite : on the farther side of the valley is the mountain called Base Brown ; while on the right, as we pass from Grey Knotts to **Brandreth**, a lovely full-length view of Buttermere and Crummock Water with Loweswater beyond reveals itself, and soon afterwards, separated from them by the bold heights of High Stile, Ennerdale Lake adds its charm to the prospect at the end of the Ennerdale valley, on the far side of which the Pillar presents as bold and formidable a front as any mountain in the district is capable of showing. Scafell Pike rises to the left of Great Gable.

From Buttermere the route we are describing may be joined about the top of Brandreth by leaving the Honister road at *Gatesgarth*, 2 miles from Buttermere, and following the course of the main beck up Warnscale Bottom, avoiding the branch which descends from Haystacks on the right hand. There are tracks on both sides of the beck. It is best to follow the pony track to the left of the beck, crossing the beck at the top just above a waterfall, where a footpath leads up the fell to Brandreth. The walk from Buttermere to the top of Brandreth will take about 2 hours.

After passing Brandreth the view down Ennerdale is very fine, extending far out to sea. There is an intermittent track, Moses's Sledgate, round the head of the valley to the dip between Great Gable and Kirkfell. Either mountain may be ascended from this depression. The track itself contours along the breast of Gable till it reaches Gavel Neese.

Green Gable is next ascended, and then a short and sharp dip brings us to *Wind Gap*, the neck of the ridge between it and its bigger and wilder brother. Beyond the gap nail-marks indicate the way up the steeply-piled boulders littering the summit of Great Gable.

3. From Ennerdale. Those who approach Great Gable from Upper Ennerdale should walk up beside the stream to Beckhead, the gap between Great Gable and Kirkfell. The walk is easy but long and rather monotonous ; there are magnificent views of the northern precipices of Gable. From Beckhead the way is mostly a scramble over boulders up the north-west side of the mountain—quite safe so long as one follows the cairns.

On a boulder near the summit cairn, facing north, is the **War Memorial Tablet of the Fell and Rock-Climbing Club** (*see also p.* 13). It consists of a tablet of bronze engraved on which is a relief map of the neighbouring peaks, those purchased by the Club and presented to the nation through the National Trust being enclosed by a delimiting line. The peaks thus indicated are Kirkfell, Great Gable, Green Gable, Brandreth, Grey Knotts, Base Brown, Seathwaite Fell, Glaramara, Allen Crags, Great End, Broad Crag and Lingmell.

Below is the inscription—

" In glorious and happy memory of those whose names are inscribed below, members of this Club, who died for their country in the European War 1914–18, these fells were acquired by their fellow members and by them vested in the National Trust for the use and enjoyment of the people of our land for all time."

View from Great Gable.—This is grand and extensive. Its principal features are Wastwater, the whole expanse of which appears close at hand, flanked by the Screes on the left and Yewbarrow on the right, and backed by the sea and the Isle of Man ; Scafell Pike and Scafell, whose headlong crags and steep grass-slopes are seen to the greatest advantage ; the Pillar mountain and rock, rising with wonderful abruptness from the wild Ennerdale valley and hiding Ennerdale Lake ; the Buttermere heights and Crummock Water ; Borrowdale, Skiddaw, and Saddleback to the north ; the Helvellyn, Fairfield, and High Street ranges to the east, and a strip of Windermere, backed by the far-off Yorkshire fells, to the southeast. The great height of the Scafell group and of Bowfell prevents an extensive prospect southward.

From a little beyond Westmorland Cairn, 150 paces southwest of that on the summit, we look down on the **Napes Ridges,** which afford some of the most popular rock-climbing in the district.

Descents.—1. *To Rosthwaite by Aaron Slack.*—Commencing in a north-easterly direction, a well-cairned route leads down to Wind Gap, the *col* between Great Gable and Green Gable. From it descend to the Sty Head Pass by Aaron Slack. For route from Sty Head to Rosthwaite, *see pp.* 198–9.

2. *To Sty Head.*—Descend south-eastward as near as may be in a line with the track between Sprinkling Tarn and Great End and over Esk Hause. Be careful to avoid getting too far to the right. This route is easier to find when ascending than when getting off the mountain. For the route to Wasdale Head, *see p.* 133 ; to Seathwaite, *see p.* 211.

3. *By Honister Pass, or to Buttermere.*—Descend north-eastward to Wind Gap as in Descent 1, but in this case climb from the *col* over Green Gable and thence continue northward along the main ridge, taking care not to descend into Gillercombe on the right or to Ennerdale or Buttermere on the left. (The alternative

route contouring along the western side of the main ridge is only slightly easier, and misses the splendid views eastward.) After passing Brandreth, whence there is a fine view over Buttermere and Crummock, the route diverges a little to the right and strikes the Honister Pass at its highest point, leaving the Crag itself on the left. The old " drum house " of the slate tramway is a useful guide.

For *Buttermere* (direct) diverge to the left from Brandreth, when you get a clear view of the two lakes of Buttermere and Crummock, and follow the course of the stream descending to them. There is a path down the steep part of it on both sides leading into the Honister road at Gatesgarth.

A variation may be made by descending from the summit of Great Gable in a north-westerly direction, to the depression, *Beckheap*, between it and **Kirkfell**. This route is very rough and it is necessary to watch closely for the cairns. A safe and simple descent from Beckhead may be made by striding down the grass northward into the head of Ennerdale, whence Buttermere can be gained by Scarf Gap.

HARTER FELL, ESKDALE, 2,140 ft.

Time for the road, 4 to 5 hrs.

The ascent can be made either by *Penny Hill Farm* from the *Woolpack* or from the crest of Hardknott Pass (*see p.* 125). This latter route is preferable as a descent because (a) the best of the scenery is in front of you ; (b) any leisure time may be spent in examining Hardknott Castle (*p.* 125) without risking being behind the clock at the end of the day.

From the Woolpack.—Leave the main road just west of the *Woolpack* by a turn to the left in 100 yards. Cross river by Penny Bridge and continue to Penny Hill farm beyond which take second cart track on right which rises and follows line of a wall part way up fellside till the track which comes up from the foot of Hardknott Pass is joined. Follow this for about half a mile, then make your way up the slope of Harter Fell till the topmost crags are reached. A short easy scramble takes one to the summit. Hands as well as feet must be used, for Harter Fell has the distinction of being the one " true peak " in the District.

View from Harter Fell.—Seaward the prospect is disappointing. The scenery tails off in that direction and Birker Moor is not a pleasing foreground. The inevitable Isle of Man, portent of bad weather, is occasionally visible. North-west is the slope of the Screes, then Pillar Fell, and then the whole grand length of the Scafell heights. What is seen of the Bowfell range is unsatisfactory, either stunted perspective or featureless slopes. In the gap over Wrynose is the Fairfield range. Red Screes and Caudale Moor are so "mellowed and mingled" that it is difficult to distinguish one from the other. Then come the Coniston Fells, gradually dropping away to the level ground near the coast. Black Combe is the most distant height seawards in this direction, a little west of south.

Descent.—From the summit proceed north-east by north, keeping if anything rather to the east till the top of Hardknott Pass is reached. There is a good deal of broken ground and care is desirable. From the Pass descend left to Eskdale (*p.* 126). Crowhow End, the craggy face on the left, contains some really good climbing.

HARTER FELL, MARDALE, 2,585 ft.

Time, 3½ to 4 hrs.

Like its namesake in Eskdale, this fell is the preserve of a particular dale, Mardale (*p.* 54). It may be conveniently included in a walk over the tops from Long Sleddale, but only as an incident. The ascent is best made by the Gatescarth Pass (*p.* 94), returning to Mardale by Nan Bield (*p.* 93).

From the indefinite top of the Gatescarth Pass turn up the slope on the right and bear away in a westerly direction, keeping if anything nearer to the Mardale edge of the slope. After a short distance a cairn is seen which commands a vista of singular beauty. Fifteen hundred feet below and seemingly at one's feet lies the head of Mardale, with Haweswater beyond. The full stretch of the upper lake is in view, most daintily set with the slopes of Guerness Wood and Naddle Forest on the right and on the left High Street at its best, presenting a striking contrast to the featureless eastern slopes. Laythwaite Crags overlook the lake and close on its head are Whelter Crags. The long rugged spur on our left is Rough Crag, with Kidsty Pike beyond and on this side the great rocky combe embracing Blea Water.

Continue steadily up the slope till a wire fence is reached with some cairns adjacent.

During the ascent the Howgill Fells near Sedbergh come into sight, and, on the right front, Saddleback and Skiddaw appear, only to be hidden by the intervening highlands. From the summit the prospect is superb. Starting from the Howgill Fells and working round by the north the most prominent heights are Crossfell, Catchedicam, Helvellyn, Dollywaggon, Fairfield, Red Screes and a peep of Caudale Moor. Then Thornthwaite Crag, close at hand, blocks the view. Next on its left come Ill Bell, Gable, Pillar, Steeple, the Scafell and Coniston ranges running down to Morecambe Bay. Further round in a southerly direction are glimpses of Long Sleddale and the lower part of Windermere with the Yorkshire fells beyond.

By following the wire fence the head of Nan Bield Pass is reached and a descent made to the right by Small Water.

HAYSTACKS, 1,750 ft.

From Buttermere, 2 hrs.

Follow the Scarth Gap route to the summit of the pass and then work your way up among the crags on the left till the summit is reached. The views are very fine, especially over Great Gable and Pillar. From one point Crummock and Ennerdale Lakes can be seen almost at full length simultaneously. The remarkable similarity of the dimensions of these lakes is now apparent to the eye. The walk may be continued round the head of Warnscale Bottom and a return made to Buttermere either by Honister Pass or over Fleetwith or by the tracks leading down the Bottom from the quarries behind Fleetwith, on either side of the beck. It should be noted that the Haystacks is a very rough fell, the summit consisting of abrupt, craggy hummocks, and that the rocks end precipitously in many places on the Warnscale side without warning. It is a really dangerous fell in a mist.

HELVELLYN, 3,118 ft.

Emergency Descent, see p. 298.

Helvellyn is, probably, more ascended than any other mountain in the Lake District. Its height, inferior to that of Scafell Pike and Scafell only, its central position, and its accessibility from favourite places of resort on all sides, mainly contribute to this result. The halo of romance, too, cast around it by Scott and Wordsworth has something to do with the magnetic influence it possesses over the minds of aspiring tourists.

Apart from these considerations there can be little doubt that many other mountains in the vicinity, of less renown, repay the climber better. The ascent from anywhere except Patterdale is somewhat tedious, and the view from the summit, though extensive in every direction, lacks that variety which is so telling from summits which bring lowland and highland, lake and encircling fell, into broad and harmonious contrast. The best part of Ullswater is not seen, and Windermere and Coniston are too far off, though the latter is, perhaps, the most beautiful feature in the panorama. The ascent by Striding Edge is by far the most interesting and quite safe for people with steady heads.

Ascents.—There are four places from which the ascent of Helvellyn is ordinarily commenced, the relative claims of which in point of time and distance will be gathered from the following table :—

	Miles.	Hours.	
1. *Grasmere*	6	$3\frac{1}{2}$–$4\frac{1}{2}$	*by Grisedale Tarn.*
2. *Patterdale*	6	$3\frac{1}{2}$–$4\frac{1}{2}$	*by Glenridding.*
3. *Do.*	4	$2\frac{1}{2}$–3	*by Red Tarn.*
4. *Thirlspot*	3	2 –$2\frac{1}{2}$	*direct.*
5. *Wythburn*	$2\frac{1}{2}$	2 –$2\frac{1}{4}$	*direct.*

The paths from Grasmere, Patterdale (by Glenridding), and Wythburn are well marked throughout, except for a short distance of the last-named rather more than half-way up, where the track is made indistinct by soft ground. The Red Tarn track is unmistakable, except near the tarn itself, where it crosses a bog; while the Thirlspot route is indicated by whitewashed stones; the sharp ridge leading up to the Low Man is a good landmark.

The nearest ascent from Keswick is by the gill beyond Thirlspot, some 6 miles on the Ambleside road. Walkers from Patterdale gain nothing by adopting the circuitous Glenridding route, unless they wish to spend a few extra hours on the mountain, in which case it is, perhaps, best to ascend by Glenridding and descend by Grisedale Tarn. They may also shorten the Red Tarn route by taking Striding Edge, on the south side of the water, instead of Swirrel Edge on the north.

Lastly we would advise those who can to take Helvellyn on the way from Keswick to Patterdale, or *vice versâ*. It forms part of what is, with the exception of the Sticks Pass, the shortest route between the two places, and no feature of interest is lost by its adoption, if Aira Force be visited separately.

1. **From Grasmere.**—Follow the Grisedale Pass route, as described on *pp.* 159–60, until you have crossed the stream issuing from Grisedale Tarn. Then take the zigzag track up the fellside to the left. About half-way up a seat, close to a welcome but easily overlooked spring. When the steep part comes to an end you are on the summit-ridge of Helvellyn. The first peak of it is *Dollywaggon Pike* (2,810 *ft.*), which the direct route leaves a little to the right. Hence, by keeping due north and near to the precipitous edge of the cliff, you will reach the summit of Helvellyn in about half an hour.

On the Grasmere side of the wire fence running up Birkside, a few yards to the left of the pony-track, is a small outcrop of rock very distinctly marked by glacial striations.

The track which comes up on the left, a short distance from the summit, is the Wythburn route.

During the walk the razor-like spurs which shoot eastward from the main ridge are seen to great advantage, and Grisedale, lying far below, between them and the steep slope of St. Sunday Crag, looks its best. The last spur before the summit is reached is *Striding Edge*, and beyond it, on the far side of the Red Tarn, are *Swirrel Edge* and the peak of *Catchedicam*.

2. **From Patterdale,** (a) *by Glenridding.*—The track is unmistakable as far as the top of the main ridge. For the first 1½ miles it follows the cart-road to the *Greenside Smelting Mills*, which leaves the Patterdale and Penrith road opposite the *Ullswater*

Hotel, and keeps the Glenridding Beck on the left the whole way. Beyond the mills the cart-road, zigzagging to the right up to the mines and the Sticks Pass, must be avoided, and the course of the main beck pursued almost to the dry bed of *Keppel Cove Tarn*, on approaching which the track zigzags to the right. The distance may be shortened by keeping the tarn on the right-hand side. When the top of the main ridge is reached, a sharp turn to the left must be made, and the top of the mountain is attained in about half an hour.

A very good alternative is the track by Gillside Farm. This ascends to the ridge of Birkhouse Moor, and joins the Red Tarn pony-track some way short of the tarn.

(*b*) *By the Red Tarn.*—This is the shortest route from the *Patterdale Hotel*, and a more interesting one than that by Glenridding from any starting-point. Take the Grasmere route, as indicated by the sign-post, just south of the bridge over Grisedale Beck. Keep along by the side of the beck for about ten minutes, and then cross it according to the instructions of another sign-post directing to Helvellyn. The road continues for a short distance at right angles to the Grisedale road, by the side of an iron fence, and then turns to the left and ascends the side of the fell. A gateway, conspicuous nearly two miles ahead, is the point at which the Striding Edge spur is crossed, and the path to it is well marked, zigzagging in places to modify the steepness.

For the **Striding Edge** route follow the ridge all the way from the gateway. The views down on both sides are very striking. The last few hundred feet up the breast are steep. The way off the edge on to Helvellyn is a little nasty.

After passing through the gateway the *Red Tarn* is seen a little way ahead. Some boggy ground has to be crossed here. Leave the tarn on the left hand, and climb under Catchedicam on the right by a well-marked path up to the steep ridge of *Swirrel Edge* and thence to the summit.

3. From Thirlspot.—The pony-track commences behind the *King's Head Inn*, rounds the south side of it, and makes a wide detour in a north-easterly direction almost to *Fisher Gill*, within a short distance of which it turns sharp to the right, and keeps, with little variation, a direct line to the summit, having for some distance the southern branch of Fisher Gill on the left-hand side, and working round some craggy ground which rises above Thirlspot eastwards. This angle may be avoided by keeping the crags on the left. After about an hour's walk the ridge of the mountain is attained, and a sharp climb by a well-defined path along it leads to the summit of Helvellyn *Low Man*, whence the *High Man* is reached in about ten minutes.

A shorter though steeper way is up by Helvellyn Gill (*see Map*).

4. From Wythburn.—The track leaves the high road close to the church, and about a thousand feet up works round below Dabyside crags, which it keeps on the right, bending left again when it has reached the level of the crags, and joining the Grasmere route in the last depression of the main ridge, before the actual summit is reached. The gill, which is close at hand on the left when the start is made from Wythburn, remains more or less distinct on the same side during its entire course. When the comparatively level ground beyond the crags is reached, the track is indistinct for some time. In a fog be careful not to descend on the left. Six hundred yards before the Grasmere track (*see Map*) is joined, there is close to the track, on the left, a spring, reputedly the highest in England, " The highest fountain known on British land " (Wordsworth : *Michael*).

The View (*see Panorama on pages 318–19*).—Windermere and Coniston are seen to the south, with Esthwaite Water between them, and a wide stretch of Morecambe Bay behind all three. In the north-west is a portion of the Cumbrian sea-board ; also the Solway Firth and the Dumfriesshire hills. The nearest visible lake, with the exception of the Red Tarn, which lies 700 feet below, and apparently within a stone's throw, is Ullswater, whose upper reach, however, is hidden by the numerous spurs of Helvellyn itself shooting out in that direction. Thirlmere is just out of sight. To see it you must walk some way west, or better, north-west, to the *Low Man*. A few yards' walk in the same direction brings Bassenthwaite also into view. Northward is the dry bed of Keppel Cove Tarn, and the one to the west, some distance farther off, Harrop Tarn, which, if the sunshine happens to be playing upon it, is a welcome relief to the mass of somewhat uninteresting fell all round it. Beyond it is a grand skyline of huge hill-tops, the most striking of which are Scafell Pike, some distance to the left of the tarn, and Great Gable and the Pillar more nearly over it. North of them the Buttermere Fells, High Crag, High Stile, and Red Pike show a hog's back centre-piece with a peak at each end. Bowfell, and the line of fells extending thence to the Coniston Old Man, continue the range to the south of Scafell Pike. Black Combe peeps up over the Wrynose Gap to the north of the Coniston Fells. North of Red Pike, and nearer, is Dale Head, succeeded by a strip of Grasmoor, Whiteside, and the graceful cone of Grisedale Pike. Due north is Saddleback, with Skiddaw in all its glory to the left of it, and on the right the smiling Eden valley, backed by the somewhat wearisome-looking ridge of the Pennine chain, in which Crossfell may be described as the best of a bad lot. Then, extending southward from the far shore of Ullswater, comes the High Street range, an almost level ridge except for the cone of Ill Bell. To the left of High Street, Angle Tarn gleams high up among the fells. Close at hand, and in the direction of High Street, is St. Sunday Crag, and to the right of it Fairfield, Caudale Moor and Red Screes appearing over the dip between the two. Ingleborough, in Yorkshire, rises flat-topped far away in the south-east.

Lastly, the tourist may exert his ingenuity to identify the " huge nameless rock " of Scott's well-known lines on Gough and his dog,

and then to pose himself so as to get it into the right place, relatively
to the surrounding heights, ascribed to it by the poet :—

> " On the right Striding Edge round the Red Tarn was bending,
>   And Catchedicam his left verge was defending ;
>   One huge nameless rock in the front was ascending,
>   When I mark'd the sad spot where the wanderer had died."

Possibly Scott mistook Swirrel Edge for Catchedicam, and dubbed
the latter " a huge nameless rock." More probably he refers to the
face of Helvellyn between the two Edges, locally the Red Screes:
not to be confused with the Fell by the Kirkstone Pass. There is
another Red Screes on this range north of Wanthwaite.

Descents.—1. To Grasmere.—Follow the track southwards for
about 1½ miles, avoiding the turn to Wythburn at the bottom
of the first depression. At the diverging point the first few
yards of the Grasmere track are not very distinct, and in a fog
apt to be missed altogether. If in doubt, keep along the ridge-
line. Hence, leaving the peak of *Dollywaggon Pike* a little on
the left, the path zigzags down to the north-east corner of *Grisedale Tarn.* Here again it is for a few yards almost lost in swamp.
There is a direction-stone, and the thing to avoid is getting too
far down the clearly-marked track towards Patterdale. Hence
the route is the same as the Grisedale one from Patterdale to
Grasmere (p. 219).

2. To Patterdale, *(a) by Glenridding.*—The pony-track, keeping
to the ridge for 1½ miles, takes a wide circuit round *Keppel
Cove*, to the level of which it descends by a series of zig-zags.
Walkers may scramble down by the right-hand side of the tarn.
In either case the miners' road is hit at the disused *Smelting
Mills*, and the main Patterdale road opposite the *Ullswater
Hotel.*

(b) By the Red Tarn.—From the top of the mountain a *gateway*
is visible beyond the Red Tarn, and at the end of the sharp part
of Striding Edge. Whether the descent be by Swirrel Edge,
on the north of Red Tarn, or by Striding Edge on the south,
this gateway must be made for. From it the pony-track is
clearly marked to the bottom of the *Grisedale valley*, which it
reaches about half a mile short of the main Patterdale road.
The latter is joined close to the bridge over Grisedale Beck, ½ mile
north of the *Patterdale Hotel*, and ⅔ mile south of the *Ullswater.*
A short cut direct from the Red Tarn to the *Ullswater Hotel* may
be made by Gillside Farm. The early part of the route is marked
by white uprights. (The descents both to Swirrel and Striding
Edges involve a little mild scrambling.)

3. To Thirlspot.—Proceed from the summit, in a north-westerly
direction, over the *Low Man*, and thence descend the ridge
until you have *Keppel Cove* almost at right angles to you on
the east. Then go north-west again in the direction of Bassenthwaite Lake, until you can comfortably descend to the *King's*

Head Inn, a long white house by the roadside, or take a shorter cut down by Helvellyn Gill. The pony-track, marked by white stones, takes a circuit to the right, not descending the steep part to the inn until it has almost reached *Fisher Gill.*

4. To Wythburn.—Bend to the right out of the Grasmere route about ten minutes' walk from the summit. Six hundred yards farther there is a spring on the right (*see p.* 242). The path soon afterwards becomes indistinct for a while, but if care be taken not to descend into the gill on the right until it is again traceable, no mistake can be made. Some time after its reappearance, the track turns sharp to the right, avoiding some crags in front, round the base of which it descends to the church at Wythburn.

HIGH STREET, 2,718 ft.

Emergency Descent, see p. 304.

From Windermere Village	..	..	3½–4½ *hours.*	9 *m.*
,, *Ullswater (Patterdale Hotel)*	..	3–3½	,,	7 *m.*
,, *Mardale*	..	..	2–3 ,,	3 *m.*
,, *Ambleside by Caudale Moor*	..	4–5	,,	7 *m.*

High Street is in itself one of the least interesting of the Lake mountains, being simply the highest part of a long range of fells which extend in an unbroken line from within a few miles of Penrith to Windermere village. Its summit is scarcely distinguishable, and there is no cairn upon it. The columnar one at the head of Troutbeck, which seems to mark the top from Windermere, and which commands by far the finest view southwards, crowns Thornthwaite Crag, and is upwards of a mile distant from and 150 ft. lower than the actual summit. The excursion, however, from any one to any other of the starting-points above named, is of very great interest, and discloses some of the most striking views in the Lake District. It is also very easy.

1. From Windermere or Bowness.—*By the Garburn Pass and Ill Bell, see p.* 249. (For this route allow an extra hour.) *By Troutbeck* : Follow the Patterdale road as far as the cross-roads half a mile beyond Troutbeck Church. Here take the right turn, and proceed up the lane for 1½ miles towards a farm called *Troutbeck Park,* crossing first the main stream, and then a tributary beck. After passing the latter a short cut may be made by inclining to the right and crossing a field diagonally to a stile at the corner of a stone wall, beyond which the track is again entered by the side of *Hag Gill* (very pretty), the eastern branch of the Upper Troutbeck valley, which is cut in two by a long hill called the *Tongue.* Proceed up Hag Gill, with the stream on the right, and, when the track bends to the left, go straight on till you pass through a sheepfold, whence you begin to climb steeply alongside a wall. When the wall diverges slightly to the left, keep straight on. The track disappears or becomes intermittent, but by keeping a straight and ever-ascending course along the flank of Froswick (the steep grass-slope on the right), the Roman road will be found, and the southern spur of High Street, **Thornthwaite Crag,** surmounted by a columnar cairn, is easily reached.

View from Thornthwaite Crag.—From the cairn the feature of the view is Windermere, the whole of the lake being seen except that part of it which is hidden by Wansfell Pike. The islands and the long-drawn vista of the lower reach give the lake a charm as attractive as it is unique. There is also a fine mountain-prospect, beginning with Black Combe to the south-west, to the right of which are the graceful skylines of the Lancashire fells—the Old Man, Carrs, and Wetherlam. The rocky peak of Harter Fell fills up the gap to the right of Carrs. Then, after the nearer fells on the other side of the valley have intercepted the view for a short distance, the main range is continued by Crinkle Crags, Bowfell—recognisable by its graceful peak—and the two Scafells, separated from each other by the deep ravine of Mickledore. The Langdale Pikes assume quite a subordinate aspect under Bowfell. Great Gable is more bold than elegant, to the right of Scafell Pike, and still farther to the right a fragment of the Pillar peers over Caudale Moor. Then come, nearer at hand, Fairfield and the Helvellyn range, whose landmark is the conical summit of Catchedicam. Helvellyn proper is to the left of the last-named height, and to the right of it Skiddaw and Saddleback appear in the far distance. Eastwards, Harter Fell appears over the Nan Bield Pass, and the long, even-topped Pennine range calls for no description of its separate heights.

To reach the actual top of **High Street,** the highest point being indicated by an Ordnance Survey pillar, diverge somewhat to the right from the cairn, and keep more or less near a wire fence till another wall trends northward over the summit-level. Traces of the Roman road are again discernible to the left of the wall and the highest part of the ridge. During the walk we look down into the uppermost part of Kentmere, with its reservoir, on the right, and the deep valley lying between us and Grey Crag on the left. The precipitous sides of Ill Bell and Rainsbarrow Crag descend with fine effect into the former dale. Then, on reaching the highest part of the vast sheep-walk which constitutes the top of High Street, formerly the scene of an annual fair at which horse-racing was a leading feature, we look down into the almost Stygian waters of Blea Water, the finest of the numerous tarns of that name in the district, and catch sight of the farther end of Haweswater held up by the Great Dam. The view northwards has greatly opened up, and extends far over the Eden valley to the Crossfell range and the Solway Firth. Southwards, Windermere is still seen, through the depression to the right of Froswick ; but the view in this direction is not so fine as from our first standpoint at the cairn, the attractive foreground of the Troutbeck valley being lost. Due eastward stretches the limb of the mountain called Rough Crag, between Riggindale and the upper part of Mardale, which lie left and right of it respectively. The precipitous northern side of Harter Fell is a striking object beyond Blea Water.

Recrossing the wall, we look down upon Hayeswater (a reservoir for the Penrith district) and Patterdale, and over Grey Crag we catch a glimpse of the Buttermere Fells.

By continuing about three miles northwards Howtown on Ullswater may be reached by descending into Fusedale on the left. From High Street to Howtown is about 2 hours' walk (*see p.* 223).

2. From Patterdale.—Follow the Windermere road (*p.* 216) till it turns to the right for the Kirkstone Pass, a quarter of a mile after crossing the stream issuing from Brothers' Water. Then proceed through the hamlet of Low Hartsop, and straight along a cart-track, which crosses and recrosses the beck flowing out of Hayeswater within a mile, taking care not to diverge into the right-hand valley, just after passing the hamlet. The second crossing is within a few hundred yards of the foot of Hayeswater. A fairly well-defined track then zigzags to the top of the ridge, leaving the Knotts, a peak overlooking Hayeswater, on the right. On reaching the ridge, Kidsty Pike is in front, and High Street nearly a mile to the right. Between them, in an easterly direction, extends the deep valley of Riggindale, at the top of which is a gateway in the wall, through which it is possible to pass from Patterdale to Mardale without ascending either High Street or Kidsty Pike, though the drop on the Mardale side is an excessively steep one.

3. From Mardale.—There are four easy ascents of High Street from Mardale Green—viz., by Kidsty Pike ; by the Blea Water Beck and the eastern ridge of the mountain over Rough Crags, the shortest and finest ascent—grand views right and left ; by the ridge between Blea Water and Small Water ; and by the Nan Bield Pass. The nearest and quickest route to Windermere, irrespective of mountain-tops, is over the ridge between Blea Water and Small Water. Those who take this route avoid the dip into the Kentmere valley.

(*a*) *By Kidsty Pike.*—Leaving the path west of the lake at a point near Riggindale ascend to the rocks which form the eastern buttress of Kidsty Pike, the pointed summit at the head of the valley, on the right. Climb these rocks, keeping them rather on the left than on the right hand, and then follow the ridge. Towards the summit small cairns and single stones mark the route.

From the top of **Kidsty** there is a fine view, the points of which will be understood from the foregoing description of that from High Street itself. Hence the latter height will be reached in less than half an hour by working round the top of the Riggindale valley by the narrow portion of High Street known as the Straits

of Riggindale. Views into Rampsgill, debouching on to Ullswater, and peeps of Ullswater itself, reveal themselves on the
way.

(b) *By Blea Water Beck.*—Cross the stream and follow a rough
track till opposite the confluence of the Small Water Beck.   Then
keep the Blea Water Beck still on the left, till you come in sight
of the tarn itself, whence climb to the grassy dip between High
Street and its eastern spur, Rough Crag, and gain the summit by
the steep and rough ridge which there commences.

(c) *By the ridge between Blea Water and Small Water.*—Follow
the Nan Bield route (*pp.* 224–5) till it crosses the beck issuing from
Small Water.   Then climb the grass slope to the right, working
your way up through some small crags which form a kind of
buttress to this shoulder of High Street.   A track will be found
at the steepest part, and a cairn a little way above it.   Hence,
bearing to the right round the ridge which overlooks Blea Water,
you will reach the summit in about 20 minutes.   To reach Windermere, a direction more to the left, and towards the columnar
cairn on Thornthwaite Crag, should be followed, rounding the
head of Kentmere Valley.   This route should not be attempted
in doubtful weather, because of the craggy portion above Small
Water.

(d) *By Nan Bield Pass.*—Turn sharp to the right about the
top of the pass (*pp.* 224–5), and keep to the highest ground, in a
north-westerly direction, till you reach the summit, passing near
the cairn mentioned in the last ascent.

4. From Ambleside *by Caudale Moor.*—Follow the route past
Stock Gill Force along a road which becomes gradually rougher
and, in about two miles, narrows to a field-path.   It emerges on
the Windermere–Patterdale road at the foot of Woundale Fell.
Here turn to the left and, at the junction of the Ambleside and
Windermere coach-roads, the *Kirkstone Inn* is reached.   A short
distance beyond the Inn turn to the right through a field-gate
and ascend to the ridge-line by a short scramble.   This route
is less tiresome than the diagonal course marked on the map.
Follow the ridge-line in a northerly direction by a wall till the
broad summit of Caudale Moor is reached.   The course now lies
in a north-easterly direction, but time will be well spent in
wandering about the plateau for the sake of the views from
this most easily-ascended fell of its height in the district.   These
are similar to those from Red Screes (*p.* 275) except that that
fell, looking its best from the north-west edge of the plateau,
occupies the foreground in that direction.   For High Street
cross the moor, negotiating one or two walls *en route,* in the
direction of the conspicuous cairn on Thornthwaite Crag.   From
the plateau a steep scramble leads down to Threshthwaite Hause
(or Mouth), from which delightful views may be obtained of

Windermere and Ullswater. From the hause a steep, shaly ascent leads to the summit of Thornthwaite Crag.

Descents.—1. To Troutbeck and Windermere.—Follow the course of the wall southwards till you come to the wire fence on the right, leading towards the columnar cairn on the top of Thornthwaite Crag, the most prominent part of the mountain visible from Windermere. Hence drop to the dip between High Street and Froswick, and then descend diagonally and not in too great a hurry in the direction of Troutbeck village, leaving the steep narrow ridge of Froswick and Ill Bell on the left. A track more easily seen from a distance than close at hand drops to Hag Gill, the depression lying eastward of Troutbeck Tongue. Here you reach a grass-path bordered by bracken, and a furlong after passing through a sheepfold enter a horse-track, which continues along the right-hand side of the beck for about a mile, and then turns sharp to the right to Troutbeck Park Farm. By crossing a stile at the turn, and a field beyond it to its farthest extremity, you will cut off a corner, and enter the road from the farm to Troutbeck village, just where it crosses the stream. About a mile farther, the stream having been recrossed meantime, a lane to the right leads up in a few hundred yards to the *Queen's Head* at Troutbeck. The direct route enters the Patterdale and Windermere main road about half a mile farther on. By the latter route there is no inn till Windermere is reached.

2. **To Patterdale.**—Follow the ridge northwards, to the head of Riggindale, and continue round the Knott, about half a mile farther on, leaving *Kidsty Pike* considerably on the right. Then descend by a peat-track to the lower end of *Hayeswater* and *Hartsop* hamlet, whence the road down Patterdale to Ullswater is unmistakable.

3. **To Mardale.**—The most direct descent is by Rough Crag, the ridge running due east from the summit of High Street. The commencement of the descent to the ridge is steep and the latter part steep and rough. This is hardly a route to be recommended to nervous tourists. The ridge-line may be left at the first dip and a descent made by Blea Water.

Other routes are (a) over *Kidsty Pike*, whence the descent must be continued along the ridge until the last rocks are passed and then to the bottom of *Riggindale* : and (b) by the top of the *Nan Bield Pass*, or the ridge between Small Water and Blea Water. For either of the last two, make for the cairn about a mile to the south-east of the summit, and thence keep along the main shoulder for Nan Bield, or pick your way carefully down to the Nan Bield track, at the outlet of Small Water.

4. **To Ambleside.**—Reverse the route described on *p. 247*. Apparent alternatives are longer and more fatiguing. From the *Kirkstone Inn*, however, the road may be taken direct to Ambleside.

ILL BELL, 2,476 ft.

Emergency Descent, see p. 304.

From Windermere, 6 m. (time, 3 to 3½ hrs.) ; Garburn Pass, 1 to 1½ hrs.

Ill Bell, though not the highest point, is the most pronounced peak in the range to which it belongs, and the ascent is one which no sojourner at Bowness or Windermere should omit to make. There is no severe climbing, but the views both from the summit and during the descent (which we shall describe into Troutbeck) are amongst the most beautiful in Lakeland. An artist who wished to paint an ideal picture of fairyland could hardly obtain from nature a more perfect model than the full length view of Windermere, with its islands, sylvan shores, and graceful hill-outlines, which ravishes the eye during almost the whole of this descent ; while in strong contrast, north, west, and east, stand out the sterner features—mountains and deep-set valleys—of the District.

Ascent.—Follow the Kentmere road (*p. 92*) as far as the top of the Garburn Pass (1–1½ hrs. from Windermere). Another route is to take the Kendal road for ⅔ mile from Windermere Station, and then, turning to the left, to gain the top of Garburn by the route shown on the map (*p. 71*). The fault of the latter route is that to begin with it takes you a little outside the district.

From the top of **Garburn** (1,450 *ft.*), where the Kentmere track turns square to the right, turn north on to the open fell and go straight ahead towards the highest part of the ridge in front of you. The ground is uneasy walking and sometimes boggy until an ascent is made on to Yoke. A divergence to the right is worth making for the sake of looking down the noble Rainsborrow Crag. After crossing a slight depression a steepish pull uphill lands you on the summit of Ill Bell, which is marked by three cairns. The view is much the same as from Thornthwaite Crag (*p. 245*). Windermere is the feature, and the look down the steep craggy side of the mountain into Upper Kentmere is very fine.

In descending, walk for about a quarter of a mile south from the depression between Ill Bell and Yoke and then incline diagonally to the right in a south-westerly direction, following the natural line of descent down by Lowther Brow.

The route may, with very little rise and fall, be continued from Ill Bell over Froswick to Thornthwaite Crag or High Street (*p. 245*). or from Froswick the Roman road track (*see Map*) may be joined,

KIRKFELL, 2,631 ft.

Emergency Descent, see pp. 297-8.

For a grand if not comprehensive view this mountain is hardly second to the Gable.

Ascents.—(*a*) From Wasdale Head by Black Sail to summit

of pass (*p.* 207). Thence the climb is rather tricky, the iron fence which keeps to the ridge from the Pillar to Kirkfell ascending amongst awkward crags.

(*b*) Follow the Black Sail route for a few hundred yards ; then make for the steep grass slope on the right, keeping the village and the lake in a line behind—a very stiff grind. From the top of this slope the way to the summit is over grass and scree.

(*c*) After crossing the bridge at the foot of the Sty Head Pass ascend the very steep ridge of Great Gable, Gavel Neese, which comes down on the left. At about the height of Beckhead, the depression between Gable and Kirkfell, a prominent splinter of rock is seen and from near this a cairned track bears away to the left to Beckhead Tarn. Thence turn left and follow the wire fence to the summit.

(*d*) Go straight up from the bridge in Ennerdale (between Black Sail and Scarth Gap), keeping to the left of the Black Sail *col.*

The View.—The features are Scafell and Scafell Pike towering grandly over Lingmell, with Mickledore intervening : then, the Screes and a full-length view of Wastwater. Westward the Pillar and his companions over Mosedale. Across Ennerdale the Buttermere fells, and beyond these Robinson, Hindscarth, and Dale Head. Gable is, perhaps, the gem of the whole. From no other point does its precipitous character show to such advantage.

N.B.—It must be remembered that Kirkfell is a mountain of great bulk, and perhaps easier to get astray on in thick weather than any other in the district. In such conditions the wire fences descending to Black Sail and to Beckhead may be an invaluable guide.

THE LANGDALE PIKES (Harrison Stickle, 2,401 ft. ; Pike o' Stickle, 2,323 ft.) and HIGH RAISE.

Emergency Descents, see p. 300.

Time, from 3 *to* 5 *hours up and down.*

The ascent of the Langdale Pikes from Dungeon Ghyll is a delightful walk, but those whose anticipations are based on the wonderful impressiveness of the twin peaks as seen from the Windermere end of the district will probably be disappointed with the view from the top. The two towering crags—which, when looked at from below, have seemed the most prominent figures in the mighty fell phalanx all around—are completely dominated by their fellow heights when their summit-level is attained. On one side Bowfell rears its rocky head 500 ft. above them, and on the other, at a greater distance, the huge mass of Helvellyn narrows the view to a range of eight or ten miles, while northwards they are overtopped by uncharacteristic fells— High Raise ; in fact, in this direction the view is perhaps a little monotonous. The entire strength of the mountain lies in its craggy and bold southern swoop into Langdale, across which the prospect of Windermere, Esthwaite Water, and the far Yorkshire hills atones for any shortcomings in other directions. There is no difficulty in the ascent, but the direct descent is very awkward in consequence of the crags about half-way down and should be avoided. A deviation is necessary down to the dip, but care should be taken on account of the boggy stretch of ground between the two pikes. (*See p. 300.*)

Ascent.—This is nearly always begun from one of the Dungeon Ghyll hotels. From other sides, except Grasmere, it is tame and laborious. The best route is to ascend by Dungeon Ghyll and to descend by Stickle Tarn.

The routes from the two hotels converge at the foot of Dungeon Ghyll (*p. 118*), whence either side of the ghyll may be pursued. The track on the left-hand side is, perhaps, to be preferred. It winds up with the fall on the right-hand side, and then skirts the top of the crags, looking down on the *Old Hotel*: soon working round to the right again, and always keeping the ghyll on that side. One or two picturesque falls come into view during the climb, and the retrospect over the Langdale valley is very pleasing. When the top of the lower spur of the mountain is reached some boggy ground has to be crossed to the foot of the peaks themselves, which are separated by a gully. The way then is to skirt Loft Crag on the left hand of the gully, climbing, if so disposed, Pike o' Stickle as well as Harrison Stickle. Skiddaw presents a most imposing appearance from Pike o' Stickle.

A simpler route is by the path up the left side of Mill Ghyll, and then to the right of Stickle Tarn, noting Jack's Rake, the narrow diagonal ledge running from north to south upwards across the face of the crags, the gullies, and other features of Pavey Ark, reaching the Pikes by a circuitous route over the slopes on far side of Pavey Ark, and crossing its summit right to left. A more direct but steeper ascent is between Pavey Ark and Harrison Stickle.

View from Harrison Stickle.—Skiddaw and Saddleback appear in the north, over the long and dreary range which stretches from the pike itself to Castlerigg over Derwentwater. Then comes the range extending from Catbells, on the west side of Derwentwater, to Dale Head. On the right of the latter is the cone of Grisedale Pike, and on its left Grasmoor. Then, nearer at hand, comes the Glaramara range, backed by the fells between Buttermere and Ennerdale, to the south of which the Wasdale shoulder of the Pillar rises. Between the latter and Scafell Pike, which is directly over Pike o' Stickle, Great Gable asserts a strong individuality. South of Scafell the graceful peak of Bowfell is a never-failing landmark, and the range is continued to the Coniston Old Man. The southward prospect includes Windermere, Esthwaite Water, Blea Tarn, and Elterwater. The flat-topped hill far away in the south-east is Ingleborough. The Helvellyn and High Street ranges, with St. Sunday Crag, Fairfield, and Red Screes, close the prospect eastwards, St. Sunday Crag filling up the gap between Dollywaggon Pike, the most southerly shoulder of Helvellyn, and Fairfield, and rising immediately over Seat Sandal.

Descents.—The most inviting descent into Langdale, on the score of variety as well as safety, is by Stickle Tarn. In fact, the direct descent to Langdale is by no means to be recommended, for reasons given on the previous page. With care one may also reach Grasmere or Borrowdale without encountering any serious intervening depression.

1. *To Langdale.*—By Stickle Tarn. The route is unmistakable. Turning one's back to Langdale, the tarn lies below on the right, and the usual course is round it over the summit of *Pavey Ark* (*see above*). The shorter and more direct descent between Harrison Stickle and Pavey Ark is quite simple, provided one keeps as near as possible midway between the two. The grass should be kept to the whole way. If crag is encountered on the left hand, bend to the right ; if on the right hand, bend to the left.

2. *To Grasmere.*—After descending from Pavey Ark, cross the stream which feeds the tarn, and then, bearing slightly to the left, climb again for a little way. The height on the left hand, crowned by a columnar cairn, is *Sergeant Man*. Strike the ridge about half a mile south of this cairn. From the summit you will look straight down to Grasmere village over *Codale* and *Easedale Tarns*. The latter is the larger and more conspicuous of the two, and the former, which lies on your way to it, is only intermittently visible. Keep both of them on your left. Descend direct to the old stone hut at the foot of Easedale Tarn immediately after crossing the summit of the Crags of Blea (Castle) Rigg that fall precipitously towards the tarn. From it there is a good pony-track all the way to Grasmere (*p.* 196). The whole descent will take from 2 to 2½ hours.

3. *To Borrowdale.*—By passing behind Pike o' Stickle you will hit the Stake Pass (*p.* 130) at about its highest point, or by continuing along the ridge northwards for nearly an hour over **High Raise,** whence there is a splendid panorama (*see below*), you will reach the place where the track from Grasmere to Rosthwaite, by *Far Easedale* and *Greenup Edge*, crosses. Where there is no path, small cairns mark the direction of this track. For the descent thence to Rosthwaite, *see p.* 157.

HIGH RAISE

(*Emergency Descent, p.* 300) is the moorland which stretches northward from the dip behind the Langdale Pikes to Greenup Edge. Distinction of outline so characteristic of Lakeland fells is almost entirely lacking, although from certain points in Borrowdale and from the Portinscale meadows it appears to possess a low, blunt summit at either end of the plateau. On certain maps it is described as High White Stones, which is actually a slightly-marked elevation a little south of Greenup Edge, but the fell is usually known as High Raise. Low White Stones is the rocky portion overlooking the head of Easedale.

High Raise is generally considered to be the centre of the Lake District.

Ascents.—From the Langdale Pikes (*see* 3, *above*). From Grasmere by Blea Rigg and Sergeant Man, as above. From Grasmere by Far Easedale. Follow the route (*p.* 157) as far as Greenup Edge and turn left. From Keswick by Borrowdale and Greenup. Follow the Keswick to Grasmere route (*p.* 195) to Greenup Edge and turn right. For descents to Grasmere or Keswick reverse the routes of ascent (the wire fence running north and south is a useful guide in thick weather). For descents by the Langdale Pikes, *see* p. 300.

View.—From its central position and the absence of loftier heights for a long distance round, High Raise commands a most comprehensive panorama, not so beautiful as many others by reason of the tameness of the foreground, but perhaps the best of all standpoints for a lesson in the geography of the Lake District. Looking due north we have Saddleback on the right and Skiddaw on the left, and then, over Bassenthwaite Lake, the Scottish coast, with Criffel near Dumfries conspicuous. Next, the fells between Derwentwater, Buttermere, and Crummock, the gracefully-peaked Grisedale Pike and the rude bluff of Grasmoor amongst them ; then, in a line, the Buttermere heights of which High Stile is the chief. Just to the right of them the precipice of Honister Crag is a very marked feature. Westward are the Pillar, Great Gable, and the Scafells. In this direction Gable is the "monarch of mountains." Next comes Bowfell. Southward the Coniston group blocks the way, the sharp point of Dow Crag being noteworthy. Windermere and Morecambe Bay are the next objects of interest ; and, far away in the south-east, rise the Yorkshire fells, with the flat-topped Ingleborough as their chief. Then, to the east, appear Ill Bell, Red Screes, Fairfield, the gap of Grisedale Pass with St. Sunday Crag on its right, succeeded by the Helvellyn range, which prevents a farther view in a north-easterly direction.

THE OLD MAN (*see pp.* 281–2).

THE PILLAR, 2,927 ft.

Emergency descent, see p. 300.

From Wasdale Head .. .. .. 2½–3½ *hours.*
From Ennerdale (Anglers' Hotel) .. 4–4½ *hours.*

The ascent of the *Pillar Mountain* or *Fell* is most interesting and perfectly safe. It must not be confused with the climb of the *Pillar Rock*, a prominent craggy pinnacle on the Ennerdale

side of the fell, a short way below the summit (*see p.* 258).
Pedestrians from Wastwater to Ennerdale, or *vice versa*, are
strongly advised to adopt the route over the Pillar Mountain.
There is a somewhat shorter cut over *Windy Gap*, a depression
of about 500 feet, between the Pillar and the Steeple; but this
route, besides missing the best views, is so excessively steep on
the Wastwater side that no saving of fatigue results from adopting it.   The approaches to the *Pillar Rock* are for mountaineers
only.

1. From Wasdale Head and down to Ennerdale (*car park*
(6 *to* 7 *hrs*).—Follow the Black Sail route (*p.* 207) till Gatherstone
Head has been left behind.   The ordinary route may be followed
to the top of the Pass and a turn to the left made over **Lookingstead,** or the steep side of Lookingstead ascended to the ridge
from some point short of the Pass head—an outcrop of rock
where the track becomes stony is a good starting-point.   Once
on the ridge the way to the summit of Pillar is rough and occasionally steep, but marked by a path more or less distinct.   The wire
fence must in all cases be kept on the right, as the Ennerdale face
of the fell is precipitous.   Good views across Ennerdale to the
north and Mosedale to the south.   The Ennerdale Valley is
finely fenced in by the richly-coloured screes of Red Pike and
the barren slopes of High Crag and High Stile, beyond the former
of which the bulky red bluff of Grasmoor appears.   The track
over Scarth Gap is seen climbing the other side of Ennerdale and
beyond it Skiddaw makes a striking skyline.   Great Gable rises
majestically at the head of Ennerdale.   To the right is the
Scafell group, with a barren moorland below, relieved by Burnmoor and Eel Tarns and backed by the fells beyond Eskdale.
The most striking features of the scene, however, are the deeply
rifted crags which descend wildly from the gazer's feet into the
depths of Ennerdale, surpassing in chaotic grandeur anything
else of the kind in the district.   The summit of Pillar is grassy and
almost level.

View from the Pillar.—Superb.   In addition to the features
enumerated, a wide prospect westwards opens, including the whole
of Ennerdale Lake, the champaign country between it and the sea,
the sea itself and the Isle of Man.   Saddleback appears to the right
of Skiddaw and the Helvellyn range bounds a great deal of the view
eastwards.   Black Combe and Morecambe Bay are the limits of
the southward outlook.   The most interesting feature, however,
is the Scafell group, the crags and recesses of which are magnificently
displayed.

Those who wish to cross *Windy Gap* without climbing to the top
of Pillar Fell must follow the Black Sail route to where the path
forks.   Here they must take the left branch and, after passing

through a gate and sheepfold, make straight for the top of the Gap, taking care not to mistake for it a depression more to the left from which the main stream of Mosedale descends. The last part of the ascent is very rough and steep.

For Ennerdale from the summit cairn proceed in a south-westerly direction, disregarding the trend of wire fences, to Windy Gap, which is reached after a steep drop of 500 feet in about 20 minutes. From the Gap descend the steep slope on the right through Windy Gap Cove to *High Beck*, the lateral stream which you will see flowing into the main valley. During the first part of the descent the crags of the *Steeple* have a very striking appearance high up on the left, and will remind many travellers of the famous " corries " of the Cuillin Hills in Skye. It is then advisable to keep to the forest ride running parallel with High Beck, as Forestry Commission woods have now made the slopes here almost impenetrable, and have, indeed, altered and obliterated many of the old paths in this part of the Ennerdale Valley. The track leads to a bridge over the Liza; here turn left, along the lane leading to *Gillerthwaite Farm* in about a mile. Cross a stone wall and continue by a footpath along the shore of the lake, round the foot of a headland—Bowness Point—passing some picnic tables and, finally, joining the road which should be followed for nearly two miles. The walk from the top of the Pillar to the foot of the lake will take from 2½ to 3 hours.

2. From Ennerdale Lake, and down to Wasdale Head.—The ascent of the Pillar in this direction may be made either by exactly reversing the previous route, or by joining it at the top of the Black Sail Pass, and there turning sharp round to the right, so as to travel along the summit-ridge to Windy Gap. We recommend the former of these alternatives to those who wish to cross to Wasdale Head, and the latter to such as are returning to Ennerdale Lake car park.

The ascent from *Wasdale Head* having been fully described, it is only necessary to give chief landmarks of the reverse route.

Leaving the lake car park, keep along the shore of the lake for rather more than a mile. Then rise for a few yards through a lane with a cottage on the left, and across an unenclosed patch of green, to the cart-road, a few yards in front of a gate. Proceed along this road for nearly two miles, till, about a mile onwards from *Gillerthwaite Farm*, you see a bridge over the river on the right. Cross this, and follow the forest ride ahead, leading upwards, by the side of High Beck (*see* p. 255).

To make the ascent by Black Sail do not cross the river, but follow the track through the plantations as far as the Youth Hostel, 3¼ miles past Gillerthwaite. Hence the way up Black Sail is described in the Buttermere and Wasdale Head route (*pp.* 202–3), and from the top of Black Sail to the Pillar in the foregoing description. It is a long and rather monotonous walk.

After exploring High Beck, climb right away in the direction of Windy Gap, the depression to the right of the Pillar, and between it and the Steeple. From the *col* of Windy Gap a steep climb of 500 feet to the left lands you on the top of the Pillar. (For the view, *see* p. 254.) The descent is along the top of the ridge, eastward over Lookingstead, to the top of the Black Sail Pass, keeping, as much as possible, both the Ennerdale and Mosedale valleys in view at the same time. For the concluding part of the route, from Black Sail to Wasdale Head, *see* p. 203. A corner may be cut off by descending to the right some distance short of Black Sail.

RED PIKE (Buttermere), 2,479 ft., and HIGH STILE, 2,643 ft.

Emergency Descent, see p. 301.

From Buttermere Village by Sour Milk Gill .. 1½–2½ hrs.
,,   ,,   ,, *by Scale Force* .. 2½–3¼ ,,

This mountain must not be confused with another Red Pike which lies between the Steeple and Yewbarrow, overlooking Wasdale. The Buttermere Red Pike commands more lakes in the immediate foreground than any other mountain in the District, and is for that reason worthy of special consideration on the part of the tourist.

There are three ways of climbing Red Pike from Buttermere—by Scale Force, by Sour Milk Gill, and by Ruddy Beck.

Those who wish to combine *Scale Force* with the excursion will do best to adopt the first route, but such as have already visited Scale Force are recommended to try the second, as being shorter and less tedious. The Scale Force route is particularly devoid of interest from the force itself almost to the summit, the only compensation being the thoroughness of the " *coup d'œil* " when the highest point is reached.

Ascents : 1. By Scale Force.—The route to Scale Force is described on *p.* 182. From the force either side of the beck may be taken, the climb being at first steep, and then over a monotonous grass-slope. If the right-hand side be chosen, the beck should be crossed near a little runnel entering it on the same side, and a gradual ascent made in a south-easterly direction. By taking the left-hand side of the beck, a slight angle may be cut off, but in either case the top of the mountain is not seen for some time, the highest point visible being *Starling Dodd* (2,085 *ft.*), more than a mile to the right of it. This must be left well to the right, and from the point on the moorland where the beck forks the direction is uphill, inclining to the left. There is no particular path. When the ridge of the grass-slope is attained, the some-what pointed summit of Red Pike is unmistakable, and is reached by about a quarter of an hour's steeper climbing.

2. By Sour Milk Gill.—After crossing the stream which connects Buttermere and Crummock Water (*p.* 182) turn to the left. Almost immediately beyond Sour Milk Gill, which runs down into Buttermere at its very foot, a track will be seen running diagonally up the fell-side. Follow this until near the wall which comes down from High Stile and then turn up the steep slope to the right. The angle soon eases and a wall is crossed by a gap. Thence turn sharp to the right and cross Sour Milk Gill again, close to Bleaberry Tarn, disregarding a cairned track to the left which leads in the direction of High Stile Crags. After crossing the stream take the most convenient route by the grass and reddish screes to the summit of Red Pike high up on the left.

3. By Ruddy Beck.—Ruddy Beck is the streamlet descending from Ling Combe into Crummock Water close to its head.

Follow the foot-track for Scale Force (*p.* 182) until you come near the south-western corner of Crummock Water, where Ruddy Beck flows into it. Then climb, keeping the beck on the right hand. The first 1,000 feet or so of the ascent are steep, but not difficult. When the slope eases, bend to the left till the spur which separates Ling Combe from Bleaberry Combe is reached and ascend the ridge of the spur to the summit. This route presents no advantages over route 2, either as an ascent or descent.

The View.—The feature of this prospect is the number and diversity of the lakes, which appear in almost every direction ; not narrow strips of water glimmering in the distance, as is the case with the view from many mountain-tops noted for the mere number of lakes comprised in it, but real substantial lakes, each one, by virtue of the space it presents to the eye, and the distinctness with which the windings and varieties of its shores are traceable, taking a prominent part in the whole panorama.

Looking towards the north-east we see Bleaberry Tarn, nearly 1,000 feet below, but so near that one could almost roll a stone into it ; beyond it, Buttermere, with Hassness on the far side. A spur of Red Pike itself partly hides the strath between Buttermere and Crummock Water, but over it we see Buttermere Hause and the

Newlands valley stretching away to Derwentwater, beyond which the clear-cut brow of Blencathra makes a striking skyline. Skiddaw is seen to the left of Blencathra (Saddleback), and above the range which stretches eastwards from the sturdy red bluff of Grasmoor, overhanging Crummock Water, to the slope of Causey Pike. The sharp-pointed peak filling up the depression to the right of Grasmoor is Grisedale Pike, and the near one, in a line with it, Whiteless Pike. To the left of Grasmoor, Whiteside appears, flanking the rich vale of Lorton. Then comes Melbreak, dipping to the western margin of Crummock and Loweswater, the highest and smallest of the triad sisterhood of lakes which feed the river Cocker. Loweswater empties its waters into Crummock. Beyond it, the Solway Firth and Scotch hills may be visible. Then, to the west, the upper part of Ennerdale Lake appears, with the valley itself stretching away eastwards under the towering heights of Steeple and Pillar. The Scafell group appears in the distance, immediately left of the Pillar, and then the loftier summit of High Stile, rising close above us, bars further prospect towards the south-east. To the left of it, Honister Crag and Dale Head appear, right and left of the Honister Pass respectively, and the Helvellyn range closes the view in this direction. Helvellyn itself is the par of it almost due east, and just to the right of the pointed summit of Catchedicam. St. Sunday Crag and Fairfield are to the right of Helvellyn.

Those who do not intend to drop directly into Ennerdale, or to proceed along the ridge over **High Stile**, will do well, before commencing the descent, to walk for about ten minutes in a southwesterly direction, past a rocky knob, till the bottom of the Ennerdale valley comes into view. By so doing they will gain an adequate impression of the grandeur of the cliffs which descend from the Pillar into Ennerdale. The Pillar Rock is a noble crag several hundred feet below the top of the Pillar Mountain.

Descents.—There are various available routes for descending Red Pike. The shortest ones, to Buttermere village, require careful observation, because the lowest and steepest part of the mountain is not visible from the summit, and the shoulder, which extends exactly in the direction of the village, is dangerously steep and craggy in its lower parts.

1. To Buttermere Village direct.—Reverse either the Ruddy Beck or Sour Milk Gill routes, choosing one for the ascent and the other for the descent according to fancy. The Ruddy Beck route, however, is steeper and rougher and many prefer the Sour Milk Gill route both up and down.

2. To Ennerdale.—Ennerdale is easily reached in less than an hour from the top by making south-west for the farm-house of *Gillerthwaite*, a mile above the head of the lake, whence to the *Anglers' Hotel is* 3½ *miles (p. 255).*

3. To Buttermere, by High Stile and High Crag.—In clear weather this is a most delightful and by no means fatiguing round. The only needful instruction is to proceed from Red Pike, along the ridge overlooking Buttermere, till the top of the

Scarth Gap Pass is reached by a steep descent. A wire fence which should be kept on the left is a useful guide. High Stile is about 150 feet higher than Red Pike, and commands a more extensive if not so beautiful a view. From 3 to 4 hours should be allowed for the distance by this route between Red Pike and Buttermere village. For the part of it beyond Scarth Gap, *see p. 207.* The walk may be continued from Scarth Gap over the Haystacks and Green Crag, round the head of Warnscale Bottom, and so over the top of Fleetwith Pike by Gatesgarth to Buttermere, a full day's excursion, but not at all fatiguing, and affording delightful views.

A quite practicable ascent of **High Stile** from Buttermere is direct from Bleaberry Tarn, leaving that sheet of water on the right. It entails a little scrambling.

SADDLEBACK (Blencathra), 2,847 ft.

Emergency Descent, see p. 302.

Saddleback, or Blencathra, is a very fine and strongly-individualised mountain. Its contour, though diverging but little from the straight line, is more sharply cut than that of any mountain in the district ; and the series of lateral spurs (especially Sharp Edge above Scales Tarn) shooting out southwards from its main ridge approach still nearer to the razor-edged formation which always contrasts finely with smooth grass slopes. The walk over the mountain, from end to end, is very delightful, but it should always be taken from east to west ; otherwise, the traveller will have the view behind him all the way. The feature of the prospect from the top is the vista of St. John's Vale and Thirlmere, the latter possessing that indescribable charm which attaches itself to long and narrow lakes, when seen at full neighbouring heights.

The shortest ascent from Threlkeld is by the centre one of the three ridges which lie on the south face, *Narrow Edge*, or " Hall's Fell Top." It really is narrow. That on the west, *Gategill Fell*, is quite broad. It affords one of the most tedious descents in the district. That on the east, *Doddick Fell*, is quite easy, and finishes just above Scales Tarn.

Most walkers will prefer to do the whole tour of the mountain, descending either to Threlkeld or straight to Keswick, whereto the best route is by a wooded lane north of the Greta and under Latrigg. The entire circuit, beginning and ending at Threlkeld Station, will take about from 4 to 5 hours. To reach Keswick again on foot, another hour should be added.

From **Threlkeld** (*see p. 188*) follow the Penrith road for 1½ miles, as far as the *old toll-gate*, whence, after crossing a bit of waste ground, a path is seen, with a wall on the right, rounding the shoulder of the mountain. Continue in this direction for about half a mile, and then turn to the left up the shoulder The route is then unmistakable, if you continue to climb, keeping the southern cliff of the main ridge on your left when it appears, and *Scales Tarn* some distance below on the right. The narrow ridge on the far side of the Tarn is Sharp Edge and requires some care in negotiation because of even steeper sides than Striding Edge on Helvellyn. In wild weather the shoulder of the mountain may be rounded by an unmistakable track, and Scales Tarn reached at the foot. Beautiful views open up across Derwentwater to the Newlands and Buttermere mountains. Once on the top ridge, you have only to keep to it. The view southwards becomes very charming when St. John's Vale opens, backed by Thirlmere, and, in the far distance, Coniston Fells. Northwards is an expanse of moorland, and westwards Skiddaw presents its least interesting side. The grand sweep of the Scafell group and Great Gable closes the prospect between Thirlmere and Derwentwater, the latter lake vying with the former in the distinctive beauty which it adds to the panorama. South and south-eastwards the Helvellyn and High Street ranges appear, and due east, over a foreground of featureless moorland, are seen the Eden valley and the Crossfell range.

The descent may be made down the steep lateral spur, *Doddick Fell*, which drops towards the Helvellyn range, or preferably the cliffs may be skirted in a south-westerly direction, and, when they are passed, the green round shoulder of the mountain traversed. In the latter case, if Threlkeld be aimed at, turn to the left, and go down in a southerly direction; if Keswick, keep the islands of Derwentwater straight in front. By this route at the foot of the shoulder you will go through some enclosures, past a farm-house, and by a footbridge over the *Glenderaterra Beck*, which separates Saddleback from Skiddaw. On the other side, take the cart-road to the left for a few hundred yards. Then turn sharp to the right, and keep the road through the Brundholme woods north of the Greta until you cross it by a bridge about half a mile short of Keswick.

ST. SUNDAY CRAG, 2,756 ft.

Emergency Descent, see p. 296.

From Patterdale, Elm How, ¾ hr.; top, 2 hrs.

Leave Patterdale by the Grasmere bridle-path (*p. 219*) and follow the road, which soon becomes a mere cart-track, keeping the Grisedale Beck on the right-hand side throughout, to *Elm How* farm-buildings. Two minutes farther, a beck descends on the left. Cross this and make for the top of the ridge by the dip between St. Sunday Crag on the right and its northern spur: a stiff climb. Thence turn right, and an easy climb will land you on the summit, which is not actually visible until it is nearly reached. The peak on the left, marked by a cairn, is Gavel Pike.

As an alternative ascent take a track past Mill Moss at the

back of Patterdale village and, ascending gradually, enter Glemara Park. Continue till there is a stream in front, then turn up left through the trees on to open ground. Climb an iron ladder over a wall to Trough Head, carry on past the end of Birks Fell, turn up right to a cairn, whence a good peat path leads forward to the foot of the last steep pitch.

The View.—St. Sunday Crag commands Ullswater better than any other mountain, both the upper and middle reaches being visible. The crags of the Fairfield range are seen to great advantage beyond the sombre hollow of Deepdale. On the other side, Helvellyn, with the sharp ridge of Striding Edge and the cone of Catchedicam, looks its best, the rocky buttresses and combes overlooking Grisedale forming an impressive foreground. In the gap between the two ranges appear the western fells from Coniston Old Man to Scafell Pike, the graceful peak of Bowfell conspicuous. Away to the east are the High Street range and the Pennine Chain.

In descending, the line of ascent may be reversed or the walk continued to the end of the ridge and then by a steep and tortuous path through Glemara Park into Grisedale close to its junction with the high road ; or a descent may be made by Deepdale Hause to the head of Grisedale Pass.

SCAFELL PIKE, 3,210 ft.

Emergency Descent, see p. 303.

Scafell Pike, in itself, worthily supports its adventitious fame as the monarch of English mountains. Though not so fascinating in outline or so individually conspicuous as several others in its immediate vicinity, it has so much rugged grandeur about it— it is such a perfect example of the wildest workings of Nature— that no one who ascends it can fail to acknowledge that he has obtained one of the genuine mountaineer's first objects—the farthest possible removal from the associations of his everyday life. Indeed, with the exception of the Cuillin Hills in Skye and the Teallach group in Ross-shire, it is doubtful whether the British Isles contain anything more majestically wild than the region of Scafell Pike and Scafell. All that part of the group which is above the 2,000-ft. contour line is now the property of the National Trust (*see p.* 13).

Between Scafell Pike and Scafell itself, and a few hundred feet below the respective summits, is a ridge called **Mickledore**, steep on both sides, but quite easy to walk along, and by no means so razor-like as either Striding Edge on Helvellyn, or narrow as Sharp Edge on Saddleback. On the Scafell side of this the crags rise in sheer precipices. For the route by it to **Scafell**, *see p.* 268.

There are many ways of ascending Scafell Pike, safe and easy, though fatiguing, in clear weather ; but the peculiarly rough nature of the summit, and the crags and precipices which abound on almost every side, render it in bad weather a particularly dangerous mountain for anyone who is not intimately acquainted with the district.

We shall describe the principal **Ascents,** giving approximately the time required for each. The descent takes about two-thirds of the time occupied in the ascent.

The following is a list of the ordinary routes up the mountain :—

1. *From Dungeon Ghyll Hotels* .. .. .. $3\frac{1}{2}$–$4\frac{1}{2}$ hrs.
2. ,, *Rosthwaite or Seatoller, Borrowdale* .. $3\frac{1}{2}$–$4\frac{1}{2}$,,
3. ,, *Wasdale Head (direct)* .. .. .. $2\frac{1}{2}$–3 ,,
   ,, ,, ,, *(by Esk Hause)* .. 3–$3\frac{1}{2}$,,
4. ,, *the Woolpack Inn or Boot (Eskdale)*.. $3\frac{1}{2}$–$4\frac{1}{2}$,,

Routes 1, 2, and 3 are marked by path or cairn all the way; route 4 an indifferent and slightly-intermittent track, as far as the steep climb to Mickledore. The Wasdale Head route is the easiest as well as the shortest.

1 and 2. **From Langdale** (6 *to* 7 *m.*), **or Rosthwaite** (7$\frac{1}{2}$ *m.*).— These routes converge on the summit of Esk Hause. For a description up to that point of the path from Langdale *see* p. 131; and of the Borrowdale track, to the point where it diverges from the Sty Head track, *p.* 198.

A slightly shorter route up from Borrowdale to Esk Hause is *via* Grain Gill. Immediately on crossing *Stockley Bridge* turn to the left through an opening in the wall and follow a track on the right of the beck. The route crosses the beck and then, becoming extremely sketchy, leads up a green tongue : then to the left of what seems the bed of an old tarn, underneath Allen Crags on the left, and so across Ruddy Gill on to the track a little short of Esk Hause. There is also a track on the other side of the beck. Great End grandly fills up the gap in front as we ascend the valley from Stockley Bridge.

If the regular footpath route by Sty Head Tarn be taken, branch off to the left after passing the tarn. The path is boggy at first especially if one branches off too soon after passing the tarn ; but it soon becomes clearly marked. **Sprinkling Tarn** is passed on the left, and the crags of *Great End* tower over the pass on the right. There is a splendid view of Borrowdale and Derwentwater through the vista of Grain Gill.

Further description applies to the two routes equally. A shelter erected by the Lake District Association on the top of Esk Hause is intended as a protection against wind.

Looking westward from **Esk Hause** we have on the right the path up from Sty Head ; then overlooking it and occupying the centre of the view, Great End. The path to Scafell works up the gentler slopes of Great End towards the left. A series of small cairns mark the way. In a few minutes a streamlet is crossed, the last water during the ascent, and the track works up the combe between Ill Crag and Great End. At the head of the steepest bit of the way we suddenly get a fine view north-westward. The Pillar, Steeple, and Mosedale valley are well seen, and it is worth diverging from the path for the full-length view of Great Gable. Beyond this point we pick a way up the boulder-strewn side of Broad Crag : the cairns must be watched, though if descending in a sudden mist the nail-marks on the rocks may be easier to discern. Beyond a rather surprising and almost level stretch of gravel, scantily covered with herbage, come the big stones again. There is a slight dip and a beautiful peep of Crummock Water on the right, with Criffel in Kirkcudbrightshire beyond, through the depression between Great Gable and Kirkfell. Another and a greater dip has to be made, and then, by a steep climb of ten minutes up a narrow ridge with a plain winding path the summit is reached. There is much loose soil near the summit and climbers should beware disturbing it to fall on others following.

(2a.) *The Corridor route.*—A pleasing alternative, entailing much less hard work, is to start from the cairn on the Sty Head Pass, cross the bog to the rock beyond, and then turn along a faint path west to Wasdale. In a few yards this drops down to grass on the right. Here bear up to the left in the direction of Great End and a constant line of small cairns will soon be sighted. This line sweeps below the ravine of Skew Gill and above the two Greta Gills—care is required at this point—and so on across grass to a narrow track near the head of Piers Gill. From this point the *col* between Scafell Pike and Lingmell can be reached near the dilapidated wall (*see* below) or by bearing to the left a direct ascent of the Pike made by working a way up amongst the crags right ahead. This track is preferable as a return route, as one then has the best of the scenery in front. It is, however, important to remember that starting from the wall it is essential to keep up to the right and away from Piers Gill. On no account should this route be taken except in clear weather.

3. From Wasdale Head.

(a) **The Lingmell Route.**—From the hotel follow the road as far as old school, beyond which turn to the left and pass through a gate at sign-post. A beck is crossed, then climb the wall by an iron stile, and follow an unmistakable path round Lingmell shoulder. From the ridge the path then falls slightly, crosses a wall by another iron stile, and so on to the foot of *Brown Tongue,* crossing the northern branch of Lingmell Gill beck. The crags of Scafell are grand objects in front. The Tongue is grassy and easy climbing. At the top of the Tongue you come to boulder-strewn ground—Hollow Stones—on which are several tracks. The correct route lies to the left. An unmistakable landmark is the gully-seamed bastion of Pike's Crag which stands up directly ahead. This must be left on the right and an ascent made to the dip between Lingmell and Scafell Pike, across which runs a tumble-down wall. Here turn sharp to the right. The rest of the way is over rough stones and boulders, by a track which is marked by a succession of small cairns.

A noticeable feature of these ascents is that Scafell itself is throughout a much more prominent object than Scafell Pike.

(b) **The Piers Gill Route.**—*An ascent to be undertaken in fine weather only.* 1. Just beyond Burnthwaite a lane leads to the right to a bridge. Cross this and with Lingmell Beck on the left follow a somewhat sketchy track along the slopes of Lingmell to the point where the stream issues from the ravine of Piers Gill. 2. After crossing the bridge at the foot of the Sty Head Pass, turn right where the pass begins to rise, and cross Lingmell Beck by a footbridge (erected 1973) and proceed to the junction of Piers and Greta Gills. Here cross Greta Gill if convenient. If the streams are full it is preferable to walk on to where Greta Gill forks and cross the channels in succession. From the mouth of the ravine the path, which is slight and intermittent, bears upwards to the left in a wide curve. Soon some rocky bluffs are reached which should be turned on the left. Soon after, the track again approaches Piers Gill. A stream is crossed and should be immediately followed up towards some rocks, where it is recrossed so as to reach a gap in the skyline. From this point the route lies uphill till the cairns on the " Corridor " route (*see 2a*) are reached. On no account must this route be used as a descent. *Nor must it be attempted with the Gill on the left.* Many parties have been entangled hereabouts and in 1921 an experienced fell-walker slipped into the ravine and remained there for eighteen days, although search parties were seeking him high and low. He was providentially discovered by accident in time to save his life.

4. From the " Woolpack " (7 m.) or Boot (8 m.), Eskdale.

This ascent of Scafell Pike is considerably longer than that from Wasdale Head, but full of interest the whole way, and though there is some stiff climbing during the last hour, there is nothing to appal even a timid mountaineer. During the journey the beauties of Upper Eskdale and the crags which form the southern buttress of the Pikes and Scafell itself are seen to the greatest advantage.

The main road up the valley must be followed for 1¾ miles from Boot, and thence a private road to the left, indicated by a sign-post, to *Taw House Farm* (*National Trust*), a long half-mile farther.

Or the main road may be followed for another ¾ mile, crossing the Esk, till a rough road to the left leads to *Butterilket.* Ascend the valley to Esk Falls (*p.* 126), and there cross the bridge and keep the stream on the left (immediately on the west of the defile is impassable) till a convenient crossing offers some quarter of a mile below Cam Spout Crag, where the main track (*see below*) is rejoined. This crossing is impossible except when the river is low. (Esk Falls make a pleasant objective for a short separate excursion.)

Beyond Taw House a cart-track crosses some fields, keeping the river on the right, to a couple of sheepfolds, 100 yards or so beyond which it crosses a beck by a stone bridge. Here are a couple of beautiful falls, one above and the other below the bridge. The pyramidal summit in front, which fills up the head of the valley, is Bowfell. Beyond the bridge, the road, which is now a peat-track, leaves the valley, and zigzags up the steep slope on the left. When, after about half an hour's walk, it comes to an end at a peat-bog, cross some swampy ground a little to the right of its most depressed part. In a few minutes indications of a foot-track reappear. This track (which may easily be missed) is marked by a series of small cairns, and is separated from the crags of Scafell by a low line of hill. Care must be taken not to descend into the moss at the side of the river when the latter again appears on the right. The crags of Scafell tower nobly on the left, and in front the Pikes look their very best. It is only from this side one realises what a grand mountain they really form. A couple of sheepfolds and some huge detached boulders are passed, and a prominent crag down which a cataract, Cam Spout, pours, is rounded. A wide ravine now opens on the left. Cross the stream and work up the ravine, with the stream on the left as far as may be, till Mickledore, the ridge connecting Scafell Pike with Scafell, is reached. It is a stiff ascent. The top of the **Mickledore** ridge is narrow but not dangerous, and from it a direct descent may be made into Wasdale. The summit of Scafell Pike rises directly to the right, and will be reached after another twenty minutes' hard climb over a course in comparison with which the ruins of Petra would be smooth walking.

From **Boot** to the summit of Scafell Pike there is a variant which keeps Whillan Beck on the left and turns away from it sharp to the right a little short of Gill Bank, and passes first Eel Tarn on the right and then Stoney Tarn on the left, dropping into the hollow of Cowcove. On the far side of this, across the stream, the zigzag track before mentioned, is joined. By the adoption of this route, however, the beauty of mid-Eskdale is lost.

View from Scafell Pike.—The prospect is more of a mountain than a lake one. Only the lower end of Wastwater is visible, one side of Derwentwater, and a part of Windermere ; but Skiddaw and Saddleback beyond Derwentwater, Great Gable on the other side of Wasdale, and the Pillar at the head of the Mosedale Valley in the northwest, are grand objects. Grisedale Pike rises over Great Gable, whose cairn exactly cuts the line of the summit of Robinson. Between Great Gable and the Pillar is Kirkfell, beneath which, and close at hand, the craggy top of Lingmell is just visible. Between Grisedale Pike and the Pillar the chief heights are Grasmoor, with its red, burly front, and the Buttermere Fells of High Stile and Red Pike. On both sides of the last-named group are the Solway Firth and Scotland. Merrick, the summit of the Galloway hills, has been distinguished in clear weather. The range of the Pillar is continued westwards by Steeple and Haycock, the latter rising over Low Tarn. Then comes Seatallan, sinking gradually to the crags of Buckbarrow, which, in their turn, drop abruptly to the plain of West Cumberland.

The Isle of Man (*p.* 269) rises out of mid-ocean beyond Scafell, and Black Combe and the Duddon estuary are seen to the left of the same mountain.

Under certain weather conditions Ireland can be seen, the chief height visible being *Slieve Donard* (2,796 *ft.*) in County Down. It rises north of Snaefell (2,034 *ft.*), the crowning peak of the Isle of Man, and is 100 miles distant. The Welsh Carnedds—Dafydd and Llewelyn—90 miles away, are also among the possibilities, just over Black Combe.

Almost due south, to the left of the Duddon estuary, the Coniston range appears—continued nearer at hand by Crinkle Crags and Bowfell. Then comes a peep of Windermere, with the Yorkshire fells far away in the south-east, the flat-topped Ingleborough rising slightly above. Parts of the High Street range are distinguishable behind the nearer ridge of Fairfield and Red Screes by the Kirkstone Pass. The top of Ill Bell, its most southerly peak, just cuts the line of Harter Fell on the farther side ; then the range, disappearing to the north of Red Screes, is continued by the long, slightly-curved top of High Street itself, and the sharp point of Kidsty Pike. In the gap between Fairfield and Helvellyn, St. Sunday Crag appears, and between the long Helvellyn ridge and Saddleback the eye wanders away to the Eden valley and the almost level skyline of the Pennine range.

The prospect from Scafell Pike is not so good as that from many other points in the same range which are fortunately within easy reach. Consequently the tourist will do well to devote a long day to the excursion. It is little over a mile, as the crow flies, from the Pike itself to **Great End**, its north-eastern buttress, and there is no intervening depression of more than a few hundred feet. Generally speaking, in this direction the view increases in interest all the way, Borrowdale and Derwentwater coming more and more into the line of it, and Windermere revealing itself more fully over the Langdale valley. The only strong points lost are the view of the cliffs of Scafell itself, and the wide champaign of land and sea beyond them.

The summit of Scafell Pike is a memorial to the men of the English Lake District who fell in the Great War 1914–18. It was presented to the National Trust by Lord Leconfield. A memorial tablet, facing north, is built into the summit cairn.

Descents 1 and 2. To Langdale or Borrowdale.—The general direction of both these descents is north-eastwards, as far as Esk Hause. There is a plain track where the nature of the ground admits of one, but many parts of the route are over huge masses of rocky *debris*, and here the landmarks are a succession of small cairns, of which the tourist should be particularly careful not to lose sight. The penalty of so doing may be an awkward descent into Wasdale on the left hand, or Eskdale on the right, both of which valleys are separated from Keswick and Langdale by one or more formidable passes. Eskdale, especially, is a trap into which many unwary tourists fall. Once in it, the alternatives are a long trudge down it to the *Woolpack*, between which and Langdale rise the passes of Hardknott, Wrynose, and Blea Tarn, or a fatiguing grind up to the top of Esk Hause, which is out of the question late in the day. Failing the cairns, one may get some guidance from the nail marks on the rocks.

During the route to Esk Hause two depressions have to be crossed, the first and deepest immediately after leaving the summit, and the second, 15 or 20 minutes' walk farther on. The path across these depressions is clearly marked. After the second of these a plateau is traversed, at the end of which a rough descent is made to the grass-land under **Great End.**

The ascent of **Great End** from here is perfectly simple and worth the extra half-hour for the glorious view it commands—Borrowdale, Derwentwater, and Windermere.

A streamlet, descending from Great End into Eskdale, is crossed near its source (the nearest water to Scafell Pike summit), after which the path, still indicated by cairns, and traversing the comparatively level ground to the right of Great End, quickly reaches *Esk Hause.* Care must be taken not to descend the slopes on the right.

Hence the route to *Langdale* is described on *pp.* 205–6 ; that to *Borrowdale* on *p.* 132, as far as its junction with the Sty Head Pass.

A short cut to Borrowdale may be made down **Grain Gill**, the first depression on the right after leaving Esk Hause by the path to Sty Head (*see ascent, p.* 262). From the point of divergence (where the stream has eaten away a deep channel known as Ruddy Gill) there is a lovely view over Derwentwater to Skiddaw and Saddleback. The regular Sty Head route is joined at *Stockley Bridge*, a mile short of Seathwaite hamlet.

3. To Wasdale Head.—Start north-westwards in the direction of the Pillar and Mosedale valley, and passing a succession of small cairns, in about 10 minutes, when the lower slopes of the mountain come into view, bend to the right in the direction of Lingmell, descending to the swampy ground between that mountain and Scafell Pike, and turn left again when you approach an old tumble-down wall.

Hence you may ascend **Lingmell** and obtain a splendid view straight down the Seathwaite arm of Borrowdale. From the summit return on your tracks and regain the original route of descent.

From this point keep left to the green tongue, called *Brown Tongue*, that falls between the two branches of Lingmell Beck, which descend from Lingmell and Mickledore respectively. During this descent, as one rounds Pike's Crag, the Scafell precipice comes into view with magnificent effect. A little short of the meeting of the two you cross the right-hand branch and proceed by a track, which crosses a wall by an iron stile, coasting round Lingmell shoulder, and crossing another stone wall by another iron stile, regains the main road near the school.

4. To the Woolpack Inn or Boot (Eskdale).—This is a long but very interesting walk. There is no track whatever until the bottom of the valley is reached. From the summit make for the ridge of Mickledore between the Pikes and Scafell itself.

(Owing to magnetic rock the compass hereabouts is liable to deviation.) On attaining the far side of this, go down the screes on the left, a steep but safe descent. Continue down a wide ravine, with the stream on the left till Eskdale opens up in front and a conspicuous cataract, Cam Spout, is seen on the right. Cross the stream near the foot of this, and then keep well up by a faintly-marked track, with the boggy land between it and the Esk river on the left. You will pass some big green-clothed boulders. Where the stream flows farther away to the left, keep straight on, passing two sheepfolds. Half an hour's more walking will bring you to a peat-bog, whence a cart-track zigzags down to the valley, crossing a bridge, on either side of which are beautiful falls. Hence the route goes through two more contiguous sheepfolds, and, passing the farmstead of *Taw House*, enters the main Eskdale road about ¾ mile beyond it, and a like distance short of the *Woolpack*.

SCAFELL, 3,162 ft.

Emergency Descent, see p. 303.

From the ordinary tourist's point of view, Scafell suffers from the disadvantages of being so many feet lower than Scafell Pike, and from an ascent involving a considerable amount of extra labour from every frequented place in the district except Wasdale and Eskdale. For all that, it is in itself a finer mountain than the Pike, and, in respect of the magnificent crags and gullies which drop from its summit-level on the northern and eastern side, unquestionably the grandest height of Lakeland.

We shall deal here with the ordinary ascents only :—

1. From **Wasdale Head** by **Green How** (2½ *to* 3 *hrs.*). The natural line of ascent is to take the Burnmoor track (*p.* 209) till the level of the moorland is reached. Thence turn left till you hit off a cairned route over Green How to the summit. The ascent is tedious and the prospect in front confined to the barren mountain slope. Compensation may, however, be found in the view to the left over the Pillar and Buttermere groups, with Kirkfell and Great Gable in the foreground. To the right are the lower Eskdale Fells and in retrospect the Screes and Wastwater.

2. From **Wasdale Head direct**, 2 *to* 2½ *hrs.*, as in route (*a*) up the Pikes (*see p.* 263) as far as *Brown Tongue*, whence ascend the steep grass slope of Scafell on the right before reaching the crags, and bear to the left above the crags to the summit ; or keep straight up Brown Tongue towards Mickledore (*p.* 265), a little below which strike up a slope of scree debris on the right and join the following route at the foot of Lord's Rake. From this point to the top of Lord's Rake exercise approximates to exertion.

3. From **Scafell Pike** (*about* 1½ *hrs.*) drop down to Mickledore,

(15 *min.*), and cross it to the face of Scafell; then (a steep but interesting and not difficult scramble) turning to the right descend a short way to a grass ledge running along the bottom of the crags a little above the screes, and follow this to the foot of **Lord's Rake.** This is a scree-track ascending across the side of the mountain in the Wastwater direction. The route is unmistakable. It begins with a very steep scree-gully rising between the mountain and an outstanding crag or buttress. The best footing is found on either side of the gully rather than in the middle. Ascend this gully to just below its summit, which is partially blocked by a large boulder (the imposing gully to the left is Deep Gill). Thence the track falls a short way, rises again behind a second buttress, and again descends; then keeps more or less on a level across the top of screes that slope down to the valley on the right, and finally ascends behind a third buttress. This third ascent brings you out at the end of the cliffs. Bear back to the left up the slope, and the summit is easily reached.

We are now about ¼ mile from the topmost cairn and 250 feet below it. Bearing to the left, almost square with the course of the Rake, we shall in 8 minutes or so reach a point which commands a view into Eskdale, whence another 2 or 3 minutes will land us on the cairn itself.

View from Scafell.—It cannot be said that one can see from Scafell very much that one cannot see from the Pikes. Wastwater is better seen, but Windermere has vanished, and Derwentwater and Borrowdale are not so well to the fore. Burnmoor Tarn and Miterdale are but indifferent substitutes. The charm of the mountain lies in the splendid precipices and gullies which drop from the comparative plateau of its summit on the north and east sides. In clear weather the Isle of Man is conspicuous; the chief heights (north to south) being North Barrule, over Ramsey, Snaefell, and the fells north of Port Erin. From the lower cairn descend a few steps to the north-west for a splendid view down Deep Gill, with the Pinnacle immediately on the right.

4. From the **Woolpack, Eskdale** (*a*) *by Cam Spout,* 3 to 3½ *hrs.* Follow the route to the Pikes (*p.* 264) till you approach the screes descending from Mickledore; then break out through a wide opening to the left and scramble steeply up a rough ascent to the top. There are many choices of route here, but the best is to follow the left or southern branch of the Cam Spout stream till the screes are reached. At the top of these turn to the right along the ridge for the summit.

(*b*) *By Burnmoor,* 2½ to 3 *hrs.* Take the Burnmoor route (*p.* 127) by *Eel Tarn* until it turns to the footbridge near Burnmoor Tarn. Then bear away up the long slope to the right.

Descents.—These will be understood from the descriptions of ascents. The Burnmoor route is much less tiresome to descend than to ascend. If you descend by the *Lord's Rake* note particularly the description of the ascent, and remember that it consists of two short and one longer drop, with slight ascents between them, also that at each drop the wall of rock is broken on the left by screes, which fall abruptly into Wasdale. Care is required.

SKIDDAW, 3,054 ft.

Emergency Descent, see p. 304.

6 m.　Time (up and down) 3 to 4 hrs.

Of Skiddaw only the southern and western sides are, strictly speaking, within the limits of the region which it is our province to describe. The eastern descent is broken by the wide moorland of Skiddaw Forest, and the northern slope terminates in the comparative champaign which extends to the shores of the Solway. There is no more shapely mountain in the district, but for some reason the fact that it is easy of ascent seems to discount, in the eyes of some people, its beauty of outline.

The ascent of Skiddaw from Keswick is easy and consequently to some people monotonous, and assuredly it misses entirely that exceptional charm of the district, any sudden burst of surprise. The best views are from the lower skirts of the mountain. The actual summit, though commanding a most extensive panorama, lies too far back from the near objects of interest to give them due prominence in the prospect.

For all this, Skiddaw is, and doubtless always will be, one of the favourite mountain ascents in the country. To many people its simplicity is a powerful magnet ; to still more its name and fame.

Ascent.—Follow the road to Latrigg (*p.* 169) through Lower Fitz Park, and take the second turn to the right up Spoony Green Lane. The lane goes straight at first, and then works round Latrigg, ending on the north side of it, and almost on a level with its summit, at a gate which leads into another lane coming up from Applethwaite. This lane also ends at a gate, a few yards to the right of the first one. Pass through it, then left along a narrow fenced track beside a plantation, recently felled, to a stile which leads on to open fell. Follow the track to the left which leads up a steep hill continuing along a well-marked track over the fell.

Hence is a steep but simple climb to the angle of the wall. The retrospect during this part of the ascent is very fine. Derwentwater exhibits its full beauty in the foreground, and the surrounding fells, near and far, make up with it a varied and harmonious whole. Most of them will be recognised from the description of the view from Castle Head (*p.* 164). In addition, the Pillar appears over the depression between Robinson and

Hindscarth in the south-west, and the Coniston mountains due south, beyond the Langdale Pike o' Stickle, which from this point looks like a thimble. The long Helvellyn range closes the prospect to the south-east.

Where the wall bends sharply to the right it must be quitted, and the track to the left followed. A stone " man " indicates the route. After about five minutes' climb an almost level sheep-walk commences, terminated by Skiddaw **Low Man** (2,837 *ft.*). The pony-track leaves this height some way on the left, and passes through an iron fence, beyond which it becomes a broad, clearly-defined path again. The pedestrian will probably prefer to climb the Low Man on his way, especially as the view from it is decidedly finer than from the High Man.

By following the wall to the right for about half a mile and crossing it to the right, the top of **Lonscale Fell** is reached, a far better view-point than Skiddaw itself.

The distance from the Low to the High Man is about a mile, and the route unmistakable. The desolate, undulating track of *Skiddaw Forest* stretches far away to the right. There is a slight drop before the summit is reached, and the usual disappointment at finding that the top is not the top. Before the real one is reached Keswick disappears, but the view in the other direction becomes very extensive, Scotland, the Solway Firth, and the Isle of Man forming parts of it.

The View.—Attention has already been drawn to the objects which successively come into view during the ascent, and a description of the prospect from the top would be mere repetition. Its features are the long serried ranks of fell-tops which form the sky-line southward, and the wide tract of land and sea to the north and west. In clear weather the chief summits of the Scottish Lowlands are in view, from their monarch—Merrick in Kirkcudbrightshire—to Hart Fell and the other heights of Moffat and Ettrick Dales. The nearest and most conspicuous height is Criffel.

Descents.—The shortest and most picturesque is by Carl Side Descend the slate screes on the west side of the mountain, from a point some way south of the High Man, working round the head of a deep combe on the left, and then making a slight ascent to the summit of Carl Side, which is a conspicuous object all the way from the top. Hence descend the ridge, following as near as may be the line of the west side of Derwentwater. and being careful to keep another combe, which shortly appears, on the left hand. The route is in places rocky. At the foot of the steepest part a wood appears in front. Diverge a little, so as to leave this on your right, and a few hundred yards farther you will enter a by-lane at *Millbeck*, whence Keswick is reached by road in 2¼ miles.

From the summit of Carl Side an exhilarating walk over Long-side brings you out on the main road half-way down Bassen-thwaite.

Millbeck may also be reached by an uninteresting descent of

Millbeck Gill, leaving the summit ridge between the High Man and the Low Man.

For Applethwaite, the quickest descent is from the summit of the Low Man down Howgill Tongue, a steep but joyous scamper. The ordinary way down needs no description, save that, after passing the Low Man, it is well to incline generally to the right. Otherwise you may land out on Lonscale Fell.

THE WASTWATER SCREES, 1,978 ft.

Emergency Descent, see p. 303.

The Wastwater Screes are somewhat neglected. They are in fact handicapped by the proximity of Scafell, Scafell Pike, Great Gable and Pillar, which, it must be admitted, outclass them in every respect save one, that being the view from the skyline of the escarpment down to the lake. In this attraction the Screes have the pre-eminence, not only over every fell in the Lake District, but over every mountain south of the Border. On this account alone they are worth a visit.

Whether started from Wasdale or Eskdale, the walk should be taken from the Irton Fell end of the ridge in a north-east direction so as to have the best of the scenery in front all the way.

1. From Wasdale Head (4½ to 5 hrs. ; *about an hour may be saved if a conveyance is taken to Wasdale Hall, not to be confused with Wasdale Head Hall*). Follow the shore road until it leaves the lake and, before crossing a cattle grid, cross a wooden stile lower down towards the lake and follow the lakeside path until a bridge across the Irt is reached. After crossing this a short divergence to the left of a few minutes is abundantly worth the making for the sake of the incomparable view up Wastwater from the opening where the Irt exits from the lake (*see p.* 128). Above, on the right, is the magnificent lower bastion of the Screes. Retracing your steps, make for Hawl Gill, a conspicuous ravine with red scarps in the fell-side beyond the crags, and ascend to the skyline. From this point as far as the other end of the lake the route is unmistakable. Keep as near the edge of the Screes as possible. The views down the gullies are very grand. Between Whin Rigg and Illgill Head are some limestone sinks, and the limestone is again apparent on the left on the descent from Illgill Head.

2. From Boot in Eskdale (5 to 6 *hrs.*). Whin Rigg may be reached (1) by leaving the road just between Eskdale Green Station and the Tatie Garth Inn through a field gate and by a path crossing the line by a bridge to a farm. Keep left at the farm and then up a grassy bridle track to Siney and Blea Tarns. In misty weather it is easy to stray a good deal on this route. (2) From Eskdale Green, crossing Miterdale by the Miterdale Plantations on to the open moor. (3) From Irton Road Station, turn left down the main road for a few yards, then right up a lane at the Police house. Follow this lane until it is joined by the road from Eskdale Green. Cross a stile on the left, over the River Mite, and continue through the wood by a well-defined path which rises up the fellside. At its highest point, cross another stile to join a path which follows the side of the wall. Turn right and follow this path to the top of Whin Rigg. The return from the far end of the ridge is by the Burnmoor track (*see p.* 127).

View.—On the right on the far side of Eskdale is a range of low fells culminating in the pyramidal Harter Fell. Beyond is the not so rugged side of the Coniston Fells and to the left of these, during the early part of the walk, Crinkle Crags are visible. On the left across the lake are the buttresses of Buckbarrow, Middle Fell, and Yewbarrow, backed by Seatallan, Haycock, Scoat Fell, and Pillar. Later glimpses of the Buttermere Fells are obtained, then Hindscarth, with Skiddaw on the horizon and Sail between. As one approaches the end of the ridge, Great Gable stands up magnificently. At one point the gap between it and Kirkfell is filled in by Brandreth. In front the view is blocked by the Scafell group. The view westward is most extensive, including the Isle of Man and, possibly, the dim outlines of the Irish coast.

DAYS ON THE FELLS

These fell walks may of course be reversed at the discretion of the tourist, but he will be well advised to follow the routes here outlined. For a note on the estimated times, *see p. 29*.

1. Ambleside to Ambleside, over Red Screes, Hart Crag, Fairfield, Great Rigg, and Nab Scar. *Map at end of the book. For Fairfield, see also pp. 160, 291.*

For a variation of this in the opposite direction—Patterdale to St. Sunday Crag, Fairfield, and Red Screes; thence straight down to the *Kirkstone Inn*— *see pp. 290 and 226.*

To Red Screes, 1⅓ *hrs.; Scandale Head,* 2 *hrs.; Hart Crag,* **3** *hrs.; Fairfield,* 3½ *hrs.; Great Rigg,* 4 *hrs.; Nab Scar,* 5 *hrs.; Ambleside,* 6 *hrs. About* 12 *m.*

This is a delightful mountain excursion, and the most practicable one from Ambleside. A whole day should, if possible, be devoted to it. The views, both near and distant, are of a very high order during the entire round.

Leave Ambleside by the Kirkstone road, and after ascending the " Struggle " for nearly a mile, turn on to the fell through a wicketgate on the left, and climb between two straggling walls. At first, Ill Bell and Froswick fill up the gap over the top of the Troutbeck valley on the right, and the head of Windermere, backed by the Coniston Fells, appears behind. When the ridge is reached, and a view down into Scandale obtained, the Bowfell range, with the graceful peak of Bowfell itself predominant, comes into view. Rydal Water, with its wooded island, and the far side of Grasmere, soon give an additional charm to the near prospect, and farther back, the Langdale Pikes, though still striking features in the landscape, begin to acknowledge their inferiority in point of height to the Scafell group behind them. Between them and Bowfell, Scafell Pike appears, and over their left arm Great End.

After about half an hour's climb there are one or two walls, in which the gaps of one year may be the most troublesome crossing-places of the next. The best direction is to keep to the ridge as nearly as possible, about in a line with the lower reach of Windermere, only diverging a little when gaps appear. Coniston Lake soon shows itself in the rear, and Great Gable peers over the fells to the north of Grasmere. To the south is Morecambe Bay.

After negotiating various characteristic obstacles, *e.g.* walls, boggy ground, etc., we come upon soft velvety grass and reach the first cairn. The second, and highest, is less than half a mile farther on.

The prospect from the top of **Red Screes** is exceedingly fine, being marked by that variety which Windermere, when seen at full length, imparts to mountain-scenes more effectively than any lake in the kingdom. The whole of the lake lies mapped out before the eye, except a portion of the upper reach hidden by Wansfell Pike. The islands clustering in the centre serve to prevent any impression of monotony, without interfering with the dignity of the lake as a whole. The rest of the panorama will be to a great extent familiar from the descriptions which have been given of its various features during the ascent. In addition to these we have, if we move eastwards to the edge of the crags, the Kirkstone Pass, with its little inn immediately below us to the south-east, and its descent northward to Brothers' Water, beyond which are Patterdale and a strip of Ullswater. Saddleback appears over the eastern limb of Helvellyn.

The High Street range rises beyond Caudale Moor, the latter descending, to all appearance, precipitously to the Kirkstone Pass. The Yorkshire hills are seen far away to the south-east, and westward a long array of fell-tops, extending from the Coniston Old Man to the Newlands mountains between Derwentwater and Crummock, the most prominent peaks in which, not hitherto mentioned, are the Pillar, High Stile, and Grasmoor, all to the north of Scafell Pike, and occurring in the order named. Fairfield, Helvellyn, and St. Sunday Crag constitute a formidable and nearer barrier to the north-west.

By ordinarily active persons the highest cairn may be reached by a far more exhilarating ascent from the top of the Kirkstone Pass, a little above the Inn. The ascent is very steep, but a route can easily be found by working in and out among the crags. The long pull by the turnpike road up to the Inn may be avoided by taking the road *past* Stock Gill Force and the Grove Farm till the Troutbeck road is reached a few hundred yards from its junction with the Kirkstone Pass. As a descent this is not recommended.

Descending from the cairn, pursue a north-westerly course in the direction of Fairfield to the hause between Scandale and the Caiston Glen. The latter is separated from the Kirkstone Pass by the steep shoulder of Red Screes called Middle Dodd. The general inclination is slightly to the left till one reaches the wall, which serves as a guide as far as the hause.

From the hause a descent may be made to the left back again to *Ambleside* by Scandale and Sweden Bridge (*p.* 112), or to the right into the *Kirkstone Pass* at the *Brothers' Water Inn* (*p.* 218).

The rocky height just beyond the hause is **Little Hart Crag.** Leave this on the right, and when you come to a point where a wire fence on the same side turns down into the valley, attack the slope in front, bending slightly to the left. This lands you on **Dove Crag,** a stony and abrupt height, from which there is a characteristic view down Dovedale to Brothers' Water. A tumble-down wall is now reached, which extends southward along the ridge of Scandale Fell, almost to Low Sweden Bridge (*p.* 112), close to Ambleside. (This is an easy way to start the Fairfield round from Ambleside if it is not desired to include Red Screes in the same excursion.)

Continuing in a north-westerly direction, there is a dip in the ridge and then **Hart Crag** is soon gained, whence there is another fine view on the right, into Deepdale. The Ullswater side of the fells we are now traversing is much bolder and more precipitous than the Windermere side. Windermere has again come into view with telling effect, and St. Sunday Crag has an imposing aspect on the other side of Deepdale. Greenhow End, a precipitous bastion of Fairfield, is a fine feature in the foreground.

Our route now drops, and then rises abruptly and roughly to the broad, almost level sward of **Fairfield,** and here the tourist may wander about at his leisure, admiring first, it may be, the grand eastern precipices and razor-backed ridges of Helvellyn to the north. The nearest of the Helvellyn ridges is Striding Edge, and above it rises the peaked summit of Catchedicam. Westward and southward the view is very similar to that from Red Screes (*p.* 275). From the north-western edge of the plateau, Grisedale Tarn and Grisedale Valley, leading down to Ullswater, may be seen, and a wee bit of the lake itself; while in the distance, over the tarn, the Buttermere and Newlands mountains again crop up. The top of the Grisedale Pass, just south of Grisedale Tarn, may be easily reached by descending westwards and following the course of a wall.

To reach St. Sunday Crag direct from Fairfield looks difficult, but is not so, though care is required. There is a path over the sharp ridge (Cofa Pike), and then a rough drop to Deepdale Hause.

From the top of Fairfield our route turns southward, across a slight depression, to the summit of **Great Rigg,** whence there is a fine view to the right front over Grasmere.

From this point to reach *Grasmere* itself follow the ridge to the right of the next depression southward; when the descent becomes steep a pony-track will be discovered, leading into a lane which joins the Windermere and Keswick road close to the *Swan Hotel.* Alternatively a descent may be made down the bottom of Greenhead Gill.

For Nab Scar, continue due southward along the ridge overlooking the Rydal glen. The first height reached is *Heron Pike,* and from it to Nab Scar the route is rough but unmistakable. Any sense of fatigue is qualified by the ever-increasing beauty of the prospect southward. From **Nab Scar** itself the Rothay valley, with the long reach of Windermere beyond it, and the peaceful lakes of Rydal and Grasmere at its head, forms a picture of exquisite beauty.

From the rocky summit of Nab Scar turn somewhat to the left, down the ridge in the direction of Rydal village. The descent is steep at first, by a kind of natural staircase, and then between two stone walls to a road which descends through Rydal village to the Windermere and Keswick high road, 1½ miles from Ambleside.

Reverse Route, Grasmere to Fairfield (4 *m. to top*, 4 *to* 4½ *hrs. up and down*). Take the road that goes north-eastward from the south side of the *Swan* and becomes a lane at cross-roads, continuing up a shady gill. In ⅓ mile it bends to the left, leaving the beck, and then zigzags through the bracken up a very steep slope over Greenhead Gill (on the right), between two walls, crossing the pipe-track of the waterworks and then bending to the right on to the open fell, where, after doubling the shoulder of Stone Arthur, it continues northward and joins the route described on *p.* 276 on Great Rigg, a good mile short of Fairfield top.

2. Ambleside, Coniston, or Grasmere over Wrynose Gap, Crinkle Crags, and Bowfell, to Ambleside, Coniston, or Grasmere. *Map at end of the book.*

Distances to Wrynose Gap :—From Ambleside, 8½ *m., p.* 123; *Coniston (by Tilberthwaite),* 6½, *p.* 136 *; Grasmere, by Elterwater,* 7½.

Time from Wrynose Gap :—Crinkle Crags, 2¼ *hrs. ; Bowfell,* 3¼ *hrs. ; Dungeon Ghyll Hotel,* 5 *hrs.,* 7 *miles.*

Dungeon Ghyll Old Hotel to Ambleside, 7½ *m. ; Coniston,* 8 *; Grasmere,* 5½.

In fine, clear weather, this is one of the most remunerative mountain-walks in the district. The craggy character of the ground, however, on the eastern side, and the utter absence of accessible accommodation on the western, render it a particularly undesirable one for wet or foggy days. Its features are the exquisite and strongly-contrasted views of the Langdale, Eskdale, and Duddon valleys, the crags on the southern side of Scafell and Scafell Pike, and the glorious summit of Bowfell itself.

The road must be left at a conspicuous cairn a little short of the **Three Shire Stone** (*p.* 124). A cairned track now leads uphill in a north-westerly, not northerly, direction, through ground diversified by swamps and streams. Care must be taken not to diverge to the right as the cairns are also part of a track from Wrynose to Langdale by Red Tarn, under Pike o' Blisco. **Cold Pike**, the peak which rises slightly to the left, is the objective, and Red Tarn must be kept on the right. Some time before Cold Pike is reached, Skiddaw comes into view to the right, almost due north, showing its bold clear-cut outline to full advantage.

[If, at the cost of about three-quarters of an hour's extra tramping, it is desired to include the Pike o' Blisco in the expedition, the Wrynose Pass should be left just beyond the bridge a little more than half-way up. By following the stream upwards and bending slightly left at its source, in less than an hour the broken summit of Pike o' Blisco is reached. The view is fine and extensive, a special feature being the Crinkles and Bowfell.

Below, a little west of south, lies Red Tarn, a small sheet of water. For Cold Pike descend, keeping the tarn on your right. For Great Langdale and Dungeon Ghyll a descent *may* be made by either Browney Gill or Kettle Gill to Great Langdale and Dungeon Ghyll, but both paths are steep at times.

Then, when the ridge is reached, the **Duddon Valley** appears far down to the left, with its one or two sycamore-guarded little home-steads, its stream meandering in a succession of graceful curves through pastures of emerald green, till it loses itself in the bracken-clad fells of the Broughton district ; beyond it, Black Combe, the Wrekin of the Lake District, and the glimmering sea. Our first height is Cold Pike, and only ungoverned, unappreciative haste will prevent us halting a while, and giving its due meed of admiration to the wonderfully-diversified scene around us. Perhaps the most striking feature is the contrast between the rich verdure and foliage of the Little Langdale and Brathay valleys, winding down to Windermere on the east, and the simple rustic beauty of the Duddon to the south-west. Southward the Lancashire group of fells still closes the view, and Pike o' Blisco hides Great Langdale. Exactly over Pike o' Blisco Fairfield is seen, and between it and the Lang-dale Pikes, which from this elevation lose all that grandeur of form which they possess when looked at from below, extends a great part of the Helvellyn range, more conspicuous than beautiful from this side. Then, above and beyond the obliquely-peaked High Raise, which is the real summit of the Langdale plateau, are Saddleback and Skiddaw. Glaramara has on its left the red precipitous-looking screes of Grasmoor descending into Crummock Water. Westwards a little inclined to the south, the rough Hardknott Pass is seen, and over it Devoke Water shines high and bright amid the hills, and, farther still, the sea extends over the sands of Ravenglass to the horizon.

And now proceeding on our way, still in a north-westerly direction, we make a slight dip. Soon Great Langdale comes into view on the right, and Eskdale on the left. We leave the highest ridge of Great Knott to our right, and make straight for the first **Crinkle,** which is conspicuous before us. The summit reached, fresh scenes appear.

Above Eskdale, Devoke Water, with its solitary little island, still gleams. To the right of it, where the valley spreads out into the open sea-board, is the estuary of the Esk, crossed by a many-arched railway-bridge. Here lies Ravenglass. Still more to the right, far across the sea, is the Isle of Man, with Snaefell prominent among its heights. In front appear Scafell and the Pikes, separated by the ravine of Mickledore—masses of rugged precipice and screes, with here and there a few blades of grass to keep alive the adventurous sheep which spend a happy-go-lucky existence on their desolate sides. Just below us, the *col* separating the waters of the Duddon from those of the Esk is very plain. The Old Man, too, has come into view southwards, between the two chief summits of the Seathwaite fells. The sharper peak to the right of the Old Man is Dow Crag. The sandy, straggling estuary of the Duddon is very plain to the eye, while the chimneys of Askham and Barrow on one side and Millom on the other side of it give evidence of the industry of the Furness district. Over the left shoulder of Wetherlam a strip of Esthwaite Water is visible. Eastward the sharp peak in the distance, directly over the centre of Great Langdale, is Kidsty Pike, and the long-backed ridge next to it on the right, High Street. Between Helvellyn and Fairfield, St. Sunday Crag appears. Looking northwards, towards the dip between Skiddaw and Saddleback, we see the Stake Pass wending its way into Langstrath and Borrowdale. Take one more look into Eskdale and, if the day be bright, you will notice a gill running down into its upper reach on this side of Devoke Water. The lower part of this beck is Stanley Gill, which contains the finest force in the district. A mile or so nearer, on the right of the river, just visible against the trees, is Boot in Eskdale.

Look down the length of Dunnerdale, and in the clearest of weather you may detect Snowdon, just over 100 miles distant.

There is a steep dip between the first of the *Crinkle Crags* and the second, which is the highest by some 80 feet. To attain the latter, strike a little to the left, and make for a pillar of stones lying in a slight depression to the left of the highest point. Precipices make a straight track impracticable to all but cragsmen. There is but little change in the prospect, except that Bowfell comes into prominent view. A narrow neck of very small depression connects the second and highest with the third **Crinkle** (there are actually five Crinkles), whence, unless you wish to incur the toil of climbing up and down several more similar heights, without any compensation in the way of fresh views, you will do well to turn down to the left, in the direction of Scafell[1] Pike, for a few minutes, till you double a rather prominent rock,[1] from which to the dip immediately below Bowfell is rough but simple walking with Shelter Crags on the right. In this dip are several clear little pools, one in particular near the eastern declivity—a basin entirely enclosed by rock, suggesting a miniature copy of Loch Coruisk. This group is called the **Three Tarns**, though there are four all told. Hence an admirably-cairned route leads for some 600 to 700 feet, plentifully bestrewn with rocks and boulders, to the summit of Bowfell.

From Three Tarns an easy descent can be made into Eskdale, or Langdale over the Band route on the shoulder of Bowfell.

Bowfell is itself a splendid peak, and the view from it highly attractive, though, strangely enough, it only embraces three lakes, Windermere, Esthwaite, and Devoke Water. The Lancashire fells hide Coniston, Scafell Wastwater, and Glaramara Derwentwater. Skiddaw and Saddleback stand out strikingly in the north, and their smooth though marked contour contrasts finely with the wild ruggedness of Scafell, the Langdale Pikes, and the other nearer mountains. The tourist has already, during his walk, become familiar with most of the surrounding objects.

[1] In the case of mist it will be found better to descend west into Eskdale rather than east into Langdale, but Crinkle Crags is really a place to be avoided on a day when the fells are cloud-capped.

One or two fresh ones have, however, appeared. Especially has the view northward opened up. To the left of Skiddaw in that direction are seen the Solway Firth and the Dumfriesshire hills. To the left of them, the smooth red-looking fells are Causey Pike, west of Derwentwater, Sail, Eel Crags, and Grasmoor ; then again Solway and Scotland. The rocky continuation of Bowfell to the north-west is Esk Pike ; and, beyond it, Great End, the north-eastern buttress of the Scafell ridge. Behind Great End is Great Gable, almost hidden. Esk Hause lies between Esk Pike and Great End.

By keeping well up the ridge the tourist may, if so inclined, and time permits, continue his journey over rough ground by Hanging Knott and Esk Pike, and, joining the track from Esk Hause (*p*. 132), proceed over Scafell Pike to Wasdale Head. From Bowfell to Wasdale Head this route would take from $3\frac{1}{2}$ to 4 hours. A descent from Esk Hause may also be made by Sty Head for Wasdale, or by Grain Gill for Borrowdale. These routes will be found fully described in the ascents of Scafell Pike (*p*. 261). A short, steep descent by Ewer Gap between Hanging Knott and Esk Pike brings the tourist on to the track leading from Rossett Gill to Esk Hause. From Esk Hause down Eskdale there is no track till you approach Esk Falls (*p*. 126), and no inn till you get to the *Woolpack*, about 7 *m*. To reach this would take about 3 hours.

Those who are not gluttons at climbing will, after resting on the comfortable seat afforded by a huge flat stone eastward of the cairn on Bowfell, be glad to descend to Dungeon Ghyll. The best way of doing so is to keep as nearly as possible the ridge of the shoulder, called the *Band*, which extends eastward with a slight tendency to the south, separating Mickleden from Oxendale and Hell Gill, the latter a wild ravine commencing near the dip between Shelter Crags and Bowfell. For the *Band* descend by the Three Tarns route until an obvious opening with a cairn on either side is seen on the left. Or you may descend again almost to Three Tarns, and then work round on to the *Band*.[1] The first part of the descent is rough, but an easy path is to be found working its way through the crags. The winding road from Dungeon Ghyll to Blea Tarn will be seen directly in front, and it is best to keep in a straight line with this, until, towards the end of the descent, a wall with a gap in it crosses the ridge. This gap is one of the " traps " of the expedition, and leads to crags from which one has to extricate oneself by an awkward scramble to the right. The true path, which may be overlooked, turns down to the right through the bracken several yards short of the wall. Pass by the farm at *Stool End*, cross the Oxendale stream, and in a few minutes more the *Old Dungeon Ghyll Hotel* appears to the left ; the *New Hotel* is some $\frac{3}{4}$ mile farther on.

[1] Or you may keep nearer *Hell Gill* (*p*. 119), and get a view of the fine force therein.

3. Coniston to Coniston, or to Ambleside, Dungeon Ghyll, or Grasmere, over the Old Man and Wetherlam. *Map at end of the book. See p. 299.*

Coniston Village to the top of the Old Man, 2 hrs. ; Wetherlam, 4 hrs. ; Coniston, 5½ hrs., 10 to 11 m.

Little Langdale Village, 5½ hrs., 10 to 11 m. ; Little Langdale to Ambleside, 5½ m. ; Dungeon Ghyll, 4 ; Grasmere, 4½. To Dungeon Ghyll the distance may be shortened 2 miles by joining the Coniston and Blea Tarn road (pp. 140–1) near Fell Foot.

The ascent of the Old Man is deservedly one of the favourite mountain excursions of the Lake District. It is true that commerce has wrought sad havoc with this fine fell, disfiguring it with unsightly mines and slate refuse. Nevertheless the natural sovereignty of the mountain is still pre-eminent.

We have preferred to treat the Old Man as the first summit of a range of fells which together form a most enjoyable and by no means over-tiring day's excursion, rather than as a separate peak. Those, however, whose time or inclination prompts them to confine their wanderings to the Old Man himself, will find no difficulty in descending by any of the routes described in ascending.

On the front overlooking the village the mines and quarries have together established an almost labyrinthine system of tracks, some of them blind ones, and others such as will ultimately place the traveller in a position to climb the last steep pitch without difficulty ; that is, supposing the weather to be clear; if it be thick and misty the usual routes are very perplexing.

(*a*) For the **Old Man,** from the Church turn by the *Black Bull Inn,* leaving it on the left, and follow a lane uphill. Soon after passing through a gate the deep ravine of Church Beck opens on the left and a short distance farther on is a bridge over some falls, now sadly diminished in volume owing to the demands of the electric-lighting of Coniston. Cross this bridge and pass through a gate almost opposite on to the fell-side.

(*b*) The same point may be reached by taking a not very obvious turning to the right immediately beyond the *Sun Hotel.* This lane passes through a gate, crosses a field, after which it ascends the southern bank of Church Beck to the gate near the bridge. The summit of the Old Man is now visible on the left. From the gate a track leads round in the direction of the Old Man. One or two awkward stiles over walls are crossed and the cart-track from the Walna Scar route is joined. Do not turn left but keep on steadily ascending by the main track, which inclines to the right (the left track is a false one and leads to a quarry) till it reaches *Low Water,* a charming tarn in a beautiful natural setting of wild crags. From Low Water the track bends up to the left and so gains the ridge whence another ten minutes of steep ascent will bring you to the cairn on the top.

(*c*) Follow the Walna Scar route (*p.* 142) till Boo Tarn is reached. A track will be seen on the right which may be followed, but, as a matter of fact, from almost any point at the base of the southern shoulder of the fell the summit cairn may be attained without difficulty by the simple process of walking uphill.

(d) Continue along the Walna Scar track till, about a quarter of a mile short of Torver Beck, a path strikes upward to the right through the bracken and, after partly following a track to some quarries, leads to a hollow marked by a conspicuous white cairn, whence a short scramble amongst boulders takes you to the solemn recess of *Goats (Gaits) Water*, overlooked by the sombre bastions of Dow Crags. From the foot of the tarn ascend the grassy slope on the right to the summit cairn. This route is a trifle longer in the matter of time, but entails the least collar work. From either of these two last routes the magnificent prospect from the summit cairn springs to the eye with all the delight of a surprise view.

The View.—The contrast between the almost savage ruggedness of the north and the broad and bright sea expanse, the rich woodlands, and far-reaching pastures of the south, gives it a charm of variety to which the central mountains of the District cannot lay claim. Perhaps the gem of the scene is the lake of Coniston itself, spread out beneath in its entire length and breadth. Very pleasing, too, is Tarn Hows (p. 135), while beyond it the parts of Windermere visible give the impression of two if not three lakes. To the south, over Morecambe Bay, Morecambe itself and Fleetwood are visible ; then, to their right, the broad sands of Duddon and the whale-backed Black Combe. In the direction of the latter it is quite possible, if the day be very clear, to discern the tapering cone of Snowdon. The industrial Furness district is in the middle distance. To the west appear Devoke Water, high up amid the fells ; the sea again and, beyond it, the Isle of Man. Scafell and Scafell Pike, with the chasm of Mickledore between them, are prominent in the north-west ; Skiddaw due north, with Saddleback on its right, and then the long swelling ridge of Helvellyn, with indications here and there that suggest to the eye of the practised mountaineer that its farther or eastern front is not wholly innocent of precipices. In the north-east are High Street, with the columnar-shaped cairn on Thorn-thwaite Crag, and the cone of Ill Bell, the latter rising beyond Ambleside and the head of Windermere. Over the southern spurs of the Ill Bell range appear Kentmere Pike (the southern ridge of Harter Fell, Mardale), and farther still an alluring array of high-lands, the Howgill Fells above Sedbergh, the Barbon Fells beyond Kirkby Lonsdale, and a wilderness of the Yorkshire limestone hills, with the table-topped Ingleborough conspicuous.

The precipice to the west is **Dow Crag**, and the tourist—unless he has used route (d) above—should make a slight detour in that direction till he comes in sight of the dark and deep-set tarn, **Goats Water**, lying immediately at the foot of it, and 1,000 ft. below him.

Those who do not wish to continue their mountain-walk to one or more of the other Lancashire peaks have a choice of descents. They may diverge slightly to the left and make for the ridge which connects the Old Man with **Dow Crag**, thence either descending to the rough track which skirts the east shore of Goats Water and in another mile joins the Walna Scar road ; or, climbing again to Dow Crag, whence is a fine view of the Duddon valley, they may keep along the southern shoulder of the mountain till the same road is reached at the top of Walna Scar. They may take a northerly direction till they are opposite *Lever's Water* (*see p.* 299), and then descend by Townson Cove to the west side of it ; or they may return as they came. In short, with ordinary prudence, and in clear weather, they may choose what direction they like. Should the weather take a bad turn—and the Old Man is very whimsical in this respect—we recommend a southerly course to the Walna Scar road.

Proceeding from the summit in a northerly direction over Brim Fell, we traverse a slight grassy depression loosely known as **Fairfield,** and then, ascending again along the rocky ridge of Great How Crags, reach the rounded elevation of **Swirl How** (2,630 feet), only three feet lower than the Old Man and scarcely inferior as a view-point, especially in consideration of the retrospect towards the Old Man itself. The large sheet of water to the left is *Seathwaite Tarn* (a reservoir for Barrow-in-Furness) ; by it a descent may be made into the Duddon valley.

From the summit of Swirl How the route turns in a north-easterly direction—to the right—along the watershed of the Coniston streams to the south and the Little Langdale streams to the north. The descent to the gap in this ridge, Swirl Hause, is here and there somewhat awkward. When in doubt, keep to the right. For the ascent of the opposite slope it is easier to work a little to the left. From the summit first attained, **Black Sails,** a ridge runs down towards Coniston. The descent of this is not recommended owing to the open mine-shafts about its foot. **Wetherlam** is a little farther on to the north-east, separated from the present elevation by a shallow depression.

View from Wetherlam.—This is very fine, though not so extensive or varied as that from the Old Man, who himself shuts out a good deal of the southerly landscape. The fresh features are the exquisite little Brathay valley, winding under the southern slopes of Loughrigg to Windermere, and the upland dale in which Wordsworth's Blea Tarn reposes, backed by the grand outline of the Langdale Pikes. High up, and sheltered from the north by the precipitous right shoulder of these twin peaks—Pavey Ark—Stickle Tarn gleams with a silvery radiance, if the day be bright. Little Langdale Tarn lies below us, to the north-east ; Elterwater to its right, and beyond it the dip between Loughrigg and Silver How, behind which lies Grasmere.

Grey Friar and Carrs.—If time permits, and the divergence does not occupy more than an hour's easy going, it is well worth while from the top of Swirl How to turn due west and cross the depression leading to Grey Friar, from which there is an excellent view of the lower Duddon Valley, with Black Combe in the background. In the opposite direction, north, the Pike o' Stickle can be seen. From Grey Friar, retrace your steps in a north-easterly direction to Carrs, from which the original route over Swirl How may be regained in a few minutes by following the ridge-line in the direction of Coniston.

Descents.[1]—*Wetherlam to Coniston.*—From the cairn the route lies in a southerly direction. Continue till a grassy depression is reached with a rather abrupt rise beyond. Here turn to the right and a track will be picked up leading past the copper-mines and down by Church Beck.

Wetherlam to Little Langdale (and for Ambleside or Grasmere). —A north-easterly direction must be pursued, holding slightly to the right down the first steep bluff, a dip of about 800 feet. A wall running in a straight line with us along the ridge, some way down the fell, is not a bad guide. From the base of the bluff diverge to the left, and descend obliquely to the cart-road leading down from the *Greenburn Copper Works*, striking it near a gate a few hundred yards below them. As we get lower, the contour of the Langdale Pikes over the Blea Tarn depression is very striking. Half an hour's walking along the road, during which we must be careful not to climb to the right, takes us down to some cottages at Hall Garth. A few yards farther a footpath leads across the Slater's Bridge (*p.* 116) and through the fields into the Wrynose–Little Langdale road. Almost exactly opposite is the branch road for Elterwater and Grasmere. For Little Langdale village turn right. The village may also be reached from Hall Garth by continuing past the Slater's Bridge to the Tilberthwaite–Little Langdale road. Cross the beck by the footbridge and in seven minutes you reach the Post Office and the *Tourist's Rest*.

Wetherlam to Tilberthwaite.—From the foot of the " first steep bluff " (*see* foregoing paragraph) incline to the right (eastward) over Birkfell and then south to the head of Tilberthwaite Gill.

Carrs to Wrynose Pass and Little Langdale.—From the summit keep almost due north till opposite Pike o' Blisco. From this point a quick descent may be made to the Three Shire Stone. Or the ridge of Wet Side Edge may be further followed to Rough Crags. Just before reaching these incline to the right till Greenburn Beck is reached. The left bank of the stream should be followed to a stile in a wall which lands you on the road from Fell Foot to Tilberthwaite. The special feature of this descent is a grand view of the Bowfell Range away on the left. The prospect in front, however—the Ill Bell heights and the Yorkshire Fells—is glorious throughout.

4. Keswick to Buttermere, over Catbells, Maiden Moor, Eel Crags,[2] Dale Head, and Robinson. *Map at end of the book. See pp.* 301–2.

To Catbells, 2 hrs. ; *Maiden Moor*, 2½ hrs. ; *Eel Crags*, 3½ hrs. : *Dale Head*, 4½ hrs. ; *Robinson*, 5½ hrs. ; *Buttermere*, 7 hrs. ; 13 m.

---

[1] The slopes of Wetherlam need special care because of disused mine-shafts.
[2] Not to be confused with the *Eel Crag* named in the next excursion.

There are few, if any, finer mountain excursions in the Lake District than this. A large number of the chief mountains—including Scafell, Great Gable, the Pillar, Skiddaw, Saddleback, and Helvellyn—are seen to a great advantage from it. It commands the whole of Derwentwater and Bassenthwaite, and during the latter part of it fine views are obtained of Buttermere, Loweswater, and Crummock. Care must be taken to start in good time. The journey may be shortened by descending at various points, and a return may be made direct from Robinson to Keswick, but by far the most enjoyable plan is to arrange to stay the night at one of the hotels at Buttermere. Two miles of the distance may be saved by hiring a boat from the landing-stage at Keswick to Hawes End, at the foot of Catbells.

Take the field-path to *Portinscale*, which commences on the far side of the Greta Bridge (*p.* 163), and the road to the left which diverges just beyond *Derwentwater Hotel.* In another half-mile is the turn down to Nichol End Landings. Next comes a private road through Fawe Park. A few yards farther a signpost on the left directs to Catbells and Brandelhow Park through Fawe Park Woods. The track runs first up and then down for a considerable distance till it crosses a road. On the far side of this is an iron swing gate, and the track goes on with private grounds on the left for about 150 yards and the wood on the right till it emerges into a meadow by a stile with a hayshed on the right. (This is a useful landmark on the reverse route.) The meadow is crossed and the wood again entered by another swing gate, from which the path leads out on the Derwentwater and Grange road. This may be followed, but it is preferable to cross the road and, skirting a coppice, come out on the west side of Catbells. Here turn to the left over the shoulder until a good zigzag track up the fell-side is reached. **Catbells** is deceptively steep when viewed upwards, and its smooth slope of short grass makes it hard work for those who try short cuts. From the summit there is a fine view of Derwentwater to the east, and the green pastoral valley of Newlands to the west. The top of Helvellyn appears in the former direction, with the pyramid of Catchedicam to its left. The bell-shaped peak southward is the Langdale Pike o' Stickle. Between Catbells and Maiden Moor is a slight depression traversed by a track from Newlands to Grange in Borrowdale. Thence succeeds the gradual ascent of **Maiden Moor.** As the cairn is reached, Scafell and Great Gable come into view between Eel Crags and Dale Head.

Beyond the cairn on Maiden Moor the track skirts the sheer crags which descend into the wild Newlands valley. From another cairn, slightly to the left of the direct route, a fine view is obtained into the lower end of Borrowdale, the village of Grange lying immediately below, and the Bowder Stone close to a cottage on the right of it. Still more to the right, the branches of Borrowdale leading over High Rise to Grasmere and over the Stake

Pass into Langdale are noticeable, separated by Eagle Crag. The Pillar, on the far side of Ennerdale, has come into view over the dip between Dale Head and Hindscarth.

A large cairn marks the summit of **Eel Crags.**[1] Few precipices in the district have a more formidable appearance than these, when looked at from above. A sharp descent to the depression at the head of the valley on the right succeeds. Beyond it a small pond, dignified by the name of *Dale Head Tarn*, is visible. From this depression, Rigg Head, a descent may be made either into the Newlands valley on the right or to Rosthwaite or Seatoller in Borrowdale on the left ; or by going right ahead the Honister Pass may be gained near its summit.

The walk up the **Newlands Valley** to this point, though inferior to Borrowdale and the ridge walk under consideration, is nevertheless very fine. The way lies from Hawes End, starting along the western side of Catbells, and is unmistakable. From Bull Crag the route lies along the foot of two miles of unbroken precipice, in this respect without parallel south of the Border, and the head of the Dale, with the bastion of Gable Crag prominent, approximates to grandeur. The Newlands Falls below it are well worth a divergence, but it must be admitted that the screes leading up from the valley are cruel.

To reach **Dale Head,** go round by the far side of the tarn (from the south or left side of which a wire fence strikes up over Dale Head and to Robinson), and climb the slope, bearing slightly to the left till the ridge is attained. A cairn marks the summit. The view from it is fine, but not so good as from a little way farther on, where the ridge narrows to a few yards' width, and the deeply-scooped valleys of Honister on the left and Newlands on the right vie with one another in precipitous wildness. Buttermere appears at the foot of the former, and on the other side of it are High Crag, High Stile, and Red Pike, presenting from this point rather an angular appearance. Scafell, Great Gable, and the Pillar form a nobly-set group southward, the first-named looking its best and highest. Bowfell terminates the ridge to the left. The distant fells which have been for some time visible between the latter and Pike o' Stickle are in Yorkshire.

A steep grass slope descends to the right between Dale Head and Hindscarth, at the foot of which two streamlets are formed. To the right of the right-hand one, looking down, is a mine, with a cart-track ascending to it from the bottom of the valley.

Hindscarth projects nearly half a mile to the right of the direct route from Dale Head to Robinson. There is nothing particular to be gained by diverging to it, though there is a very pleasant descent to Newlands by the Hindscarth ridge over Scope End. Before commencing the gradual grassy ascent of **Robinson**, there

---

[1] The actual fell is Scawdell Fell. Eel Crags are the precipitous west face.

is a considerable dip to be made, from the bottom of which the
climb is somewhat akin to that of an easy staircase. The best
views are obtained by working round the left side of the ridge.
The summit is a gritty plateau. From it Crummock and Loweswater are seen, the former cut in two by Rannerdale Knott;
but to get a view of Derwentwater, the summit-level must be
traversed for some distance to the right. Directing his gaze
southward, the tourist may notice that Scafell Pike has disappeared. Great Gable, however, is prominent with its cairn, close
to which a keen eye will detect another cairn. That is the
summit of Scafell Pike. There is, of course, nothing remarkable
in the larger mountain being exactly behind the smaller, but it
is not a little singular that the two cairns should be in the direct
line of vision, so placed that by walking a few yards one can be
made to hide the other exactly. Robinson is 2,417 feet high,
Great Gable 2,949, and Scafell Pike 3,210. From these data
our mathematical friends may amuse themselves by calculating
the distances between the respective peaks, that from the first to
the last being 6 miles horizontally. The northern face of Pillar
Mountain, furrowed with gullies, presents probably the finest
full-face view of any single mountain in the district.

Those who wish to return direct to **Keswick** must descend the
mountain in the direction of the lower ridge of Hindscarth, and
follow the stream which issues from the hollow between the two
mountains. A track will soon be reached on the left-hand side of it,
leading past the church and joining the main Newlands road near
some buildings.

In descending to Buttermere, care is required. The village
is not visible from the top of the fell, being hidden by a boggy
plateau some 800 feet below, called Buttermere Moss. Descend
to this, keeping to the left, in order to avoid crags, and traverse
it to its ridge, which rises slightly again above the level of the
morass. From near the north or lower end of this second ridge
a sledge-track, once used for bringing down peat, will be observed
descending a shoulder of the fell in the direction of Buttermere
church. The track joins the road from Keswick by Newlands,
a little distance short of the village. A simple alternative, which,
however, misses the charming view from the brow of Buttermere
Moss, is to bear to the right on reaching the level of the moss in
the direction of Whiteless Pike. A track will soon be found just
west of a stream which leads down to the road a little short
of Buttermere Hause.

5. Keswick to Keswick, over Grisedale Pike, Grasmoor, Sail, and Causey Pike. *Map at end of the book. See p. 296.*

*To Grisedale Pike, 3 hrs.; Grasmoor, 4 hrs.; Sail, 5 hrs.;
Causey Pike, 5½ hrs.; Keswick, 7½ hrs.; 15 m.*

This is also a beautiful excursion, especially during its latter
part. From the hause between Grisedale Pike and Grasmoor a

direct descent may be made to the *Scale Hill Hotel* by the narrow V-shaped depression which separates Grasmoor from Whiteside, or Buttermere may be reached from Grasmoor by an easy descent over Whiteless Pike. As the direct route from Keswick to Scale Hill by the Coledale Pass is closely connected with this route, we have included a description of it.

From Keswick, follow the Whinlatter route (*p.* 184) as far as the turn to the right, just beyond *Braithwaite Village*, and then strike up the fell by a path commencing a few yards past an old barytes mine.

The **Force Crag** route starts up the valley just at the above-mentioned turn in the road, and proceeds almost straight along the side of Grisedale Pike, the broad upper track being kept to throughout, and up the pony-track, with Force Crag on the right. So far the route is shut in and uninteresting. It next crosses the *col* between Grisedale Pike and Grasmoor at its lowest point, 1,800 ft. Here the route over Grisedale Pike converges and a very interesting descent by the Coledale Pass to Scale Hill may be commenced. The valley, Gaskell Gill, is very narrow, and it is best to keep the beck on the left hand all the way. The crags of **Whiteside** are noteworthy features on the right, and Grasmoor is an effective barrier on the left. The route emerges from the narrow pass on to the Buttermere and Cockermouth road, almost opposite the commencement of that to *Scale Hill* through *Lanthwaite Wood.* The total distance from Keswick to *Scale Hill Hotel* by this route is about 9 miles.

From the *col* above Force Crag it is a grand walk along **Whiteside**, descending at the end to the right of the cairn (leave crags well to left) to the *Scale Hill Hotel.* The ridge is in places very narrow, but quite safe. Fine views of the Solway Firth and Galloway hills.

The path up **Grisedale Pike** goes in turn right and left at first, to ease the gradient; then, keeping an extensive plantation on the right hand, it ascends almost in a straight line to the top of the mountain, climbing the ridge obliquely at first, through heather and bilberry bushes, and becoming somewhat steep before reaching the top. A wide and beautiful view to the south is gradually revealed, Derwentwater and the lower part of the New-lands valley playing an important part in the foreground. Range above range of overlapping fells appear, the farthest being the Scafell group. When the summit is reached, Scafell Pike rises just over Great Gable. The loftier ridge of Grasmoor hides a good deal to the south-west, but between it and Eel Crag the Buttermere Red Pike pops up very effectively. Northward the view over the Whinlatter Fells, extending to the Solway Firth and Scottish hills, is extensive. Helvellyn and Fairfield bound the south-eastern prospect, the sharp peak above the former ridge being Catchedicam. Only a strip of Bassenthwaite is visible, but Skiddaw shows himself from head to foot. The thimble-like peak of Pike o' Stickle appears to the south-east.

Leaving Grisedale Pike, you must keep the ridge, with a wall on the right, for some time, ascending a minor height called **Sand Hill**, and then inclining to the left near the top of a deep corrie on the right, which is worth viewing for the sake of the fine-looking, but extremely brittle, Hobcarton Crags.

There is considerable local confusion as to the place-names hereabouts. The 2,525 ft. peak at the east end of Whiteside is frequently called Hobcarton, and the same name is applied to the nameless ridge running north from Grisedale Pike to Hobcarton End (2,010 ft.). The correct name of the 2,525 ft. peak is Hope Gill Head, for which Hobcarton Pike may be a convenient alternative out of deference to expressed local desires. Hobcarton can apply to the valley only. The ridge running from Grisedale Pike to Hobcarton End might with advantage be called Hobcarton Ridge.

From a point where the stone wall changes to a fence, you will see a runnel in front, descending from Grasmoor to the top of the Coledale Pass. Follow the direction of this streamlet, and at the top of the pass—whence is a rough descent to Scale Hill, as described in the last digression—commence the ascent of Grasmoor. Before reaching the pass there is a peep at Loweswater between Grasmoor and Whiteside.

The summit of **Grasmoor** lies to the right of the course of the stream, about a mile beyond its source. There can be no difficulty in reaching it. The top of Grasmoor is flat and grassy, though grise (*wild boar*) rather than grass is probably the origin of the name. On the far side, however, the mountain descends with striking steepness to the Vale of Lorton and Crummock Water There are three cairns, and each should be visited. As a mountain view-point Grasmoor is scarcely surpassed, though from Wandhope, the spur running down towards Whiteless, the prospect is artistically even more beautiful. Red Pike and High Stile rise over Buttermere, and beyond them the Pillar, Great Gable, and Scafell present a most imposing front.

The descent from Grasmoor to Buttermere village is along the narrow ridge which connects the former with **Whiteless Pike**, to reach which the tourist must retrace his steps almost to the runnel above mentioned, and then diverge to the south, following the ridge over the top of Whiteless (2,159 ft.), leaving the summit on the left, and thence down to the village. The descent is very steep, but without danger.

In returning to Keswick, you have only to recollect that the ridge, along which your route lies, runs almost due east, and is separated in its latter part from the one by which you ascended by another ridge of inferior height. After leaving the plateau of Grasmoor, which must be almost exactly retraversed, a steep slope leads to **Eel Crag,** whose rough summit commands a splendid view. From this point the path is along a narrow ridge. When the ridge spreads out again you may adopt various routes, but the most satisfactory conclusion to the expedition is to keep along the top of the main ridge, as far as **Causey Pike,** and then to descend south-east to the *Newlands* hamlet, or still along the ridge by Rowling End to *Stair*. The former is 4½, and the latter nearly 4 miles from Keswick. The ridge may be quitted at Scar Crags by an old cart-track that runs down on the left below Outerside to Stonycroft and Stair.[1]

6. Patterdale to Patterdale, over Hart Crag, Fairfield, and St. Sunday Crag. *Map at end of the book. See p. 295.*

Patterdale Hotel to divergence from road, 20 min. ; Hart Crag, 2½ hrs. ; Fairfield, 3 hrs. ; St. Sunday Crag, 4 hrs. ; Patterdale 6 hrs. ; 12 miles. For reverse direction, see p. 274.

This is the pleasantest of all the fell excursions from Patterdale, displaying more grandeur and variety of prospect than the more ambitious round of Helvellyn by Glenridding and Grisedale. The route may be varied in many ways—*e.g.*, (*a*) Deepdale, scrambling up between Hart Crag and Fairfield ; (*b*) Dovedale, a finer but considerably stiffer route (*p.* 226), scramble steeply up to **Dove Crag**, keeping the precipice close by on the right ; (*c*) Caiston Glen (*p.* 113), which leads to the depression between Red Screes and Dove Crag, a little south-east of Little Hart Crag (*see also p.* 275) ; or by descending direct from Fairfield to the top of the Grisedale Pass ; but, taken as a whole, the round, as we are about to describe it, is the finest and, except the descent of St. Sunday Crag by Glemara Park, the easiest.

Quitting Patterdale follow the Kirkstone road for three quarters of a mile. Where the road bends left at the foot of a short hill go through a gate on the right and past four separate houses to a yellow-washed farm-house, Deepdale Hall, where directions will be given for the ascent of the ridge—a most unpleasantly wet and boggy route—**Hartsop-above-How**, which, about a mile beyond the trees, bends to the right. During the ascent the view back to Ullswater, and over Brothers' Water up the Hayeswater valley to High Street, is very charming. **Deepdale**, backed by St. Sunday Crag, is on the right, and Dovedale on the left. The cliffs of Fairfield, at the head of Deepdale, present a strong contrast to the grassy slopes of the same mountain, as seen from Windermere, and on the left Dove Crag sends down a fine craggy front. A steep climb now leads up to **Hart Crag**. During the ascent, the precipitous eastern side of the Helvellyn range on the right becomes a prominent object over the dip between Fairfield and St. Sunday Crag. From the top of the ridge, to the neighbourhood of which a wall ascends from the Ambleside direction, the view southward, embracing Windermere, Esthwaite, and part of Coniston lakes, is as extensive as it is beautiful. A fine view opens westward, including Scafell Pike, Great Gable, and the Pillar—Great Gable from this direction

---

[1] Note the rough road marked on map, but not dotted red, from Stonycroft to Scar Crags. This avoids the actual ascent of Causey Pike if the route is reversed.

being conspicuous by the precipitous character of both sides.
The Pillar rises on the right, and Scafell Pike on the left of it.

Between Hart Crag and **Fairfield** there is a rough but shallow
depression, beyond which the latter shows a level top, green and
broad enough to constitute an excellent sheep-walk. The view
from the various edges of it is very fine. Windermere tapers
off to the south, very beautifully, and to the right of it appear
Esthwaite and Coniston lakes. The Old Man and Wetherlam look
very handsome on the right of Coniston ; and then comes the long
amphitheatre, comprising the humps of Crinkle Crags, the peak
of Bowfell, the bracket-shaped Scafell Pike, and the prominent
elevations of Great Gable, the Pillar, Grasmoor, and Grisedale
Pike. Then the nearer range of Helvellyn hides Skiddaw and
Saddleback, and St. Sunday Crag hides Ullswater. To the right of
the last-named height, Place Fell, backed by the Pennine chain,
and the High Street range, distinguished by the peak of Kidsty
Pike, the long flat top of High Street itself and the cone of Ill
Bell, carry on the prospect almost to our starting-point at Windermere. Morecambe Bay and the Yorkshire fells close the prospect
to the south and south-east.

A descent may be made from Fairfield to the top of the **Grisedale
Pass** by the side of a wall which drops from a point north-west of the
summit to the horsegap at the highest point of the pass, a little
distance south of the tarn. Thence Grasmere may be reached
(*p.* 219), or Patterdale (*p.* 160).

Between Fairfield and St. Sunday Crag is a narrow ridge called
Cofa Pike, which looks alarming at first, and requires care. A
very beautiful but simple climb along the summit of a grassy
ridge then leads to the top of **St. Sunday Crag.** The profound
depressions of Grisedale and Deepdale add greatly to the charm
of this part of the walk. For the descent from St. Sunday Crag,
see p. 260.

7. Wasdale Head to Wasdale Head over Red Pike, Steeple, Scoat Fell, Haycock and Seatallan, or Wasdale Head to the Anglers' Hotel, Ennerdale. *Map at end of the book. See p.* 301.

Red Pike by Mosedale, 2 *hrs. ; Scoatfell,* 2½ *hrs. ; Steeple and
return,* 3 *hrs. ; Haycock,* 3¾ *hrs. ; Seatallan,* 4½ *hrs. ; Netherbeck
Bridge,* 5½ *hrs. ; Wasdale Head,* 6½ *hrs. : Distance,* 12 *miles.*

From Wasdale Head to Dore Head, the *col* between Yewbarrow and Red Pike.

(*a*) *Very arduous.* Cross the bridge behind the Hotel and,
working through several " intacks," follow a rough track upwards
along the side of Yewbarrow to the *col.* (In order to avoid some
awkward crags, which should be kept well to the left, it is advisable to start up towards Mosedale and then work diagonally
up to the *col,* instead of following the route marked on the map.)

(*b*) Follow the Strands road for rather more than half a mile

beyond the head of the lake. A path, the commencement of
which is not easily detected, here diverges to the right. Near
Overbeck the path forks. Take the right-hand fork and contour
upwards along the westerly side of Yewbarrow to the *col*.

From the *col* a scramble, by a fascinating and admirably-
cairned route, up Stirrup Crag takes one on to the long ridge of
Yewbarrow, and those with time to burn may traverse it to the
end overlooking Wastwater, returning in their tracks. The view
is fine, but Yewbarrow is a rough fell and uncomfortable in bad
weather. It is questionable whether a special divergence repays.

(c) It is also possible to go round by the farm-house at Bowderdale and so on to the open fell. The way lies almost directly
northwards, with Low Tarn on the left and the Dore Head *col*
some distance on the right. This route is the easiest, though
longest in the matter of distance.

Routes (a), (b), and (c) all lead north-west up the shoulder of
Red Pike and soon after converge on the ridge-line. The ground
at first is somewhat rough, but soon after passing the second cairn
on **Red Pike** smooths out into turf that challenges in elasticity
that of the Sussex Downs. The view which from the commencement has been mainly confined to the fell-side in the near foreground now opens up on the right, but of more immediate interest
is the clean-cut, precipitous drop into Mosedale. A cairn is soon
reached and, a little farther on, another. Either is an effective
view-point. The outlook in the direction of the Scafell group is
similar to that from Pillar (*p.* 254), but inferior owing to the intervening ridge of Yewbarrow. On the other hand, the view of
the Screes across Wastwater through the gap between Yewbarrow
and Middle Fell is very striking. To the east Kirkfell shuts out
Great Gable and northward Pillar blocks the prospect. Over
the gap of Black Sail between the two fells appear Brandreth
and Fleetwith with Dale Head beyond and Saddleback on the
horizon. On the left and indeed throughout the walk till the
descent to Netherbeck is commenced is a remarkable green
hollow, so large that Low Tarn at the head of the High Fell and
Scoat Tarn, picturesquely tucked away under Red Pike, are but
scantly noticed. From the second cairn continue in a north-
westerly direction to the summit of **Scoat Fell**, 2,746 ft. (The
distinctions " Great " and " Little " may be disregarded : they
refer to acreage of pasture-land, not to elevation.) From this
point the route turns left but, before proceeding, it is quite worth
while continuing the original line and climbing **Steeple**, a spur of
Scoat Fell that projects into Ennerdale, for the sake of the prospect down the dale and lake to the west and the look down into
the shattered hollow of Windy Gap Cove, backed by the crags of
Pillar Fell on the other side. Returning to Scoat Fell a wall
leads in a south-westerly direction to **Haycock**. It is well to
keep this wall on the left for the sake of the view down the
ravines descending to Ennerdale. On the far side of that valley

are the Buttermere fells, mild-looking in comparison with their aspect from the north. Saddleback has disappeared behind Pillar, but Skiddaw has come into view with the Grasmoor group nearer and to the west. Closer at hand Robinson is visible beyond High Crag. The aspect of Ennerdale Lake deteriorates with every step and compensation must be sought in the prospect across the Solway to the Galloway highlands. Westward one may see the Isle of Man.

Haycock lies slightly to the left, but those who wish to reach the car park at Ennerdale should continue along the wall to the depression short of Crag Fell and thence round over Angling Crag to the dam and footbridge at the foot of the lake, time 6–7 hours. From Ennerdale Lake to Wasdale the route by Pillar Fell (*p.* 255) is more attractive.

From the summit of Haycock a fine view opens out to the south-east. Far off are the Coniston Fells with the Scafell group nearer and then the Screes overlooking Wastwater. From this point the walk deteriorates in interest. A rather rough descent leads across marshy land southward to **Seatallan,** a tame fell commanding an underrated view. There is a practicable descent from Seatallan to Greendale by striking nearly south from the summit and crossing the beck some distance below Greendale Tarn. There is a good path from this point down to the farm. The descent is now south-east. **Middle Fell,** with Greendale Tarn, looks attractive and there is no difficulty in walking to the cairn. Steps must, however, be retraced : the descent of Middle Fell anywhere in the direction of Wastwater is the most exasperating in the district. From the depression south-east of Seatallan a rough walk down the course of Netherbeck lands one on the road just below Bowderdale.

This most exhilarating expedition may be reversed, starting up Netherbeck.

DESCENTS FROM THE FELLS

THE two immediately preceding chapters should enable walkers to find their way over the Cumbrian highlands without difficulty.

Occasionally, however, it happens that one lingers too long on the fells, and finds that there is risk of being overtaken by darkness, and quite frequently one is caught by mist, rain, or bad weather. Under such conditions, clear and concise instructions as to the proper line of descent in a given direction are desirable ; and emergencies occasionally arise which make it imperative to get off the fells as quickly as possible, and in which destination becomes a secondary consideration. In these cases the easiest descent should unhesitatingly be chosen.

Tourists should bear in mind the difference between " true " and " magnetic " north. The latter—as shown by the compass—lies some $5\frac{1}{2}°$ west of the former. The edges of the map in the Guide are laid *true* north and south. The variation is very important. The angle on the compass appears slight, but when produced the divergence becomes considerable—when bearings are taken every few yards, serious.

As most tourists will read our directions in conjunction with the map, we have in the following notes given *true* bearings unless otherwise stated. Necessarily the bearings only indicate the general direction.

See also the introductory notes for fell walkers, *pp.* 228–30.

Of course, the emergency route may also be followed in fair weather.

BOWFELL

See p. 279.

This is the culminating buttress of the rugged fells that run north-west to south-east from Esk Hause. The eastern (Langdale) and western (Eskdale) sides may be considered impracticable, being much broken up, and in misty weather the Band route from the summit to Langdale cannot be recommended, as it is easy to go astray amongst the initial crags and get entangled on the Langdale face.

Emergency Route.—From summit cairn descend south-south-east by the cairned route to Three Tarns, keeping if in doubt rather to the Langdale (easterly) side. For Langdale, if below the mists, a way may be found (east-south-east) between the gills ; but as these gills cut deeply into the face, it is safer in thick weather to coast to the left till the ridge of the Band is hit, and then follow the ridge downwards. For Eskdale turn in a south-westerly direction and follow the stream.

The Band may also be reached higher up by proceeding south-south-east from the summit for about 200 yards, and then turning east. The Band affords the easiest descent to Langdale.

For Esk Hause keep along the ridge-line north-west. There are many scarps, but it is best to keep as near those on the right hand as possible. When the ground slopes north and becomes less rugged, make north for Esk Hause.

If the weather conditions make it desirable to quit the ridge-line as soon as possible it is well to descend in a northerly direction at the first marked depression with a pronounced rise beyond. This is *Ewer Gap*. In descending keep the stream on the right (it does not much signify how far on the right), and you will hit off the Esk Hause track.

The rugged southerly ridge (Crinkle Crags, etc.) is best left alone except in quite settled weather. At the first symptoms of mist or other trouble, consult map and compass, and get off the ridge as quickly as possible. Generally the safest objective is the Three Shire Stone, and it is worth remembering that whereas the eastern face of the Crinkles is precipitous, a band of moorland skirts their bases on the west.

ESK HAUSE

Esk Hause is the hub of the Lakeland fells. By general testimony it is also specially designed for beguiling tourists into taking the wrong path, even without atmospheric accessories. " Mistakes are very liable to occur. On this high ground mists are extremely frequent, and blinding rain is abundant. The only safeguard is, of course, to bear in mind that the ups and downs hereabout are considerable, and to arm oneself with map and compass." Read also the notes on the summit of the Hause on *p.* 205. Travellers from Wasdale to Langdale should remember that they have to mount again after passing Angle Tarn ; that *all* the streams lead eventually to Borrowdale ; and that if they find themselves working up an easy slope to the south, they are off the track, and *en route* for Eskdale. Travellers on the reverse route will do well to bear in mind these instructions.

FAIRFIELD AND RED SCREES
See pp. 275 and 291.

These are the bulky fells north and north-east of Grasmere. Deep glens and long grassy ridges south. Much of the north-east face scarped.

Emergency Route.—From Fairfield, west by steep scree to Grisedale Tarn ; whence for Grasmere, south-south-west, or Patterdale, north-north-east.

Emergency Route from Red Screes.—North-west down slope to Scandale Head, the first depression. Thence Caiston Glen may be followed in a north-easterly direction for Kirkstone Pass and Patterdale, or the southerly track by Scandale Beck for Ambleside, etc.

It is, however, perfectly safe and easy to follow any of the south ridges of this group for Grasmere or Ambleside.

From the ridge-line, in misty weather, the route from Hart Crag north-east to Hartsop-above-How cannot be commended, and the route from Fairfield over Cofa Pike is best left alone.

From **St. Sunday Crag** follow the ridge north-north-east to the foot of the first steep descent. Then, when the ground becomes more level, get down in a north-westerly direction to Grisedale. The beck that runs down the fell-side from the foot of the north-west slope of the summit is a fair guide.

GLARAMARA

See pp. 232-3.

This is a rugged mountain of great bulk, lying north and south at the head of Borrowdale. Precipitous on east and west sides. The summit ridge, though much broken up, is of about the same general level. Part of the north face, the head of the combe looking down Borrowdale, is quite sheer. The north-east spur, Rosthwaite or Chapel Fell, is entirely detestable.

Way Off.—Proceed slightly west of *true* north for about a mile over ground first broken, then swampy. From swamp incline slightly left to make sure of getting well past crags at head of Comb Gill, and so straight on, keeping rather on east (right) side of ridge, inclining gently right till natural slope of mountain turns you down to foot of combe.

In mist this will be found the shortest route to anywhere, as in thick weather the traverse of the summit ridge south to Allen Crag for Esk Hause is most confusing.

GRASMOOR, ETC.

See p. 287.

A bulky mountain group some twenty miles in circumference, sending out numerous spurs, narrow ridges terminating in very steep dodds. Towards Crummock Water the main mass descends with great steepness.

Emergency Route.—East to swampy depression between Grasmoor and Eel Crag. Then, in very bad weather, it may be advisable to get down the very steep scree and grass south of Eel Crag for Sail Beck, for either Buttermere (south-west) or Newlands hamlet on the Keswick road (north-east) ; otherwise, the Keswick route by the beck north to Coledale Pass. For Keswick turn east-north-east. If the track down Force Crag cannot be hit off at once, it is safer to keep along the northern slopes of Eel Crag, with the becks on the left, following them downward.

For Scale Hill turn west-north-west by pass between Whiteside and Grasmoor.

For Buttermere, south-west over Whiteless Pike, keeping rather on the right slope of the ridge till Whiteless Pike is passed. In clear weather this is the finest descent from Grasmoor. The descent from Whiteless Pike, however, is very steep, and if the grass is wet or sun-dried is hardly to be recommended.

For Eel Crag, due east up hill from swamp, and by ridge-line to Causey Pike for Newlands. Not to be attempted in a gale.

Eel Crag.—Descend west to depression below Grasmoor and then as above.

Grisedale Pike.—South-west by wall and wire fence to Sand Hill, the next slight elevation, and then south for Coledale Pass. (*See above.*)

For Keswick and Braithwaite north-east by ridge-line.

GREAT GABLE

(With Green Gable and Brandreth and Kirkfell.

See pp. 233-4.

The summit of Great Gable is a rough quadrangle covered with loose stones, steep on all sides and precipitous on most.

Emergency Routes.—From cairn follow small cairns in a north-north-easterly direction—taking care to avoid walking over the north face—and keep to the rough, stony track to Wind Gap, the depression between Green and Great Gables. Thence turn right (eastwards), and follow the stream down Aaron Slack to Sty Head Tarn.

In thick weather this is really the shortest route to anywhere except Buttermere, in which case (except in very bad weather) metal posts may be followed in a northerly direction from the north slope of Green Gable over Brandreth, whence turn north-north-east for Honister Hause. In bad weather one can get down in a north-westerly direction from Wind Gap and thence down the grass, following the infant *Liza*, to the Youth Hostel at the foot of Scarth Gap and the plain road down Ennerdale.

If caught on Green Gable, make south for Wind Gap. If caught on Brandreth, make north-north-east for Honister.

Kirkfell (*p.* 249) is sometimes visited from Great Gable. The north face is craggy, and there are numerous scarps elsewhere. Moreover, the great extent of the broad summit makes it a most undesirable fell to be caught on.

Emergency Route.—Make west, and get down the steep grass slope into Mosedale and the Black Sail–Wasdale track.

It is also possible to make eastward for Beck Head, in the

depression between Kirkfell and Great Gable (the fence is a useful guide), whence the Brandreth route may be joined by traversing in a north-easterly direction by a detestably-rough track below the north face of Great Gable.

From Beckhead one may traverse southward below Gable Screes till Gavel Neese is reached. There is a cairned track (*p.* 237).

HARTER FELL (ESKDALE)

See p. 237.

A craggy peak with slopes interspersed with numerous rocky bluffs. A bad mountain in a mist. The best way off for any destination is to make north-east for the Hardknott Pass, remembering there are scarps on the left all the way.

HARTER FELL (MARDALE)

See p. 238.

A bulky fell, terminating a long ridge running up from the south-east. North face precipitous. For Mardale or Windermere keep along in a westerly direction for the Nan Bield Pass, care being taken to avoid straying south.

HELVELLYN

See pp. 239–44.

The massive range forming the eastern boundary of the Cumberland fells runs north and south, and descends west towards Thirlmere in broken grassy slopes, but is scarped east towards Patterdale. Farther north, above St. John's Vale, the crags are west and the slopes east. For tourists the range is practically confined to its culminating point, Helvellyn.

Emergency Route.—A way can be found almost anywhere down the western slopes for Thirlmere (Wythburn or Thirlspot). Outcrops of crags, but easily rounded. Preferable to go south. After walking quarter of an hour, incline south-west for Wythburn track, just south of which are crags. If this is missed continue south-west down slope to Dunmail Raise, or the ridge can be followed south over Dollywaggon, whence a zigzag path leads down to Grisedale Tarn, Patterdale (north-north-east), Grasmere (south-south-west).

For Thirlspot or Patterdale go north over Low Man. In about a mile, just beyond next elevation, the track forks. Left incline (north-west) for Thirlspot. For Patterdale incline (east-north-east) till south slope of Raise turns you east.

Just beyond Low Man and Browncove Crags (on the left) there is a quick north-westerly descent to Thirlspot down Helvellyn Gill.

For Patterdale in calm weather, though misty, either Striding or Swirrel Edge (east-north-east) may be taken. It is impossible to miss the way once started. Both these routes entail a little mild scrambling. They are not to be recommended in winter on account of ice on Striding Edge and frequent snow blizzards. People who find the prospect of Striding Edge disagreeable may scramble down from near its juncture with the mountain into Nethermost Cove, and so into Grisedale Pass.

THE SOUTHERN (Lancashire) FELLS
Coniston Old Man, Wetherlam, etc.
See pp. 281-4.

The general outline of the main ridge of this range resembles the line of the first finger of the left hand slightly bent, the first joint, from the Old Man to Great How Crags, south to north, and the two top joints, bending north-east, terminating in Wetherlam. On the concave side scarps are numerous. Levers Water and Low Water are deeply set in precipitous walls. Wetherlam is scarped to the north and west, Carrs to the east ; Dow Crag, a ridge by itself, south-west of the summit, sends down east one of the finest precipices in the District, and there are plenty of steep places on the west side. *Besides which the slopes are honeycombed with unfenced mines and quarries.*

Emergency Routes (and for Coniston).—Follow ridge-line in a southerly direction to Walna Scar route, keeping slightly on the west slope of the range. Follow Walna Scar track east for Coniston. The ordinary route up is not recommended as a descent in bad weather on account of the quarries and the labyrinth of tracks.

From Dow Crag follow ridge-line south to head of Walna Scar (east for Coniston, west for Duddon valley). There is a descent south to Goats' Water from the head of the combe between Dow Crag and the Old Man which also reaches the Walna Scar route.

From Great How Crags, at the bend of the finger, one can retrace one's steps south to the first depression and descend roughly east, and thence by miners' track to Coniston ; or west to Seathwaite Tarn.

For Langdale (north) generally over Carrs, and so to the Three Shire Stone on Wrynose Pass for Langdale. The route forks (*see Map*) just before Wrynose, but no object is gained by taking the east variation.

Wetherlam (for Coniston). The better descent is in a south-easterly and southerly direction from the cairn till the track past the Copper Mines is reached.

For Langdale. Proceed north-east and then with the hill slope incline left to Greenburn Copper Mines. This route is most tiresome owing to the quantities of bilberry and juniper, and loose stones. The descent to Tilberthwaite Gill is quite nasty.

LANGDALE PIKES

Pike o' Stickle, Gimmer Crag,[1] Harrison Stickle, Pavey Ark.

See p. 250.

The Langdale Pikes form the pointed southern buttress of the long, featureless range of grassy fells that flanks Derwentwater and Borrowdale on the east.

From the apex, Harrison Stickle, the southern face of the group drops in very steep terraces and rocky slopes to the head of the Langdale valley. The other face is sharply set back, and falls eastwards precipitously to Stickle Tarn. A steep grass slope divides Pavey Ark from Harrison Stickle.

Emergency Route (from Harrison Stickle).—West-north-west to Stake Pass, which leads (1) south to Mickleden for Dungeon Ghyll, Grasmere, etc.; (2) north to Langstrath for Rosthwaite and Keswick. Ground swampy and very tedious, and the trudge is either far greater than it appears (on the map), or appears far greater than it is in reality. In fact, it is only recommended in case of being benighted or in execrable weather.

For Keswick. Follow **High Raise** northwards for about two miles to the foot of the first descent (a wire fence running south to north on east side of summit plateau is a certain guide). Then from gate at foot of depression north-north-west for Greenup by cairns. Towards commencement of descent avoid going too far left.

For Dungeon Ghyll. Descend between Harrison Stickle and Pavey Ark (east), keeping about midway between Harrison Stickle and the southern end of Pavey Ark (*see p. 252*). Then follow ghyll running from tarn steeply, with ghyll left. Be careful you descend between Harrison Stickle and Pavey Ark, east, and not between Harrison Stickle and Gimmer Crag, south. In fact on no account should a direct descent to Langdale be attempted. From Harrison Stickle one can also proceed north till Pavey Ark is passed, and then make a semicircular round, descending to Stickle Tarn.

For Grasmere. As for Dungeon Ghyll.

PILLAR

See pp. 253-4.

Pillar sends down a magnificent face to the north. It is also scarped to south and west.

Emergency Route.—East to head of Black Sail, keeping wire fence left; ground broken. Then follow track south for Wasdale. This is really the best route off the mountain.

For Windy Gap, south-south-west. From the Gap there is a very steep descent eastward for Mosedale and Wasdale, and north-west there is a rough way down to Ennerdale for Gillerthwaite.

---

[1] The name of the actual *Pike* of Gimmer Crag Buttress is Loft Crag.

Steeple and *Red Pike* are often included in a Pillar excursion. If caught on Steeple (precipitous), make south for Scoat Fell; thence follow ridge-line north-east for Windy Gap.

If caught on Red Pike, which falls steeply north-east, follow ridge south-east to Dore Head, whence a descent down very steep scree can be made in an easterly direction to Mosedale for Wasdale Head.

RED PIKE, BUTTERMERE, HIGH STILE, ETC.

See p. 256.

A long ridge, running south-east to north-west, bounding Buttermere on the south-west side, descending in steep slopes to Ennerdale, south-west, heavily scarped along the Buttermere side, north-east.

Emergency Route.—Follow fence south-east along summit ridge, over broken ground, to summit of High Crag. (The route curves in and out far more than indicated on the map.) Thence descend steeply by fence to gate at head of Scarth Gap. Thence north (left) by pass for Gatesgarth and Buttermere. The track south leads to the head of Ennerdale, nowhere near anywhere.

The wire fence may be followed from Red Pike, north-west, over grass to the descent (broken ground) by Scale Force Beck to Crummock Water. Care must be taken as to direction, as there are misleading fences running down to Ennerdale.

For Buttermere, from summit of Red Pike, walk a short distance north-east. Then drop down screes (right) to Bleaberry Tarn. Continue with tarn (right) along wall till slope of High Stile turns you down diagonal track in wood (left) to foot of Buttermere. The descent from Red Pike by Ruddy Beck is not recommended.

To Gillerthwaite in Ennerdale. Find summit of Red Pike by following wire fence along the summit ridge-line of High Crag, High Stile, and Red Pike; then drop down slope south-west.

Haystacks (south-east, Scarth Gap) presents one of the most confusing summits in the district, a labyrinth of low crags and shallow hollows. On first indication of bad weather get down to Scarth Gap, west. Care is required, as the descent is steep and much broken up by crags. It is, in fact, easier to get off east towards Brandreth, but the country in that direction is specially designed to make one lose one's way in mist.

Fleetwith.—Descend the grass east-south-east to Honister Hause, taking care to keep clear of Honister Crag on the left.

ROBINSON, DALEHEAD, ETC.

See pp. 286–7.

This long line of fells lies north-east of Buttermere and Honister Pass, sending out three long spurs north-eastward : High Snab Bank from Robinson, Scope End from Hindscarth, and Eel

Crags (for Maiden Moor and Catbells), just east of Dalehead. Grassy but most treacherously scarped ; grassy slopes leading down to unexpected crags. General line of summit ridge east-south-east to west-north-west.

Emergency Route.—Follow wire fence south-south-east to Honister Hause, keeping fence on right (as there are quarries on Honister side of Dalehead). From Hause descend east by road for Rosthwaite and Keswick, west for Buttermere.

Robinson (for Buttermere). Descend south-west down grass and scree till level summit of Moss is reached, then west. (*See p.* 287.) A very featureless route, and difficult in a mist. With caution the shortest route on reaching the Moss is to turn north for Buttermere Hause. Robinson is scarped on the right, and there are crags on the left at the head of Moss.

For Littledale and Newlands Vale (north-east). It is as well to avoid going much to the left in descending. In fact, if anything, keep rather east than north-east in the event of not hitting off the track at once.

Hindscarth (for Keswick). Follow ridge north. The emergency fence is south-east, and also south-east of—

Dale Head (for Rigg Head). East to Dalehead Tarn, then north to a swampy depression, whence a detestably-rough path leads north-west to head of Newlands, and a steep slope east by a trolley-track to Rosthwaite. At the foot of this track a good path leads north to Grange. From Rigg Head the ridge-line may be followed north over Eel Crags, Maiden Moor, and Catbells to Keswick. When descending from Maiden Moor to Catbells keep rather on east (right) side of the ridge-line.

SADDLEBACK

See p. 259.

Rounded grass slopes to north and west, steepening towards west. South and east sides precipitous.

Emergency Route (and for Keswick or Threlkeld).—Face west, and drop down grass slope inclining left, with slope under left elbow, till a track is reached running south.

The route up by Scales Fell, the easiest line of ascent, has nothing to recommend it as a descent.

Fair-weather Routes.—Threlkeld and the Penrith road may also be reached by any of the southern edges ; Doddick Fell, south of Scales Tarn, easiest. Halls Fell Top (narrow edge), south of summit cairn, not recommended. Gate Gill Fell (Broad Edge), farther west, is perhaps the most tedious descent in the district. Sharp Edge is definitely to be avoided in anything but fine weather.

SCAFELL, SCAFELL PIKE, GREAT END

See pp. 261–70.

Scafell.—In misty weather all routes off this mountain may be considered impracticable except that due west. On reaching the nearly level moorland—for Wasdale incline north-west; for Boot, south-west (the first stream you meet conducts you to Burnmoor Tarn, whence the pony-track leads south by west, with stream left to Boot). The long southern sloping shoulder of the mountain is of no use to anyone, and may lead to trouble.

Scafell Pike is the roughest as well as the highest mountain in England, the greater part of the surface being a chaos of boulders. *Two* cairned routes meet at the summit. Be careful which you select. The route to the west divides just below the summit rocks, that south-west leading to Mickledore; that north-west to the Lingmell *col* for Wasdale.

Emergency Route, and for Wasdale. Follow cairns in a north-west direction, and at about 80 yards fork right, and then, as the ground becomes less steep and rough, turn north, descending till you reach a swampy plateau. On nearing or reaching a " tumble-down " wall, turn downhill west-south-west to Brown Tongue and Lingmell Gill.

From **Lingmell** make for this plateau, which lies south-west from the summit.

For **Esk Hause,** *see pp.* 132 *and* 206. Follow cairns north-east over a wilderness of boulders. If you lose the cairns, keep pegging away north-east, recollecting that there are precipices on either side, and that the route is down, up, down, up, down, and then east-north-east inclining north-east. At this point it should not be difficult to hit off first the line of small cairns, and then the shelter on Esk Hause, about half-way between the summit of the ridge and the track. Do *not* follow the first and only stream you meet; it leads to *Eskdale*.[1] Do not go north of it, or you will find yourself on—

Great End, another wilderness, scarped north, north-east, and west. Descend south-east until the stream is reached. Then follow directions as above for Esk Hause—that is, east-north-east inclining north. The cairns and shelter are useful guides.

It must be remembered that the Esk Hause track lies a few hundred yards north of the summit of the Hause itself.

THE WASTWATER SCREES

See p. 272.

Descend east towards Burnmoor Tarn (*p.* 209). The entire length of the north-west face is precipitous.

---

[1] Eskdale may be reached from the Pike itself by dropping down left from Mickledore ridge.

SKIDDAW

See p. 270.

A well-defined, peaked, grass mountain, falling steeply towards Derwentwater and Bassenthwaite in long screes and grass tongues, and, in the opposite direction, in steep grass declivities. The summit ridge lies approximately north and south.

Emergency Route (and for Keswick).—From summit keep south-south-east till a wall is reached. Descend by well-marked track, on downwards, arriving eventually at Spoony Green Lane. On the way down hug the edges of the steep declivities towards Derwentwater, until the ground falls steeply south-east. This slope may be followed safely, and will lead to Keswick, but it is better to find the wall. In no case descend to the left—that is, north-east.

For Bassenthwaite Common descend north-west from northern cairn.

The descents *viâ* Applethwaite and Millbeck Gills are over exasperating screes.

The following are fair-weather routes :—

To Carl Side. Walk a few yards towards the Low Man, and then descend very steep scree to Carl Side, and thence in a line with the west edge of Derwentwater, avoiding some crags on the Millbeck (left) side. This descent gives the finest views.

THORNTHWAITE CRAG, ILL BELL, HIGH STREET KIDSTY PIKE

See pp. 245–8.

The Ill Bell range is practically the preserve of Windermere ; High Street, of Patterdale. Thornthwaite Crag is the Mecca of lost pilgrims on either.

(1) Ill Bell range, running north and south ; steep grassy slopes west, scarped east.

Emergency Route.—From Thornthwaite Crag walk a few hundred yards south, and drop down slope to Troutbeck, west.

Windermere.—Follow ridge-line south over Froswick, Ill Bell, and Yoke to Garburn Pass, where turn south-west (right).

Patterdale.—Follow wall north-west, with wall on right, to Threshthwaite Hause, a steep, shaly, slippery slope. Cross wall to right, and, after a steep rough descent, follow Pasture Beck north-north-west to Low Hartsop.

(2) High Street range :—From High Street to Kidsty Pike, north.

Chiefly steep grass ; a deal of crag, especially on the spurs. Owing, however, to the indefinite character of the range, it is impossible to indicate concisely the scarps, which are numerous, unexpected, and aggravating. Blea Water and Small Water are deeply set in semicircles of precipitous walls. In fact, throughout the Lake District, one is well advised to approach an unknown tarn with caution.

Emergency Route.—From High Street, southward to Thornthwaite for Patterdale or Windermere. (*See above.*)

For Mardale from Kidsty, east by lateral spur ; a tiresome route in mist owing to the nature of the ground—a mixture of grass and crag. It is perhaps quicker and easier to incline south-east from High Street and hit the Nan Bield Pass, care being taken to give Blea Water a wide berth, and to get well south of Small Water, as the ground between the two is much broken up.

High Street or Kidsty Pike for Patterdale. From Kidsty Pike go due west to the wall that runs north and south along the " Street," and from High Street follow it northwards till a gate is reached, whence is a track west which leads down to Hayeswater ; but the way on these featureless fells is hard to find. In fine weather the walk north-west from the above-mentioned gate over the ridge by Angle Tarn above Patterdale is pleasant though boggy ; in thick weather it is most tiresome. *Note.*—Kidsty Pike is nearly ½ a mile east of the main ridge.

Caudale Moor.—Drop down in a south-westerly direction to the Kirkstone Pass.

INDEX

₊ Where more than one reference is given, the first is the principal.

The names enclosed in [square] brackets are required to complete the postal address.

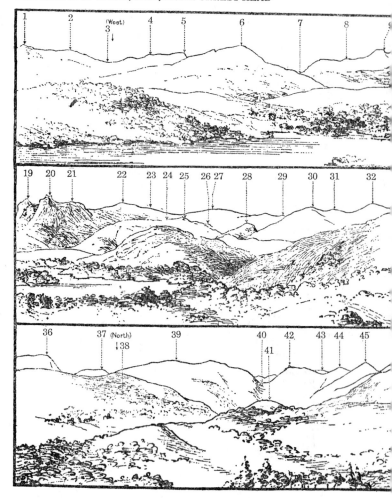

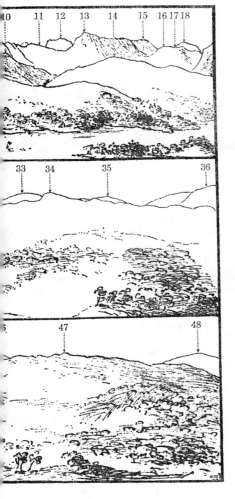

REFERENCE TO PEAKS, &c.

1. **Conniston Old Man,** 9 *miles*
2. Brim Fell.
3. Fairfield.
4. Great How Crags.
5. Carrs
6. Wetherlam.
7. Wrynose Pass (*below*).
8. Cold Pike.
9. Crinkle Crags.
10. Pike o' Blisco.
11. Shelter Crags.
12. **Scafell Pike,** 14 *miles*.
13. **Bowfell,** 11½ *miles*.
14. Lingmoor.
15. Great End.
16. Esk Hause (*below*).
17. Allen Crags.
18. Great Gable.
19. Loft Crag.
20. Harrison Stickle.
21. Pavey Ark.
22. High Raise.
23. Sergeant Man.
24. Loughrigg (*below*), 5 *miles*.
25. Blea Rigg.
26. **Silver How,** 8 *miles*.
27. Ullscarf.
28. Helm Crag.
29. Steel Fell.
30. Nab Scar.
31. Heron Pike.
32. Great Rigg.
33. Fairfield.
34. **Wansfell Pike,** 4 *miles*.
35. Dove Crag.
36. **Red Screes,** 6 *miles*.
37. Woundale Fell, Broad End.
38. Troutbeck Hundreds.
39. Caudale Moor.
40. Thresthwaite Cove.
41. Troutbeck Tongue.
42. Thornthwaite Crag.
43. High Street.
44. Froswick.
45. **Ill Bell,** 6 *miles*.
46. Yoke.
47. Garburn.
48. Harter Fell.

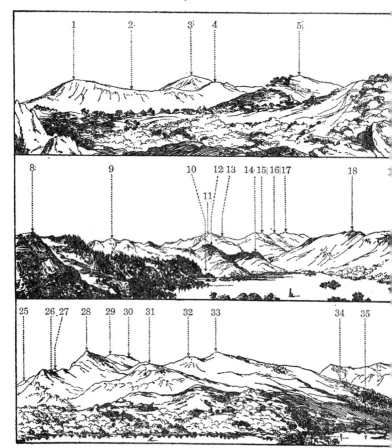

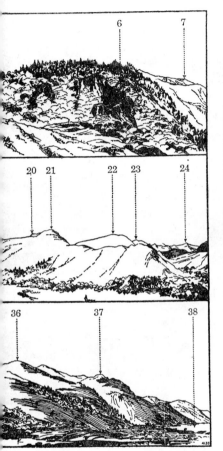

REFERENCE TO PEAKS, &c.

1. Clough Head, 4 *miles.*
2. Wanthwaite Crags.
3. Great Dodd, 5 *miles.*
4. Watson's Dodd, 5½ *miles.*
5. Causeway Pike, 1¼ *miles.*
6. Walla Crag.
7. High Seat, 3 *miles.*
8. Falcon Crag.
9. Ashness Fells.
10. Lodore.
11. Glaramara, 10 *miles.*
12. Brund Fell, 4 *miles.*
13. Esk Pike.
14. Castle Crag.
15. Great End, 10 *miles.*
16. Black Crag.
17. Scafell Pike, 11 *miles.*
18. Scawdell Fell, 5 *miles.*
19. Maiden Moor, 3½ *miles.*
20. Hindscarth, 5½ *miles.*
21. Catbells, 2½ *miles.*
22. Robinson, 6 *miles.*
23. High Stile, 8 *miles.*
24. Red Pike, Buttermere, 8 *miles.*
25. Knott Rigg.
26. Rowling End.
27. Whiteless Pike.
28. Causey Pike, 4 *miles.*
29. Sail, 5 *miles.*
30. Eel Crag, 5½ *miles.*
31. Barrow.
32. Sand Hill, 5 *miles.*
33. Grisedale Pike, 4½ *miles.*
34. Whinlatter Pass, 6 *miles* (*below*).
35. Derwentwater.
36. Lord's Seat, 5 *miles.*
37. Barff, 5 *miles.*
38. Bassenthwaite Lake.

PANORAMIC VIEW FROM SUMMIT OF HELVELLYN

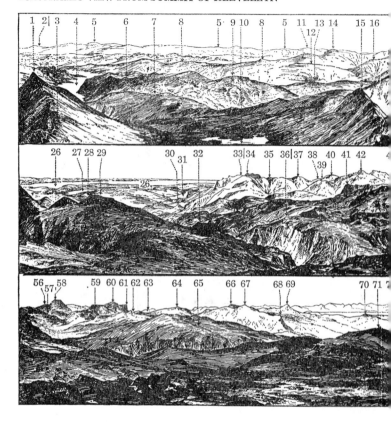

REFERENCE TO PEAKS, &c.

EAST

1. Catchedicam
2. Black Fell, Pennines
3. Swirrell Edge
4. **Ullswater**
5. **Cross Fell and Pennines**
6. Birk Fell
7. Birkhouse Moor
8. High Street Range
9. Place Fell
10. Red Tarn
11. Kirkby Stephen Fell
12. Rest Dodd
13. Angle Tarn
14. Kidsty Pike
15. **Striding Edge**
16. Gray Crag
17. St Sunday Crag
18. **High Street**
19. Harter Fell (Mardale)
20. Froswick
21. Caudale Moor
22. Ill Bell
23. Ingleborough
24. Red Screes
25. Fairfield

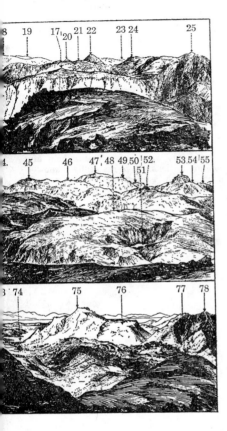

TO READERS

Since Mr. Baddeley's original writings the District has been continuously and most carefully surveyed and route descriptions mentioned are as accurate and up to date as possible. No small part of this accuracy of detail is due to kind help from readers who from time to time inform us of alterations they notice in using the book. We confidently appeal for further help of this nature. All such communications will be gratefully acknowledged and information used at the earliest opportunity.

The Editor.

Ward Lock Limited
116 Baker Street
London, W1M 2BB